Praise for *Barbarian Days*

"A hefty masterpiece." —Geoff Dyer, *The Guardian* (London)

"Terrific . . . Elegantly written and structured, it's a riveting adventure story, an intellectual autobiography, and a restless, searching meditation on love, friendship, and family. . . . A writer of rare subtlety and observational gifts, Finnegan explores every aspect of the sport—its mechanics and intoxicating thrills, its culture and arcane tribal codes—in a way that should resonate with surfers and non-surfers alike. His descriptions of some of the world's most powerful and unforgiving waves are hauntingly beautiful. . . . Finnegan displays an honesty that is evident throughout the book, parts of which have a searing, unvarnished intensity that reminded me of *Stop Time*, the classic coming-of-age memoir by Frank Conroy." —*The Washington Post*

"The kind of book that makes you squirm in your seat on the subway, gaze out the window at work, and Google Map the quickest route to the beach. In other words, it is, like Jon Krakauer's *Into the Wild*, a semi-dangerous book, one that persuades young men . . . to trade in their office jobs in order to roam the world, to feel the ocean's power, and chase the waves." —*The Paris Review Daily*

"Fans of [Finnegan's] writing have been waiting eagerly for his surfing memoir. . . . Well, *Barbarian Days* is here. And it's even better than one could have imagined. . . . This is Finnegan's gift. He's observant and expressive but shows careful restraint in his zeal. He says only what needs to be said, enough to create a vivid picture for the reader while masterfully giving that picture a kind of movement." —*Honolulu Star-Advertiser*

"That surfing life is [Finnegan's], and it's a remarkably adventurous one sure to induce wanderlust in anyone who follows along, surfer or not. . . . Lyrical but not overbaked, exciting but always self-effacing. It captures the moments of joy and terror Finnegan's lifelong passion has brought him, as well as his occasional ambivalence about the tenacious hold it has on him. It's easily the best book ever written about surfing. It's not even close." —*The Florida Times-Union*

"An engrossing read, part treatise on wave physics, part thrill ride, part cultural study, with a soupçon of near-death events. Even for those who've never paddled out, Finnegan's imagery is as vividly rendered as a film, his explanation of wave mastery a triumph of language. For surfers, the book is *The Endless Summer* writ smarter and larger, touching down at every iconic break." —*Los Angeles Times Magazine*

"Vivid and propulsive . . . Finnegan . . . has seen things from the tops of ocean peaks that would disturb most surfers' dreams for weeks. (I happily include myself among that number.) . . . A lyrical and enormously rewarding read . . . Finnegan's enchantment takes us to some luminous and unsettling places—on both the edge of the ocean and the frontiers of the surfing life."

—*The San Diego Union-Tribune*

"*Barbarian Days* gleams with precise, often lyrical recollections of the most memorable waves [Finnegan has] encountered. . . . He carefully mines his surfing exploits for broader, hard-won insights on his childhood, his most intense friendships and romances, his political education, his career. He's always attuned to his surroundings, and his reflections are often tinged with self-effacing wit."

—*Chicago Reader*

"Extraordinary . . . [*Barbarian Days*] is in many ways, and for the first time, a surfer in full. And it is cause for throwing your wet-suit hoods in the air. . . . If the book has a flaw, it lies in the envy helplessly induced in the armchair surf–traveler by so many lusty affairs with waves that are the supermodels of the surf world. Still, Finnegan considerately shows himself paying the price of admission in a few near drownings, and these are among the most electrifying moments in the book. . . . There are too many breathtaking, original things in *Barbarian Days* to do more than mention here—observations about surfing that have simply never been made before, or certainly never so well."

—*The New York Times Book Review*

"Without a doubt, the finest surf book I've ever read . . . All this technical mastery and precise description goes hand in hand with an unabashed, infectious earnestness. Finnegan has certainly written a surfing book for surfers, but on a more fundamental level, *Barbarian Days* offers a clear-eyed vision of American boyhood. Like Jon Krakauer's *Into the Wild*, it is a sympathetic examination of what happens when literary ideas of freedom and purity take hold of a young mind and fling his body out into the far reaches of the world."

—*The New York Times Magazine*

"Which is precisely what makes the propulsive precision of Finnegan's writing so surprising and revelatory . . . Finnegan's treatment of surfing never feels like performance. Through the sheer intensity of his descriptive powers and the undeniable ways in which surfing has shaped his life, *Barbarian Days* is an utterly convincing study in the joy of treating seriously an unserious thing. . . . As Finnegan demonstrates, surfing, like good writing, is an act of vigilant noticing."

—*The New York Review of Books*

"Finnegan is an excellent surfer; at some point he became an even better writer. That pairing makes *Barbarian Days* exceptional in the notoriously foamy genre of surf lit: a hefty, heavyweight tour de force, overbrimming with sublime lyrical passages that Finnegan drops as effortlessly as he executed his signature 'drop-knee cutback' in the breaks off Waikiki. . . . Reading this guy on the subject of waves and water is like reading Hemingway on bullfighting; William Burroughs on controlled substances; Updike on adultery. . . . Finnegan is a virtuoso word-smith, but the juice propelling this memoir is wrung from the quest that shaped him. . . . A piscine, picaresque coming-of-age story, seen through the gloss resin coat of a surfboard."

—*Sports Illustrated*

"Overflowing with vivid descriptions of waves caught and waves missed, of disappointments and ecstasies, and gargantuan curling tubes that encir-cle riders like cathedrals of pure stained glass . . . These paragraphs, with their mix of personal remembrance and subcultural taxonomies, tend to be as elegant and pellucid as the breakers they immortalize. . . . This memoir is one you can ride all the way to shore."

—*Entertainment Weekly*

"[A] sweeping, glorious memoir . . . Oh, the rides, they are incandescent . . . I'd sooner press this book upon a non-surfer, in part because nothing I've read so accurately describes the feeling of being stoked or the despair of being held under. But also because while it is a book about 'A Surfing Life' . . . it's also about a writer's life and, even more generally, a quester's life, more carefully observed and precisely rendered than any I've read in a long time."

—*Los Angeles Times*

"Gorgeously written and intensely felt . . . With Mr. Finnegan's bravura memoir, the surfing bookshelf is dramatically enriched. It's not only a volume for followers of the sport. Non-surfers, too, will be treated to a travelogue head-scratchingly rich in obscure, sharply observed destinations. . . . Dare I say that we all need Mr. Finnegan . . . as a role model for a life fully, thrillingly, lived."

—*The Wall Street Journal*

"An evocative, profound, and deeply moving memoir . . . The proof is in the sentences. Were I given unlimited space to review this book, I would simply reproduce it here, with a quotation mark at the beginning and another at the end. While surfers have a reputation for being inarticulate, there is actually a fair amount of overlap between what makes a good surfer and a good writer. A smooth style, an ability to stay close to the source of the energy, humility before the task, and, once you're done, not claiming your ride. In other words, making something exceedingly difficult look easy. The gift for writing a clean line is rare, and the gift for riding one even rarer. Finnegan possesses both."

—*San Francisco Chronicle*

"Finnegan writes so engagingly that you paddle alongside, eager for him to take you to the next wave. . . . It is a wet and wild run. He makes surfing seem as foreign and simultaneously as intimate a sport as possible. . . . Surfing is the

backbone of the book, but Finnegan's relationships to people, not waves, form its flesh. . . . [A] deep blue story of one man's lifelong enchantment."
—*The Boston Globe*

"Finnegan's epic adventure, beautifully told, is much more than the story of a boy and his wave, even if surfing serves as the thumping heartbeat of his life."
—*The Dallas Morning News*

"That's always Finnegan's M.O.: examining the ways in which surfing intertwines with anthropology, economics, politics, and, of course, writing. Finnegan is a sober, straightforward author, but the level of detail, emotion, and insight he achieves is unparalleled. . . . A must-read for all surfers—not just because of its unblinking prose and subtle wit, but because it's the only book that properly details what it's like to cultivate both an award-winning career and a dedicated surfing life."
—*Eastern Surf Magazine*

"Finnegan describes, with shimmering detail, his adventures riding waves on five continents. Surfing has taken him places he'd never otherwise have thought to go, but it also buoyed him through a career reporting on the politics of intense scarcity, limitless cruelty, and unimaginable suffering. It's a book about travel and growing up, and the power of a pastime when it becomes an obsession."
—*Men's Journal*

"Fearless and full of grace."
—*Outside*

"It's always fabulous when an incredible writer happens to also have a memoir-worthy life; *Barbarian Days* bodes well."
—*GQ.com*

"[A] lyrical, intellectual memoir. The author touches on love, on responsibility, on politics, individuality, and morality, as well as on the lesser-known aspects of surfing: the toll it takes on the body, the weird lingo, the wacky community. Finnegan's world is as dazzling and deep as any ocean. It's a pleasure to paddle into and makes for a hell of a ride."
—*The Millions*

"As it progresses the whole book turns into a portal. . . . It's tempting to say that *Barbarian Days* will bring readers as close as they'll get to the surf, short of actual surfing. But I had a stronger reaction: the book brought me closer than I'd ever been, or expected to get, to the real, unfathomable ocean."
—*Bookforum*

"A dream of a book by a masterful writer long immersed in surfing culture. Finnegan recaptures the waves lost and found, the euphoria, the danger . . . the allure."
—*BBC.com*

PENGUIN BOOKS

BARBARIAN DAYS

William Finnegan is the author of *Cold New World, A Complicated War, Dateline Soweto*, and *Crossing the Line*. He has twice been a National Magazine Award finalist and has won numerous journalism awards, including two Overseas Press Club awards since 2009. A staff writer at *The New Yorker* since 1987, Finnegan lives in Manhattan.

Grajagan, Java, 1979

BARBARIAN DAYS

A Surfing Life

WILLIAM FINNEGAN

Penguin Books

PENGUIN BOOKS

An imprint of Penguin Random House LLC
375 Hudson Street
New York, New York 10014
penguin.com

First published in the United States of America by Penguin Press,
an imprint of Penguin Random House LLC, 2015
Published in Penguin Books 2016

Photograph credits
Page vi: © Mike Cordesius
220: © joliphotos
408: © Ken Seino
430: © Scott Winer
Other photographs courtesy of the author

ISBN 9781594203473 (hc.)
ISBN 9780143109396 (pbk.)
ISBN 9780698163744 (eBook)

Printed in the United States of America
1 3 5 7 9 10 8 6 4 2

Designed by Meighan Cavanaugh

for Mollie

He had become so caught up in building sentences that he had almost forgotten the barbaric days when thinking was like a splash of colour landing on a page.

—EDWARD ST. AUBYN, *Mother's Milk*

CONTENTS

BARBARIAN DAYS

ONE

OFF DIAMOND HEAD

Honolulu, 1966–67

I HAD NEVER THOUGHT OF MYSELF AS A SHELTERED CHILD. STILL, Kaimuki Intermediate School was a shock. We had just moved to Honolulu, I was in the eighth grade, and most of my new schoolmates were "drug addicts, glue sniffers, and hoods"—or so I wrote to a friend back in Los Angeles. That wasn't true. What was true was that haoles (white people; I was one of them) were a tiny and unpopular minority at Kaimuki. The "natives," as I called them, seemed to dislike us particularly. This was unnerving because many of the Hawaiians were, for junior-high kids, alarmingly large, and the word was that they liked to fight. Orientals—again, my terminology—were the school's biggest ethnic group. In those first weeks I didn't distinguish between Japanese and Chinese and Korean kids—they were all Orientals to me. Nor did I note the existence of other important tribes, such as the Filipinos, the Samoans, or the Portuguese (not considered haole), let alone all the kids of mixed ethnic background. I probably even thought the big guy in wood shop who immediately took a sadistic interest in me was Hawaiian.

He wore shiny black shoes with long sharp toes, tight pants, and bright flowered shirts. His kinky hair was cut in a pompadour, and he looked like he had been shaving since birth. He rarely spoke, and then only in a pidgin unintelligible to me. He was some kind of junior mobster, clearly years behind his original class, just biding his time until he could drop out. His name was Freitas—I never heard a first name—but he didn't seem to be related to the Freitas clan, a vast family with a number of rambunctious boys at Kaimuki Intermediate. The stiletto-toed Freitas studied me frankly for a few days, making me increasingly nervous, and then began to conduct little assaults on my self-possession, softly bumping my elbow, for example, while I concentrated over a saw cut on my half-built shoe-shine box.

I was too scared to say anything, and he never said a word to me. That seemed to be part of the fun. Then he settled on a crude but ingenious amusement to pass those periods when we had to sit in chairs in the classroom part of the shop. He would sit behind me and, whenever the teacher had his back turned, would hit me on the head with a two-by-four. *Bonk . . . bonk . . . bonk*, a nice steady rhythm, always with enough of a pause between blows to allow me brief hope that there might not be another. I couldn't understand why the teacher didn't hear all these unauthorized, resonating clonks. They were loud enough to attract the attention of our classmates, who seemed to find Freitas's little ritual fascinating. Inside my head the blows were, of course, bone-rattling explosions. Freitas used a fairly long board—five or six feet—and he never hit too hard, which allowed him to pound away to his heart's content without leaving marks, and to do it from a certain rarefied, even meditative distance, which added, I imagine, to the fascination of the performance.

I wonder if, had some other kid been targeted, I would have been as passive as my classmates were. Probably so. The teacher was off in his own world, worried only about his table saws. I did nothing in my own defense. While I eventually understood that Freitas wasn't Hawaiian, I must have figured I just had to take the abuse. I was, after all, skinny and haole and had no friends.

My parents had sent me to Kaimuki Intermediate, I later decided, under a misconception. This was 1966, and the California public school system, particularly in the middle-class suburbs where we had lived, was among the nation's best. The families we knew never considered private schools for their kids. Hawaii's public schools were another matter—impoverished, mired in colonial, plantation, and mission traditions, miles below the American average academically.

You would not have known that, though, from the elementary school my younger siblings attended. (Kevin was nine, Colleen seven. Michael was three and, in that pre-preschool era, still exempt from formal education.) We had rented a house on the edge of a wealthy neighborhood called Kahala, and Kahala Elementary was a well-funded little haven of progressive education. Except for the fact that the children were allowed to go to school barefoot—an astonishing piece of tropical permissiveness, we thought—Kahala Elementary could have been in a genteel precinct of Santa Monica. Tellingly, however, Kahala had no junior high. That was because every family in the area that could possibly manage it sent its kids to the private secondary schools that have for generations educated Honolulu's (and much of the rest of Hawaii's) middle class, along with its rich folk.

Ignorant of all this, my parents sent me to the nearest junior high, up in working-class Kaimuki, on the back side of Diamond Head crater, where they assumed I was getting on with the business of the eighth grade, but where in fact I was occupied almost entirely by the rigors of bullies, loneliness, fights, and finding my way, after a lifetime of unconscious whiteness in the segregated suburbs of California, in a racialized world. Even my classes felt racially constructed. For academic subjects, at least, students were assigned, on the basis of test scores, to a group that moved together from teacher to teacher. I was put in a high-end group, where nearly all my classmates were Japanese girls. There were no Hawaiians, no Samoans, no Filipinos, and the classes themselves, which were prim and undemanding, bored me in a way that school never had before. Matters weren't helped by the fact that, to my classmates, I seemed not to exist socially. And so I passed the class hours slouched in back rows, keeping an eye on the trees outside for signs of wind direction and strength, drawing page after page of surfboards and waves.

I HAD BEEN SURFING for three years by the time my father got the job that took us to Hawaii. He had been working, mostly as an assistant director, in series television—*Dr. Kildare, The Man from U.N.C.L.E.* Now he was the production manager on a new series, a half-hour musical variety show based on a local radio program, *Hawaii Calls*. The idea was to shoot Don Ho singing in a glass-bottomed boat, a calypso band by a waterfall, hula girls dancing while a volcano spewed, and call it a show. "It won't be the Hawaiian Amateur Hour," my father said. "But close."

"If it's really bad, we'll pretend we don't know you," my mother said. "Bill *who?*"

The budget for moving us all to Honolulu was tight, judging from the tiny cottage we rented (Kevin and I took turns sleeping on the couch) and the rusted-out old Ford we bought to get around. But the cottage was near the beach—just up a driveway lined with other cottages, on a street called Kulamanu—and the weather, which was warm even in January, when we arrived, felt like wanton luxury.

I was beside myself with excitement just to be in Hawaii. All surfers, all readers of surf magazines—and I had memorized nearly every line, every photo caption, in every surf magazine I owned—spent the bulk of their fantasy lives, like it or not, in Hawaii. And now I was there, walking on actual Hawaiian sand (coarse, strange-smelling), tasting Hawaiian seawater (warm, strange-smelling), and paddling toward Hawaiian waves (small, dark-faced, windblown).

Nothing was what I'd expected. In the mags, Hawaiian waves were always big and, in the color shots, ranged from deep, mid-ocean blue to a pale, impossible turquoise. The wind was always offshore (blowing from land to sea, ideal for surfing), and the breaks themselves were the Olympian playgrounds of the gods: Sunset Beach, the Banzai Pipeline, Makaha, Ala Moana, Waimea Bay.

All of that seemed worlds away from the sea in front of our house. Even Waikiki, known for its beginner breaks and tourist crowds, was over on the far side of Diamond Head—the glamorous, iconic western side— along with every other part of Honolulu anybody had heard of. We were on the mountain's southeast side, down in a little saddle of sloping, shady beachfront west of Black Point. The beach was just a patch of damp sand, narrow and empty.

On the afternoon of our arrival, during my first, frantic survey of the local waters, I found the surf setup confusing. Waves broke here and there along the outer edge of a mossy, exposed reef. I was worried by all the coral. It was infamously sharp. Then I spotted, well off to the west, and rather far out at sea, a familiar minuet of stick figures, rising and falling, backlit by the afternoon sun. Surfers! I ran back up the lane. Everyone at the house was busy unpacking and fighting over beds. I threw on a pair of trunks, grabbed my board, and left without a word.

I paddled west along a shallow lagoon, staying close to the shore, for half a mile. The beach houses ended, and the steep, brushy base of Diamond Head itself took their place across the sand. Then the reef on my left fell away, revealing a wide channel—deeper water, where no waves broke— and beyond the channel ten or twelve surfers riding a scatter of dark, chest-high peaks in a moderate onshore wind. I paddled slowly toward the lineup—the wave-catching zone—taking a roundabout route, studying every ride. The surfers were good. They all had smooth, ungimmicky styles. Nobody fell off. And nobody, blessedly, seemed to notice me.

I circled around, then edged into an unpopulated stretch of the lineup. There were plenty of waves. The takeoffs were crumbling but easy. Letting muscle memory take over, I caught and rode a couple of small, mushy rights. The waves were different—but not too different—from the waves I

knew in California. They were shifty but not intimidating. I could see
coral on the bottom, but except for a couple of heads poking up far inside
(near shore), nothing too shallow.

There was a lot of talk and laughter among the other surfers. Eaves-
dropping, I couldn't understand a word. They were probably speaking
pidgin. I had read about pidgin in James Michener's *Hawaii* but, with my
debut at Kaimuki Intermediate still a day away, hadn't actually heard any
yet. Or maybe it was some foreign language. I was the only haole (another
word from Michener) in the water. At one point, an older guy paddling
past me gestured seaward and said, "Outside." It was the only word spoken to me that day. And he was right: an outside set was approaching, the
biggest of the afternoon, and I was grateful to have been warned.

As the sun dropped, the crowd thinned. I tried to see where people
went. Most seemed to take a steep path up the mountainside to Diamond
Head Road, their pale boards, carried on their heads, moving steadily,
skeg-first, through the switchbacks. I caught a final wave, rode it into the
shallows, and began the long paddle home through the lagoon. Lights
were on in the houses now. The air was cooler, the shadows blue-black
under the coconut palms along the shore. I was aglow with my good fortune. I just wished I had someone to tell: *I'm in Hawaii, surfing in Hawaii.*
Then it occurred to me that I didn't even know the name of the place I'd
surfed.

IT WAS CALLED CLIFFS. It was a patchwork arc of reefs that ran south
and west for half a mile from the channel where I first paddled out. To
learn any new spot in surfing, you first bring to bear your knowledge of
other breaks—all the other waves you've learned to read closely. But at
that stage my complete archives consisted of ten or fifteen California
spots, and only one I really knew well: a cobblestone point in Ventura.
And none of this experience prepared me especially well for Cliffs, which,
after that initial session, I tried to surf twice a day.

Path to the water, Kulamanu house, 1966

It was a remarkably consistent spot, in the sense that there were nearly always waves to ride, even in what I came to understand was the off-season for Oahu's South Shore. The reefs off Diamond Head are at the southern extremity of the island, and thus pick up every scrap of passing swell. But they also catch a lot of wind, including local williwaws off the slopes of the crater, and the wind, along with the vast jigsaw expanse of the reef and the swells arriving from many different points of the compass, combined to produce constantly changing conditions that, in a paradox I didn't appreciate at the time, amounted to a rowdy, hourly refutation of the idea of consistency. Cliffs possessed a moody complexity beyond anything I had known.

Mornings were particularly confounding. To squeeze in a surf before school, I had to be out there by daybreak. In my narrow experience the sea was supposed to be glassy at dawn. In coastal California, that is, early mornings are usually windless. Not so, apparently, in the tropics. Certainly not at Cliffs. At sunrise the trade winds often blew hard. Palm fronds thrashed overhead as I tripped down the lane, waxed board on my head, and from the seafront I could see whitecaps outside, beyond the reef, spilling east to west on a royal-blue ocean. The trades were said to be northeasterlies, which was not a bad direction, in theory, for a south-facing coast, but somehow they were always sideshore at Cliffs, and strong enough to ruin most spots from that angle.

And yet the place had a kind of growling durability that left it ridable, at least for my purposes, even in those battered conditions. Almost no one else surfed it in the early morning, which made it a good time to explore the main takeoff area. I began to learn the tricky, fast, shallow sections, and the soft spots where a quick cutback was needed to keep a ride going. Even on a waist-high, blown-out day, it was possible to milk certain waves for long, improvised, thoroughly satisfying rides. The reef had a thousand quirks, which changed quickly with the tide. And when the inshore channel began to turn a milky turquoise—a color not unlike some of the Hawaiian fantasy waves in the mags—it meant, I came to know, that the sun had risen to the point where I should head in for breakfast. If the tide was extra low, leaving the lagoon too shallow to paddle, I learned to allow more time for trudging home on the soft, coarse sand, struggling to keep my board's nose pointed into the wind.

Afternoons were a different story. The wind was usually lighter, the sea less seasick, and there were other people surfing. Cliffs had a crew of regulars. After a few sessions, I could recognize some of them. At the mainland spots I knew, there was usually a limited supply of waves, a lot of jockeying for position, and a strictly observed pecking order. A youngster, particularly one lacking allies, such as an older brother, needed to be careful not to cross, even inadvertently, any local big dogs. But at Cliffs there was so much room to spread out, so many empty peaks breaking off to the west of the main takeoff—or, if you kept an eye out, perhaps on an inside shelf that had quietly started to work—that I felt free to pursue my explorations of the margins. Nobody bothered me. Nobody vibed me. It was the opposite of my life at school.

. . .

MY ORIENTATION PROGRAM at school included a series of fistfights, some of them formally scheduled. There was a cemetery next to the campus, with a well-hidden patch of grass down in one corner where kids went to settle their differences. I found myself facing off there with a number of boys named Freitas—none of them, again, apparently related to my hairy tormentor from wood shop. My first opponent was so small and young that I doubted he was even at our school. The Freitas clan's method for training its members in battle, it seemed, was to find some fool without allies or the brains to avoid a challenge, then send their youngest fighter with any chance at all into the ring. If he lost, the next biggest Freitas would be sent in. This went on until the nonkinsman was defeated. It was all quite dispassionate, the bouts arranged and refereed by older Freitases, and more or less fairly conducted.

My first match was sparsely attended—really of no interest to anyone—but I was still scared sick, having no seconds in my corner and no idea what the rules were. My opponent turned out to be shockingly strong for his size, and ferocious, but his arms were too short to land punches, and I eventually subdued him without much damage to either of us. His cousin, who stepped up immediately, was more my size, and our sparring was more consequential. I held my own, but we both had shiners before a senior Freitas stepped in, declaring a draw. There would be a rematch, he said, and if I won that, somebody named Tino would come and kick my ass, no questions asked. Team Freitas departed. I remember watching them jog, laughing and loose, a happy family militia, up the long slope of the graveyard. They were evidently late for another appointment. My face hurt, my knuckles hurt, but I was giddy with relief. Then I noticed a couple of haole guys my age standing in the bushes at the edge of the clearing, looking squirrelly. I half recognized them from school, but they left without saying a word.

I won the rematch, I think. Then Tino kicked my ass, no questions asked.

There were more fights, including a multiday brawl with a Chinese kid in my agriculture class who refused to give up even when I had his face shoved deep in the red mud of the lettuce patch. This bitter tussle went on for a week. It resumed each afternoon, and never produced a winner. The other boys in the class, enjoying the show, made sure that the teacher, if he ever came round, didn't catch us at it.

I don't know what my parents thought. Cuts and bruises, even black eyes, could be explained. Football, surfing, something. My hunch, which seems right in retrospect, was that they couldn't help, so I told them nothing.

A racist gang came to my rescue. They called themselves the In Crowd. They were haoles and, their laughable gang name notwithstanding, they were impressively bad. Their leader was a jolly, dissolute, hoarse-voiced, broken-toothed kid named Mike. He was not physically imposing, but he shambled around school with a rowdy fearlessness that seemed to give everyone but the largest Samoans pause. Mike's true home, one came to understand, was a juvenile detention center somewhere—this schoolgoing was just a furlough, which he intended to make the most of. He had a younger sister, Edie, who was blond and skinny and wild, and their house in Kaimuki was the In Crowd's clubhouse. At school they gathered under a tall monkeypod tree on a red-dirt hill behind the unpainted bungalow where I took typing. My induction was informal. Mike and his buddies simply let me know I was welcome to join them under the monkeypod. And it was from the In Crowd kids, who actually seemed to include more girls than boys, that I began to learn, first, the broad outlines, and then the minutiae, of the local racial setup. Our main enemies, I came to know, were the "mokes"—which seemed to mean anyone dark and tough.

"You been beefin' with mokes already," Mike told me.

That was true, I realized.

But my fighting career soon tailed off. People seemed to know I was now part of the haole gang, and elected to pick on other kids. Even Freitas in wood shop started easing up on me. But had he really put away his two-by-four? It was hard to imagine he would be worried by the In Crowd.

DISCREETLY, I STUDIED the surfing of some of the regulars at Cliffs—the ones who seemed to read the wave best, who found the speed pockets and wheeled their boards so neatly through their turns. My first impression was confirmed: I had never seen such smoothness. Hand movements were strikingly in synch with feet. Knees were more deeply bent than in the surfing I was used to, hips looser. There wasn't much nose-riding, which was the subspecialty rage at the time on the mainland and required scurrying, when the opportunity arose, to the front of one's board—hanging five, hanging ten, defying the obvious physics of flotation and glide. I didn't know it then, but what I was looking at was classic Island style. I just took my mental notes from the channel, and began, without thinking about it, to walk the nose less.

There were a few young guys, including one wiry, straight-backed kid who looked to be about my age. He stayed away from the main peak, riding peripheral waves. But I craned to see what he did. Even on the funky little waves he chose, I could see that he was shockingly quick and poised. He was the best surfer my age I had ever seen. He rode an unusually short, light, sharp-nosed board—a bone-white clear-finish Wardy. He caught me watching him, and he seemed as embarrassed as I was. He paddled furiously past me, looking affronted. I tried to stay out of his way after that. But the next day he cocked his chin in greeting. I hoped my happiness didn't show. Then, a few days later, he spoke.

"Mo' bettah that side," he said, throwing his eyes to the west as we pushed through a small set. It was an invitation to join him at one of his obscure, uncrowded peaks. I didn't need to be asked twice.

His name was Roddy Kaulukukui. He was thirteen, same as me. "He's so tan he looks Negro," I wrote to my friend. Roddy and I traded waves warily, and then less warily. I could catch waves as well as he could, which was important, and I was learning the spot, which became something of a shared enterprise. As the two youngest guys at Cliffs, we were both, at least half-consciously, in the market for an age-mate. But Roddy didn't come out there alone. He had two brothers and a sort of honorary third brother—a Japanese guy named Ford Takara. Roddy's older brother, Glenn, was a lineup mainstay. Glenn and Ford were out every day. They were only a year older than us, but both of them could compete with anybody in the main peak. Glenn in particular was a superb surfer, with a style that was already flowing and beautiful. Their father, Glenn Sr., also surfed, as did their little brother, John, though he was too young for Cliffs.

Roddy began to fill me in on who some of the other guys were. The fat guy who appeared on bigger days, taking off far outside and ripping so hard that the rest of us stopped surfing to watch, was Ben Aipa, he said. (Years later, Aipa photos and stories began to fill the mags.) The Chinese guy who showed up on the biggest day I had seen yet at Cliffs—a solid, out-of-season south swell on a windless, overcast afternoon—was Leslie Wong. He had a silky style, and he only deigned to surf Cliffs when it was exceptionally good. Leslie Wong caught and pulled into the wave of the day, his back slightly arched, his arms relaxed, making the extremely difficult—no, come on, the *ecstatic*—look easy. When I grew up, I wanted to be Leslie Wong. Among the Cliffs regulars, I slowly got to know who was likely to waste a wave—fail to catch it, or fall off—and then how to quietly snag the wave myself without showing disrespect. Even in a mild-mannered crowd, it was important not to show up anyone.

Day in, day out, Glenn Kaulukukui was my favorite surfer. From the moment he caught a wave, gliding catlike to his feet, I couldn't take my eyes off the lines he drew, the speed he somehow found, the improvisations he came up with. He had a huge head, which seemed always to be slightly thrown back, and long hair, sun-bleached red, also thrown lushly back. He had thick lips, African-looking, black shoulders, and he moved with unusual elegance. But there was something else—call it wit, or irony—that accompanied his physical confidence and beauty, something bittersweet that allowed him, in all but the most demanding situations, to seem like he was both performing intently and, at the same time, laughing quietly at himself.

He also laughed at me, though not unkindly. When I overpowered a kickout, trying to put a flourish on the end of a ride, slicing awkwardly over the shoulder and into parallel with his board in the channel, Glenn said, "Geev 'um, Bill. Geev 'um da lights." Even I knew that this was a pidgin cliché—an overused exhortation. It was also a dense little piece of satire. He was mocking me and encouraging me, both. We paddled out together. When we were nearly outside, we watched Ford catch a set wave from a deep position and pick a clever line to thread through a pair of difficult sections. "Yeah, Fawd," Glenn murmured appreciatively. "Spock *dat*." Then he began to outsprint me toward the lineup.

One afternoon Roddy asked where I lived. I pointed east, toward the shady cove inside Black Point. He told Glenn and Ford, then came back, looking abashed, with a request. Could they leave their boards at my house? I was happy for the company on the long paddle home. Our cottage had a tiny yard, with a stand of bamboo, thick and tall, hiding it from the street. We stashed our boards in the bamboo and washed off in the dark with a garden hose. Then the three of them left, wearing nothing but trunks, dripping wet, clearly stoked to be unburdened by boards, for distant Kaimuki.

THE IN CROWD'S RACISM was situationist, not doctrinaire. It seemed to have no historical pretensions—unlike, say, the skinheads who came along later claiming descent from Nazism and the Klan. Hawaii had seen plenty of white supremacism, particularly among its elites, but the In Crowd knew nothing of elites. Most of the kids were hardscrabble, living in strait- ened circumstances, though some had been kicked out of private schools and were simply in disgrace. Among Kaimuki Intermediate's smattering of haole students, most were actually shunned by the In Crowd as insuffi- ciently cool. These unaffiliated haoles seemed to be mainly military kids. They all looked disoriented, scared. The two guys who had watched me fight the Freitases without offering help were among them. And so was a tremendously tall, silent, friendless boy whom people called Lurch.

There were other haoles, I later realized, who were too smart to get in- volved in gang nonsense. These kids, most of them surfers from the Waikiki side of Diamond Head, knew how to keep low profiles when in the minority. They also knew losers when they saw them. And they had, in a pinch, their own mutual-assistance structures to draw on. But I was too clueless those first months to register their existence.

Adolescent cool was, as ever, mostly a mystery, but physical strength (read: early puberty), self-confidence (special bonus points for defying adults), and taste in music and clothes all counted. I couldn't see how I qualified in any category. I wasn't big—indeed, puberty seemed, to my shame, to be eluding me. I wasn't hip to fashion or music. I certainly wasn't bad—I had never even been to jail. But I admired the spunk of the In Crowd kids, and I wasn't inclined to question anybody who had my back.

I thought the In Crowd's main activity would be gang fighting, and there was certainly continual talk of impending warfare with various rival "moke" groups. But then Mike always seemed to be leading a peace delegation to some last-minute powwow, and bloodshed would be avoided through painstaking, face-saving diplomacy. Truces would be formalized by solemn underage drinking. Most of the group's energy actually went into gossip, parties, petty theft and vandalism, and being obnoxious on the city bus after school. There were a number of pretty girls in the In Crowd, and I was serially smitten with each of them. Nobody in the gang surfed.

· · ·

RODDY AND GLENN KAULUKUKUI and Ford Takara all went to
Kaimuki Intermediate, it turned out. But I didn't hang with them there.
That was a feat, since the four of us spent nearly every afternoon and
weekend together in the water, and Roddy was soon established as my new
best friend. The Kaulukukuis lived at Fort Ruger, on the north slope of
Diamond Head crater, near the cemetery that abutted our school. Glenn
Sr. was in the Army, and their apartment was in an old military barracks
tucked in a little kiawe grove below Diamond Head Road. Roddy and
Glenn had lived on the island of Hawaii, which everybody called the Big
Island. They had family there. Now they had a stepmother, and she and
Roddy didn't get along. She was Korean. Did I know what Koreans were
like? Roddy was ready to fill me in.

Confined to quarters after a fight with his stepmother, he poured out
his misery in bitter whispers in the stifling room he shared with Glenn
and John.

I thought I knew something about misery: I was missing waves that
afternoon in a show of solidarity. There wasn't even a surf mag to leaf
through while grimacing sympathetically. "Why he have to marry *her*?"
Roddy keened.

Glenn Sr. occasionally came surfing with us. He was a formidable character, heavily muscled, severe. He ordered his sons around, not bothering
with niceties. He seemed to loosen up in the water, though. Sometimes
he even laughed. He rode a huge board in a simple, old-fashioned style,
drawing long lines, perfectly balanced, across the long walls at Cliffs. In
his day, his sons told me proudly, he had surfed Waimea Bay.

Waimea was on the North Shore. It was considered the heaviest big-
wave spot in the world. I knew it only as a mythical place—a stage set,
really, for the heroics of a few surf celebrities, hyped endlessly in the mags.
Roddy and Glenn didn't talk much about it, but to them Waimea was
obviously a real place, and exceedingly serious business. You surfed it

when you were ready. Most surfers, of course, would never be ready. But for Hawaiian kids like them, Waimea, and the other great North Shore breaks as well, lay ahead, each a question, a type of final exam.

I had always assumed that only famous surfers rode Waimea. But now I saw that local fathers rode it too, and in time, perhaps, their sons would as well. These people never appeared in mainland magazines. And there were many families like the Kaulukukuis in Hawaii—multigenerational surfing families, *ohanas* rich in talent and tradition, known only to one another.

Glenn Sr. reminded me, from the first time I saw him, of Liloa, the old monarch in a book I loved, *Umi: The Hawaiian Boy Who Became a King*. It was a children's book, first given to my father, according to a faded flyleaf inscription, by two aunts who had bought it in Honolulu in 1939. The author, Robert Lee Eskridge, had also done the illustrations, which I thought magnificent. They were simple but fierce, like lushly colored woodcuts. They showed Umi and his younger brothers and their adventures in old Hawaii: sailing down mountainsides on morning-glory vines ("From vine to vine the boys slid with lightning speed"), diving into pools formed by lava tubes, crossing the sea in war canoes ("Slaves shall accompany Umi to his father's palace in Waipio"). Some of the illustrations showed grown men, guards and warriors and courtiers, whose faces scared me—their stylized cruelty, in a pitiless world of all-powerful chiefs and quaking commoners. At least the features of Liloa, the king and Umi's secret father, were softened at times by wisdom and paternal pride.

Roddy believed in Pele. She was the Hawaiian goddess of fire. She lived, people said, on the Big Island, where she caused the volcanoes to erupt when she was displeased. She was famously jealous and violent, and Hawaiians tried to propitiate her with offerings of pork, fish, liquor. She was so famous that even tourists knew about her, but Roddy made it clear, when he professed his belief to me, that he wasn't talking about the kitsch character. He meant a whole religious world, something from before the

haoles came—a Hawaiian world with elaborate rules and taboos and secret, hard-won understandings about the land, the ocean, birds, fish, animals, and the gods. I took him seriously. I already knew, in rough outline,
what had happened to the Hawaiians—how American missionaries and
other haoles had subjugated them, stolen their lands, killed them en masse
with diseases, and converted the survivors to Christianity. I felt no responsibility for this cruel dispossession, no liberal guilt, but I knew enough to
keep my junior atheist's mouth shut.

We started surfing new spots together. Roddy wasn't afraid of coral the
way I was, and he showed me spots that broke among the reefs between my
house and Cliffs. Most were only ridable at high tide, but some were little
keyholes, slots between dry reef—sweet waves hiding in plain sight, essentially windproof. These breaks, Roddy said, were customarily named after
the families who lived, or had once lived, in front of them—Patterson's,
Mahoney's. There was also a big-wave spot, known as the Bomb, that
broke outside Patterson's. Glenn and Ford had ridden it once or twice.
Roddy had not. I had seen waves feathering (their crests throwing spray as
the swells steepened) out there on big days at low tide, but had never seen
it big enough to break. Roddy talked about the Bomb in a hushed, strained
voice. He was obviously working up to it.

"This summer," he said. "First big day."

In the meantime, we had Kaikoos. It was a deepwater break off Black
Point, visible from the bottom of our lane. It was hard to line up, and always bigger than it looked, and I found it scary. Roddy led me out there
the first time, paddling through a deep, cross-chopped channel that had
been cut originally, he told me, by Doris Duke, the tobacco heiress, to
serve a private yacht harbor that was still tucked into the cliff under her
mansion. He pointed toward the shore, but I was too worried about the
waves ahead to check out Doris Duke's place.

Thick, dark blue peaks seemed to jump up out of deep ocean, some of
them frighteningly big. The lefts were short and easy, really just big drops,
but Roddy said the rights were better, and he paddled farther east, deeper

into the break. His temerity seemed to me insane. The rights looked closed out (unmakable), and terribly powerful, and even if you made one the ride would carry you straight into the big, hungry-looking rocks of outer Black Point. If you lost your board in there, you would never see it again. And where could you even swim in? I darted around, dodging peaks, way outside, half-hysterical, trying to keep an eye on Roddy. He seemed to be catching waves, though it was hard to tell. Finally, he paddled back to me, looking exhilarated, smirking at my agitation. He took pity on me, though, and said nothing.

I later learned to like—not love—the rights at Kaikoos. The spot was often empty, but there were a few guys who knew how to ride it, and, watching them on good days from the Black Point rocks, I began to see the shape of the reef and how to avoid, with a little luck, catastrophe. Still, it was a gnarly spot by my standards, and when I bragged in letters to my friend in Los Angeles about riding this scary, deepwater peak, I was not above spinning tall tales about being carried, with Roddy, by huge currents halfway to Koko Head, which was miles away to the east. My detailed description of scooting through a big tube—the cavern formed by a hard-breaking wave—on a Kaikoos right contained, on the other hand, a whiff of authenticity. I still half remember that wave.

BUT SURFING ALWAYS HAD this horizon, this fear line, that made it different from other things, certainly from other sports I knew. You could do it with friends, but when the waves got big, or you got into trouble, there never seemed to be anyone around.

Everything out there was disturbingly interlaced with everything else. Waves were the playing field. They were the goal. They were the object of your deepest desire and adoration. At the same time, they were your adversary, your nemesis, even your mortal enemy. The surf was your refuge, your happy hiding place, but it was also a hostile wilderness—a dynamic, indifferent world. At thirteen, I had mostly stopped believing in God, but that was a new development, and it had left a hole in my world, a feeling that I'd been abandoned. The ocean was like an uncaring God, endlessly dangerous, power beyond measure.

And yet you were expected, even as a kid, to take its measure every day. You were required—this was essential, a matter of survival—to know your limits, both physical and emotional. But how could you know your limits unless you tested them? And if you failed the test? You were also required to stay calm if things went wrong. Panic was the first step, everybody said, to drowning. As a kid, too, your abilities were assumed to be growing. What was unthinkable one year became thinkable, possibly, the next. My letters from Honolulu in 1966, kindly returned to me recently, are less distinguished by swaggering bullshit than by frank discussions of fear. "Don't think I've suddenly gotten brave. I haven't." But the frontiers of the thinkable were quietly, fitfully edging back for me.

That was clear on the first big day I saw at Cliffs. A long-period swell had arrived overnight. The sets (larger waves, which usually come in groups) were well overhead, glassy and gray, with long walls and powerful sections. I was so excited to see the excellence that my backyard spot could produce that I forgot my usual shyness and began to ride with the crowd at the main peak. I was overmatched there, and scared, and got mauled by the biggest sets. I wasn't strong enough to hold on to my board when caught inside by six-foot waves, even though I "turned turtle"—rolled the board over, pulled the nose down from underwater, wrapped my legs around it, and got a death grip on the rails. The whitewater tore the board from my hands, then thrashed me, holding me down for long, thorough beatings. I spent much of the afternoon swimming. Still, I stayed out till dusk. I even caught and made a few meaty waves. And I saw surfing that day—by Leslie Wong, among others—that made my chest hurt: long moments of grace under pressure that felt etched deep in my being: what I wanted, somehow, more than anything else. That night, while my family slept, I lay awake on the bamboo-framed couch, heart pounding with residual adrenaline, listening restlessly to the rain.

. . .

OUR LIFE IN THE LITTLE COTTAGE on Kulamanu felt makeshift, barely American. There were geckos on the walls, cane rats under the floor, huge water bugs in the bathroom. There was strange fruit—mangoes, papayas, lychees, star fruit—that my mother learned to judge for ripeness, then proudly peel and slice. I don't remember if we even had a TV. The sitcoms that had been a kind of prime-time hearth back on the mainland—*My Three Sons*, *I Dream of Jeannie*, even my favorite, *Get Smart*—now seemed like half-remembered black-and-white dreams from a world left behind. We had a landlady, Mrs. Wadsworth, who watched us supiciously. Still, I found renting grand. Mrs. Wadsworth had a gardener, which afforded me a life of leisure. My yard chores in California had seemed to take up half my waking hours.

Another thing about our exotic new life: we all squabbled less, maybe because we each remained slightly awestruck by our new surroundings. And the fights we did have never escalated into the full-dress screaming and belting and spanking that we had regularly endured in L.A. When my mother yelled, "Wait till your father gets home," she didn't seem serious now. It was as if she were slyly quoting an earlier self, or some TV mom, and even the little ones were in on the joke.

My father worked at least six days a week. When we had him with us, on the odd Sunday, we would ramble around the island—cross the sheer, dripping, wind-blasted Pali (the pass over the mountains that stood like a green wall above Honolulu), or picnic out at Hanauma Bay, beyond Koko Head, where the snorkeling on the reef was wondrous. He made it home most evenings, and on special occasions we went to a restaurant called the Jolly Roger, part of a pirate-themed chain, with burgers named after Robert Louis Stevenson characters, in a shopping mall in Kahala. One night we went to see Disney's *Snow White* at a drive-in on Waialae Avenue, all six of us in a pile in our old Ford Fairlane. I know this because I wrote to my friend in L.A. about it. I described the film as "psychedelic."

My father's Hawaii was a big, truly interesting place. He was regularly in the outer islands, herding film crews and talent into rain forests, remote villages, tricky shoots on unsteady canoes. He even shot a Pele number on a Big Island lava field. Although he didn't know it, he was building the foundation for an adjunct career as a Hawaii specialist—he spent most of the next decade making feature films and TV shows in the islands. His job involved constant battling with local labor unions, particularly the teamsters and the longshoremen, who controlled freight transportation. There was abundant private irony in these battles, since my father was a strong union man, from a union family (railroaders) in Michigan. Indeed, family legend had it that in New York City, where I was born, he spent the night of my birth in a jail cell, having been plucked off a picket line outside the CBS studios, where he worked as a newswriter, and where he and his friends were trying to organize. Though he never talked about it, our move to California, with me still an infant, had been driven by employment difficulties caused by his labor militancy. It was the heyday of Senator Joseph McCarthy.

The Hawaiian unions were, around that same time, performing postwar miracles. Led by an outpost of the West Coast longshoremen, in league with local Japanese American leftists, they even organized plantation workers, transforming a feudal economy. This was in a territory where, before the war, the harassment and even murder of strikers and organizers by management goons and police generally went unpunished. By the mid-'60s, however, Hawaii's labor movement, like much of its mainland counterpart, had grown complacent, top-heavy, and corrupt, and my father, although he came to like personally some of the union bosses he fought daily, never seemed much edified by the struggle.

His work carried us into odd orbits. A hyperkinetic restaurateur named Chester Lau, for instance, had attached himself to *Hawaii Calls*, and for years my family turned up at far-flung luaus and pig roasts and civic events organized by Chester and usually held at one of his joints.

My dad gained enough sense of local working-class culture to know that the streets of Honolulu (and perhaps the schools) might be a challenge for a haole kid. If nothing else, there was a notorious unofficial holiday called Kill a Haole Day. This holiday got plenty of discussion, including editorials (against) in the local papers, though I never managed to find out where precisely on the calendar it fell. "Any day the mokes want," said Mike, our In Crowd chief. I also never heard whether the holiday occasioned any actual homicides. The main targets, people said, of Kill a Haole Day were actually off-duty servicemen, who generally wandered in packs around Waikiki and the red-light district downtown. I think my father took comfort in seeing that my best friends were the local kids who kept their surfboards in our yard. They looked like they could handle themselves.

He had always worried about bullies. When confronted by bigger boys, or outnumbered, I should, he told me, "pick up a stick, a rock, whatever you can find." He got alarmingly emotional giving me this advice. Was he remembering ancient beatings and humiliations in Escanaba, his Michigan hometown? Or was it just so upsetting, the thought of his child, his Billy, alone and set upon by thugs? I had never taken the advice, in any case. There had been plenty of fighting, some of it involving sticks and rocks, in Woodland Hills, the California suburb where we lived, but rarely the stark encounter my dad envisioned. Once, it was true, a Mexican kid, a stranger, got me down under some pepper trees after school, pinning my arms, and squeezed lemon juice into my eyes. That might have been a good time to grab a stick. But I couldn't quite believe that was happening. Lemon juice? In my *eyes*? Put there by someone I didn't even know? My eyes burned for days. I never told my parents about the incident. That would have been a violation of the Code of Boys. Neither did I tell them (or anyone else) about Freitas and his terrible two-by-four.

My father as a scared child—that was a picture that would not come into focus. He was Dad, Big Bill Finnegan, strong as a grizzly. His biceps, a marvel to all of us, were like marbled oak burls. I would never have such arms. I had inherited my mother's string-bean build. My dad seemed scared of no one. Indeed, he had a cantankerous streak that could be mortifying. He wasn't afraid to raise his voice in public. He sometimes asked the proprietors of shops and restaurants that posted signs asserting their right to refuse service to anyone what exactly *that* meant, and if he didn't like their answers angrily took his business elsewhere. This didn't happen in Hawaii, but it happened plenty of times on the mainland. I didn't know that such notices were often code for "whites only"—these were the waning days of legal racial segregation. I just quailed and stared desperately at the ground, dying of embarrassment as his voice began to rise.

MY MOTHER WAS PAT, née Quinn. Her willowy figure was misleading. With a mostly absent husband and no domestic help, she raised four kids without seeming to break a sweat. She had grown up in a Los Angeles that no longer exists—white Catholic working-class Roosevelt liberals—and her generation, reaching adulthood after the war, was broadly, blithely upwardly mobile. Beachgoing progressives, they hitched their stars, for the most part, to the entertainment industry—husbands working in it, wives managing the suburban brood. My mother had an easygoing, tennis-playing grace. She also knew how to make ends meet. When I was little, I thought carrot, apple, and raisin salad was required fare, seven nights a week. In fact, those were the cheapest healthy foods in California at the time. My mother's people were Irish-immigrant hill farmers in West Virginia and she, even more than my dad, was a child of the Depression. Her father, an alcoholic refrigerator repairman, had died young. She never mentioned him. Her mother, left to raise three girls alone, had gone back to school and become a nurse. When my grandmother first saw my father, who was an inch shorter than my mother, she reportedly sighed and said, "Well, all the tall ones got killed in the war."

My mother was endlessly game. She didn't like sailing but spent most weekends knocking around on the succession of little boats that my father, as we got less broke, bought and doted on. She didn't like camping but went camping without complaint. She didn't even like Hawaii, although I didn't know that at the time. To her, the provincialism of Honolulu was suffocating. She had grown up in L.A., had lived in New York, and apparently found the Honolulu daily paper painful to read. She was terrifically social, and not at all snobbish, but she made few friends in Hawaii. My father had never really cared much about friends—if he wasn't working, he preferred to be with his family—but my mother missed the wide circle of other families we knew in L.A., most of them also in show business, as well as her close friends from childhood.

She hid all of that from us and threw herself into making the most of life in an insular, reactionary town. She loved the water, which was lucky (though not for her fair Irish skin). On the patch of damp sand at the bottom of our path, she would spread beach towels and lead the little ones into the lagoon with masks and nets. She got my sister, Colleen, into training for her First Communion at a church in Waikiki. She even, when possible, jumped on planes to the neighboring islands with my dad, usu-

Patricia Finnegan, Windward Side, Oahu, 1966

ally with Michael, who was three, on her hip, and some hasty babysitting arrangement in her wake. And in the outer islands she found, I think, a Hawaii more to her liking—not the Babbitty boosters and country-club racists of Honolulu. In snapshots from those jaunts, she looked like a stranger: not Mom but some pensive, stylish lady in a sleeveless turquoise shift, alone with her thoughts in the middle distance—a Joan Didion character, it seems now, walking barefoot, sandals in hand, past a shaggy wall of shorefront pines. Didion, I later learned, was her favorite writer.

I TREASURED THE BREAK from yard work. But, to my sorrow, I was coming into my own as a babysitter. My parents, ignorant of my budding career as a Kaimuki gangbanger, knew me only as Mr. Responsible. That had been my role at home since shortly after the others started arriving. There was a substantial age gap between me and my siblings—Kevin was more than four years younger, Michael ten—and I could be counted on to keep the little ones undrowned, unelectrocuted, fed, watered, rediapered. But formal babysitting duties, evenings and weekends, were a new thing, and a terrible imposition, I found, when there were waves to ride, city buses begging to be pelted with unripe mangoes, unchaperoned parties to attend in Kaimuki. I took my revenge on poor Kevin and Colleen by sourly reminiscing about the good old days before they were born. It was a golden age, really. Just Mom and Dad and me, doing what we pleased. Every night out at the Jolly Roger. Cheeseburgers, chocolate malts. No crying babies. Those were the days.

I tried to lose my job one blazing Saturday with Colleen. She was scheduled to receive First Communion the next day. Saturday was dress rehearsal for the big ceremony. Mom and Dad were away, probably at a Chester Lau function. Colleen was in head-to-toe white lace regalia. She was supposed to make her First Confession that day—although what, even generally, a seven-year-old girl would have to confess in the way of mortal sins is hard to imagine. The Saturday rehearsal was, in any case, mandatory. The Roman Catholics in those days did not fool around. If you missed the rehearsal, you would not make your First Communion. Come back next year, little sinner, and God save your soul in the interim. Because I had been raised in the cold bosom of the church, I knew what tough nuts the nuns could be. Therefore, when Colleen and I contrived to miss the once-an-hour city bus to Waikiki on the day of her rehearsal, I knew exactly what the stakes were. And because I was still, deep down, little Mr. Responsible, I panicked. I put my tiny sister out in the middle of Diamond Head Road in her showstopping costume, flagged down the first Waikiki-bound vehicle, and got her to the church on time.

I WAS STARTING TO GET my bearings in Honolulu. From the lineup at Cliffs, you could see the whole south coast of Oahu, from the Waianae Mountains in the west, beyond Honolulu and Pearl Harbor, to Koko Head, which was a sort of second-rank Diamond Head—another parched-looking crater at the water's edge—in the east. The city filled a plain between the coast and the Ko'olau Range, whose steep green peaks were usually buried in clouds and mist under brilliant, billowing thunderheads. The mountains sent rain clouds out to water the city, though most burned up before they reached the coast. Rainbows littered the sky. Beyond the mountains was the Windward Side, and somewhere out that way was the fabled North Shore.

Directions in Honolulu were always given, though, in terms of local landmarks, not the compass, so you went mauka (toward the mountains) or makai (toward the sea) or ewa (toward Ewa Beach, which was out past the airport and Pearl Harbor) or diamondhead. (Among those of us living on the far side of Diamond Head, people just said kokohead—same difference.) These picturesque directions weren't slang or affectations—you saw them on official maps and street signs. And they were also, for me— and my sense of this was unformed but strong—a salient piece of a world more unitary, for all its fractiousness, a world more coherent in its mid-

Pacific isolation than any I'd known before. I missed my friends in L.A. But Southern California, in its sprawling, edgeless blandness, was losing its baseline status in my mind. It was no longer the place by which all other places had to be measured. There was a kid in the In Crowd, Steve, who groused endlessly about "the Rock." He meant Oahu, although he made it sound like Alcatraz. Steve's urgent ambition was to escape the Rock, ideally to England, where his favorite band, the Kinks, played. But anywhere "mainland"—anywhere not Hawaii—would do. I, meanwhile, wouldn't have minded staying in Da Islands forever.

IN OLD HAWAII, before the arrival of Europeans, surfing had religious import. After prayers and offerings, master craftsmen made boards from sacred koa or wiliwili trees. Priests blessed swells, lashed the water with vines to raise swells, and some breaks had *heiaus* (temples) on the beach where devotees could pray for waves. This spiritual awareness did not preclude raucous competition, even large-scale gambling. "One contest between Maui and Oahu champions involved a wager of four thousand pigs and sixteen war canoes," according to the historians Peter Westwick and Peter Neushul. Men and women, young and old, royalty and commoners surfed. When the waves were good, "all thought of work is at an end, only that of sport is left," wrote Kepelino Keauokalani, a nineteenth-century Hawaiian scholar. "All day there is nothing but surfing. Many go out surfing as early as four in the morning." The old Hawaiians had it bad, in other words—surf fever. They also had plenty of what we would call leisure time. The islands were blessed with a large food surplus; its inhabitants were not only skilled fishermen, terrace farmers, and hunters, but built and managed elaborate systems of fishponds. Their winter harvest festival lasted three months—during which the surf frequently pumped and work was officially forbidden.

This was not what the Calvinist missionaries who began arriving in Hawaii in 1820 had in mind for the islanders as a way of life. Hiram Bingham, who led the first missionary party, which found itself in a crowd of surfers before it had even landed, wrote that "the appearance of destitution, degradation, and barbarism, among the chattering, and almost naked savages, whose heads and feet, and much of their sunburnt swarthy skins, were bare, was appalling. Some of our number, with gushing tears, turned away from the spectacle." Twenty-seven years later, Bingham wrote, "The decline and discontinuance of the surfboard, as civilization advances, may be accounted for by the increase in modesty, industry or religion." He was not wrong about the decline of surfing. Hawaiian culture had been destroyed, and the people decimated by European diseases; between 1778 and 1893, the Hawaiian population shrank from an estimated eight hundred thousand to forty thousand, and by the end of the nineteenth century surfing had all but disappeared. Westwick and Neushul count Hawaiian surfing less a victim of successful missionary zeal, however, than of extreme demographic collapse, dispossession, and a series of extractive industries—sandalwood, whaling, sugar—that forced the surviving islanders into a cash economy and stripped them of free time.

From this terrible history modern surfing is descended, thanks to the few Hawaiians, notably Duke Kahanamoku, who kept the ancient practice of *he'e nalu* alive. Kahanamoku won a gold medal for swimming at the 1912 Olympics, became an international celebrity, and started giving surfing exhibitions around the world. Surfing caught on, slowly, on various coasts where there were ridable waves and people with the means to chase them. Postwar Southern California became the capital of the emerging surf industry largely because a local aerospace boom provided both new lightweight materials for board-building and an outsized generation of kids like me, with the time and inclination to learn to surf. Not that the local authorities encouraged us. Surfers were typecast as truants and vandals. Some beach towns actually banned surfing. And the trope of the surf bum—brother to the ski bum, sail bum, climbing bum—has never been retired, for good reason. Jeff Spicoli, the stoned-out Sean Penn surf dude in *Fast Times at Ridgemont High*, muddles on righteously in beach towns all over the world today. Hawaii was different, though. At least it felt different to me. Surfing wasn't subcultural or imported or oppositional—even though its survival represented enduring opposition to the Calvinist business values of Hiram Bingham. It felt deeply woven into the fabric of the place.

GLENN AND RODDY INVITED ME to a meeting of their surf club, the Southern Unit. All I knew about the club was that its members wore green-and-white aloha-print trunks, and that every Southern Unit guy I'd seen in the water, mainly out on good days at Cliffs, surfed notably well. The meeting was held in Paki Park, a little public square on the diamond-head side of Waikiki. It was nighttime, and crowded, and I hung back in the shadows. A short, loud, middle-aged man named Mr. Ching ran the show—rattling off old business, new business, contest results, upcoming competitions, all while jousting with the crowd and getting laughs, though the repartee was too quick for me.

"No get wise," Mr. Ching yelled, wheeling on a boy creeping up behind him.

That, Roddy told me, was his son, Bon Ching. He was our age, but he surfed as well as Glenn. There were only a few haoles on hand, but one of them I recognized: Lord James Blears. He was a burly, golden-maned ex-wrestler and local TV host with a theatrically trained, possibly even authentic British accent. Lord Blears, besides everything else, surfed, in a ceremonial sort of way. Roddy pointed out his teenage daughter Laura, who surfed well, he said, and who seemed to me impossibly beautiful, and her brother Jimmy, who later became a famous big-wave rider.

There were other kids at that meeting who grew up to make names for themselves in the wider world of surfing, including Reno Abellira, then a Waikiki urchin heckling Mr. Ching from the shadows, later a top international competitor, renowned for his low, crouching style and blinding speed. What dazzled me, though, were the jackets. Several people wore

green-and-white Southern Unit windbreakers. These were even more de-
sirable, if possible, than the club trunks. When Roddy urged me to volunteer for a fund-raising project being touted by Mr. Ching, I swallowed my
self-consciousness and approached him for an assignment.

I had never been in a surf club. In California you heard about Windan-
sea, which was based in La Jolla and had some big-name members. There
was also a club, supposedly based in Santa Barbara, called Hope Ranch,
that for some reason sounded like very heaven to me and my friends.
None of us knew anyone who belonged to it. We didn't even know its
colors. Maybe it didn't exist at all. Still, the idea of Hope Ranch hovered,
immaterial, a dream of supercoolness in our geeky, overheated wannabe
brainpans.

Now, though, for me it was the Southern Unit. The admissions process
was unclear. Did I have to go out and win a contest? I had never surfed in
a contest—just a few dorky "surf-offs" against other guys from my junior
high in California. I was not averse to more formal competition. But first,
apparently, there was fund-raising. Roddy found an excuse to not appear,
but I dutifully showed up on a hot Saturday morning at the pickup spot.
Mr. Ching drove a group of us, including his son Bon, to a posh-looking
subdivision high in the hills above Honolulu. We each got a heavy sack of
Portuguese sausage and basic instruction in door-to-door salesmanship.
We were raising money for our surfing club—a wholesome cause, like the
Boy Scouts. Mr. Ching said "the Southern Unit," and the kids laughed,
because he pronounced it haole-style, standard English, though it was
usually said "da Soddun Unit." Sales territories were assigned. We were to
meet at the bottom of the mountain at the end of the day.

With lonely bravado, I threw myself into the job. I banged on gates and
doors, ran from angry dogs, talked loudly to old Japanese ladies who gave
no sign that they spoke English. A couple of haole ladies took pity on me,
but I made few sales. The day got hotter. I drank from yard hoses, but I
had brought no food. Finally, famished, I tore into one of my sausages. It
wasn't tasty, but it was better than nothing. Ten minutes later I was on my

knees, retching into a storm drain. I didn't know that Portuguese sausage had to be cooked. I wondered, between heaves, if I was getting closer to or farther from the glory of surf-club membership.

RODDY WAS TRANSFERRED, for some reason, into my typing class. Listening to him report to the teacher, I was stunned. Like Mr. Ching in his fund-raising spiel, Roddy abandoned, briefly, his normal pidgin and spoke standard English. But this wasn't for comic effect; it was just for the occasion. Glenn, I learned later, could do the same thing. The Kaulukukui boys were bilingual; they could "code switch." There just weren't many occasions in our daily rounds—indeed, almost none—when they had to drop their first language, the Hawaiian creole known as pidgin.

But keeping my two worlds separate got suddenly trickier. Roddy and I started hanging out at school, far from the In Crowd's monkeypod. In the cafeteria, we ate our saimin and chow fun together in a dim corner. But the school was a small pond. There was nowhere to hide. So there should have been a scene, a confrontation, perhaps with Mike himself—*Hey, who's this moke?*

There wasn't, though. Glenn and Ford were around then too. Maybe Glenn and Mike hit it off over some shared laugh, nothing to do with me. All I knew was that, seemingly overnight, Glenn and Roddy and Ford were showing up not only at the In Crowd's school yard spot under the monkeypod but also at Mike and Edie's house in Kaimuki on Friday nights—when Mike's uncle supplied the Primo (local beer) and mod Steve supplied the Kinks. The In Crowd had been integrated, with no visible fuss.

This was at a time when the Pacific Club, the leading local private club, where much of Hawaii's big business was conducted over cocktails and paddle tennis, was still whites-only. The Pacific Club, apparently unmoved by the fact that Hawaii's first U.S. representative and one of its first two senators were Asian American (both were also distinguished veterans of World War II; one of them, Daniel Inouye, had lost an arm), still formally banned Asian Americans from membership. This sort of bald discrimination wasn't un-American—legal segregation was still in force in much of the country—but it was badly out of date in Hawaii. Even the low-rent haole kids in the In Crowd were more enlightened. They saw that my friends were cool guys—particularly, I think, Glenn—and, at least for gang purposes, just let the race thing go. It wasn't worth the trouble. It was radioactive crap. Let's party.

Not that kicking it with the In Crowd was the fondest ambition of Glenn, Ford, or Roddy. From what I knew, which was a lot, it was no big deal to them. It was only a big deal to me. In fact, after Roddy got to know a couple of the girls I had been telling him about—In Crowd girls I had agonized over, and had very occasionally canoodled with—I could see he was unimpressed. If the term "skank" had been in use then, he might have used it. Roddy had been suffering his own romantic torments, which I had also heard much about, but the object of his affections was a modest, notably old-fashioned, quietly beautiful girl whom I would never have noticed if he hadn't pointed her out. She was too young to go steady, she said. He would wait years, if necessary, he said wretchedly. Looking at my erstwhile girlfriends through his eyes, I didn't like them any less, but I began to see how lost they were, in their delinquent, neglected-child glamour, their sexual precocity. In truth, they were far more sexually advanced than I was, which made me timid, which made me unhappy.

And so I developed a disastrous crush on Glenn's girlfriend, Lisa. She was an older woman—fourteen, in ninth grade—poised, amused, kind, Chinese. Lisa was at Kaimuki Intermediate but not of it. That was how I saw her. She and Glenn made sense as a couple only because he was a natural-born hero and she was a natural-born heroine. But he was a wild man, an outlaw, a laughing truant, and she was a good girl, a good student. What could they possibly talk about? I didn't really want an answer to that question. "There was a joy of life in him and a kind of tenderness untainted by the merely gentle." When I read that line, written by James

Salter, many years later, I thought of Glenn. Lisa, as I imagine her, might have too. No, I thought, I would just wait, impatiently, for her to come to her senses and turn to the haole boy who struggled to amuse her, and worshipped her. I couldn't tell if Glenn noticed my hapless condition. He had the good grace, anyway, to say nothing off-color about Lisa within my hearing. (No "Spock *dat*"—which means "Look at that," and which boys were always saying to each other, popping their eyes at girlish rumps and breasts.)

Lisa helped me see Ford. I knew he was unusual for a Japanese kid. Glenn sometimes teased him, saying things about "da nip-o-nese" and what a disappointment Ford, who cared for nothing except surfing, must be to his family. But he rarely got a rise out of him. Ford had a powerful inwardness about him. He could not have been more different, I thought, from the Japanese kids in my academic classes. They looked to teachers, and to one another, blatantly, fervently, for approval. I had become friendly with some of the funnier girls, who could be very funny indeed, but the social wall between us stayed solid, and their brownnosing in class still offended my sense of student-teacher protocol. Ford, on the other hand, was from my planet.

He had pale skin, a blocky build, with hard, chiseled-looking muscles, and a stiff, efficient surfing style that carried him swiftly down the line (across, that is, a wave's horizontal expanse). His and Glenn's friendship seemed to revolve around the surf, where they were near equals, but it also included a shared sense of the ridiculous, which Ford, who never said much, expressed with small, dry smiles at Glenn's jokes. Then there was the refuge that the Kaulukukuis provided Ford from family pressures. That was what Lisa explained. She knew Ford's family, including his hard-driving parents and college-bound siblings. The Japanese had surged to the fore politically in postwar Hawaii, moving rapidly off the sugar plantations that they— like the Chinese and Filipinos and other groups—had originally been brought to the islands to work. And they were rising commercially too. They were generally resented for their insularity—unlike the Chinese, say, they were in no hurry to marry outside their ethnic group. But their collective attitude, it seemed safe to say, especially among the older generation, was that they were not going to get ahead in America by hanging out with Hawaiians and having fun. And this, Lisa said, was what Ford rebelled against daily. No wonder, I thought, his jaw always seemed so firmly set.

FLYERS WENT UP for a surf contest, to be held at Diamond Head Cliffs. The organizer seemed to be just a kid at Kaimuki Intermediate—Robert, a small, smooth-talking ninth-grader who didn't even surf. But Roddy and Glenn said he was legit, that he came from a family of sports impresarios. The contest could not have been more small-time—none of the local surf clubs was involved, and the only category seemed to be Boys Under 14. But that was me. I entered.

On contest day, the surf at Cliffs was a sunny, windblown mess on a rising swell. None of the kids who showed up to compete were Cliffs locals—I didn't recognize them, anyway, except for a couple from school. But they all seemed to know their way around the contest rigamarole of heats and jerseys. Some had parents with them, who had gamely made the climb down from Diamond Head Road. I hadn't even told my parents about the event—too embarrassing. Roddy, to my dismay, didn't show up. Glenn was there—he had been drafted to serve as a judge—but he said Roddy had been compelled to go to work that morning with their father, at Fort DeRussy, in Waikiki. I had been counting on seeing Roddy win the contest.

Robert read out the heat lists. When we were not surfing, we huddled under thornbushes on the hillside, squeezing into patches of shade. The judges sat higher up the slope. Some of the surfers looked pretty good, I thought, though none could touch Roddy. One kid wore Southern Unit trunks, but his wave selection was terrible, and he bombed.

I surfed two or three rounds. I was nervous and paddled hard, paying no attention to anyone else. The surf was coming up slightly, which was good, but little Robert did not have the power to clear a contestants' area, so we were surfing in among the usual Saturday crowd. I knew the reefs at Cliffs well by then, so I moved off by myself, ewa side, where a slab of coral sat outside, at a good angle for this swell. Over there I found set waves that connected cleanly through the main part of the break. Robert had a flag system that was supposed to tell surfers when their heats were over, but he neglected to change the flags as the finals ended, and I kept surfing till Glenn paddled out to get me. It was over, he said. I got second place. A haole kid named Tomi Winkler got first. Glenn was grinning. "That drop-knee cutback," he said. "Every time you do one, bwaah, I give you big points."

It was a startling result in three ways. First, Robert actually gave us trophies, some weeks later, greatly surprising my parents, who were hurt that I hadn't invited them. Second, who the hell was Tomi Winkler? He was, it turned out, one of the low-profile haoles at Kaimuki Intermediate—a sweet, sunny guy and, as I came to know, a better surfer than me. Third, Glenn liked my drop-knee cutback. It was a cold-water maneuver, practically unknown in Hawaii, and if I had been systematically shedding my mainland style it would have been one of the first moves to go. But I was apparently still doing it, and my idol, Glenn, actually saw some grace, or at least some novelty, in it. That settled it—the drop-knee stayed.

But this business of style, mainland versus Hawaiian, was complicated. This was true both in surfing as a whole, in every era, and in my little world. I had often heard Glenn tease Roddy about the way he surfed—"too Island kine." He imitated his brother by crouching, sticking his ass out, extending his arms in exaggerated speed arcs, squinting like an angry samurai. It was unfair and inaccurate, but funny. Glenn would even do it sometimes while riding waves, though the war cry then was always "Aikau!" The Aikaus were a local surfing family known for their traditional styles. Like Ben Aipa and Reno Abellira, the Aikaus would later become famous in the international surfing world—renowned for, among other things, their pure Hawaiian styles in big waves. But I had never heard of them. Ford and Roddy found Glenn's parodies irresistible. "You see the Aikaus," Ford told me. "You see why we laugh."

Author, Queens, Waikiki, 1967

MY FIRST TRIP to the North Shore, I made with my family. It was spring, and the big swells from the Aleutians that sent huge surf to the North Shore were finished for the year. We stopped at the fabled big-wave spot, Waimea Bay. Except for the fact that the sea was flat, it looked just like its pictures. We hiked up the canyon behind the beach and swam in a freshwater pool. Dad, Kevin, and I jumped off a cliff into the cold brown water, daring each other to go higher. In feats of stupid physical daring, I had, I realized, surpassed my father, although he was athletic, not timid, and not yet forty. My family, I thought, knew less and less about me. I had been leading a clandestine life, particularly since we moved to Hawaii. Much of that was down to surfing, and it had begun back in California.

Why had I even started surfing? In one picture-book version, the hook had been set on a shining afternoon in Ventura when I was ten. Ventura

was on the coast north of Los Angeles. There was a diner on the pier. My
family ate there on beach weekends. From our booth by the window, I
could see surfers out at a spot known as California Street. They were silhouettes, backlit by low sun, and they danced silently through the glare,
their boards like big dark blades, slashing and gliding, swift beneath their
feet. California Street was a long cobblestone point, and to me, at ten, the
waves that broke along its shelf seemed like they were arriving from some
celestial workshop, their glowing hooks and tapering shoulders carved by
ocean angels. I wanted to be out there, learning to dance on water. The
snug fracas of the family dinner felt vestigial. Even my chiliburger, a special treat, lost its fascination.

In truth, there were plenty of siren songs playing at the time, each calling me toward surfing. And my parents, unlike Ford Takara's, were willing to help me start. They got me a used board for my eleventh birthday.
They gave me and my friends rides to the beach.

Now, though, I seemed to be on my own. Nobody asked where I went
with my board, and I never talked about good days at Cliffs or my triumphs over fear at Kaikoos. When I was little, I liked to bring my wounds
home, liked hearing my mother gasp when she caught sight of blood
trickling down my leg. *What are you gasping about? Oh, that.* I enjoyed
being fussed over, injured but nonchalant. Once, I recall, I even got a per-
verse pleasure from being accidentally burned by another mother's cigarette while riding in a boat. The attention, the remorse—the pain was
worth it to me. Where did that guiltmongering little killjoy come from?
He's with me still, no doubt, but as I entered my teens I suddenly moved
on, psychically, from my family. Tripping back down the trail at Waimea
in swimsuits, I knew we looked like six kindred souls, blood-tied, a brood,
but I felt like the odd one out. A cold gust of pubescent separation seemed to
have caught me prematurely. Of course, when I dove face first into a coral
head—this happened the following summer, at Waikiki—it was still my
mother to whom I was carried, and she who took me to get sewn up.

. . .

I say that my dad was not yet forty. The ages of adults are absurd, of course, to kids, the numbers too large, mostly meaningless. But my dad's age was weirdly constant, in a way that even I knew was odd. You could see it in the family photo album. One moment he was a dark-haired, watchful boy, skating and sledding, playing trumpet in a dance band. Then, at twenty, discharged from the Navy, he was suddenly middle-aged. He smoked a pipe, wore a fedora, looked intent at a typewriter, contented at a chessboard. He married at twenty-three, became a father at twenty-four. That in itself wasn't strange in my parents' world, but my dad seemed to take on adulthood with unusual relish. He *wanted* to be forty. It wasn't that he was a cautious, measured person; if anything, he was moody and rash. He just seemed to want to put youth behind him.

I knew he had hated the Navy, the claustrophobia of shipboard life (the war was over—he had just missed it—but he was in the Pacific on an aircraft carrier). He hated, especially, the helplessness of the ordinary seaman. "They don't call them petty officers for nothing," he said. What I didn't know then was that his early childhood had been a horrorshow. His birth parents were itinerant drunks. Their two sons ended up in the care of elderly aunts. My dad was lucky, landing in small-town Michigan with Martha Finnegan, a sweet-tempered schoolteacher, and her husband, a railroad engineer known as Will. But my father was haunted his entire life by the turmoil and terrors he suffered before his first set of parents gave him up.

My parents were both, not surprisingly, abstemious drinkers. Even in the heyday of the martini, I never saw either one of them tipsy. One of their abiding fears was that their kids would be alcoholics.

They wanted a big family, and they got off to a quick start with me. We lived in a fourth-floor walk-up on Second Avenue in Manhattan. They paid a dollar a month to park my baby carriage in the barbershop downstairs. They hoped to move to Levittown, the prototypical suburb, then brand-new, on Long Island—a tragic idea, in retrospect. Luckily, they moved to Los Angeles instead. My mother then had three consecutive miscarriages. One may have been a stillbirth. Single pregnant Catholic girls, dispatched by some wing of the church, looked after me. When my mother got pregnant with Kevin, she went to bed for six months. This all happened during the purported golden age.

During that same age, my dad seemed to have a thousand jobs. He was a set electrician, a set carpenter, a gaffer, a gofer, on shows live and taped and stage. Of all his jobs, my favorite was gas station attendant. He worked at a Chevron station in Van Nuys—not far from Reseda, where we lived then—and we could deliver him lunch. He wore a white uniform to pump gas; all the attendants did. I thought the chevron insignia on the uniform's starched short sleeves was dashing in the extreme. He worked as a stage manager on a children's TV program called *The Pinky Lee Show*, which my mother and I watched mainly for glimpses of him offstage in his headset. Even I understood dimly that my father was frantic about supporting us, which was why he was nearly always at work. I also got, at some level, that even though he was our household hero, out in the big world wearing headsets and chevrons, he was also, in his own way, as dependent on my mother's support as I was.

We were dutiful, if not particularly enthusiastic, Catholics. Mass every Sunday, Saturday catechism for me, fish sticks on Friday. Then, around my thirteenth birthday, I received the sacrament of confirmation, becoming an adult in the eyes of the church, and was thunderstruck to hear my parents say that I was no longer required to go to Mass. That decision was now mine. Were they not worried about the state of my soul? Their evasive, ambiguous answers shocked me again. They had been big fans of Pope John XXIII. But they did not, I realized, actually believe in all the doctrine and prayers—all those Oblatios, Oratios, frightening Confiteors, and mealymouthed Acts of Contrition that I had been memorizing and struggling to understand since I was small. It was possible that they didn't even believe in God. I immediately stopped going to Mass. God was not visibly upset. My parents continued to drag the little ones to church. Such hypocrisy! This joyful ditching of my religious obligations happened shortly before we moved to Hawaii.

AND SO, on a spring Sunday morning, I found myself slowly paddling back from Cliffs through the lagoon while my family sweated it out up at Star of the Sea in Waialae. The tide was low. My skeg gently bumped on the bigger rocks. Out on the mossy, exposed reef, wearing conical straw hats, Chinese ladies, or maybe they were Filipinas, bent, collecting eels and octopus in buckets. Waves broke here and there along the reef's outer edge, too small to surf.

I felt myself floating between two worlds. There was the ocean, effectively infinite, falling away forever to the horizon. This morning it was placid, its grip on me loose and languorous. But I was lashed to its moods now. The attachment felt limitless, irresistible. I no longer thought of waves being carved in celestial workshops. I was getting more hardheaded. Now I knew they originated in distant storms, which moved, as it were, upon the face of the deep. But my utter absorption in surfing had no rational content. It simply compelled me; there was a deep mine of beauty and wonder in it. Beyond that, I could not have explained why I did it. I knew vaguely that it filled a psychic cavity of some kind—connected, perhaps, with leaving the church, or with, more likely, the slow drift away from my family—and that it had replaced many things that came before it. I was a sunburnt pagan now. I felt privy to mysteries.

The other world was land: everything that was not surfing. Books, girls, school, my family, friends who did not surf. "Society," as I was learning to call it, and the exactions of Mr. Responsible. Hands folded under my chin, I drifted. A bruise-colored cloud hung over Koko Head. A transistor radio twanged on a seawall where a Hawaiian family picnicked on the sand. The sun-warmed shallow water had a strange boiled-vegetable taste. The moment was immense, still, glittering, mundane. I tried to fix each of its parts in memory. I did not consider, even passingly, that I had a choice when it came to surfing. My enchantment would take me where it would.

HERE'S HOW RIDABLE WAVES FORM. A storm out at sea churns the surface, creating chop—smaller and then larger disorganized wavelets, which amalgamate, with enough wind, into heavy seas. What we are waiting for on distant coasts is the energy that escapes from the storm, radiating outward into calmer waters in the form of wave trains—groups of waves, increasingly organized, that travel together. Each wave is a column of orbiting energy, most of it below the surface. All the wave trains produced by a storm constitute what surfers call a swell. The swell can travel thousands of miles. The more powerful the storm, the farther the swell may travel. As it travels, it becomes more organized—the distance between each wave in a train, known as the interval, increases. In a long-interval train, the orbiting energy in each wave may extend more than a thousand feet beneath the ocean surface. Such a train can pass easily through surface resistance like chop or other smaller, shallower swells that it crosses or overtakes.

As waves from a swell approach a shoreline, their lower ends begin to feel the sea bottom. Wave trains become sets—groups of waves that are larger and longer-interval than their more locally generated cousins. The approaching waves refract (bend) in response to the shape of the sea bottom. The visible part of the wave grows, its orbiting energy pushed higher above the surface. The resistance offered by the sea bottom increases as the water gets shallower, slowing the progress of the lowest part of the wave. The wave above the surface steepens. Finally, it becomes unstable and prepares to topple forward—to break. The rule of thumb is that it will break when the wave height reaches 80 percent of the water's depth— an eight-foot wave will break in ten feet of water. But many factors, some of them endlessly subtle—wind, bottom contour, swell angle, currents—

determine exactly where and how each wave breaks. As surfers, we're just hoping that it has a catchable moment (a takeoff point), and a ridable face, and that it doesn't break all at once (close out) but instead breaks gradually, successively (peels), in one direction or the other (left or right), allowing us to travel roughly parallel to the shore, riding the face, for a while, in that spot, in that moment, just before it breaks.

THE SURF CHANGED as spring progressed. There were more swells from the south, which meant more good days at Cliffs. Patterson's, the gentle wave between wide panels of exposed reef out in front of our house, started breaking consistently and a new group of surfers materialized to ride it— old guys, girls, beginners. Roddy's younger brother, John, came too. He was nine or ten, and fantastically nimble. My brother Kevin began to show some interest in surfing, perhaps influenced by John, who was about his age and kept his board in our yard. I was surprised. Kevin was a terrific swimmer. He had been diving into the deep end of the swimming pool since he was eighteen months old. Pigeon-toed, he had a piscine ease in water, and was an expert bodysurfer already at nine. But he had always professed indifference to my obsession: it was my thing; it would not be his. But now he paddled out at Patterson's on a borrowed board and within days was catching waves, standing, turning. He was clearly a natural. We found him a used board, an old Surfboards Hawaii tanker, for ten dollars. I was proud and thrilled. The future suddenly had a different tinge.

With the first big south swell of the season, the Bomb broke. I stood with Roddy on the seawall to watch it. The main peak was so far out, we could see only the first wave of each set break. After that, it was all just shining walls of whitewater and spray. The surf was giant—at least ten feet, the biggest waves I had ever seen. Roddy was silent, staring desolately out to sea. Surely this was out of the question for him. There were two guys out there. Did he know them?

He did.

Who were they?

Wayne Santos, he sighed, and Leslie Wong.

The surfers were only occasionally visible, but we saw each of them drop into monsters. They surfed intently but stylishly, didn't fall, and each kicked out at high speed over the reef beyond Patterson's. Wong and Santos were amazing surfers. They were also adults. Glenn and Ford were out at Cliffs. Surely this wasn't the day for Roddy to make his debut at the Bomb. Sighing deeply, he agreed it wasn't. We tossed our boards in the water and started the long paddle to Cliffs, which would be plenty big for us on a swell like this.

Kevin got hurt—hit in the back by a board at Patterson's. I heard people calling me. *It's your brother.* I paddled in, frantic, and found him on the beach, people standing around him. He looked bad—pale, in shock. Apparently he had gotten the wind completely knocked out of him. Little John Kaulukukui had saved him from drowning. Kevin was still breathing heavily, coughing, crying. We carried him up to the house. Everything hurt, he said, every movement. Mom cleaned him up, calmed him down, and put him to bed. I went back out surfing. I figured he would be back in the water in a few days. But Kevin never surfed again. He did resume bodysurfing, and as a teenager became one of the hotshots at Makapuʻu and Sandy Beach, two serious bodysurfing spots on the eastern tip of Oahu. As an adult, he has had back trouble. Recently an orthopedist, looking at a spinal X-ray, asked him what exactly had happened when he was a child. It looked like he had suffered a massive fracture.

EVERY SCHOOL HAD A BULL—a toughest guy. Kids from different schools would ask each other, *Who da bull at your school?* The bull at Kaimuki Intermediate when I arrived was a guy named, unbelievably, the Bear. It was like some bad Wall Street joke—Da Bear was Da Bull—except nobody had heard of Wall Street. The Bear was huge, naturally. He looked about thirty-five. He seemed benign, even befuddled. He was Samoan, I think. He was always surrounded by a deferential retinue, like a Mafia don. But the Bear's group dressed like slobs—they may actually have inspired my early impression of Kaimuki "natives" as poor and raggedy. They looked, really, like sanitation workers who had just finished work and were looking forward to that first beer. They were all far too old for junior high. Scary-looking but usually in the safe middle distance, they seemed timeless.

Then something happened. It had nothing to do with the Bear, but it caused him to be deposed. And for me, it changed everything. I didn't see how it started, exactly, although I was right there. It was lunchtime. The In Crowd was in its usual spot. I was talking to Lisa, with the usual stars no doubt in my eyes. Lurch, the haole outcast giant, passed by. Somebody said something, and Lurch replied. He had a deep, shy voice and he did look like the TV character he'd been cruelly named after—the lugubrious butler on *The Addams Family*. He had sad eyes, a broad forehead, a wisp of mustache, and he walked hunched over, hoping to disguise his height. Normally he skulked away from insults, but this time something must have gotten under his skin. He stopped. Glenn was standing near him. He told Lurch to keep moving. Lurch didn't move. Glenn approached him. They got into a shoving match. Then they started throwing punches.

It was a strange sight, a comic mismatch. Glenn wasn't short, but Lurch was a full foot taller. Glenn couldn't reach his opponent's chin except by getting in very close. Lurch was clumsy and couldn't land a punch, but he saw his chance, wrapped Glenn in a bear hug, then lifted him off his feet. He spun Glenn against his chest, one huge arm around his neck. Now the gathering crowd could see Glenn's face. Lurch was choking him, really choking him. Glenn's eyes bugged out. It was clear that he couldn't breathe. He was thrashing, but Lurch's grip was unbreakable. A very long moment passed, with Lisa screaming, Glenn thrashing, and no one else moving.

Ford Takara appeared. He walked up to Lurch, cocked a fist quickly, and hit him very hard under the jaw. Lurch's eyes rolled up in his head.

He dropped Glenn. Then he collapsed himself, falling straight down, and as he fell Ford landed a second shot to his temple. Then the truly weird thing happened. Ford led the gasping, injured Glenn away, and the In Crowd set upon the fallen Lurch. We kicked, punched, scratched. Lurch, probably more from despair than physical incapacity, put up little defense. I remember Edie, Mike's sister, raking his arms with her nails, then lifting her hands triumphantly, like a fairytale harpy, to show the blood she had drawn. Other girls were gouging at his face, pulling his hair. This blood-frenzy went on for a good while until the cry went up, "Chock!" We scattered. Mr. Chock was the school's vice principal for discipline, and he was hurrying to the scene.

When did I realize that I had taken part in a disgusting crime? Not soon. In the immediate aftermath, I was elated. We had defeated the evil giant, or some such crap. In retrospect, I had perhaps exorcised for myself some of the terrors of life without a gang—my time at the business end of a two-by-four, say. Of course, Ford was the hero of the day. And his performance had been so dramatic, so decisive, that people were already starting to say he was the new bull of Kaimuki. I found that confusing. Would he not have to fight the Bear to claim that title? Apparently not. These things turned on popular emotion, not organized competition. But did Ford even want to be the bull? I doubted it, and I knew him better than all the kids who were just learning his name did. Still, maybe there was a Ford I didn't know—a killer, who craved power. There was clearly a me I didn't know—a rabid rodent of some type.

The official fallout from the mauling of Lurch was asymmetrical. Ford was not punished. Lurch became scarce around school. Glenn became a wanted man. The rest of us were not punished, although Mr. Chock seemed to come around more and give us long looks known locally as "da stink eye." Glenn ran away from home. Mike, always good for an escapade outside the law, became Glenn's accomplice, helping him hide. The two of them would appear brazenly on campus at lunchtime to show the colors. Mr. Chock would come barreling down the road in his car, chasing the

two boys across the cemetery and into the kiawe grove where the Kaulukukuis lived. Cop cars would sometimes join the hunt. This cat-and-
mouse seemed to go on for weeks, although it was probably just a few
days.

STEVE, WHO LOVED THE KINKS, was over at our little house. He surfed
competently, and we were changing into trunks, headed out to Patterson's.

His fiery contempt for Oahu aside, Steve was a sweet kid. He was
brown-skinned and pigeon-breasted, with a tiny body, a big square head,
enormous eyes, and a middle-class command of English. His father was a
rich, grumpy haole, and his dark-skinned birth mother long gone. Like
Roddy, Steve hated his stepmother, who was Asian. They lived in Kahala.
Steve's worldliness let him pass as haole—he certainly wasn't anything
else. But he had a gift for mimicry, and he could speak many brands of
pidgin.

"I like see," he said, in a voice that was part geisha, part pure island
naïf. And with that he lifted my T-shirt and studied my bare boy parts. I
was too shocked to react. "Nice," he said softly, then dropped my shirt.

I was in a phase of desperate shame about my balky puberty and could
not take the compliment. Steve's suave sensuality was from some border-
less, unknown world.

I still didn't have even the reproductive basics straight, and my parents
were too shy on the subject to be any help. I discovered the miracle of
ejaculation by myself, one agitated night. That was helpful, and quickly
became a habit. I was like most boys my age, no doubt, except none of the
boys I knew discussed it. My constant erections were a source of constant
embarrassment, confusion, and intense fondness for doors that locked. I
pioneered a new solo route, on small days, from Cliffs back to our house
near Black Point, circling outside the reefs rather than inside through the
lagoon. Out there, in the blue depths, no one on the beach or in the houses
behind the beach could see me. I rolled off my board in azure water, tak-

ing a break from the long paddle for a delirious bit of what some pidgin speakers called, unpoetically, "hammer skin."

ONE NIGHT there was a tremendous rainstorm, the kind that seems to happen only in the tropics. In my bed, above the din of the rain, I started hearing hollow, familiar bumps. It was the noise, I realized, of surfboards colliding. I jumped up, ran outside, and saw five or six boards floating out of our yard and into a river that had formerly been our lane to the beach. Our street, Kulamanu, and our lane formed, it seemed, a main funnel for local storm runoff. I chased the boards down the hill in the dark, pulling them from the hedges, or from wherever they briefly hung up, lugging them to safe ground in neighbors' yards. There was Roddy's bone-white Wardy, my slate-blue Larry Felker, Ford's baby-blue Town and Country. There was John's board, Kevin's old tanker. Where was Glenn's board? Ah, jammed nose first under the landlady's steps. None of the boards reached the ocean, where the stream running down the path could be heard emptying loudly even as the rain let up. My shins were bruised, my toes stubbed. The boards were probably all dinged, but no skegs were broken. I caught my breath, then carried each board slowly back up to our yard, wedging them all more firmly in their bamboo enclosure, although the deluge was over. Trash cans littered the street. It had been a downpour for the record books. Why did I seem to be the only person in Honolulu who had woken up?

THEY CAUGHT GLENN. He was sent to the Big Island. This, Roddy said, was better than "juvey," which was where they sent Mike. Glenn Sr. had convinced the authorities that Glenn would be strictly monitored by his old-fashioned aunties on the Big Island, which Roddy said was true. He probably wouldn't even get to surf. That seemed to me sickeningly harsh. But everything felt a bit queasy without Glenn. Roddy and John were subdued. Lisa looked like she had been seriously ill. Roddy wasn't as free to surf Cliffs as he had been before—his dad always seemed to need him down at Fort DeRussy. Really, I thought, he just wanted to keep an eye on Roddy. Maybe he blamed himself for Glenn's running wild. Nothing seemed like a colorful woodcut of old Hawaii now.

Sometimes Roddy invited me down to DeRussy. It was an interesting place, at least when we weren't stuck sweeping sand off walkways, which was his dad's preferred way to keep us busy. DeRussy sat on prime Waikiki beachfront property, flanked by high-rise hotels. Thousands of servicemen ("jarheads," we called them) showed up every week there, on R&R from Vietnam. Glenn Sr. worked as a lifeguard. Roddy and I would sneak into the gardens and lobbies of the neighboring hotels, and while one of us stood lookout, the other would dive in and plunder fountains and wishing wells for coins. Then we'd go buy chow fun, malasadas (Portuguese doughnuts), and pineapple slices from a street cart.

But the most interesting part of DeRussy, by far, was the surf out front. Summer was coming, and the Waikiki reefs were starting to come alive. Roddy introduced me to Number Threes, Kaisers Bowl, and Ala Moana. These were some of the surf spots I had heard about before we moved to Hawaii. They were crowded and, in the case of Ala Moana, frighteningly shallow, but they were beautiful waves, and the trades blew offshore on this side. Riding those breaks made me feel, as the pidgin phrase has it, "big-time," at least when I surfed decently.

I also started surfing Tonggs, down at the diamondhead end of the long swoop of city shoreline that includes Waikiki. This was where Tomi Winkler, winner of the Diamond Head Surf Contest, lived with his mother. The wave at Tonggs seemed to be nothing special—a short, crowded left that couldn't handle much size, breaking in front of a row of high-rises and a seawall. But a lot of good surfers, including Tomi and his buddies, were locals, and they urged me to wait for nearby spots that would light up on big days, particularly a fearsome right peak known as Rice Bowl. Rice Bowl, they said, was town's answer to Sunset Beach—the great wave on the North Shore. I wondered how Rice Bowl compared with the Bomb, but something told me not to ask. All the guys I met at Tonggs were haoles. Everybody I knew from Cliffs and Kaikoo's was what the Tonggs guys would call a moke. Maybe these haoles had never heard of the Bomb. (They had, but they called it Brown's.) Maybe Rice Bowl was a haole wave. (It wasn't.) Maybe everything would be simpler, I thought, if the Southern Unit just gave me a pair of club trunks and I confined myself to surfing with Roddy and Ford. I never got those club trunks, though.

Ford seemed lost without Glenn. He still surfed Cliffs daily, but it was different. He would take his board from our yard without even checking to see if I was home. At school he seemed to have no interest in exercising any of the droits de seigneur that came with being the bull—a title that the Bear had reportedly relinquished with a weary smile. Ford was too shy even to claim a girlfriend, which seemed to me insane, especially since the school year was about to end.

When the next big south swell hit—it was the biggest swell yet—I found myself at Rice Bowl. The wave broke on the ewa side of Tonggs, across a channel and farther out, and I watched it from the seawall. It looked to be what people said—a small-scale Sunset. Not that I had ever surfed anything on the scale of either break. But there were a couple of guys out at Rice Bowl, and I thought it looked manageable. The wind was light, the channel looked safe. The waves were big and hard-breaking but makable, even precise. The whole setup seemed far less wild than the Bomb. I paddled out. I don't remember any companions.

For a while, things went fine. The other guys acknowledged me curiously. They were much older. I caught a couple of clean waves, each of which startled me with its power and speed. I tried nothing fancy. I just stayed over my board, drawing a prudent line down the face and toward the shoulder. Paddling back out, watching other waves—peering into the area that surfers call the impact zone, or the pit—I could see that Rice Bowl broke very hard indeed. The noise alone was something new to my ears.

Then a big set came, waves in a category for which I was not remotely prepared. We were already surfing a very long way from shore, I thought, but I started paddling seaward from what I had believed was the main takeoff spot. I had obviously been wrong about where I was on the reef. Rice Bowl had another personality, which it was now revealing—vast, horizon-blotting power, the whole ocean seeming to gather itself toward one outer reef. Where could such a set have come from? Where were the other guys? They had vanished, as if forewarned. I was a fast paddler—light on my board, with long arms—and in my skittishness I had gotten an early start. I knee-paddled, digging hard, angling toward the channel now, trying to keep my breathing deep and even. When the first wave of the set began to feather, it was still far outside, and I felt my strength start to flag. Was I going in the wrong direction? Should I have started for shore when these silver death mountains first appeared in the distance? Had I been heading for the worst possible place all along—the outer reef where these waves would actually break? It was too late to change course. I paddled on, my mouth sour with nausea, my throat dry with panic, my breath short.

I made it over the set, which had four or five waves. It was a close enough thing that I went airborne over the top of at least one, and was drenched with offshore spray by each of them, and I was shaken to the core by the sound of the waves detonating a few yards behind me. I was convinced that if I had been caught inside, I would have died. This conviction was a first for me. This was the fear line that made surfing different, here underscored extra-heavily. I felt like Pip, the cabin boy in *Moby-Dick* who falls overboard and is rescued but loses his mind, undone by visions of the ocean's infinite malice and indifference. I paddled far, far around the Rice Bowl reef, on the Tonggs side, light-headed, humiliated, back to shore.

And that was the overwhelming memory of surfing in Hawaii that I took back to the mainland the following week, when the first season of *Hawaii Calls* wrapped up and we abruptly packed and moved. I would be back, I told my friends. Write. Roddy said he would, but he didn't. Steve did. Lisa did. But she was starting high school. I tried to accept it: she would never be mine. A big sister, at best. I started ninth grade at my old junior high in L.A. I surfed, I surfed. Ventura, Malibu, even Santa Monica, anywhere my friends and I could get somebody to drive us. I preened here and there about surfing in Hawaii, but I never mentioned Rice Bowl. Nobody was interested in my stories anyway.

Then we moved back, exactly a year after leaving. My dad got a job on a feature called *Kona Coast*, starring Richard Boone—crusty old haole fisherman gets enmeshed in Polynesian intrigues of some sort. We couldn't get our old Kulamanu house back, and ended up in another cramped cottage farther down Kahala Avenue, with no good surf nearby.

The day we arrived, I took the bus to Roddy's house. The Kaulukukuis had moved. The new tenants had no information.

The next day, I got my mother to drop me with my board on Diamond Head Road, climbed the trail down to Cliffs, and, to my joy, found Ford out surfing, still on his baby-blue board. He seemed genuinely happy to see me—more talkative than I had ever seen him. Cliffs had been good all spring, he said. Yes, the Kaulukukuis had moved. To Alaska.

To Alaska?

Yeah, the Army had transferred Glenn Sr. there. That seemed too crazy, too cruel, to be true. Ford agreed. But that's what had happened. Glenn, back from the Big Island, had run away again rather than move. But Roddy and John had gone glumly along with their dad and stepmom. They lived on some military base in the snow. This picture refused to come into focus. Where was Glenn, then? Ford made a strange face. In Waikiki, he said. You'll see him around.

I did. But not right away.

Waikiki became my home break. That was partly the season, partly logistics. The surf was good in summer all the way from Tonggs to Ala Moana, and there were lockers at Canoes, a central spot, right on Kalakaua Avenue, where I could keep my board for the price of a combination lock. So I left my board in the outdoor lockers at Canoes and caught the bus or, if my allowance was exhausted, quietly hitchhiked around Diamond Head each morning at dawn. I spent long days learning the breaks off the crowded, hotel-lined beaches.

Each spot had its locals. I made some friends. Waikiki was a dense nest of hucksterism, tourists, excitement, crime. Even the surfers all seemed to have hustles—some of them legitimate beach jobs, like taking tourists out to ride waves in outrigger canoes or giving them surf "lessons" on giant pink paddleboards; others much shadier, involving gullible tourist girls or friends who worked in the hotels and could get room keys. The kids I met in the water mostly lived in a ghetto called the Waikiki Jungle. Some were haoles, usually living with waitress moms; most were locals with big multiethnic families. There were hot surfers at every break—guys to study and emulate. I asked everybody I surfed with about Glenn Kaulukukui. And everybody said they knew him. He was around, they said. They just saw him last night. Where was he living? Not clear.

Finally, out at Canoes one afternoon, I heard, "Focking Bill." It was Glenn, paddling up behind me, laughing, grabbing my rail. He looked older, a little haggard, but dauntless, still himself. He peered at my board. "What's this?"

It was a nose-rider—a new model known as the Harbour Cheater, with a "step" in the deck that supposedly made it plane better when one was up on the nose. The board was my most prized possession, earned by endless hours of weed pulling after school. It was tinted—not pigmented—a pale yellow. Transparent tints were the style that year. I even loved the discreet black triangular Harbour sticker. I held my breath while Glenn checked out my board. At last he said, "Nice." He even seemed to mean it. I exhaled, unnerved by the vastness of my relief.

He was evasive about his living arrangements. He was working as a waiter, he said, living in the Jungle. Not going to school. He would show me the restaurant where he worked, slip me a teriyaki steak. Roddy was doing okay in Alaska. Cold. They would all be back "bye'm'bye"—but Glenn gave the pidgin expression a darker turn than the singsong treatment it usually got. He actually sneered, not trying to hide his anger toward the Army.

We surfed together, and I was startled to see that Glenn had improved dramatically. He wasn't just a good young surfer anymore. Still smooth, he was now a showstopper.

But I never saw the restaurant where he supposedly worked. Indeed, I rarely saw him on land. We surfed Canoes and Queens and Populars and Number Threes together, and I actually had trouble understanding some of what he was doing on waves, he was surfing so fast, turning so hard, transitioning so quickly, especially off the top. Climbing and dropping, stalling into the tube, squaring up to the breaking lip in a stable, high-velocity crouch. There was something new happening in surfing, and Glenn seemed to be in its vanguard.

Nose-riding was, I suspected, not part of it. I had become adept at hanging five, hanging ten, cross-stepping up to the tip and back as a wave allowed. I had the right ultra-light frame for it. David Nuuhiwa, the world's best nose-rider, and one of my heroes, was also tall and thin. But my Harbour Cheater was far from the most radical specialty model being ridden that summer, 1967. There were others, like the Con Ugly, that had sacrificed all other aspects of performance to maximum time on the tip.

Still, for all its ethereality, its improbability and technical difficulty, I was starting to lose interest in nose-riding. Mixed in with the slow, gentle, outrigger-bearing, tourist-clogged mush at Waikiki, there were shallow reefs, at Kaisers and Threes and even Canoes, that produced, particularly at low tide, hollow waves—waves that created, as they broke, honest-to-God tubes. And I began that summer to find my way into the spinning blue bellies of a few waves, and even to emerge, occasionally, on my feet. Everybody talked about getting "locked in," but the thing itself, these tube rides, had the quality of revelation. They were always too brief, but their mystery was intense, addictive. You felt like you had stepped through the looking glass for an instant, and you always wanted to go back. The tube, not nose-riding, felt like the future of surfing.

People said Glenn was on drugs. That seemed plausible. Drugs—marijuana, LSD—were everywhere, especially in Waikiki, most especially in the Jungle. It was the Summer of Love, whose epicenter was San Francisco, and we seemed to get a steady traffic of envoys from there, each bringing new music, lingo, and dope. I knew kids my age who smoked pot. I was too timid to try it myself. And when my little friends and I found ourselves once or twice at parties in tumbledown surfer shacks in the Jungle, where strobe lights wheeled, the Jefferson Airplane thundered, and big guys were probably getting laid in the back rooms, we stole beers and fled. We were only ready for so much experience. I wondered where the hell Glenn lived.

My parents, as with Kaimuki Intermediate, seemed to know nothing about my demimonde life in Waikiki. But I almost got them involved after Dougie Yamashita stole my surfboard. I was beside myself with rage, fear, frustration. Yamashita, a Canoes fixture and street punk a bit older than me, had asked to borrow my board for a few minutes, then never brought it back. I was persuaded by savvier Waikiki hands to keep adults out of it. Instead, I enlisted a broad-shouldered kid known as Cippy Cipriano to find Dougie and get my board back. Cippy was a hired gun—he would beat up other kids, no explanation required, for five bucks. He surprised me and took my case for free. People said he had other scores to settle with Dougie. In any event, my beloved yellow Cheater was soon returned, with only a couple of new little scratches. Dougie, I was told, had been on acid when he took it, and should not therefore be held responsible. I didn't buy that. I was still livid. But then, the next time I saw him, I found I didn't have the nerve to confront him. This wasn't junior high school. I didn't have the In Crowd behind me. Dougie no doubt had a large family full of tough guys, always happy to stomp little haoles. He ignored me, and I returned the favor.

I saw almost no one from the In Crowd. Steve, still stuck on the Rock, said the gang had broken up. No one, he said, could fill Mike's shoes. For some reason, we laughed ourselves sick at the image. There had been something clownlike about Mike. I phoned Lisa regularly, but always hung up, mortified, when I heard her voice.

"Gloria," by the Irish rock band Them, had been the big song on the local hit parade when I was at Kaimuki Intermediate. We all went around singing it. "*G-L-O-R-I-A, Glo-o-o-o-r-ria.*" In 1967 the song on the radio in Honolulu was "Brown-Eyed Girl," by Them's singer-songwriter, Van Morrison. It wasn't a big hit, but its lyrics had the kind of Gaelic poetry that killed me in those days, and the tune had a rushing plangency too, almost Island-style. It was an elegy for lost youth, and for years it always made me think of Glenn. The song had something of his fugitive, laughing beauty in it. What I pictured was him remembering Lisa. She was the brown-eyed girl. I didn't really know what had happened between them, but I idolized them both, and I liked to think that they had once been happy "*standing in the sunlight laughing / hiding behind a rainbow's wall.*" But it was typical of me, somehow, to put all this into other people, to romanticize their affairs. And it was typical, too, of the perversity of pop culture to start recycling "Brown-Eyed Girl" decades later as elevator music, supermarket music, until I couldn't stand to hear it. Every band on earth has covered it. George W. Bush had it on his iPod when he was president.

My parents had to make a choice. *Kona Coast* wasn't finished, but the school year was starting. They had learned enough about Hawaii by then to know that public schools weren't such a hot option, particularly not for high school, which I was now entering. We would head back to the mainland in time to start school there.

On cue, my surfboard was stolen again. My combination lock, cut through by hacksaw, lay in the sand by my locker. Clearly the thief had known we were leaving. This time I did involve my parents. But time was short, and no one knew anything. Both Dougie and Cippy were away, sorry. Their families weren't sure about their plans. And so we flew back to the mainland minus one key piece of luggage.

My parents loaned me the down payment for a new Harbour Cheater, which would be identical to the stolen board, right down to the yellow tint. I went to work pulling weeds for a neighbor, at a dollar an hour, after school. With tax, the board would be $135. I figured I could have the money by November.

With my mother, Santa Monica, 1953

TWO

SMELL THE OCEAN

California, ca. 1956–65

I WAS IN LAGUNA BEACH, CALIFORNIA, A FEW YEARS AGO, DRIV-ing south in a rental car down the main street, Pacific Coast Highway. It was foggy, damp, deserted, ocean to my right, its midnight smell, the aqueous lights of businesses closed for the night flanking the road. I was tired, but not unalert. Passing an old, decrepit-looking motel, I heard a horrible cry. I knew what it was: a memory, not a crime or a heartbeak in progress. But the rawness of the remembered shriek made my scalp prickle. It was my father, as a young man. He had dislocated his shoulder in that motel, playing with me in an indoor pool. It was the first indoor pool I had seen. It was the first time I had heard my dad cry out in pain. He never cursed or complained when he got cuts, scratches, bruises. Indeed, he usually laughed. So this was bad—terrifying, really, for me. He was helpless, desperate. My mother was called. An ambulance came. What were we doing in a motel in Laguna? I don't know. We had friends in Newport Beach, the next town north, not Laguna. I was four at the most—still in that purported Eden before siblings.

Dad's shoulder continued to dislocate every few years. The last time it happened, he was out at the Bomb. He didn't surf, so what was he doing, on a surfboard, out at the Bomb? Apparently he paddled out just to have a look, to see big waves at close range. Then a set closed out the channel. He lost the board. And his shoulder came out of its socket. He went down once, twice, couldn't stay afloat. A Hawaiian surfer saved him. I wasn't there. I was in exile then, a college dropout. At the hospital, they opened up his shoulder, repaired the capsule, and tightened the surrounding muscles. It would not dislocate again. Neither would he be able to raise his arm above his head. Decades later, driving south through Laguna, I found myself hoping that my daughter, then four, never heard me bellow helplessly.

WE LIVED FAR from the coast when I was small. I was not a beach kid. How, then, did surfing become the tumbling center of my tender years? Let me take you down some of the alleyways where the great wet driving reverb of the surf guitar first found me.

There were the Beckets. They were ocean people. They were the family friends who lived in Newport Beach, which is an old fishing and yachting town fifty miles south of Los Angeles. They had six kids, and the oldest, Bill, was exactly my age. Family photos show the two of us as infants, on our bellies at the beach, each fascinated by sand. My mother said the adults, all new to parenthood, gave us orders, "Play!" Behind us, lounging in period bathing suits, our impossibly young parents throw back their heads and laugh. I can still hear Coke Becket's big, cascading chortle. She and my mother had knocked around together before they were married, working as maids in Yosemite Park and, for reasons they could never precisely recall, as secretaries in Salem, Oregon.

Big Bill Becket was a fireman. He kept hundreds of lobster traps in their backyard, and on calm days he set them from his dory on certain rock reefs off the Orange County coast. Little Bill quickly acquired four sisters and then a brother. The Beckets were more hard-core Catholics than we were. They bought a little two-story shingled saltbox on Balboa Peninsula, a densely built finger of sand that ran between the ocean and

Newport Bay. Their street, 34th, was three blocks long, ocean to bay-channel. We tried to rent a cottage for a week each summer, usually on the bay side, where it was cheaper.

I started staying with the Beckets from a young age. Little Bill and I fished with handlines for smelt, filled buckets with crabs and clams, borrowed an ancient paddleboard from his dad to explore the maze of bay-channels, paddling tandem out past Lido Island into the open waters of Newport Bay. We commandeered a tiny sailboat and beached it on a barren, sandy island near the highway, claiming the land for ourselves and fighting off other kids who tried to land there. In late afternoon, trapped by a sea breeze against the highway bridge, which was lower than our mast, we tacked frantically back and forth, losing ground each tack, finally tying up on the last possible private dock.

Mainly, we bodysurfed in the waves off 34th Street. That was our home base, a universe complete: the cold blue ocean, the hot white sand, the crashing south swells.

Little Bill had a closet-sized room, with barely enough space for a single bed, and we slept in it heading opposite directions, kicking each other in the face. We showered together, even peed together, snickering swordsmen crossing our streams in toilet-bowl battle. He was a true beach kid, with a crew cut bleached white by sun, feet with soles like wood, and a back that in summer went black as tar. He knew what the tide was doing at any moment, no matter where we were, as if he could smell it on the air. He knew when the grunion were running—mysterious fish that washed up in the shorebreak to spawn, but only at night, an hour after high tide, and only in certain months and certain phases of the moon. With a flashlight, you could fill a gunnysack with grunion in an hour. Floured and deep-fried, they were considered a delicacy. Walking on Newport Pier, Bill poked around in the buckets of fishermen without permission, putting them at their ease with offhand, wharf-rat encouragement. "Nice corbina."

Bill, like his father, prided himself on being unflappable. He was sardonic, almost aggressively relaxed—the essential California oxymoron.

From an early age, he had a cracker-barrel expression for every occasion. Becket was never simply busy—he was always "busier 'n a one-armed paperhanger" or "busier 'n a bad raccoon." He could be overbearing. He tried to order his sisters around, with mixed results. They met his imperiousness with sarcasm, and there were four of them, each the proud little owner of an acid wit. The Beckets' house overflowed with full-time residents, and yet it somehow doubled as a community center. There were always neighbors in and out, platters of tacos arriving from the kitchen, someone barbecuing fresh-caught fish in the backyard, live lobsters going in the pot. Among the adults, the wine and beer and liquor flowed.

Coke Becket played the accordion, and the family songbook was prodigious. Even the little kids could belt out "Remember Me," "She's More to Be Pitied," "Sentimental Journey," and "Please Don't Sell My Daddy No More Wine." A vein of showmanship ran through the clan. Coke's mother, Ardie, who lived off in the hills somewhere, showed up one afternoon on 34th Street, but not in a car, as my grandmother would have. She had instead parked her truck and horse trailer around the corner and arrived on 34th Street standing, in a tight beaded buckskin costume and a feathered headdress, on the back of a horse. She paraded up the street, waving serenely at the people popping out of houses. The Becket kids were excited to see her, but not amazed by the circus entrance. They had seen it many times.

Big Bill came from downtown Los Angeles. He was part of a loose group of young guys who had made their way to the coast south of the city after the war. He was wry and intense, slow-talking, good-looking, with basset-hound eyes and a deep tan. Good with his hands, he could build a seaworthy boat from a pile of lumber. He surfed. He played the ukulele. In fact, he and Coke had gotten married in Hawaii. Big Bill had carved the coffee table in their tiny upstairs living room out of his own old redwood surfboard. It was teardrop-shaped, heavy as lead. Little Bill and I liked to visit his dad at the firehouse, where he was a captain. He seemed to be always out behind the station, working on a boat, putting on another coat of varnish in the sun.

Little Bill had not just chores but real jobs. At dawn he baited hooks for the dory fishermen at the pier. It was nasty work, pressing stinking anchovies onto rusty barbs fixed every couple of feet on eighteen-hundred-foot coils of line, $2.50 for six hundred hooks, but he could finish by midmorning with some help, so I would go along, and both our hands would stink all day. One summer he had a job at a place called Henry's, also by the pier, renting hard rafts to tourists. They were wonderful rafts, and Becket's friends and I would help ourselves to the stock, risking his job. The rafts were heavy canvas, with heavy yellow rubber ends, and so hard you could almost ride them standing up. Styrofoam bellyboards were popular, but Henry's rafts were faster and more maneuverable.

Surfboards were also around, but in Newport their use was restricted to designated areas and early mornings only, at least in summer. More to the point, boardsurfing was intimidating. It was for big guys, we believed, not us. We saw surfers around town. They had sun-bleached hair, drove old station wagons, wore plaid Pendleton shirts, white jeans, *huaraches*—Mexican sandals with soles made from old car tires—and they rioted, we heard, on weekend nights way down the peninsula at the Rendezvous Ballroom, where Dick Dale and the Del-Tones played seductive, subversive music.

Becket lost his job at Henry's not because of our unauthorized rentals but because he got bored one afternoon waiting for a tourist kid who was just lying with his raft on the beach. It was the only raft still out. Becket wanted to close up the stand. We were all waiting around. The tourist kid, who was pale and plump, seemed to be asleep. Finally, one of Becket's buddies produced a slingshot. Becket, loading up a pebble, nailed the torpid customer on an exposed flank. The boy cried much louder than seemed warranted. We fled. The boy's mother, to our astonishment, called the cops. From our hiding places, we watched Becket's little tennis-ball head ride away in the backseat of a police car. Henry fired him, and Becket's friends started calling him JB, for Jailbird. Not that he—son of a popular fire captain—spent a minute in a cell.

Becket's friends were all Catholics. They even went to Catholic schools. The older ones were on their way to becoming altar boys. They rode their bikes to Sunday Mass, and swaggered around like they owned the church grounds. I was impressed and ashamed, thinking of my timid Sunday visits to St. Mel's, our church at home, always with my parents. The Newport boys showed me how to sneak into the balcony at the back of the church, where the choir sang at High Mass, and we watched the service from up there. This required a lot of hiding in the pews so that the priest,

First Communion class, St. Mel Catholic Church,
Woodland Hills, 1960 (author, third row, third from right)

on the altar, would not spot us when he turned to the congregation. It was tricky because my companions very much wanted to catch the eyes of their friends who were serving as altar boys, to try to make them laugh. I was agog at all this mischief, then mortified when a redheaded kid named Mackie hissed at me to shut up—I had apparently, after the priest intoned, "*Dominus vobiscum*," been murmuring, out of habit, "*Et cum spiritu tuo.*" Growing bored, a couple of boys started silently spitting on the parishioners below us, leaping back to hide after each thick loogie, as we called them, was dropped. Now I was truly scandalized. Did these boys not believe in hell? They did not, as was made clear to me in jeering conversation out on the oceanfront after Mass. I still did, though, and I was horrified by what I had seen that morning—genuinely, religiously afraid. Evidently it took Catholic school to turn young kids into fearless, hardened apostates. I was a public school wimp, still cowed by nuns.

I LOVED NEWPORT, but I loved San Onofre more. It was forty miles farther south, a little patch of undeveloped shore surrounded by a big Marine base. The Beckets stuffed their Volkswagen bus full of kids and gear and headed down there on weekends. San Onofre had been one of the early outposts of California surfing, and the dedicated beach bums who camped there to surf and fish and hunt abalone had somehow convinced the military to let them keep going in after the base was built. There was a dirt road to the coast blocked by a guardhouse, but members of the San Onofre Surfing Club were allowed through. Big Bill was a founding member. The beach was nothing special—narrow and treeless, rocky beyond the water's edge—but the families who camped there shared the place with a palpable, low-key pleasure. Many of them seemed to have PhDs in having fun. Surfboards, fishing rods, snorkel gear, old sea kayaks, inflatables— everything pointed toward the water. Panel vans with faded awnings and tiki huts built from driftwood provided patches of shade. Bridge tournaments and volleyball gave way, after sundown, to bonfires and hootenannies, and martinis were legal tender.

Then there were the waves. San Onofre's waves were passé by the '60s, when I came along—too slow, too mushy. In surfing's early modern era, however, when boards were huge, very heavy, and generally did not have fins, riding straight toward shore with a minimum of turning was the preferred (indeed, the only possible) technique, and San Onofre offered perhaps the best wave in California for that style of surfing. The rides were long and smooth, with enough rock-reef variety to keep them inter-esting. Many of the surfers who went on to modernize board design after World War II cut their teeth at San Onofre—it was the Waikiki of the West Coast, minus the hotels and hoopla. And it remained an excellent place to learn to surf.

I rode my first waves standing up there, on a borrowed green board, one summer day when I was ten. I don't recall anyone giving me instruc-tions. There were other people out, but San Onofre is a roomy spot. I paddled out alone, bowing my head and hanging on through gentle, sil-very lines of whitewater. I watched other surfers riding by. It was monkey see, monkey do. I turned the board toward shore. The waves were nothing like the thumping beachbreaks that I had been bodysurfing for years. But the tide was low and the wind light, which made the approaching swells easy to read. I found a wide, crumbling, evenly crested wall and stroked like mad into the trough. The acceleration as the board, lifted, caught the wave, was less dramatic, less violent than catching waves at the beach-breaks on a raft or bodysurfing. But then the sensation, particularly a feeling of speed, of skipping across the water's surface in front of the wave, just went on and on. This sense of weighty momentum was new. I wob-bled to my feet. I remember looking to the side and seeing that the wave was not weakening, and looking ahead and seeing that my path was clear for a very long way, and then looking down and being transfixed by the rocky sea bottom streaming under my feet. The water was clear, slightly turquoise, shallow. But there was room for me to pass over safely. And so I did, again and again, that first day.

But I was, to my enduring shame, an inlander. Woodland Hills, where we lived, lay in the northwestern reaches of Los Angeles County. It was a world of dry hills—the foothills of the Santa Monica Mountains—at the west end of the San Fernando Valley, which was a beige lake of smoggy sub-divisions. My year-round friends didn't know anything about the ocean.

Their families had moved west from landlocked regions—Pennsylvania, Oklahoma, Utah. Their fathers went to work in offices. Except Ricky Townsend's dad, Chuck. He had an oil rig in the hills out toward Santa Paula. Ricky and I would go there with him. He wore a hard hat and filthy work shirts and big work gloves. His rig worked night and day, pumping and banging, and he was always fixing something. I figured the goal was a gusher, a sudden explosion of black gold. In the meantime, there wasn't much for Ricky and me to do. The rig had a tower, with a little plywood-floored cab way up in the girders, and Mr. Townsend let us climb up there. So that was where Ricky and I sprawled around a transistor radio, listening to Vin Scully call Dodgers games late into the night. Koufax and Drysdale were in their primes, striking out the world, and we thought that was normal.

We lived in a cup of hills. And there was an insularity to our neighborhood, to my elementary school, an atavism that was reinforced by the topography. It felt like a small town, a hollow, and it was run by xenophobic hardheads. The John Birch Society was strong. My parents and their liberal, cosmopolitan friends were a minority—lovers of Adlai Stevenson in a Sam Yorty town. (Yorty was the mayor of L.A.—a tough, grinning, ignorant Red-baiter from Nebraska.) My parents subscribed to *I.F. Stone's Weekly* and passionately supported the civil rights movement. They fought a local ballot measure that would allow housing owners to racially discriminate. NO ON 22, said the sign on our lawn. They lost. Woodland Hills Elementary remained 100 percent white.

The best part about the hills was the hills. They were full of rattlesnakes, hobos, coyotes. They were where as boys we took long treks out past Mulholland Drive, which was still a dirt road then, to old shooting ranges and horse ranches. We had tree forts and rock forts scattered through the hills and canyons we claimed as ours, and we fought bands of boys from other hollows whom we met in unclaimed lands. More immediately, the hills were chutes. We swooped down them on bicycles, scraps of cardboard, rubber-wheeled Flexible Flyers ("From vine to vine the boys

slid with lightning speed"), and, once they became available, skateboards.
Even the paved streets, though, were absurdly steep. Ybarra Road was such
a precipice that unwitting drivers stopped when they saw it, reversed, and
sought alternate routes.

INTO THIS SMALL, bounded world, a dashing lad named Steve Painter
rode. I first noticed him standing watching me beat up a classmate of
mine. I was in the habit of inviting classmates home, strapping boxing
gloves on them, and going a few rounds. What seems odd now is that we
used to fight on a patch of grass right next to the sidewalk and the street.
That patch was my boxing ring. I don't think any part of the arrangement
would be acceptable today. Then, however, nobody interfered with us.
Boxing was what boys did. Steve Painter, after watching me knock my
classmate around, quietly offered to put on the gloves. He was no bigger
than me, so I confidently agreed. He beat me to my knees. It turned out
he was three years older than me.

He was from Virginia, and he called my mother "ma'am" and grown
men "sir." He had thick, wavy black hair, olive skin, and a dark purple scar
under one eye that he said had come from a hockey puck. He did play ice
hockey, it turned out, but that didn't stop me from imagining that the
gash on his cheekbone was really a Civil War scar. Besides being in seventh grade—in junior high school!—Painter had a natural air of command, some pubic hair, two webbed toes that for some reason impressed
me greatly, plus many ideas and swear words that were new to us. He also
had an enviable indifference to pain that, along with his strength, allowed
him to dominate our games, particularly the mainstay, tackle football. He
quickly became the top dog in our little neighborhood pack, displacing a
surly, sallow kid from Pittsburgh named Greg.

Painter liked to pick on me, even physically torture me—I was the
youngest member of the pack—but he also took me under his wing. He
joined a hockey team that played out of Tarzana Ice Rink. Tarzana—

named after an actor resident who was one of the early movie Tarzans—was the next suburb east. Painter, once he had made the hockey team, persuaded me to try out. Hockey was not a big sport in Los Angeles then, and the members of our league's far-flung teams tended to be kids recently moved to the area from Canada or Wisconsin, Scandinavians who could skate rings around us locals. Painter did what he could to sharpen my game, firing pucks at me in his garage. But I knew I had no hockey future—I still saw myself ending up most likely as a pass receiver for the Rams, although I was not ready to rule out pitching for the Dodgers. I only lasted one season on the ice.

But that season gave me the chance to see my father skate. He came down to the rink when he could to watch our early Saturday practices, and once or twice stayed for the first public session of the day. I had seen his skates, rusted and neglected, in our garage forever. They were old-fashioned speed skates, with extraordinarily long blades, Hans Brinker gear. The Tarzana Ice Rink had nothing like them, certainly. Now he got them down and polished them up, and after my practice we took to the fresh ice together. He skated bent forward at the waist, with his hands clasped behind him, pushing off effortlessly, smiling to himself. Slowly he picked up the pace, and the rink began to seem small as he took the straightaways in a few flashing strokes. The routine for public sessions was to alternate the mood and rules with each song on the rink's P.A., so that Couples Only skated to sappy doo-wop, Girls Only skated to "Big Girls Don't Cry," and so on. Men and Boys Fast skated, for some reason, to Dion's "Runaround Sue," a song I loved, and I urged my dad to light the afterburners for those three minutes. He didn't seem too sure about that, but he started pumping his arms and cross-stepping on the turns, and I was very sure that I had never seen anyone skate so fast. On the way home, I demanded tales of all the races he had won back in Michigan as a kid. Later I convinced myself that if it hadn't been for World War II canceling the key Games, he would definitely have gone to the Olympics—if not as a skater, then as a miler, or a ski jumper.

· · ·

STEVE PAINTER ALSO HELPED turn me toward surfing. His interest was unrelated to the old-school involvement with the ocean of people like the Beckets—or, for that matter, the Kaulukukuis. It derived instead from the fad that had swept America a few years before—the *Gidget* movies and their spin-offs, surf music, surf fashion. Large numbers of kids on both coasts had bought boards and started surfing. Magazines, particularly *Surfer*, had become the main conduit of the surf subculture's self-celebration, and Painter and his junior-high friends read the mags avidly and talked, with increasing authority, in the new language they found there. Everything was "bitchen" or "boss" and anyone they didn't esteem was a "kook" (an insult usually reserved for an incompetent surfer—the term derives from *kuk*, a Hawaiian word for excrement).

It didn't strike me at the time, but it was telling that I never saw a copy of *Surfer* in the Beckets' house. They would have been interested in it— hell, a friend of theirs from San Onofre had started it—but they undoubtedly had better things to do with seventy-five cents.

For most inlanders, the road to surfing ran through skateboarding. This was certainly true in Woodland Hills. We all got skateboards, and turned certain steep streets into skate parks. The emphasis was on speed, carving, kick turns, and tail spins, not jumps. Handstands were considered a bitchen trick, though hard on knuckles. The upper playground at my school turned out to have a long, bowled asphalt bank that provided a great facsimile of an ocean wave. From its apex behind the handball courts, it was a big, fast, relatively short right or, going the other way, a long, steep, perfectly tapered hundred-yard left. Skating the school bank on weekends was so exciting it felt illegal. Actually, it was—we had to climb the fence to get in. The pleasures of riding that bank, especially the left, which we called Ala Moana, were only a few notches below the thrill of riding a wave standing up at San Onofre.

Getting to the coast from Woodland Hills was difficult. It was twenty miles away, over the mountains. Painter and his friends were old enough to hitchhike; I wasn't. My mother, with her passion for the beach, had started taking us to Will Rogers Beach State Park as soon as she got her own car. I must have been seven or eight then. The car was an elderly, sky-blue Chevy, and we used to drive through Topanga Canyon. Just before the canyon's mouth, we would hit a wall of sea fog. As we turned south on Pacific Coast Highway, my mother would say, "Smell the ocean. Doesn't it smell good?" I'd mumble, or say nothing. I never liked the smell of the ocean. Something was apparently wrong with me. A fishy stench enveloped the coast, seeming to emanate from the pilings under the flat-roofed houses jammed together on the ocean side of the road. My nose curled against it.

The ocean itself was another story. I waded into the waves at Will Rogers, diving under pummeling lines of foam, thrashing toward the main sandbar, where the brown walls of the big waves stood and broke. I couldn't get enough of their rhythmic violence. They pulled you toward them like hungry giants. They drained the water off the bar as they drew to their full, awful height, then pitched forward and exploded. From underwater, the concussion was deeply satisfying. Waves were better than anything in books, better than movies, better even than a ride at Disneyland, because with them the charge of danger was uncontrived. It was real. And you could learn how to maneuver around it, how long to wait on the bottom, how to swim outside, beyond the break, and, eventually, how to bodysurf. I learned actual bodysurfing technique in Newport, watching and imitating Becket and his friends, but I got comfortable in waves at Will Rogers.

Still, it was not a proper surf spot, and there was little chance that outings with Mom would ever take us to one. But then my father developed an interest in Ventura, an old oil town forty miles north of Woodland Hills. Specifically, he noticed that one could buy an old duplex rental unit a few blocks from the beach in Ventura for eleven thousand dollars, which is what he did. After that, I spent what seemed like the majority of my weekends weeding and gardening in a cold sea breeze around that duplex on Ayala Street. Other modest investments followed, and then a leap into new-house construction: identical two-story rental duplexes, all with carports and a newfangled rough-wood exterior. Ventura had no allure then as a beach town—too cold and windy, too far from anything. But my father saw the future—freeways, a marina, overpopulation—and he talked friends into co-ventures that allowed him to keep building. Meanwhile, I began to notice that Ventura was wave-blessed. I had that vision over a chiliburger on Ventura Pier.

The Finnegans, Ventura, 1966

FOR MY ELEVENTH BIRTHDAY, my father took me to the Dave Sweet Surfboards shop on Olympic Boulevard, in Santa Monica. From the rack of used boards, I chose a solid, sunbrowned 9'0" with blue-green paneled rails and a fin built with at least eight different types of wood. It cost seventy dollars. I was five feet tall, weighed eighty pounds, and could not reach my arm around it. I carried it to the street on my head, feeling self-conscious and scared of dropping the board, but as happy as I had ever been.

It wasn't an easy winter, trying to learn to surf. Even though the Beach Boys' "Surfin' USA" (*"Let's go surfin' now, everybody's learnin' how"*) was on the radio, I was the only kid at my backwater school who had a board. We spent most weekends in Ventura, so I got in the water regularly, but California Street was rocky and the water was painfully cold. I got a wetsuit, but it had short legs and no sleeves, and neoprene technology was still in its infancy. At best, the little wetsuit took some of the sharpest chill off the afternoon wind. My father liked to tell a story about a day when I got discouraged. From the warmth of the car, he had been watching me flounder—I imagine him smoking his pipe, wearing a big fluffy fisherman's sweater. I came in, my feet and knees bleeding, stumbling across the rocks, dropping my board, humiliated and exhausted. He told me to go back out and catch three more waves. I refused. He insisted. I could ride them on my knees if necessary, he said. I was furious. But I went back out and caught the waves, and in his version of the story, that was when I became a surfer. If he hadn't made me go back out that day, I would have quit. He was sure of that.

In the seventh grade, I finally moved on from the hill-girdled intimacy of my elementary school to an enormous, anonymous junior high out on the floor of the valley proper. There I started making friends on the basis of a shared interest in surfing. Rich Wood was the first. He was short, aloof, a bit roly-poly, sarcastic, a year older than me. But he had a tidy, graceful style that suited the long, satiny, gently folding waves at California Street, and he slipped into the scrum of a surrogate family—mine—with an ease that was surprising at first, considering how reserved he was, how little he had to say for himself. It made more sense after I met his family. His parents were a matched set of short, leathery golfers who were rarely around. Rich had a much older brother, and it seemed like their parents had already checked out on raising kids, moved on to some internal Florida. Rich's big brother, Craig, could certainly have driven them to it. He was a hard-charging, muscle-bound hot-rodder of some sort, cocky and loud. He claimed to surf, but I never saw him in the water.

Craig had named his penis Paco and he always had stories about Paco's adventures with women.

"Paco been doing some damage, *cabrón*!"

When Rich started going with a girl, Craig would demand to smell his fingers when he came home from dates—he wanted to verify his kid brother's sexual progress. Rich and Craig could not have been less alike.

Rich and I studied California Street together. He was strangely circumspect about where he had learned to surf. He had learned his chops somewhere, obviously. But he was vague. "Secos, County Line, Malibu. You know." I didn't, really, except from the mags and from Steve Painter. We applied ourselves, anyway, to California Street together—the lineups, the locals, the tides, the invisible ribs of rock under the dark kelpy water, all the idiosyncrasies of a long, somewhat tricky wave. Nobody spoke to us, and we found takeoff spots that were intermittent or overlooked and that suited our abilities, so that we could surf without interfering with anyone. But we also studied with fanatical intensity the moves of the top local guys, and discussed them into the night in our bunks in the duplex that my family had started using as a beach house. We got to know a few of their names: Mike Arrambide, Bobby Carlson, Terry Jones. How did Arrambide sideslip through all those middle sections? What was that crazy, quick-step first turn that Carlson did on the drop? Was he really switching stance (going from right-foot-forward to left-foot-forward)? Rich and I were still mastering the basics—clean takeoffs, hard turns, tight trimming, walking the nose—but we had to learn from the big guys because there were few kids our age at California Street, and none, we realized, who surfed better than us.

I actually got as much pleasure from watching Rich himself surf as from watching anyone else. His balance was solid, at times impeccable, his hands expressive, his footwork refined. He rode a big board that was pigmented a solid white. He got far less confident, less aggressive, when the surf was over four feet, but he had the makings of a small-wave master, and I was proud to surf with him. We would always be outsiders in small-town Ventura, but in time we were getting curt nods of acknowledgment in the water from some of the regulars.

My parents took to dropping us off at dawn, when it was often foggy and always glassy, and only picking us up in the late afternoon. There was no beach at C Street, as we learned to call it, just rocks and a low, crumbling bluff, huge oil storage tanks, grimy fields, and, farther up the point, some abandoned fairgrounds. Even farther up the point, in a grove of trees, was a hobo jungle, which meant you had to keep an eye out for shabby characters coming down the shore from that direction, since our towels and lunches were stashed in the rocks while we surfed. The onshore sea breeze usually sprang up and ruined the waves by lunchtime. That made for long afternoons huddling around driftwood fires under the bluff, waiting for our ride. Once, when the wind was particularly biting and wet, we dragged old tires into a pile and lit those. The heat was magnificent, but the thick, stinking column of black smoke blowing into town brought a police car, and we ran with our boards—not easy—and hid in the fairgrounds. At the end of those days, finally back at the duplex, Rich and I, still in our wetsuits, would share a hot outdoor shower, thirty seconds a turn, the one in the cold counting off the time aloud, then knocking the other guy out of the stream, until the hot ran out.

THE CLOSE, PAINSTAKING STUDY of a tiny patch of coast, every eddy and angle, even down to individual rocks, and in every combination of tide and wind and swell—a longitudinal study, through season after season—is the basic occupation of surfers at their local break. Getting a spot wired—truly understanding it—can take years. At very complex breaks, it's a lifetime's work, never completed. This is probably not what most people see, glancing seaward, noting surfers in the water, but it's the first-order problem that we're out there trying to solve: what are these waves doing, exactly, and what are they likely to do next? Before we can ride them, we have to read them, or at least make a credible start on the job.

Nearly all of what happens in the water is ineffable—language is no help. Wave judgment is fundamental, but how to unpack it? You're sitting in a trough between waves, and you can't see past the approaching swell, which will not become a wave you can catch. You start paddling upcoast and seaward. Why? If the moment were frozen, you could explain that, by your reckoning, there's a fifty-fifty chance that the next wave will have a good takeoff spot about ten yards over and a little farther out from where you are now. This calculation is based on: your last two or three glimpses of the swells outside, each glimpse caught from the crest of a previous swell; the hundred-plus waves you have seen break in the past hour and a half; your cumulative experience of three or four hundred sessions at this spot, including fifteen or twenty days that were much like this one in terms of swell size, swell direction, wind speed, wind direction, tide, season, and sandbar configuration; the way the water seems to be moving across the bottom; the surface texture and the water color; and, beneath these elements, innumerable subcortical perceptions too subtle and fleeting to express. These last factors are like the ones that the ancient Polynesian navigators relied upon when, on the open seas, they used to lower themselves into the water between the outriggers on their canoes and let their testicles tell them where in the great ocean they were.

Of course, the moment can't be frozen. And the decision whether to sprint-paddle against the current, following your hunch, or to stop and drift, gambling that the next wave will defy the odds and simply come to you, has to be made in an instant. And the deciding factors are just as likely to be non-oceanic—your mood, the state of your arm muscles, the deployment of other surfers. The role of the crowd is, in fact, often critical. Other surfers can signal approaching waves. You watch someone paddle over the top of a swell and you try to assess, in the last instant before he disappears, what he sees outside. It helps if you know the paddler—whether he is liable to overreact to the sight of a big wave, whether he knows the spot well. Or you may look down the line, upcoast or downcoast, at someone who may have a better view of what's in store for you than you have, and try to gauge his reaction to what he sees. He may even try to signal which way you should be moving—to give you a jump on whatever is bearing down on you. For the most part, though, the crowd is just a nuisance, a distraction, distorting your judgment while you jockey to get a wave to yourself.

At California Street, Rich Wood and I were just young apprentices. But we were serious about the work, which did not go unnoticed by the more experienced hands, who began to give us waves occasionally. The way Rich and I pooled our notes, studied each other, quietly competed—this too was, for me, fundamental. Surfing is a secret garden, not easily entered. My memory of learning a spot, of coming to know and understand a wave, is usually inseparable from the friend with whom I tried to climb its walls.

I TOOK OBSESSIVE CARE of my old Dave Sweet, fixing every ding, every shatter that cracked or broke the surface before it could soak up seawater. California Street, especially at high tide, was hard on boards. The basic ingredients of a ding-repair kit were polyester resin, catalyst, fiberglass cloth, and a block of polyurethane foam, but I slowly accumulated a workbench full of tools and supplies: saws, files, brushes, a power sander, all grades of wet and dry sandpaper, masking tape, acetone. I could do hot coats, gloss coats, quick-and-dirty overnight jobs, or patches so painstaking they became invisible. The elaborately inlaid fin on my beloved Sweet was always getting battered on rocks, and so I built up, over many nights in a cold garage, an inch-wide "bead" of fiberglass strands around its outer edge to protect it. It was the memory of similar labors, I believe, and the desire not to repeat them, that caused surfers to enlarge their reputations among other beachgoers as madmen by sprinting across sharp rocks after lost boards, unconcerned about damage to their feet.

Author, Rincon, 1967

But the time came, eventually, for me to get a higher-performance board than my clunky Sweet. Steve Painter weighed in. It would have to be a new board, he said, and it would have to be a Larry Felker. Painter and I never surfed together. I still listened to his stories about tearing apart ten-foot Topanga, which was a pointbreak south of Malibu that I had not surfed mainly because the coast there was closed to the public. Somehow Steve and his friends had become, at least in his stories, mainstays of the elite Topanga crew, and the waves there were, according to him, often huge and always superb. For me, our lopsided friendship in the neighborhood had ended one summer night when a bunch of us were sleeping out on the lawn in someone's backyard and, to the horrified delight of our companions, he urinated in my mouth. That was a torture too far. I stopped hanging around with him.

But I still deferred to him in certain matters of surf cool, and so I went to see Felker, who had the only surf shop in Woodland Hills. Felker was not a well-known shaper, but he did make beautiful boards. My parents agreed to pay half—this would be my thirteenth birthday present—and so I ordered a slate-blue 9'3", with a white glass fin and an inlaid wooden tailblock. It would take months to deliver. I went to work cutting lawns and pulling weeds for money.

WHAT HAPPENED TO RICH WOOD? A door opened, a door closed—my unconcern seems strange only now. A new school was built and I was sent there on the basis of my address; he was not, and I never saw him again. My family continued to go to Ventura. The Beckets, on a rare foray north, visited us there—fourteen people piled into a two-bedroom place.

My new surf partner was Domenic Mastrippolito, who was as formidable as his name. He was the uncrowned king of our class at the new school. He had an older brother, Pete, who was dark-haired and rowdy—Domenic was blond and calm—and it was Pete and his roughneck ninth-grade friends who first brought me to Domenic's attention. Like cockfighting aficionados, Pete and his gang enjoyed sending younger boys into battle. They even bet on the outcomes, it was said. When I was twelve, they roped me into fighting a skinny, snaggletoothed badass named Eddie Turner. The bout was held in a three-walled handball court at school, with a blood-thirsty crowd forming the fourth wall. There was no escape, and the fight went on approximately forever, with no one's bloodlust left unslaked. I was the underdog, but somehow prevailed. And my name was thereby attached, in certain circles, for years to Eddie Turner's, although he went on to much bigger things, like prison, while I returned to obscurity. Domenic, when we became friends later, would tease me about Eddie Turner—all the money Pete had lost on that fight, and how poor Turner was never the same.

It was odd becoming Domenic's friend. He was the best athlete in our class—fast, broad-chested, strong. Girls found him painfully handsome. When we got older, I heard him compared in art class to Michelangelo's *David*. And he had that sort of masculine beauty, even some of that hero's presence. I felt, popularity-wise, quite out of my league. But Domenic also surfed. Through Pete, he had access to big guys who had driver's licenses, which meant he could get to the beach. And yet it was obvious that the guys in Pete's crowd weren't serious surfers, and that Domenic was included on their jaunts basically as a mascot. So when he started coming with my family to Ventura, and trying to find his place in the C Street lineup, it was as if his real surfing career was just starting. He was keen. He didn't have the ballroom dancer's talent of a Rich Wood, nor any of my skinny-kid nimbleness on the deck. He was more like a hard-hitting linebacker on a surfboard. But he took his spot around the driftwood fires, and in the thirty-second hot-shower drills. I found my balance beside his charisma by becoming a niche comedian, specializing in self-mockery. I made fun of myself and was rewarded by his sharp, brayed guffaws. We were inseparable for years.

It was to Domenic that I wrote daily letters after we first moved to Hawaii.

RECALLING ALL THIS, I'm struck by how much violence defined my childhood. Nothing lethal, nothing horrifying, but basic to daily life in a way that seems archaic now. Bigger guys bullied, even tortured, smaller guys. It didn't occur to me to complain. We boxed in the street; adults didn't bat an eye. I didn't actually like to fight—certainly not to lose—and I don't think I've been in a serious fight since I was fourteen. But it was so much the Middle American (not to mention the Hawaiian) norm when I was a boy that I never gave it a critical thought. There was no gruesome violence on TV then—and no video games of any sort—but the cartoons we watched on Saturday mornings were old-school sock-'em-ups and we blithely carried that antic aggression into the world. I had a friend when I was very small, Glen, whom I could "take" in wrestling. He got so frustrated that he got his mother to buy him a can of spinach, which he ate straight from the can, just like Popeye did when he needed strength. We wrestled immediately. I won, but I told Glen that he definitely seemed stronger, which was not true.

It wasn't all antic, of course. I watched one or two very bloody fights between older guys—donnybrooks even worse than my brawl with Eddie Turner. They had a pornographic fascination. Such fights were theater of cruelty, devoid of empathy among the watchers—a distilled, super-dramatic version of the merciless ostracism to which certain kids were subjected. Mobthink. Lurch. My politics—which are my father's, basically: a hatred of bullies—have their roots in the horrors of those adolescent days, and in the searing glimpses of myself I caught.

Straight-up carnage had a fascination that was different, less social. Ricky Townsend's parents had a book—an art book, I think—that contained a painting of a soldier in World War II at the moment his body was destroyed by a shell. He was still running, his eyes wide in agony, with his limbs and torso just a waterfall of blood. A group of us would sneak into the room where the book was kept. A guard would be posted while we studied the forbidden image. It was shatteringly intense, a shame-filled treat. So this was what the moment of death looked like. We played army all the time, with little plastic G.I.s. But the reality of war, which some of our fathers knew firsthand, was never broached with us. It was a secret that the adults kept from us, for good reason.

Some dads were brutes, ready to turn their full strength against their kids. Not mine, thankfully. But corporal punishment was still the rule, at home and at school, even at the Saturday catechism classes I was obliged to take, where the nuns brought a wooden ruler down hard on trembling, outstretched knuckles. At school it was "swats" from the boys' vice principal—grab your ankles, try not to soil yourself or cry. My fourth-grade teacher, who had been in the military, as she often reminded us, pulled my ears so hard when she was annoyed that she left me feeling deformed. Again, it never occurred to me to complain. Nobody, as far as I knew, thought that what she was doing was wrong.

At home, because my father worked long hours, most of the physical discipline fell to my mother. She sometimes threatened to kill us, usually while she was driving—that would shut us up—but the beatings she gave us were not especially wild or brutal. Her spankings hurt less and less, in fact, as I got older. And so she started using a thin belt, then a thicker belt, then a wire coat hanger—those hurt more. I never fought back, but these were primal power struggles, quite painful emotionally for me, and probably for her too. Still, I thought they were normal. Irish Catholic normal, anyway. But then there came a day, when I was probably twelve, when my mother could no longer make me cry. She wore herself out. I would not whimper or cower. She wept, as I recall. And that was the end of it. Nobody hit me again.

Not long after that, what was considered normal changed. Kevin got his full share of beatings, I think, but Colleen much less, and Michael none at all. The social consensus on hitting kids had been collapsing in America for a while. Dr. Benjamin Spock's revolutionary *Baby and Child Care*, published in 1946, was my mother's go-to advice manual—Dr. Spock himself was one of her heroes—and its popularity had been slowly shifting public opinion against spanking. When the culture wars of the '60s heated up, Spock was prominent on the antiwar left, and beating children came to seem, at some point, to many people, including my parents, medieval. I liked to tell myself that the old-fashioned thrashings I got had been good for me, that they had made me tough, and I half believed it. Mr. Responsible always had a constructive take. Certainly I never blamed my parents. But their behavior was, as I see it now, not a small part of the ambient low-grade violence I lived in as a midcentury kid.

Surfing had, and has, a steel thread of violence running through it. I don't mean the roughnecks one encounters in the water—or, very occasionally, on land, challenging one's right to surf some precious spot. The displays of strength, skill, aggression, local knowledge, and deference that establish a working hierarchy in the lineup—a permanent preoccupation at every popular break—are a simian dance of dominance/submission that's usually performed without any physical violence. No, I mean the beautiful violence of breaking waves. It is a constant. In small waves and weaker waves, it's mild, benign, unthreatening, under control. It's just the great ocean engine that propels us and allows us to play. That mood changes as the waves get more powerful. Surfers call power "juice," and the juice becomes, in serious waves, the critical element, the essence of what we are out there to find, to test ourselves with—to recklessly engage or cravenly avoid. My own relationship with this substance, with this steel thread, has become only more vivid over time.

THE SECOND TIME we lived in Honolulu, in that come-on-baby-light-my-fire summer of 1967, Domenic flew over to visit, staying with my family. We surfed Waikiki together. I tried to show him the sights. I even took him out to look at Rice Bowl. He had heard my tales of the Sunset Beach of the South Shore. We sat on our boards at Tonggs on a brilliant morning, looking across the channel. Suddenly, a clean set stood up and broke at Rice Bowl. It didn't look particularly big—there wasn't much swell that day. Domenic suggested we paddle over there. I said no. I was too afraid of the place. He went without me. A few more sets came through. Domenic lined it up well, considering that he was out alone and had never seen the spot before. He rode several waves without falling. It was six feet at the most. I had surfed bigger waves at Cliffs, even some at California Street. Domenic and I would ride much bigger waves in the years ahead, including more than a few at the real Sunset Beach. Still, I sat there, immobilized by terror, in the channel at Tonggs. I knew that I was failing a basic test of nerve. Defeats, humiliations—craven avoidance—burn into memory so much more deeply, at least for me, than their opposites.

THREE

THE SHOCK OF THE NEW

California, 1968

THE NEW THING IN SURFING—THAT WHICH GLENN KAULU-
kukui had seemed to me, in Waikiki, to be in the vanguard of—was, it
turned out, the shortboard revolution. By luck, I saw its foremost progen-
itor in action the following winter, just before the underground movement
surfaced. He was an Australian named Bob McTavish. I saw him at Rincon, a pointbreak north of Ventura that I had started surfing with Domenic when we could cadge a ride that far. Rincon, now known kitschily as
the Queen of the Coast, was then known simply as the best wave in California, a long, hollow, wintertime right of astonishing quality. It was a big
day, low tide, late afternoon, and we were resting on the rocks in the cove
when somebody shouted and pointed to a brawny set standing up against
the sky out at Second Point. Few people surfed Second Point, also known
as Indicator, at that size. The great wave at Rincon was First Point. One
paddled up to Second Point to escape the crowd on small days, settling for
inferior waves. There were stories about huge perfect days when it was
possible to surf all the way from Second Point through First Point and
down to the cove, some eight hundred high-speed yards, but I had certainly never seen it done.

Now someone was doing it. He was doing it, moreover, on a board that
seemed to have jets installed on the rails. My eye actually had trouble following the bursts of speed that each banking bottom turn produced. The
rider would be suddenly ten yards ahead of where he was supposed to be,
according to the physics of surfing as I understood them. He was getting
comparable acceleration off his top turns. The result was that he was making it through long, heavy sections that would normally have ended a ride.
It felt like, each time I blinked, some film in my head skipped, and the
surfer reappeared farther down the line than he should have been. If you
read some of the early published descriptions of surfing—Jack London's
and Mark Twain's, each occasioned by visits to Hawaii, are the most often
quoted—you'll find them full of clumsy efforts to render action that was
too quick, complex, and foreign to the observer's eye to make any visual sense. That was how it felt to watch McTavish thread that eight-foot
wave at Rincon. He rode through the First Point takeoff zone, past the
crowd, as if it were just another section to outwit, and continued, blazing
turn after blazing turn, all the way to the cove.

There are few corny Colosseum moments in surfing—it's not that kind
of sport—but I remember people running across the beach, me among
them, to greet McTavish as he reached the sand. We mainly wanted to see
the board. It was not like any surfboard I had seen. It was outlandishly
short by the standards of the day, and the bottom was V-shaped, with two
chines getting steadily deeper and more pronounced toward the tail. I had
no words—not even "V-bottom"—to describe what I was seeing, and no
notion who McTavish was. He was short, grinning, powerfully built. All
he said was "G'day" as he trotted past, starting the long jog back to Second Point, his homemade monstrosity under his arm.

Nothing was the same afterward. Within months the surf mags were
full of V-bottoms and other radical new designs, all dramatically shorter
and lighter than the boards people had been riding for decades. The revolution was emanating from Australia and Hawaii, its gurus McTavish and
a couple of Americans, George Greenough and Dick Brewer. Their test

riders were some of the world's top surfers, most notably Nat Young, an Australian world champ. But California, then still the sport's imperial capital, eagerly converted en masse to the new faith. Surfing itself changed, with the speed and ultra-maneuverability of the new board. Nose-riding was a dead letter overnight. (Ditto drop-knee cutbacks.) Tube rides and hard, flowing, short-radius turns, banking vertically off the lip and riding always as close as possible to the breaking part of the wave—these weren't exactly new ideas, but they were all newly elevated as the goals of progressive surfing, and they were all being realized at levels never seen before.

It was 1968. Across the West, with its restless youth, a great many things—sex, society, authority—were being rethought or sharply questioned, and the little world of surfing rose, in its way, to the insurrectionary moment. The shortboard revolution was inseparable from the zeitgeist: hippie culture, acid rock, hallucinogens, neo–Eastern mysticism, the psychedelic aesthetic. The peace movement, just entering its boom period nationally, never developed a coherent surfers' wing (the environmental movement has been another story), but the world of surfing became, however incoherently, and pace Francis Ford Coppola, broadly antiwar. Many surfers dodged the draft. Even famous surfers, guys who could hardly paddle out anywhere without being photographed, but who were now wanted by the authorities, tried to go underground.

By spring I had my first shortboard. It came from a big boardmaker named Dewey Weber, in Venice Beach, who was scrambling, like every boardmaker, to meet the new demand. The model I got was called a Mini-Feather. It was bulbous and primitive, but for the moment it was state-of-the-art. Mine was 7'0". I could carry it by the rail, in one hand. I put my hard-earned second Harbour Cheater, which hardly had a ding yet, up in the garage rafters and never rode it again. At fifteen, with a solid command of the basics, I was at a good age to make the switch to shortboards. I was still very light, but strong enough to put the Mini-Feather up on a rail, hit the lip without losing control, and make the late drops that a small board, with its poor flotation and slow paddling speed, required. (Longboards, as they were suddenly being called, float higher in the water because of their greater foam volume, and thus paddle much faster.) I knew more surfers now who were old enough to drive, and so I started ducking out of family weekends in Ventura—California Street was a bit slow and mushy for shortboards—and surfing the south-swell spots closer to Los Angeles. Secos, County Line, First Point Malibu.

First Point Malibu was the center ring of the surfing circus, and had been so since the *Gidget* days of the late '50s. It was ridiculously crowded even when it was terrible. On good days it was a beautiful wave, a long right mechanical pointbreak, peeling along a tapering rock shelf all the way to the sand. There were a few top-flight surfers who still surfed Malibu, despite the crowds, but most had fled. The undisputed king of the spot when I first surfed there was Miki Dora, a darkly handsome, scowling misanthrope with a subtle style perfectly suited to the wave. He ran over people who got in his way and scorned the mindless surfing masses in well-turned quotes in the mags, all while flogging his signature-model surfboard, Da Cat, in adjacent ads. But Da Cat was a longboard. With the arrival of the shortboard, many surf legends were shoved rudely into irrelevance. First Point Malibu became even more of a madhouse than before. With longboards, it had been possible, at least in theory, for a small number of surfers to share a wave. The frantic, quick-turning style required by shortboards, their need to be always in or very near the breaking part of the wave, meant that there was really room for only one guy on a wave now. The result was bedlam.

Oddly, I didn't mind it. I had reached a stage where I actually felt quicker, better-balanced, more capable than most of the people around me, and I enjoyed weaving through them, calling them off waves, scaring them off waves with sharp turns, snagging waves to myself, driving my Mini-Feather hard through the sweet curves of inside Malibu like a sports car through a racecourse.

The larger satisfactions of the shortboard were to be found elsewhere, away from the crowds. First and foremost were tube rides, or barrels. A shortboard could fit much deeper and tighter inside a wave than a long-board. True barrels—successful passages through the inner chambers of a hollow wave—were suddenly more attainable than they had ever been. At Zuma Beach, Oil Piers, Hollywood-by-the-Sea in Oxnard, anywhere that got hollow, hard-breaking waves, a new code of risk and reward obtained, with a blown mind, in the best sense of that ominous phrase, now a real, happy possibility. "Pulling in"—trying to find the barrel by angling close to the wave face when it broke, rather than angling shoreward, to-ward the flats—was not without its dangers, to be sure, if one didn't safely emerge from the tube, which one usually didn't. Hollow waves normally break on shallow rocks, reefs, and sandbars. Falling off in the heart of a hollow wave can lead—often does lead—to a collision with the bottom. One's own board also becomes something of an unguided missile.

The barrel disaster I remember most clearly from that first shortboard summer, though, was of a different type. It happened in Mexico, at a re-mote Baja reefbreak known as K-181. I was camping there with the Beck-ets, who by then had acquired an old school bus, which they had converted, adding bunks and a kitchen, for backcountry family use. The surf was good-sized, glassy, empty. Bill and I were exploring the performance limits of our tiny new boards. I pulled into a deep, smooth, blue-green barrel, and was straining every nerve toward the sunlight ahead, the sloping shoulder. Just as I thought I was coming out cleanly, there was a horrible *chunk*, my board stopped dead, and I flew over the nose. It seemed I had run over Becket. From inside the barrel, I never saw him paddling toward my wave, caught inside, trying to punch through. He had seen me disap-pear, figured I might still be in there somewhere, and quietly abandoned ship. So I had only struck his board, not him. Still, my fin had cut deep through his rail, nearly to the stringer. Our boards were actually stuck together, in a hideous tangle of smashed fiberglass and foam, and we had to struggle to get them apart. The damage was all on his side. He was heartsick, but he was good about it. After all, I had been looking God in the face before he got in my way.

. . .

BOARDMAKERS WERE STUCK with shops full of longboards they couldn't sell. Some surfers were stuck with new longboards, bought on the eve of the revolution. That was the predicament of two friends of mine. Call them Curly and Moe. All their savings had gone into boards that were now suddenly obsolete—beautiful but embarrassing, no longer presentable at any self-respecting surf spot. Then somebody told us about homeowners' insurance. A stolen surfboard could be claimed, it was said, and reimbursed at the purchase price, if your parents had homeowners' insurance. Curly and Moe were fairly sure their parents had it. Nobody was going to steal their boards—they could not have given them away—but maybe, we thought, we could ditch them, report them stolen, and they could collect enough money to buy shortboards. It was worth trying. And so we drove out into the Santa Monica Mountains, far up a fire road, then carried the two boards on a trail deep into the brush until we came to the top of a cliff. There may have been some ritual mumbling. Certainly there were some strong emotions. Moe's board, in particular, was immaculate—a Steve Bigler signature model, the deck a pale blue tint, the rails a solid copper—and I knew that owning and riding it had been his deepest desire for years. But he and Curly each stepped to the edge of the cliff and hurled their unfashionable boards into space. They hit the rocks far below, cartwheeling, snapping, settling horribly into gnarled manzanita.

I don't remember if the insurance scam worked. I do know that that mint-condition Bigler, simply left in a garage, would be worth thousands of dollars today. What interests me, though, is what was in my head. I know I saw nothing wrong with insurance fraud, just as I saw nothing wrong with drug smuggling, or with anything else I considered a victimless crime. Draft dodging, still well in the future for me but already upending the lives of the older brothers of friends, I vehemently endorsed. The Vietnam War was wrong, rotten to the core. But the military, the government, the police, big business were all congealing in my view into a single oppressive mass—the System, the Man. These were standard-issue youth politics at the time, of course, and I was soon folding school authorities into the enemy force. And my casual, even contemptuous attitude toward the law was mostly a holdover from childhood, when a large part of glory was defiance and what you could get away with.

But a more conscious, analytic, loosely Marxist disaffection was also taking root in my politics in my midteens. (And disaggregating, intellectually and emotionally, the mass of institutional power—sorting out how things actually worked, beyond how they felt as a whole—would turn out to be the work of many years.) In the meantime, surfing became an excellent refuge from the conflict—a consuming, physically exhausting, joy-drenched reason to live. It also, in its vaguely outlaw uselessness, its disengagement from productive labor, neatly expressed one's disaffection.

Where was my sense of social responsibility? Not much in evidence. I marched in peace marches. I was still a good student, which really proved nothing except that I liked to read and was hedging my bets. I became a math tutor for a while for a couple of nerdy African American girls in Pacoima, a poor town at the east end of the Valley. I doubt they got much from our sessions. I know I felt like an impostor—a kid their own age playing teacher. My mother, who somehow managed to stay politically active while raising four children, roped me into canvassing door-to-door for Tom Bradley, Sam Yorty's opponent for mayor, in our precinct in Woodland Hills. Bradley would be, if he won, the first black mayor of L.A., so it felt like a historic election. Bradley polled well in our precinct, and we were optimistic. Then Yorty won the election, and the precinct breakdowns showed that our neighbors had evidently been lying when they told us canvassers that they would vote for Bradley. It was a well-known phenomenon, apparently, among white voters, these voting-booth reversals. Still, I was outraged, and my cynicism about organized politics and the broad mass of what I was learning to call the bourgeoisie deepened.

Robert Kennedy was assassinated, as everyone knows, on the night of the 1968 California primary. I watched the news on a small black-and-

white TV, sitting cross-legged on the foot of my girlfriend's bed. Her name
was Charlene. We were fifteen. She was asleep, believing I had left after
our evening's usual heated, inconclusive cuddle. I had stopped, however,
to watch the TV after I saw that Kennedy had been shot. It was after midnight and Charlene's parents were out watching the voting results with
friends. They were Republican Party activists. I heard them pull in the
driveway and come in the house. I knew that Charlene's father, who was
an older man, always came in to kiss her good night, and I knew, well, the
way out her window and how to catfoot it down to the street. Still, I sat
there, unthinking yet cruelly resolved, until the bedroom door opened.
Her father did not have a heart attack at the sight of me, calmly watching
TV in my underwear, though he could have. I snatched up my clothes and
dived out the window before he said a word. Charlene's mother called my
mother, and my mother gave me a serious talk about different types of
girls, emphasizing the sanctity of "good girls," such as Charlene, who belonged to some debutante club. I was embarrassed but unrepentant. Charlene and I had never had much to talk about.

I actually spent more nights in those years at Domenic's house than at
my own. Like the Beckets' perennial beach party in Newport, it was a
looser place than the prim, do-your-homework home my parents ran. The
Mastrippolitos lived in a big, dark, rambling two-story house that dated
from the early days of the San Fernando Valley, from before the subdivi-
sions like ours came. There were still orange groves across the street. Domenic's mother, Clara, was an early devotee of right-wing talk radio, and she
and I would have blistering arguments about civil rights, the war, Goldwa-
ter, communism. She loved William F. Buckley's TV show, *Firing Line*. I
would watch only when my hero, the actor Robert Vaughn, who was not
only the Man from U.N.C.L.E. but was some kind of political scientist,
with a PhD from UCLA, came on the show. Vaughn was an articulate
liberal—he later published his dissertation, a critical history of Hollywood
anticommunism—and in my opinion he demolished the polysyllabic po-
seur Buckley.

Domenic's father, Big Dom, didn't give a damn about anything but sports. He was officially a liquor wholesaler, I think, but he was really a bookmaker. He worked from home, and always had half a dozen TVs and radios going in his den, broadcasting different games and races of special interest. He rarely wore more than his bathrobe, and was constantly distracted, constantly on the phone, scribbling figures, squinting through the smoke from his cigarette. But he would occasionally come out and join in rowdy family games of gin rummy around the dining room table. Some days the family was suddenly rich and needed to spend cash fast—buy a new car, anything. Other times were grim and money was tight, especially after Big Dom got busted and was sent away for a while. But the general atmosphere was, again, loose. Many strays collected around the Mastrippolito house—alcoholic friends of Clara's with nowhere else to go, hoodlum friends of Pete's with nowhere else to go. Me. I felt welcome always, even as a deluded commie symp. Domenic's house was worlds away from my house, where *Time* and the *New Yorker* were always neatly stacked and a third slice of bacon in the morning was verboten.

Domenic and me, Mastrippolito family picnic, ca. 1967

· · ·

MY FATHER WANTED ME TO write a magazine article. He had taken up photography, and become surprisingly good at it. Perhaps it shouldn't have been surprising, since he was in the film business and knew all about lenses and cameras. His favorite subjects were his children, and he filled albums with our pictures. He also took some surf shots of me, Domenic, and Becket at Rincon, Secos, and Zuma, and that was where he got the article idea. He saw that I was always glued to the surf mags. He knew I liked to write. If I would just write a story for a surf mag, he would supply the pictures. I tried to explain that the surf mags didn't care about writing, they cared about pictures, and that he would never in this life take a photograph they would publish—not unless he moved to the North Shore and followed the top surfers everywhere for a couple of winters and got very, very lucky. Nonsense, he said. The article was the thing. If it existed, he could supply adequate pics.

This argument drove me crazy. One reason was my dad's obtuseness and refusal to listen to me, although I knew I was right. Then there was the way it underlined for me the distance between the ordinary, merely competent surfing that my friends and I were doing and the extraordinary, newsworthy, heroic exploits of the guys one saw in the mags. Mostly, though, it was the extension of another, more general argument between us. My father saw that I was always scribbling in notebooks, writing letters, papers for school. He knew I had been in ninth grade an editor on my junior high's literary magazine (in the heyday of California public schools, even junior highs had literary magazines), where poems and stories of mine appeared. What I needed to do next, he said, was start writing for real publications. It didn't matter what it was—sports roundups, ad copy, obits. The point was the discipline, the deadlines. He was thinking, I gathered, of a local newspaper, although I didn't know if Woodland Hills even had a paper. What he was really thinking about, I guessed, was his own hometown, Escanaba, where he had gotten his start as a cub reporter.

His career in journalism had veered into TV and film production, but he still knew how it worked, or believed he did. And he probably did know; I just couldn't listen. My favorite writers in those days were novelists (Steinbeck, Sinclair Lewis, Norman Mailer!) and poets (William Carlos Williams, Allen Ginsberg!), not journalists. I had no interest in newsrooms. Also, I was petrified of being told that something I wrote was no good. So I wrote nothing for publication, not even for the high school paper.

My father, for all his Depression kid's workaholic drive, had a dreamy, beachcomber side. He loved to skulk around harbors; my earliest memories of him are full of ships, piers, seagulls. Messing about on boats really was his idea of bliss. Before he was married, he lived on a sailboat anchored in Newport Bay. It was a small, sleek wooden sloop, and I liked to study the black-and-white snaps I found of him at the tiller—eyeing the windline, the luff in the jib, pipe stuck in the corner of his mouth, intent but thrilled, age twenty-two or twenty-three. The story was that my mother's first condition for getting married was that he move off the boat. It was gone before I came along.

I didn't share my father's passion for sailing, but I did love the water, and even saw it, from an early age, as my own medium of escape from dull striving, from landlocked drudgery. I remember a summer day on Catalina Island. We had sailed over, twenty-six miles, on our Cal-20, which was the bargain-basement fiberglass sloop of choice in California at the time. We were moored in Avalon Harbor. The harbor had wonderfully clear water. When a passenger ship known as the Great White Steamer came in from the mainland, local kids would swim out to it and shout for the tourists on deck to throw coins. I was probably eight or nine and I joined them, chasing the dimes and nickels that fell near me, twisting and flashing into the turquoise depths. We stored in our cheeks the coins we snatched as we shouted and battled for more. I remember swimming back to my family's boat and spitting my haul into my hands in the cockpit. I had enough for a corn dog on shore, maybe even one for Kevin. It was nonsense, but I had this vague idea that I could be completely happy as an idler, even a beggar, around the water. I wonder if my father saw that, and if it worried him because he had some of it too.

In reality, he had built a good balance between an endlessly demanding job and a famously bankrupting hobby, sailing, and had done so on a tight budget, without sacrificing time with his family. He became a bit of a tyrant, it was true, a weekend Bligh at the helm, when things went wrong, which they regularly did. He and Kevin and I once pitchpoled a Lehman 10 after going over the falls backward on a freakishly huge wave at a normally placid boat-launch spot called Carpinteria Beach. The mast spiked the bottom, snapped, and went through the hull. The three of us were thrown like bucked-off bull riders into the rigging. While the wreckage washed in, Kevin, who was four or five, immediately started diving to the bottom, still wearing sneakers, to retrieve shiny objects like Dad's silver-plated lighter. I can still see his expression of triumphant delight each time he surfaced with some lost treasure.

What could rightly have worried my dad about me and surfing was the special brand of monomania, antisocial and ill-balanced, that a serious commitment to surfing nearly always brought with it. Surfing was still something that one did—that I did—with friends, but the club thing, the organized-sports part, was fading fast. I no longer dreamed about winning contests, as I had dreamed about pitching for the Dodgers. The newly emerging ideal was solitude, purity, perfect waves far from civilization. Robinson Crusoe, *Endless Summer*. This was a track that led away from citizenship, in the ancient sense of the word, toward a scratched-out frontier where we would live as latter-day barbarians. This was not the daydream of the happy idler. It went deeper than that. Chasing waves in a dedicated way was both profoundly egocentric and selfless, dynamic and ascetic, radical in its rejection of the values of duty and conventional achievement.

I slipped away from my family at an early age, and surfing was my escape route, my absence excuse. I couldn't go to Ventura because I had a ride to Malibu, where the waves were sure to be better. I would sleep at

Domenic's. I couldn't go sailing because I had a ride to Rincon, or Newport, or Secos, and there was a swell. My parents let me go with so little
protest, it seems strange now. But it wasn't strange then. Child rearing had
entered, at least in the suburbs where we lived, an era of extreme laissez-
faire. Of course, I could, up to a point, take care of myself, and my parents
had three younger ones to worry about. My sister, Colleen, ended up being
the sailor from our generation.

THE DREAM OF back-to-nature surfing solitude had a predictable by-
product: rank nostalgia. A high percentage of the stories I wrote in my
journals involved time travel, most often back to an earlier California.
Imagine going back to the days of the Chumash Indians, or the Spanish
missions, if you could just take a modern surfboard with you. Malibu had
been breaking exactly like this, unridden, for centuries, eons. You would
probably be worshipped as a god by the locals once they saw you surf,
and they would feed you, and you could ride great waves with perfect
concentration—uncontested ownership, accumulating mastery—for the
rest of your days. There were a couple of photos in *Surfing Guide to Southern California* that illustrated, to my mind, just how narrow a margin in
time we had all missed paradise by. One was of Rincon, taken in 1947
from the mountain behind the point on a sheet-glass, ten-foot day. The
caption, unnecessarily, invited the reader to note "a tantalizing absence of
people." The other was of Malibu in 1950. It showed a lone surfer streak-
ing across an eight-foot wall, with members of the public playing oblivi-
ously on the sand in the foreground. The surfer was Bob Simmons, a
brilliant recluse who essentially invented the modern finned surfboard.
He drowned while surfing alone in 1954.

Surfing Guide to Southern California didn't trade in nostalgia, however.
It was too optimistic and hardheaded for that. The book was a meticu-
lous, thoroughly practical breakdown of nearly three hundred surf spots
between Point Conception and the Mexican border. It was thickly illus-

trated with surf shots, aerial views of the coast, and maps, and was dense with specific information about swell directions, tidal effects, underwater hazards, and parking regulations. But its greatest pleasures were in its clear, dry prose, its sage judgments about the quality of different breaks, its little puns and inside jokes, and its discreet but deeply felt enthusiasms. Obscure local heroes like Dempsey Holder, who had been riding alone, for decades, a spooky deepwater big-wave spot called Tijuana Sloughs, hard by the Mexican border, quietly got their due from the guide's authors, Bill Cleary and David Stern. And Cleary and Stern kept a sense of wry perspective in the face of the contemporary mess. Their caption for a shot of a large swarm of kooks struggling to ride the same six-inch ripple: "Surfing, an individual sport, in which lonely man pits his hard-won skill against the wild forces of the mighty ocean . . . Malibu, west swell."

DOMENIC'S GRANDPARENTS had made a barnful of wine from a vineyard that no longer existed, and it was all turning to vinegar in blue plastic Purex jugs in the barn behind Domenic's house. We took to helping ourselves to a jug on weekend nights, drinking it slug for gasping slug in the dark on the edge of a storm culvert behind the barn. The warm valley night would turn woozy, hilarious. I loved Domenic's imitations of his addled, goodhearted grandpa, whose favorite exclamation was, for some reason, "Murphy, Murphy, Murphy!" I once tried to make my own contribution to our drinking cache by raiding my parents' liquor cabinet, pouring half an inch from each bottle into a milk carton. Never mind that I was mixing bourbon with crème de menthe with gin—the tiny individual thefts would never be noticed. And they weren't. But Domenic and I got sick as dogs from the concoction. Only the loose supervision at his house let us get away with our heaving and hangovers.

Not that drinking was considered a big deal there. Wine flowed at meals, European-style. The contrast with my house was, as usual, stark. My parents were both, for reasons noted, very light, cautious, social drinkers. They had plenty of friends who could put it away, and their liquor cabinet was always stocked, but their kids never got even a whiff of wine. Half noticing their abstemiousness as a teenager, I marked it as just another symptom of their "uptightness."

But it was marijuana that drew the line between us and them, that bright generational line between the cool and the uncool. My timidity about pot, as I first encountered it in Hawaii, vanished when, a few months later, during my first year of high school, it hit Woodland Hills. We scored our first joints from a friend of Pete's. The quality of the dope was terrible—Mexican rag weed, people called it—but the quality of the high was so wondrous, so nerve-end-opening, so cerebral compared to wine's effects, that I don't think we ever cracked another Purex jug. The laughs were harder and finer. And music that had been merely good, the rock and roll soundtrack of our lives, turned into rapture and prophecy. Jimi Hendrix, Dylan, the Doors, Cream, late Beatles, Janis Joplin, the Stones, Paul Butterfield—the music they were making, with its impact and beauty amplified a hundredfold by dope, became a sacramental rite, simply inexplicable to noninitiates.

And the ceremonial aspects of smoking pot—scoring from the million-strong network of small-time dealers, cleaning "lids," rolling joints, sneaking off to places (hilltops, beaches, empty fields) where it seemed safe to smoke, in tight little outlaw groups of two or three or four, and then giggling and grooving together—all of this took on a strong tribal color. There was the "counterculture" out in the greater world, with all its affinities and inspirations, but there were also, more immediately, the realignments in our personal lives. Kids, including girls, who were "straight" became strangers. What the hell was a debutante, anyway? As for adults—it became increasingly difficult not to buy that awful Yippie line about not trusting anyone over thirty. How could parents, teachers, coaches, possibly understand the ineluctable *weirdness* of every moment, fully perceived? None of them had been out on Highway 61.

Becket, living down in ultra-conservative Orange County, got the word slightly later than we did in suburban L.A. He had grown eight inches in a year and was suddenly, at six foot five, a varsity high school basketball player. His teammates were a crew-cut, God-fearing lot, and they didn't believe me when I told them, on a visit to Newport, that pot, the evil weed that was then all over the news, was also in their upscale beach town. If they gave me ten bucks and a ride to the pier, I said, I could score them an ounce in an hour. They called my bluff, and I got them an ounce in half an hour. We got loaded in the point guard's parents' house on Lido Island, and I went home the next morning.

Two months later, asleep in the little room that I shared with Kevin and Michael, I heard a tapping at the window. I looked outside, and there was Becket. It was a Friday night, and he and his friends had a house for the weekend, he whispered, no adults around—I should come with him back to Newport. His friends were waiting down the driveway in a car. This midnight visit, this proposal—the situation was unprecedented. But what snapped me awake was Becket's shirt. It was diaphanous—very thin and rather shiny in the moonlight. The shirt was so utterly not him, it told me everything I needed to know. Apparently it had been a long two months on the Newport Harbor High basketball team. The mass conversion to stonerdom by the players struck me at first as funny. Later, though, as some of them crashed out of the program, and even out of school, I was not proud of my role, however incidental, in the collision between some of Newport's teenagers and their families and the global social shock waves of 1968.

It wasn't so different at my school, William Howard Taft High. The campus was already riven by Kulturkampf, mainly because of Vietnam. Team sports were effectively out of the question for students opposed to the war—the coaches were the most rock-ribbed members of a generally conservative, pro-war faculty and administration, and they were not shy about ragging on kids they suspected of being commies. I had two English teachers, Mr. Jay and Mrs. Ball, who changed my life's course by introducing me to the difficult pleasures of Melville, Shakespeare, Eliot, Hemingway, Saul Bellow, Dylan Thomas, and, most devastatingly, James Joyce. I saw now, in Ventura, the snotgreen sea, the scrotumtightening sea. The hobos from the old fairgrounds at C Street now came scuttling out of *Dubliners*. I became, in my own mind, Stephen Dedalus, privately sworn to silence, exile, cunning. (Regrettably, my hero was afraid of the ocean.) Los Angeles was a pallid stand-in for Ireland. But it had its own cultural bogs and treacheries.

I did go out for the track team, strangely, in the tenth grade, competing as a pole vaulter. Vaulters formed a little team within the team. The coaches knew little about vaulting, and were not about to risk their necks trying to demonstrate good technique. So we basically taught ourselves. We were excused from the grueling fitness drills the rest of the team performed, and our practices, we were often told, bore an unfortunate resemblance to long, lazy bull sessions. It was something about the vast amounts of lounging we did on the big foam-filled turquoise cushions that served as pits. Vaulting was a glory sport in those days, and vaulters were considered prima donnas. In fact, the flashy, antiauthoritarian vaulters were suspiciously regarded, often with reason, by the coaches and their more loyal athletes as Thoreau-reading, dope-smoking, John Carlos–loving hippies. I loved vaulting—the smooth upward snap and twist when you got the pole-plant right (not the rule with me), the never-long-enough moment when you threw back your arms, flicking the pole back the way you came, at the apex of the vault. But I did not go out for track again the next year.

More important, even to me, Domenic did not go out for football. In the tenth grade, he and I had been split up—sent to different high schools because of our respective addresses. He went to Canoga Park High, where Pete, who was a football player, had been ballyhooing the arrival of his fast, brawny little brother. So Domenic played. He was a halfback, and he liked the game, but practices were long, and the conditioning season started in summer. Football was eating up time when he could be surfing.

Also, he and I missed each other. When he told me that he was transferring to Taft, I was delighted. But I was unnerved when he said that the main reason he was transferring was me. I would have done the same for him, I think, had it occurred to me. Still, I worried I might disappoint him. In any case, he said, he was finished with football. Life was too short to spend another day running wind sprints for the Man.

With Caryn Davidson, in front of Kobatake's
rooming house, Lahaina, 1971

FOUR

'SCUSE ME WHILE
I KISS THE SKY

Maui, 1971

"YOU KNOW WHAT YOUR PROBLEM IS? YOU DON'T LIKE YOUR OWN kind."

This blunt assessment of me came from Domenic in 1971. Our respective politics, it seemed, were diverging. We were eighteen. It was springtime. We were camping on a headland at the west end of Maui, sleeping in a grassy basin under an outcrop of lava rocks. A little pandanus grove helped block the view of our campsite from the pineapple fields up on the terrace. This was private property, and we didn't want the farmworkers to spot us. We were raiding their fields at night, trying to find ripe fruit they had missed. We always seemed to be camping on somebody else's property in those days. Here, we were waiting for a wave.

It was late in the season, but not too late for Honolua Bay to break. That was our hope at least. Every morning at first light we would stare out across the Pailolo Channel, toward Molokai, trying to will the north swells to appear, their dark lines latticing the warm gray waters. It felt like something was stirring, but that could have been wishfulness on our part. After sunrise, we hiked around the point into the bay, studying the shorebreak against the red cliffs. Did it seem stronger than yesterday's?

Our lives, Domenic's and mine, had been like an unraveling braid for the past couple of years. The proximate cause of our disengagement was a girl: Caryn, my first serious girlfriend. She and I had found each other as high school seniors. My plans to bum around Europe with Domenic after high school became plans to bum around Europe with Caryn. We all ended up going, but we didn't see each other over there as much as we had planned. Then I went back to start college, at the University of California, Santa Cruz, and Caryn came with me. Domenic stayed on in Italy, living with relatives in the village where his father was born, in the eastern Appenines, working in a vineyard, learning Italian. (Domenic liked his own kind fine. I envied that.)

Now Domenic was living, for reasons that undoubtedly made sense then, in a converted milk truck at a beach park on Oahu—scraping by on odd jobs in paradise. I was on my freshman spring break, and my family was living in Honolulu again, so Domenic and I had reconvened there. Both of us had, like everyone who grew up on surf mags, dreamed since childhood of surfing Honolua Bay. But it was odd, in a way, that we were here, waiting on waves, since we had both quit surfing years before.

It happened when I turned sixteen. It wasn't a clean break, or even a conscious decision. I just let other things get in the way: car, money to keep car running, jobs to make money to keep car running. The same thing happened with Domenic. I got a job pumping gas at a Gulf station on Ventura Boulevard, in Woodland Hills, for an irascible Iranian named Nasir. It was the first job I had that wasn't devoted exclusively to the purpose of paying for a surfboard. Domenic also worked for Nasir. We both got old Ford Econoline vans, surf vehicles par excellence, but we rarely had time to surf. Then we both fell under the spell of Jack Kerouac and decided we needed to see America coast-to-coast. I got a job working graveyard shifts—more hours, more money—at a grubby little twenty-four-hour station on a rough corner out in the flatlands of the San Fernando Valley. It was a place where Chicano low riders would try to steal gas at 5 a.m.—*Hey, let's rip off the little gringo*. I got a second job parking cars at a restaurant, taking "whites" (some kind of speed—ten pills for a dollar) to stay awake. The restaurant's patrons were suburban mobsters, good tippers, but my boss was a Chinese guy who thought we should stand at attention between customers. He badgered and finally fired me for reading and slouching. Domenic was also stacking up money. When the school year ended, we pooled our savings, quit our gas station jobs, said good-bye (I assume) to our parents, and set off, zigzagging east, in Domenic's van. We were sixteen, and we didn't even take our boards.

We got as far south as Mazatlán, as far east as Cape Cod. We dropped acid in New York City. We subsisted on Cream of Wheat, cooked on a Coleman camping stove. It was 1969, the summer of Woodstock, but the flyers for the festival plastered around Greenwich Village mentioned an admission charge. That sounded lame to us—some kind of artsy-craftsy weekend for old people—so we skipped it. (My newsman's intuition, never great, was then unborn.) I kept uninteresting journals. Domenic, a nascent photographer, was in his Walker Evans period, shooting white street kids in South Philly, runaway girls asleep on the banks of the Mississippi. Years later, Domenic's first wife, a worldly Frenchwoman, refused to believe that we slept chastely side by side all summer in that van. We did, though, and our friendship flourished in the daily onslaught of the unfamiliar. I felt less compelled to self-mock; Domenic seemed relieved to be rid of the popularity that defined him at school. We relied on each other completely; the perils and the laughs were shared. In Chicago we met a scary guy who we later decided must have been Charles Manson. I got served my first drink in a bar—it was a Tom Collins—in New Orleans. I read Edith Hamilton's translation of *The Odyssey* propped on the steering wheel while driving across North Dakota. We got too close to grizzly bears in the Canadian Rockies. We surfed only twice that summer—once on borrowed boards in Mexico, and once in East Coast slop in Jacksonville Beach, Florida.

This is what I mean by quitting surfing. When you surf, as I then understood it, you live and breathe waves. You always know what the surf is doing. You cut school, lose jobs, lose girlfriends, if it's good. Domenic and I didn't forget how to surf—it's like riding a bike that way, at least when you're young. We just diversified, and I, for my part, plateaued. That is, I had been steadily improving since I started, and at fifteen, while hardly a contender, I was a little ripper. My rapid progress stopped when I got interested in the rest of the world. We didn't surf in Europe. Santa Cruz, a beach town in Northern California, has good waves, so I had been getting in the water, but on my own schedule, not the ocean's. The old nothing-else-truly-matters obsession was in abeyance.

HONOLUA BAY was about to change that. We didn't hear the swell start to hit in the night because the trades were offshore, blowing the rumble of waves striking the headland's boulders back out to sea. But Domenic, taking a piss at first light, saw the surf. "William! We got waves." He called me William only on serious occasions, or as part of a joke. This was a serious occasion. We had run out of food the night before, and had been planning a run to Lahaina, the nearest town, which was twelve miles away, for provisions. That plan was postponed indefinitely. We scavenged for nutrients—gnawing old mango rinds, scraping out soup cans, choking down bread previously rejected as moldy. We grabbed our boards and jogged around the point, screaming "Fuck!" and hooting nervously at each gray set that passed the headland, darkening on the final turn into the bay.

We couldn't tell how big it was, even after we got there. The bay itself was unrecognizable, at least to us, who had only seen it flat. There were waves breaking clear from the point to the cove, hundreds of yards, waves so beautiful that, as they hurled themselves into the offshores, they made me a little queasy. But this was not a classic pointbreak, in the mold of a Rincon. There were big sections, especially outside, that looked unmakable, and a rock bluff maybe fifty feet high that stuck out into the surf

line, with a narrow beach that had formed just above it, at the bottom of
the cliffs. There was certainly no obvious place to paddle out. Too impatient to hike all the way to the palm grove at the bottom of the bay and
paddle from there, we picked our way down a steep trail to the narrow
beach between the point and the bluff. The surf looked solid but not huge.
The sun was still not up. We waited for a lull, dancing in the broken coral
rocks rolling in the shorebreak. Then we sprint-paddled into the lines of
whitewater, angling away from the point but keeping a wary eye on the
bluff just downcoast.

We made it out to clear water. Slapped fully awake by the few sharp
blows of whitewater received on the push-through, we paddled around in
circles, trying to see the reef in the still-faint light. Where was the takeoff
spot? We seemed to be straight off the big bluff, but the water depth was
hard to gauge. Faint boils appeared around us as small sets rolled through,
exploding against the cliffs. Then the first real set arrived. It came straight
to us. Meaning: the waves, visible from half a mile off, first stood up and
broke near the point, reeling but uneven, and then formed a long, unmakable wall, at the downcoast end of which was a broad, heartstopping
hump—a great bowl section that feathered for a good while before it
broke. And that was where we were waiting, straight off the bluff, in the
middle of the big bowl section. It was the prime takeoff spot.

We each caught a wave in that first set, each pushing bug-eyed over a
heaving ledge. The drop was challenging, the acceleration intense—there
was a moment of unwanted weightlessness—but the faces were smooth
and there was actually time, in the course of a drawn-out, skittering first
bottom turn, to get a good look down the line. And the wave tapered
cleanly away from the takeoff section, flawless as a nautilus shell. It was
exactly what you hoped to see after such a drop. We each rode far down
into the bay. The wave, as it stood up along the reef, bent sharply toward
the cliff but never seemed to get any closer to it, speeding up across shallow slabs, slowing down in deeper water, then speeding up again, getting
glassier and smaller all the way, though still with a light offshore plume.

Domenic must have been on the second one, because I remember pulling out far inside and seeing him half crouched in a peeling, gray-blue hook, dragging one hand in the face.

Honolua Bay was, of course, a famous spot. That was why we were there. But no one else showed up, and as the sun rose we continued to surf alone. The waves weren't big—six feet on the sets—and the swell probably wasn't showing up yet in those populated parts of the Maui coast where the surfers lived. Forecasting surf had not become the popular, computerized science it is today—most people just got up and looked at the waves, as we had. Still, surfing a great wave like Honolua on an immaculate day with only two people out was very unusual, which made it hard to relax. For hours we windmill-paddled from the cove out to the takeoff spot, desperate not to miss a set, too tired to speak, just shouting odd imprecations. "Jesus fucking Christ!" "Murphy, Murphy!" Once we were in the lineup, if we had a lull, we might rehearse our rides and pool our research on the reef, which had some scary parts, especially as the tide began to drop.

Domenic was riding a small blue twin-fin. It seemed to love the waves. But he didn't know the board well, and it turned out that at high speeds one of the fins began to hum. It was a homemade board, and twin-fins were a new thing, and there seemed to be an alignment problem that had not been evident in slower waves. The hum was distracting for him, and got so loud that I could hear it as he surfed past me. He didn't think it was as funny as I did—this fly in the ointment of perfection—and he begged me to switch boards. I rode a couple of waves on the horrible hummer and gave it back. Eventually, even Domenic was laughing, trying to sing along with his underfoot zither as he rode. He always had a well-developed sense of the absurd—even, I would say, a philosophy that was anchored in a sense of imperfection, in a classical sense of the possible, and of the gods toying with us. I've never known where he got that.

Why did he say that thing about my not liking "my own kind" while we were camping at Honolua? He was saying lots of critical, dismissive things about me then. I had become, to be sure, an obnoxious, pretentious college student, taking a backpack full of books by R. D. Laing, Norman O. Brown, and other fashionable authors of the day even on a surf-camping trip. (I was studying literature with Brown in Santa Cruz.) I had probably just bored him with a lecture lifted from Frantz Fanon. (At least he didn't call me a self-hating white boy.) I had certainly developed a weak spot for anticapitalist, even Third Worldist politics. All this made me an impractical egghead, as far as Domenic was concerned, and he never tired of pointing out my (real, but not exceptional) mechanical incompetence. He exulted in the contrast with his own ingenuity around engines and other contraptions. I imagine he was feeling competitive, even insecure, as I increasingly went my way and he his. Also, perhaps, hurt. I thought he had been incredibly understanding and uncomplaining, though, after I took up with Caryn, throwing so many of his and my long-established habits and plans in the dustbin. Separation is a bitch. He and Caryn had even become friends.

In fact, Domenic, who was about to turn nineteen and was not in school, was having trouble with his draft board, and he had settled on a scheme to avoid conscription that involved a quick trip to Canada, and Caryn, who was also not in school, had volunteered to hitchhike up there from California with him. I, in my innocence, thought that was damn nice of her.

Finally, around midday, other people started showing up at Honolua. Cars appeared on the cliff top, guys scrambled down the trail. The crowd never got bad, though, and the waves, if anything, got even better. I was riding an odd-looking, ultra-light, homemade board. It was odd-looking mainly because the deck was full of big dents. In a misguided attempt to reduce weight, some backyard glasser in Santa Cruz had glassed the deck so lightly that my chest and knees when I paddled, and even my feet when I stood up, left permanent impressions. But the bottom, the planing surface, was smooth and hard, the rocker subtle and sure, and the shape was clean, with undented, slightly downturned rails and a gently rounded tail,

and the board turned quickly and flew down the line and the fin held in
the barrel, and those were the things that mattered. The board was actually too light for Honolua, especially when it got bigger and windier in the
afternoon. But fighting it down the late drops, and banking it through the
slight chop, and then setting it into the face under the high, screamingly
fast, backlit hook, I was unusually conscious of the technical challenges
involved in each maneuver. More generally, I knew I had never ridden
waves so powerful on equipment so flimsy before, and while I might have
preferred a different board out there, I could not imagine a more soul-
stirring wave. I wanted more of it. All I could get. Plato could wait.

THREE MONTHS LATER, I had dropped out of college and moved to
Lahaina. UC Santa Cruz was an exciting place, but it was easy to leave. It
was a new campus, a hotbed of academic experimentation. There were no
grades, no organized sports. Professors weren't authority figures but co-
conspirators. Maximum self-direction was encouraged. All of this suited
me, but the place had no institutional gravity.

Caryn, although dubious, came along. She had zero interest in surfing,
but she was adventurous, and I could not live, could not breathe, I believed, without her. Fortunately for me, she had no other plans. The flight
from Honolulu to Maui cost, as I recall, nineteen dollars, and the hard
fact was that on arrival we could not, between us, afford a single plane seat
back to Honolulu. We slept on the beach that night, wrapped in beach
towels, with crabs scuttling across us. The crabs were harmless yet weirdly
terrifying. Then it rained, and we shivered till daybreak. My parents,
when we'd passed through Honolulu, had made their unhappiness with
my decision to leave school painfully clear. Now Caryn made her unhappiness with me clear as well, in the Lahaina dawn. In the year and a half
we had been together, I had dragged her around on the basis of cracked
ideas and whims of mine quite a lot. Now she was supposed to become a
homeless, hungry surf chick?

I knew a guy, I told her. And I did, very slightly. I had met him on the street three months before, while on a supply run to town with Domenic, and he had pointed out where he lived. Now, by trial and error, through the muddy back blocks of Lahaina, I found my way to his place. I went inside. Caryn waited in the alley. She was surprised, I think, when I emerged with a set of car keys. I know I was. But the car's owner—a surfer, scholar, and stunningly kind older gentleman of twenty-two named Bryan Di Salvatore—had welcomed me like an old friend and, hearing about our tenuous situation, had immediately loaned us his 1951 Ford. All the waves this time of year were in town, he said, and he worked in town, so he didn't need a car. We could live in it while we looked for jobs. The car's name, he said, was Rhino Chaser. It was the turquoise beast parked under the banana tree.

If Caryn had been in a better mood, she would have said, with a grin and a smirk, "God provides." But she was still feeling suckered and skeptical. I took her on a car tour of the old whaling town turned tourist town, including the food-stamp office, where we collected an emergency monthly ration for two—thirty-one dollars, as I recall—and a series of hotels and restaurants, all of which were taking applications. Caryn quickly scored a job as a waitress. I had my eye on a bookstore on Front Street. We couldn't afford the gas to drive out to Honolua Bay, but I promised her she would love it.

"Why, because it's pretty?"

Among other reasons, I said.

In the meantime, we had to park at night in dark farm roads near town, with Caryn trying to sleep in the front seat, me in the back, and my board under the car. (I slept with one door open and a hand on the upturned fin, to discourage thieves.) We used the facilities at public parks, Caryn washing her waitress uniform in the sinks. I surfed a couple of the town breaks; she read, and seemed to relax. I was still in the doghouse, I could tell, though, from the sex we were not having. Fortunately, I landed the job at the bookstore.

It was a strange place, called the Either/Or, after Kierkegaard, although more immediately after a larger store in Los Angeles, of which it was an offshoot. The owners, a nervous couple, were on the run from the law, and so was their one employee, a red-bearded draft dodger who went by a variety of names. They needed help, but all regarded me warily. Did I look like a federal agent? I was eighteen, rail-thin, with scraggly shoulder-length hair, a sardonic girlfriend, worn-out flip-flops, sun-faded trunks, a disintegrating T-shirt. They decided to take a chance. They had a comprehensive book-knowledge test, imported from the L.A. store. All prospective workers had to pass it. (The retail book business has changed since then.) The test was written, and was not take-home. Caryn spent an evening drilling me on titles and authors. It occurred to me that she had a better chance of passing the test than I did. (She later worked in a French-language bookstore near UCLA.) She was, in fact, the most widely read teenager I knew. As I surfed in the afternoon glare off Lahaina Harbor, she curled up on the seawall with Proust, in French. Still, I took the Either/Or test, and I got the job.

On my first day behind the counter, Bryan Di Salvatore rushed in. He was leaving town, he said. Something about a letter from an old friend on a ranch in the Idaho panhandle had made him realize his time on Maui was up. He scribbled an address on an Aloha Airlines ticket folder. I should pay him for the car when I had the money, send it care of his parents in L.A. Whatever I thought it was worth. He had paid $125 for it a year before. With that, he was gone.

With paychecks, Caryn and I could afford gas, though not yet rent. We started camping on the coast out west and north of Lahaina. It was a serpentine series of bays and headlands. There were rows of old cane shacks—worker housing, red paint peeling—at the edges of cane fields that ran up a long terrace to sheer, rain-dark mountains. Puu Kukui, the highest peak of the West Maui range, was the second-wettest spot in the world, people said. We found secluded coves where we could build campfires, and beaches with water as clear as gin. I showed Caryn how to find ripe mangoes, guavas, papayas, wild avocados. We scrounged masks and snorkels and explored the reefs. I still remembered the names of some Hawaiian fish. Caryn especially liked the *humuhumunukunukuapua'a*—not the fish itself, which isn't much (a blunt-nosed triggerfish), but the name. She would surface from a dive, pull out her snorkel, and ask, "*Humuhumu?*" The word developed many meanings. I might look at the angle of the sun and answer, "*Hana hana.*" That means "work" in Hawaiian. We had to get to our jobs. Caryn did like Honolua Bay, as it turned out, which was a relief. The bay was too far from town for every-night camping, but the diving was good, with brilliant fish. And the place was undeniably pretty. There would be no waves there till fall, but neither of us had anywhere else to be.

Caryn should by rights have been a stability freak—an ant, not a grasshopper (or gracehoper, vide Joyce). Her mother and her mother's parents were German Jews and Holocaust survivors. Caryn's own life had imploded when she was thirteen, after her parents got into LSD and split up. She and I had been school friends at the time, and what I pictured was a suburban wife-swapping party presided over by Timothy Leary. Caryn disappeared into something called the Topanga Free School, the first of the "alternative" schools in our part of the world. When I next ran into her, she was sixteen. She seemed sad and wise beyond her years. All the giddy experimentation with sex, recreational drugs, and revolutionary politics that was still approaching its zenith in countercultural America was ancient, unhappy history to her. Actually, her mother was still in the midst of it—her main boyfriend at the time was a Black Panther on the run from the law—but Caryn, at sixteen, was over it. She was living in West Los Angeles with her mother and little sister, in modest circumstances, going to a public high school. She collected ceramic pigs and loved Laura Nyro, the rapturous singer-songwriter. She was deeply interested in literature and art, but couldn't be bothered with bullshit like school exams. Unlike me, she wasn't hedging her bets, wasn't keeping up her grades to keep her college options open. She was the smartest person I knew—

worldly, funny, unspeakably beautiful. She didn't seem to have any plans. So I picked her up and took her with me, very much on my headstrong terms.

I overheard, early on, a remark by one of her old Free School friends. They still considered themselves the hippest, most wised-up kids in L.A., and the question was what had become of their foxy, foulmouthed comrade Caryn Davidson. She had run off, it was reported, "with some surfer." To them, this was a fate so unlikely and inane, there was nothing else to say.

Caryn did have one motive that was her own for agreeing to come to Maui. Her father was reportedly there. Sam had been an aerospace engineer before LSD came into his life. He had left his job and family and, with no explanation beyond his own spiritual search, stopped calling or writing. But the word on the coconut wireless was that he was dividing his time between a Zen Buddhist monastery on the north coast of Maui and a state mental hospital nearby. I was not above mentioning the possibility that Caryn might find him if we moved to the island.

WE RENTED A ROOM in town from a crazy old man named Harry Kobatake. One hundred dollars a month for a roach-infested sweatbox with a toilet down the hall. We cooked our meals on a hot plate on the floor. The rent was high, but Lahaina had a housing shortage. Also, Kobatake's rooming house was directly across Front Street from the harbor, where two of the best local waves broke. Bryan had been right—the good summer waves were all in or near town. One spot, called Breakwall, needed real swell to be ridable. Over four feet, it could produce sweet lefts and rights on a jagged reef straight off a rocky breakwater that ran parallel to shore. The other spot, known as Harbor Mouth, was a crisp, ultra-consistent peak on the west side of the harbor entrance channel. It was good even at one foot, crowded, and picked up every hint of south swell. The crowd was largely haole, not local. That became my bread-and-butter spot.

I would get up in the dark, tiptoe down the stairs barefoot with my board, and jog across a little courthouse park to the wharf, hoping to be the first one out. I often was. A lot of mainland surfers had fetched up in Lahaina that year, but they were a hard-partying lot, which cut down on the number of guys ready to hit it at dawn. Caryn and I were by contrast a sober pair, and knew few people. I closed the Either/Or at nine. From her job she brought me tinfoil packages of aku and mahimahi that customers hadn't touched. And those were our evenings, eating and reading and killing cockroaches that got too bold. We named the geckos that patrolled the ceiling. I was so indifferent to bar life that when a tourist asked me the legal drinking age in Hawaii, I had to admit I didn't know.

Harbor Mouth had a short, hollow right that got longer and more complicated as the surf got bigger and the takeoff moved farther out the reef. Still, it never got very complicated. It was a wave that one could get wired—could come to understand deeply—in a summer dedicated to the task. I loved it at five feet and up, when, with clean conditions, the outside wall presented a perfectly even face and people often got fooled, moving too deep or too far out on the shoulder, unsure where to take off. There was a deep spot from which a six-foot wave, caught early and ridden correctly, could nearly always be made, and I got to know where that was, even though it gave no visual clues. Harbor Mouth's signal feature, though, its claim to whatever fame it had, was the end-section on the right (there were also longer, less shapely lefts, running away from the channel). It was a very short, thick, shallow, highly reliable chunk of wave that almost always stayed open. If you timed it right, that section was as close to a guaranteed barrel as any wave I've seen. Even at two feet, you could squeeze through it and come out dry. For the first time in my surf career, I became accustomed to the view from inside, looking out from behind a silver curtain toward the morning sun. I had sessions where I got tubed on half my rides. I would trot back to Kobatake's, where Caryn was still asleep on our pallet on the floor, my brain aflame with eight or ten brief, sharp glimpses of eternity.

I took to surfing Harbor Mouth in the black of night, after work. The tide had to be high, and the swell good-sized, and a moon could help. Even so, it was a fairly insane thing to do. It was basically surfing blind. And I usually wasn't the only one trying to do it. But I thought I knew the break so well, after a while, that I could feel—from the shadows, from the pull of the current—where to be, which way to go, what to do. I was often wrong, and spent a great deal of time hunting for my lost board in the shallows. That was the reason it had to be high tide. The lagoon inside Harbor Mouth was broad and shallow, with sharp coral covered with cruel sea urchins. In daylight I knew the little rivulets in the reef that one could float down, eyes open underwater, chest full of air for maximum flotation, skimming over the purple urchin spines, even at lower tides, in pursuit of a lost board. At night, however, one could see nothing underwater. And a search for the faint glistening ellipse of one's board, bobbing in the lagoon among all the bathtub chop dancing in the glare from the seafront street-lights, could take a whole different type of eternity from the one glimpsed in the tube. Giving up was not an option, though. I had only one board, and I always found it.

THE BOOKSTORE WAS three small rooms on a rickety old pier at the west end of the seawall. There was a bar next door. Ocean sloshed under the floorboards. The couple who owned the store trained me and, having picked up danger signals from local authorities, fled Hawaii for the Caribbean, leaving me to run the place along with the draft dodger, one of whose names was Dan. It was a terrific store for its size. Its fiction, poetry, history, philosophy, politics, religion, drama, and science sections were lively and thorough, with room for only single copies of most titles. Every book ever put out by New Directions or Grove—my favorite publishers in those days—seemed to be there. And we could get almost any title we didn't have in a matter of days, on special order. All this stock and capacity were courtesy of the big store in L.A.

And yet nobody wanted to buy all the wonderful books we had. What we mainly sold were coffee-table volumes to tourists: high-markup fifty-dollar monsters, stuffed with bright photos of coral reefs and local beauty spots. Then, every two weeks, tall stacks of *Rolling Stone* and, every month, even taller stacks of *Surfer*. Those were our profit centers. Our occult, astrology, self-help (though we may have called it self-realization), and Eastern mysticism sections also sold smartly. Some of the authors we had to order in bulk were old-school frauds like Edgar Cayce; others were nouveau gurus like Alan Watts. Then there were the counterculture best-sellers, which we ordered by the case and sold out quickly. One was *Be Here Now*, by Baba Ram Dass (formerly Dr. Richard Alpert), which came from Crown and, I recall, sold for the occult sum of $3.33. It counseled a heightened consciousness, with many diagrams. Another major seller was *Living on the Earth*, by Alicia Bay Laurel, which was large-format, hand-illustrated, and offered practical guidance to people trying to live gently and penniless in the countryside, without electricity or flush toilets.

There were many such people on Maui at the time, virtually all of them newly arrived from the mainland. They were living up narrow mountain valleys, off dirt roads or jungle footpaths. Or they were living somewhere on the broad slopes of Haleakala, the enormous old volcano that defined the eastern half of the island, or out on remote beaches along the bone-dry southeast coast. Some were making a serious go of commune life and organic tropical farming. Some surfed. There were also plenty of new arrivals scraping by in towns and villages, like us in Lahaina. Or like Sam at his monastery, which was reportedly on the north slope of Haleakala.

What about local people? Well, none of them came into the Either/Or, that was certain—when I told Harry Kobatake I had a job there, he said he'd never heard of the place, and he'd lived in Lahaina, which was a very small town, for sixty years. Our customers were all tourists, hippies, surfers, and hippie-surfers. Without particularly thinking about it, I began to dislike all four groups. I found myself proselytizing from behind my little bookstore counter, trying to get people interested in reading literature, history, interested in anything besides their souvenirs, their chakras, their pit latrines. I got nowhere, and my college-kid arrogance began to harden into disgruntlement. I felt suddenly old, like some kind of premature anti-hippie. Caryn, who had been there ideologically for years, thought it was funny.

The beautiful people were also starting to make appearances locally, mainly by yacht. Here came Peter Fonda's ketch, there went Neil Young's schooner, with "Cowgirl in the Sand" blaring from the deck speakers as it sailed off toward Lanai at sundown. Caryn felt intimidated by the leggy groupies who stalked off these luxe vessels until she had a reassuring experience in a public restroom at the harbor across from Kobatake's. Someone was giving the loudest, most fetorous performance ever in one of the women's stalls. Caryn tried to hurry her own ablutions to avoid the embarrassment of encountering the woman, but she wasn't quick enough, and, of course, the blushing starlet who emerged was straight off some rock god's boat.

The rock star who cheered me up, socially speaking, was Jimi Hendrix, as he appeared in a curious film called *Rainbow Bridge*, about a concert he had given the year before on Maui. The film was rough, and the sound bad, as Hendrix and his band played in a scrubby field in a howling trade wind. There was a sketchy, cinema-verité romance between Hendrix and a willowy black woman from New York. She was holding the Maui hippie commune scene at arm's length, and Hendrix was holding it farther away than that. His slurred, throwaway lines made me laugh. A passive-aggressive commune leader named Baron got so annoying that Hendrix was obliged to pick him off a balcony with a rifle. The movie ended with a no-budget sequence about "space brothers" from Venus landing in the crater at Haleakala. I took the ending as pure spoof. But the more talk I heard, in the bookstore and elsewhere, about "Venusians," the more I realized that mine was a minority interpretation.

We weren't entirely at odds with our little makeshift community,

Caryn and I. There was another movie, a hard-core surf film, that I dragged her to. Hard-core surf films are essentially meaningless to anyone who doesn't surf. An old ramshackle movie house in Lahaina, the Queen Theater, played them occasionally, always to sold-out, stoned-out crowds. I remember a few sequences (though not the title) from this particular film. One sequence was of giant Banzai Pipeline, and the filmmakers, lacking a soundtrack, played the Chambers Brothers' slow-building anthem "The Time Has Come Today" full blast. Everyone in the movie house seemed to be on their feet screaming with disbelief at the screen. It was electrifying, for people like us, to watch guys pulling into such apocalyptic waves. But I remember being surprised to see Caryn also on her feet, her eyes popping.

Then there was a sequence of Nat Young and David Nuuhiwa surfing one of our local spots, Breakwall, to a much gentler score. Nuuhiwa had been, a few years before, the world's best nose-rider, and Young had been the first great shortboarder, and it was moving to the point of tears to see them surfing together, both on shortboards now, both still absolute maestros—the last dauphin of the old order and the strapping, revolutionary Aussie, playing a kind of sun-drenched duet in waves we all knew well. I doubted that Caryn got all the implications of the Nuuhiwa-Young set, but she definitely got the bit that followed. The filmmakers had, on poor advice, tried to include some comic land segments—always a bad idea in a hard-core surf film. One involved a villain running around wearing a face-distorting mask made from a nylon stocking. The crowd groaned and somebody bellowed, "Fuck you, Hop Wo!" Hop Wo was a Lahaina shopkeeper with a reputation for surliness and tightfistedness. The bad guy in the nylon did bear a resemblance. Caryn laughed along with the surf mob, and "Fuck you, Hop Wo" became a complex, sweet refrain between us.

I sent Bryan Di Salvatore $125 when I had it. I didn't hear back from him directly, but an elegant woman named Max often came by the bookstore and sometimes had news of him. He was in Idaho, then England, then Morocco. I couldn't figure Max. She was boyish, in a fashion model sort of way, with a low voice and an amused, direct gaze. She seemed out of Lahaina's league—like she should be in Monte Carlo or somewhere. She and Bryan had clearly been an item, but she seemed quite cheerful about his absence. I wondered what she thought when she saw his old car. Caryn had painted a huge flower on the trunk, at my instigation. It was a well-painted flower, but still. It was no longer a car you could call Rhino Chaser. I say I was becoming anti-hippie, but I retained certain tendencies.

I heard very little from my parents. Their objections to my leaving school still rang in my head. My father had insisted that 90 percent of all college dropouts never returned to get a degree—"Statistics show!" They were probably also worried, understandably, about my draft status. What they didn't know was that I had never registered. My sense of civic obligation, never strong, was nonexistent when it came to the military. Maybe, if the feds came looking for me, I'd end up in the Caribbean with the Either/Or's owners. In the meantime, I never thought about it. My folks had also insisted that Caryn and I sleep in separate rooms while we stayed with them in Honolulu. That had been the crowning insult.

Our neighbors at Kobatake's were a rowdy, dope-smoking crew, prone to skateboarding in the hall, loud music, and louder sex. They seemed to be constantly playing Sly and the Family Stone; I would never enjoy the band's albums again. I embarrassed Caryn by frequently flying out of our room, book in hand, to glare at noisy debauchees. Actually, I didn't know then that she was embarrassed. She only told me years later. She even showed me her journal, and there I am, "our fervent scholar" sticking my "crazed head out in the hall" and causing her "endless chagrin." I didn't mind being disliked, but she did—yet another inconvenient point I didn't trouble to notice.

Everybody at Kobatake's got food stamps. Indeed, everybody who had ever lived there seemed to have gotten them. "At the usual time of the

month, the pink came," was how Caryn's ever-mordant journal put it. She
meant the dozens of pink government checks that arrived for residents
both current and departed. This mass reliance on food stamps carried,
among our loose group of peers on Maui, no particular assumptions, I
thought, about the welfare state. Food stamps were viewed as just another
hustle—strangely legal and easy but decidedly minor. I later lived among
young able-bodied dole bludgers in England and Australia (some of the
latter were surfers) who saw their government checks as essential suste-
nance and a type of right.

One day when we were both off work, Caryn and I went out in dribbly
surf at a spot called Olowalu. It was a shapeless little reef southeast of Lahaina, off a flat part of the coast where the road ran next to the shore.
Caryn had no interest in learning to surf, which I thought sensible. People
who tried to start at an advanced age, meaning over fourteen, had, in my
experience, almost no chance of becoming proficient, and usually suffered
pain and sorrow before they quit. It was possible to have fun, though,
under supervision, in the right conditions, and today I had talked her into
trying the slow, tiny waves on my board. I swam alongside, propelling her
out, getting her into position, pushing her into waves. And she was in fact
enjoying herself, getting long rides on her belly, yipping and hooting. I
was just trying not to get cut on the rocks—the water was shallow and did
not look or smell particularly clean. There was no one else around, only
cars whizzing by on the road to Kihei. Then, as Caryn finished a ride,
slipping down the wave's back as it passed into the inshore lagoon, I saw
four or five dorsal fins beyond her: sharks cruising parallel to the shore.

They looked like blacktips—not the most aggressive local species but
still an extremely unwelcome sight. They didn't look big, though it was
actually impossible to tell from where I was. They were right next to shore;
I was thirty yards out. Caryn, who was just a few yards from the beach,
obviously didn't see them. She was splashing, trying to turn the board
back out toward sea. I put my head down and swam in her direction as
hard, without thrashing, as I could. Caryn was saying something, but the

blood roaring in my ears drowned her out. When I reached her, I saw that the sharks had turned around. They were still cruising close to shore, now coming back toward us. I stood up, in waist-deep water, trying to see their bodies, but the water was muddy. I kept my face averted as they passed us. I didn't want Caryn to see my expression, whatever it might be. She was surprised, I imagine, when I turned her toward shore and started a fast march for the beach, ignoring the rocks I had been so careful about not touching on the way out. Still, I don't recall her saying a word. I angled the board so that I blocked her view of the sharks, and so that we would reach the beach well behind them, assuming they didn't turn again too soon. They didn't turn, at least not while we were crossing the lagoon or scrambling onto the sand. I didn't look back after that.

Caryn and I were in weird territory. I was deeply involved with my old mistress, surfing. I was waiting with passionate expectation for Honolua Bay to start breaking in the fall—tuning up, tuning up, surfing every day. Caryn, who had never seen me in this state, didn't seem jealous. In fact, she began making discreet inquiries about the technical aspects of my ideal Honolua board. This was a line of questioning so unlikely that she was forced to confess her plan: she wanted to get me a new board for my birthday. With our food-stamp-qualified incomes, this was no small gift. So I was waiting for Honolua, and she accepted that. But what exactly, again, was she doing on Maui? She had quit her waitress job and was now scooping ice cream at an awful new resort outside Lahaina called Kaanapali. We had made some effort to find her father, driving over to Kahului and Paia, asking around at a monastery and an outpatient clinic, but we hadn't followed up on the slim leads we got. I had started to wonder if she really wanted to ambush him. It could be painful, to say the least. Lahaina had its charms. They were subtler than those of the west Maui coast and countryside—old Chinese temples, some amusing eccentrics, coral-block prison ruins baking in the sun—and yet Caryn was alive to them. She even made a few friends among the other surf migrants—what she called "the bands of blond suncreatures." But the weirdness between us began with our failure—my failure, really—to make any serious distinction between her desires and mine.

We had been merged, fused, our hearts' boundaries dissolved, at least in my mind, since we got together in high school. Physically, we were an unlikely pair. I was more than a foot taller. Caryn's mother, Inge, liked to call us Mutt and Jeff. But we felt like one body. I experienced our separations deep in my chest. When we were still in high school, and Inge's nights had seemed to be one long middle-aged orgy, Caryn and I were the resident young Puritans—quaintly monogamous, devoted entirely to one another. Their apartment was an unusual household even then—a place where the kids were free to have sex yet pitied for their unadventurousness. It took me a while to get used to that freedom, after an adolescent love career of dodging (or failing to dodge) watchful, sometimes irate dads. My parents never did get used to it, throwing fits, after I took up with Caryn, when I failed, as I often did, to come home at night. Their ire surprised me. For years I had felt like what Caryn called, with mock solemnity, "a free agent of God." Now, at seventeen, I suddenly had a curfew? My own sullen diagnosis: parental sexual panic.

Then Caryn and I got in a car accident. We were on a camping trip up the coast when a speeding drunk rear-ended my van. The van was totaled. We were both unhurt. But we got a small insurance settlement, and we took that money, bought dirt-cheap charter-flight tickets, and split for Europe, skipping our high school graduations. This abrupt exit settled my parents' hash, I thought. Its potential cruelty never crossed my mind. Had my parents been looking forward to the graduation of their firstborn? If so, they didn't mention it. Inge, for her part, seemed to wake up and freak out just as we left, making me promise to take care of her little girl.

I didn't really do that, though. We had started to quarrel, Caryn and I, and we didn't fight well. On the road, moreover, I turned into a tyrant, setting a merciless pace as we bummed around Western Europe, living on crackers and fresh air, sleeping under the stars. There was always someplace new, someplace better, we had to be. I dragged her on grueling pilgrimages to rock festivals (Bath) and surf towns (Biarritz) and the old haunts (and graves) of my favorite writers. Caryn, less callow, did not see the reason for all the hurry. She pressed dried flowers in her journal, went to museums, and, already fluent in French and German, undertook to learn each language we encountered. She finally dug in her heels on the western Greek island of Corfu after I announced that I had a burning desire to see more "Turkish influence." I could go hunt for Ottoman minarets on my own, she said. And so I up and left her on the remote, mountain-backed beach where we were camping au naturel. Neither of us, I suppose, believed I would really do it, but I had become adept at, if nothing else, moving quickly through strange territory at low cost, and within a week I was in Turkey itself, newly intent on traveling overland to India. Motion, new companions, new lands were my drugs in those days—I found they did wonders for the adolescent nerves. Turkish influence fascinated me for about half an hour. Then only Tamil influence would do.

This folly came to a grubby halt on an empty beach on the south coast of the Black Sea. Mediocre surf, brown and misty and blown out, was

Istanbul, 1970

rolling in from the general direction of Odessa. I was stumbling along through brushy dunes. What, exactly, was I doing? I had left my true love alone in the boondocks of Greece, abandoned her on the roadside. She was seventeen, for Christ's sake. We both were. My lust for new scenes, new adventures, vanished in a bitter puff as I sat there in the Turkish scrub, not bothering to make camp. Dogs barked and darkness fell and I suddenly saw myself not as the dauntless leading lad of my own shining road movie but as a hapless fuckup: deadbeat boyfriend, overgrown runaway, scared kid in need of a shower.

The next morning I started back toward Europe. Europe turned out to be harder to reenter than it had been to leave. There was a cholera scare, and the borders with Greece and Bulgaria were reportedly closed. I bounced around Istanbul, walking along the Bosporus, sleeping on hotel roofs (cheaper than a room). I tried to go to Romania, but Ceaușescu's sentinels reckoned I was a decadent parasite and refused me a visa. Then the police raided a flophouse where I was staying. They arrested three Brits, who were convicted the next day of hashish possession and sentenced to several years each. I moved to another roof. I wrote brave, boastful postcards: *Hey, no photograph could do justice to the beauty of the Blue Mosque.*

But I was frantic about Caryn. Although she had said that she would find her way to Germany, where we had friends, I kept imagining the worst. I bought her a cheap purse in the Grand Bazaar. I befriended other stranded foreigners. Finally, I broke down and phoned home. It took all day, hanging around the vast old post office, to get through. Then the connection was awful. My mother's voice sounded terribly frail, as though she had aged fifty years. I kept asking what was wrong. I told her I was in Istanbul, but I still hadn't asked for news of Caryn—nor mentioned that I hadn't seen her in weeks—when the line went dead. Now the post office was closing. I wrote many cards and letters, but that was the only call home I made that summer.

In the end, I teamed up with other desperate Westerners, bribed some Bulgarian border guards, made my way through the Balkans and over the

Alps, and, with the help of an American Express office message board in Munich, found Caryn in a campground south of the city. She seemed fine. A little wary. I was scared to ask too much about what she'd been up to. Yes, I said, I'd got my fill of Turkish influence. She accepted the purse. We resumed our rambles: Switzerland, the Black Forest, a supremely strange visit to Caryn's mother's hometown on the Rhine. There, old people kept mistaking her for her mother, and then denouncing neighbors in whispers to us as ex-SS. In Paris we spent our first night sleeping on the ground in the Bois de Boulogne. In Amsterdam we heard that Jimi Hendrix would be playing in Rotterdam. We planned to go. But then the show was canceled and, five days later, Hendrix was dead. (The Maui film about him had been shot just a few weeks before.) Janis Joplin and Jim Morrison, two more heroes of mine, were also dead by then.

We flew back to California and camped together, Caryn illegally, in my tiny dorm room in Santa Cruz. It was a funky arrangement, with me stealing food for her from the cafeteria, but we weren't the only hippie outlaw freshman couple doing it. For me, at least for a while, it was ideal. I was awash in books and great teachers, pacing barefoot through the redwoods, arguing Aristotle, with my beloved never far away. Caryn was auditing classes, hitchhiking here and there (L.A., fornicating Canada), and starting to think about her own college career. Then I got the luminous, numinous idea of Maui, and dragged her there.

We were bound together tightly, inevitably, during those first months. When Kobatake tried to raise our rent—or to fine us over some imaginary theft of his chickens, or to evict us when he thought he had some suckers on the line willing to pay more—we fought back together. When people we knew talked, straight-faced, about Venusians, we had each other. We were fellow skeptics—rationalists, readers of books in a world of addled, inane mystics. Still, we were quarreling again. It was usually hard to say about what, but arguments would escalate, spin out of control, and one of us would storm off into the night. Makeup sex could be sublime, but that was starting to be all the sex there was.

The weirdness deepened after Caryn got pregnant. We never discussed having the child. We were still children ourselves. I was also immortal, I secretly believed. There would be time for all that—many lives from now. Caryn got an abortion. In those days, that involved a night or two in the hospital in Wailuku. After the procedure she looked awful, curled in a ball in a ward bed, her face drawn, her eyes injured. We drove back to Lahaina in silence. That, as I understand it now—I was nowhere near understanding it then—was pretty much the end of us.

ONE OF THE FLOWER-CHILD tendencies I retained, even in this period of antiutopianist reaction, was a closet communardism. I wanted, in an ill-defined way, to gather a group of friends in some soulful place and all live happily ever after. Maui, which seemed to be getting sillier and more touristy by the day, didn't entirely fit the bill, but I enticed a series of friends, including Domenic and Becket, to come stay with us in Lahaina nonetheless. They came, and squeezed in with us for weeks at a time on the floor at Kobatake's. It seemed clear, later, that I was unwittingly hoping to reconstitute a kind of family circle. I had left home, effectively, at a very young age, and for many years felt a poorly understood compulsion to build myself a new shelter from the world—even as I declined to start a biological family with Caryn and seemed to roam the globe under an opposite compulsion. Still, in Lahaina I made no real effort to find digs more suitable for a bigger group, probably because I knew a communal house wouldn't really work. Caryn and I were too shaky. Also, she was the only girl.

Certainly Domenic knew it wouldn't work. It became obvious, when he stayed with us, that something had happened on his and Caryn's draft-evasion lark to Canada in the spring. Obvious to me, that is. They already knew all about it. I never asked for details. I was horrified, and furious, but I tried to put the best face on things. Maybe we could comprise a ménage à trois. Hadn't we all seen *Jules and Jim*? Sung along with the Grateful Dead, "*We can share the women, we can share the wine*"? Domenic, with his Senecan grasp of the possible, bowed out and went back to Oahu, where he now had a job working for my father, who was producing the TV series *Hawaii Five-0*.

Domenic was a gardener on the show's set on Diamond Head Road—hot, nasty work—but he and my father seemed to have an understanding. I was vehemently uninterested in the film business; Domenic did not share my antipathy. My father, who admired Domenic's readiness to work, wanted to help him get a leg up in Hollywood's tightly closed craft guilds. Domenic took the help gladly. He eventually moved back to Los Angeles, became a film editor, then a cameraman, then a director. Many years later, in a *Godfather* moment at his wedding, his father, Big Dom, thanked my father with tears in his eyes. He was happy, I think, that his son had not gone into his business. Did young Domenic see the career opportunity when he moved back to Oahu? I doubt it. I know I watched him go with mixed feelings, which included astonishment that he could bear to leave Maui before Honolua Bay had started breaking.

I should say something here about Los Angeles, moving back to. It was an article of faith among our circle of young ex-residents that L.A. equaled living death. If Ireland was the sow that ate its farrow, L.A. was the John Wayne Gacy of cities, smothering its children with a toxic beach towel of poisoned air, mindless growth, and bad values. Whatever we were looking for—beauty, wisdom, uncrowded surf—it wasn't there. Or so we believed. (When I later learned that Thomas Pynchon, one of my undergraduate literary heroes, had apparently lived in Manhattan Beach, in the dreaded South Bay, in the late '60s and had found its grubby, bleached-out vitality inspiring, I suddenly saw it differently. I felt brought up short by my own shortsightedness, my unoriginality. Then again, I loathed the novel that his South Bay research ultimately produced.) The persistent nostalgia that infected most surfers, even young ones—the notion that it was always better yesterday, and better still the day before—was related to this dystopian view of Southern California, the suburban megalopolis that was, after all, the capital of modern surfing and head office of the nascent surf industry. But we took this nostalgia with us wherever we went. In Lahaina my imagination was captured by the news that the town had once contained a great river, big enough for whaling ships to sail up and take on freshwater. It made sense. If Puu Kukui, straight up the mountains, was the second-rainiest spot in the world, where was all the runoff? Diverted for irrigation by the corporations that grew the sugarcane all over west Maui, of course. Modern Lahaina was, as a result, parched, dusty, and unnaturally hot.

By the time Becket joined us, Caryn and I, exhausted from fighting, were practically on the rocks. She got a room of her own in a collapsing warren of worker housing next to an old sugar mill on the north side of town. Lahaina had a gender imbalance, at least among its young arrivistes—there were way more men than women—and I was certain I saw a lot of the dudes around town taking note that the tasty little dark-haired haole girl from the ice-cream parlor was now living alone. Even Dan, the simpering draft dodger at the Either/Or, started putting the moves on her. I had been writing an epic poem, full of stormy tropical imagery, called "Living in a Car." Now I turned my hand to a short story about a Filipino canecutter in Hawaii who spends his best years in a single-sex barracks, then falls in love with a blow-up sex doll. My situation wasn't quite that dire, but I was not happy.

CARYN, WITH HER SOFT HEART, was still intent on getting me a new board. So I settled on a shaper, Leslie Potts. He was the reigning monarch of Honolua Bay, a leathery, soft-spoken surf wizard and blues-rock guitarist. I tried to tell him what I wanted—something light, quick, fast—but found myself tongue-tied. He wasn't interested anyway. He had seen me surf Harbor Mouth. More than that, he knew Honolua in all its moods, demands, and supreme possibilities. He was going to shape me a thick, unfashionably wide 6'10" that would handle the drops, carve short-radius turns, and go like the wind. It was not the shape or length I would have chosen, but I trusted Potts. He was the consensus best surfer on Maui, and people said that when he could be bothered, he shaped as well as he surfed. Surprisingly, he delivered my board in good time. And it did look like it might be magic. Something about the arc of the rocker made the shaped blank look alive.

I had more control over the glassing. Potts's glasser was a quiet, bespectacled guy named Mike. I wanted a single layer of six-ounce glass on the bottom, six and four on the deck, with a rail overlap. This was considered foolishly light for a Honolua board, if only because of the terrible punishment that the cliff administered to lost boards, but I wanted to compensate for the bulk in the foam. Mike followed my directions. I ordered honey-colored solid pigment for the deck and rails, with a clear bottom. There would be no sticker: Potts was strictly underground.

Becket and I checked the northwest shore daily. It was now early fall; the North Pacific was starting to stir. Some people said there was never a Honolua swell before the humpback whales arrived in November. We prayed they were wrong. Becket had shown up on Maui looking wan— easily the palest I had ever seen him. He had had a difficult couple of years. A caper in Mexico had gone wrong and left him with amoebic dysentery, ending both his high school and his basketball careers. More recently, kidney surgery had kept him in bed for months. He was now good to go, he said, but he was obviously weak. We surfed around Lahaina, and he slowly seemed to regain strength. He was riding a little pintail only a couple of inches longer than he was tall. He had developed a forward-leaning, dropped-hands style that was new but seemed to work. It wasn't clear if he was in Hawaii on vacation or intended to stay. He had a few shekels saved, as he put it, and was not yet looking for a job. It was clear, though, that the islands suited him, temperamentally, down to the ground. He would shamble along the Lahaina waterfront, looking in the buckets of fishermen, just as he had as a kid on Newport Pier. The town had yachts and groupies, two of his favorite things, in healthy numbers. More generally, the pig-roasting, ukulele-picking, sea-centered rhythms of rural Hawaii appealed naturally to a child of San Onofre, now pursuing his own PhD in having fun. Like the rest of us, Becket was in spiritual flight from Southern California—Orange County was growing even faster and more grossly than L.A. Domenic had taken to saying that Becket would end up a fireman, like his dad. In fact, he had inherited his father's woodworking talent, and that would be his trade.

Honolua began to break, in a marginal sort of way. Becket and I surfed it stupidly close to the cliff, keeping death grips on our boards. I started getting used to the Potts, which snapped smoothly out of the hardest turns I could conjure. Indeed, it turned so sharply off the bottom that in small waves I often wasn't quick enough to change rails—shift my weight off the inside rail, the toe rail, to my heels—and unintentionally flew out over the top. It wasn't a big-wave board—the shape was too rounded, too ovoid—but it was plainly built for fast, roomy, powerful waves.

One day I saw a heart-stirring thing in a surf mag. It was a photo of Glenn Kaulukukui at Pipeline. I had heard nothing about him for years, and now here he was, instantly recognizable in silhouette on a glittering, extremely serious wave. You couldn't see his expression, but I was sure it contained none of his old irony, no playful ambivalence. This wave was the big time. Very few surfers would ever ride anything comparable. No one could take it lightly. The picture meant that Glenn had grown up, had survived, and was now surfing at a very high level. His stance in the closing jaws of the Pipeline beast was stylish and proud—almost Aikau. Years later, I saw another shot of him in another mag. Again, he was in silhouette, this time surfing Jeffreys Bay, a pointbreak in South Africa. It was a great picture, classically composed, expressively lit, with strong offshores raking an endless wall, and it had a powerful subtext because Glenn, in profile against the backlit wave, looked African, and these were still the bad old days of apartheid. According to a story that accompanied the photo, a Hawaiian team, which included Eddie Aikau, had gone to Durban for a surf contest and had been barred from a whites-only hotel. I showed the Pipeline picture to Caryn, who, with my narration, studied the image closely. "He's beautiful," she said finally. Thank you.

SOMETIME IN OCTOBER, Honolua started breaking in earnest. The setup was the same one we had surfed in the spring: long outside wall with warbles and sections, then the big bowling section of the main takeoff, then a roaring blue freight train all down the reef, deep into the bay. It was, once again, a glorious wave, with hues in its depths so intense they felt like first editions—ocean colors never seen before, made solely for this wave, this moment, perhaps never to be seen again. To surf the place intelligently would require long study, clearly, an apprenticeship of years. But the Honolua local guild was no longer taking applications: the spot already had an outsized coterie of devotees. They came from all over Maui and, on big swells, from Oahu as well. The crowd at Honolua had more dark faces than Lahaina lineups did. In fact, not many of the regulars from the town spots appeared out there once the winter season got under way. The surfing was of a much higher caliber. At times, particularly when a swell was peaking, the action in the water felt completely frenzied as amped, excellent surfers pushed their limits, wave after wave, and pushed each other. It was a tough crowd. Nobody gave a newcomer a wave. But successfully picking off sweet ones was less a matter of pure dogfight aggression, I found, than of getting into the rhythm of the sets and of finding the seams in the crowd. The whole scene had the feeling of a religious shrine overrun by passionate pilgrims. I half expected people to start speaking in tongues, to flail and foam at the mouth, or monastery monkeys to bomb us with guavas.

The top guys were astonishing. Some were big names from the mags, some were local hotshots. I saw Les Potts out in the water only once that fall. He was riding a wide white board the same shape as mine. The surf was midsized, the wind light, the crowd pretty bad, and Potts stayed away from the pack at the main takeoff. He lurked instead on the inside, and used some form of advanced personal marine radar to dodge the sets and slip across the reef at improbable moments to catch large numbers of clean, fast waves that nobody else saw coming. His surfing was subtle and sure, and radical only when he saw the right moment—which did not by any means occur on every wave—to unleash some fierce maneuver. His knowledge of the reef appeared to be encyclopedic, and he concentrated on tucking himself into spiraling barrels over the shallowest inside slabs. I moved far down into the bay to watch him. The usual mob on the cliff, having come out to watch the show, couldn't even see Potts, I realized. He was down around the corner, basically surfing alone.

My new board worked well. Watching Potts, I could see what he had in mind with the shape. I would never surf with such precision, but I found I could draw rounder lines, sharper curves, going higher under the lip than I would have thought possible on a racetrack wave like Honolua. Surfing hard, putting my board up on edge, also put other people in the lineup on notice that I was not out there to watch them surf. It was a long trek up the pecking order, and I would never reach the first rank, but I began to take a place in the second rank. On certain days I was catching as many waves as anyone, and people I didn't know were even hooting me into drops—encouraging me to go hard. If my surfing had plateaued when I was fifteen, it was now on a new upward track. I probably couldn't ride small Malibu any better now than I had as a grommet, but the size, speed, and soul satisfactions of Honolua Bay were greater by orders of magnitude than any spot I knew in California, even Rincon, could offer. The wave was far more intimidating, for a start, as well as more rewarding. And my obsession with it was well timed, given how badly my life on land was going.

Caryn took up with Mike the glasser. I couldn't believe it. She told me to call him Michael. He was nicer, smarter than I knew, she said. They even turned up at Honolua together, in his shit-brown van. She sat on the cliff while he paddled out. It was windy and big—one of those rip-roaring, high-amp days. I had been in a wave-catching, mindless groove. Now I sourly watched "Michael" paddle cautiously up the bay. A set rolled through and he headed for the horizon. He was, I realized, a kook. That improved my mood. I went back to work, battling the scrum in the main bowl, intent on center stage. Maybe, if Caryn saw me ripping on the board she gave me—or at least surfing competently—she'd come to her senses and take me back. After making a high-line screamer that no one in west Maui could possibly have missed seeing, I looked for her on the cliff. But the shit-brown van was gone. Michael had somehow reached shore alive, evidently. That seemed both improbable and unfair.

Town was flat. The whole island had been flat for a week. I had the day off work; Becket had some acid. We dropped (that was the strange, sinking, truncated phrase people used for ingesting LSD) before daybreak, then stood around a fire in Kobatake's backyard and waited for dawn. Old Kobatake never seemed to sleep. He jabbed the fire with a crowbar, his face a golden oval against the velvety blackness of his yard. He cackled when Becket joked about the roosters waking up his wife. Maybe our scheming, bewhiskered landlord wasn't such a bad guy. We took my be-flowered car, the former Rhino Chaser, and headed north.

Our plan was to trip in the country, away from the madding town, until our madness subsided. Out past Kaanapali we saw the sun's first rays strike, extra-softly, the crenellated battlements of Molokai's highlands across the channel. There was a faint reddish haze in the air—from cane fires, probably, or maybe it was volcanic smoke drifting up from the Big Island. Maui people called it vog, which seemed such a bad coinage that we laughed ourselves sick. Then Becket noticed, out on the ocean's surface beyond Napili, a weird corduroy pattern. It was weird partly of its own accord, like everything else that morning, but mainly because it was so unexpected. It was, in fact, a huge north swell, steaming past the west end of Maui. Not a trace of it was showing in Lahaina. I found I couldn't catch my breath. I couldn't tell whether I was thrilled or frightened. I put the car on automatic surf pilot. It carried us swiftly down red-dirt roads through pineapple fields to the cliffs above Honolua.

The swell might have bypassed the bay if its angle were a bit more easterly. But it was swinging massively around the point, with sets breaking in places I had never seen waves break before, filling the whole north side of the bay, the entire arena we normally surfed, with whitewater. There was nobody around. I don't remember much discussion. We had our boards on the roof. We were both hardwired to surf when there were waves. We waxed up and tried to study the lineup. It was hopeless. It was chaos, unmappable, closing out, and we were now tripping heavily. Peaking, as it was said. At some point we gave up and clambered down the trail. I picture us both giggling nervously. The roaring down on the narrow beach was constant, operatically ominous. I was sure I had never heard anything like it before. The bad news, some remaining rational part of me knew, was the good news. We would never make it out. We would be driven back onto the sand, quickly defeated by the multiple walls of whitewater stacked against us

We launched from the upper end of the beach, in the lee of some big rocks. It wasn't a wise place to enter the water, normally, but we wanted to stay as far as possible from the bluff at the other end, which had a cave on its upcoast flank that ate boards and bodies on nice days, and was now being battered nonstop. We started paddling, scrambling in an eddy alongside the rocks, and then got swept counterclockwise like ants in a sucking drain, out into the broad field of big walls of whitewater. Struggling to hang on to my board, I lost track of Becket. My thoughts turned toward survival. I would spin and try to catch the next wall of whitewater, then try to hit the beach above the bluff. The imperatives were suddenly simple: stay out of the cave, don't drown. But no whitewater presented itself. I was being swept sideways across the bay, past the bluff, paddling over the shoulders of big, foamy waves. This was apparently a lull between sets. I kept paddling toward open ocean. The bad news had turned good, which was bad. I was going to make it out. Becket, for his sins, also made it. We paddled far outside, into sunlight, stroking over vast swells still gathering themselves for the apocalyptic festivities inside the bay.

Our colloquy, sitting out in the ocean on our boards, would have seemed incoherent to an onlooker, had there been one. To us it made perfect, fractured sense. I remember lifting double handfuls of seawater toward the sky and letting them cascade through the morning light, saying, "Water? *Water?*" Becket: "I know what you mean." I had dropped acid probably six or eight times before, and had usually had an awful time. The drug tended to reduce me after a while to molecular fascinations. These were okay as long as they stood at a certain angle to everyday perception, revealing its hilarious pomposity, its arbitrariness—this was the great promise of psychedelics, after all—but they were less funny when they locked into personal psychodramas, actual feelings, much distorted. Domenic had once had to carry me to a nurse we knew to get me pumped full of Thorazine, an antipsychotic, after I fell down a rabbit hole of guilt about deceiving my parents about my high school pot smoking. Caryn liked to say, quoting Walpole, that life is a comedy to those who think, a tragedy to those who feel. That pretty well nailed my problem with LSD. The cerebral part was terrific; the emotional part, not so much.

With this huge swell, the Maui surf grapevine worked faster than it did the first time I rode Honolua, when Domenic and I caught that modest new swell by camping there, and nobody turned up all morning. This time cars started appearing on the cliff not long after Becket and I got out. Nobody joined us, though. We must have looked like what we were—two fools, having made a major mistake, bobbing way beyond the waves, too scared to move in. The surf was much too disorganized to ride. Maybe it would clean up later. My fear, however, was not the usual, frantically calculating kind. It came and went, while my thoughts bounced between the troposphere and the ionosphere, with occasional swooping Coriolis detours down to the sea surface heaving beneath us. I knew I wanted to be back on shore, but couldn't seem to hold that thought long. I began to edge in toward the point, having a vague idea that I could catch a green express train there, bound for dry land. Becket watched me recede with an expression of puzzled concern.

My Potts was not a big-wave board, but it was a fast paddler. I soon found myself in front of a broad green wall sweeping around the point and crisscrossed by backwash coming off the cliffs upcoast from Honolua. I was by then straight out from an area where people surfed on good days, although I had never surfed there myself—it wasn't the classic spot, but the outer point, where swells first entered the bay. One of the backwash warbles ghosting across the big green unbroken face spoke to me. It was my door. It was a small tepee of dark water moving sideways across a huge wall of water headed shoreward. It would form a pocket of steepness where a small board could catch a big wave early. I turned and chased it. We met in the spot I envisioned. While the big wave lifted me unnervingly, I caught the small wave cleanly, jumped to my feet, and rode it over the ledge, down the big face, nice and early. The paradox did not end there. Although this was probably the biggest wave I had ever ridden—a bit hard to tell, on LSD—I surfed it like a small wave, making hard short-radius turns, never looking much beyond the nose of my board. I was completely involved in the sensations of turning—"entranced" would not be too strong a word. I might as well have been skateboarding, at an unusually high speed, when in fact I was trying to connect the outer point and the classic takeoff bowl, riding all the way through, something I had heard about but never seen done, and I probably had the wave to do it on. As it was, I arrived at the bowl, or at a very big bowl section directly out from the usual takeoff spot, still on my feet. I failed completely, however, to draw the shoreward line, to make the charge toward the bottom that might have let me keep going. Instead, I carved up the face and under the lip, still hardly looking beyond the nose of my board. I got launched, my board drifting sadly away from my feet as we fell awkwardly through the air together.

I must have got a good breath, because the wave beat me viciously and long but could not convince my body to panic and suck water. I took several more waves on the head, diving deep and feeling myself get swept into shallower water. Soon I was being thrown against the rocks on the downcoast side of the bluff. I got a handhold and clambered out of the water, but climbed only a few feet before sitting down to inspect my shins and feet, which were battered and bleeding. A wave swept me off my perch. Incredibly, I did the same thing again a few waves later. I couldn't seem to grasp that I needed to get higher up the cliff, onto dry rocks. The third time I scrambled up, a kind man who had climbed down the cliff to help grabbed me by the arm and escorted me to higher ground. I was too tired and disoriented to speak. I made my thanks known by sign language. I also inquired, by pantomime, about my board. "Went in the cave," he said.

I decided to take a nap. I climbed the cliff, ignored the stares, found my car, got in the backseat, and lay down. Sleep wouldn't come. I flew out of the car, increasingly disoriented. I looked for Becket. He was still out there, halfway to Molokai, still alone. I decided to go down to the innermost part of the bay, where the ocean was always calm, to wait for him. Caryn and I had used to picnic there. You had to walk through creek-bottom jungle from the road. But I decided to drive. Somehow I crashed the old car through the jungle to the beach. But then the beach didn't feel safe. There were very tall coconut palms, and falling coconuts were dangerous. I waded out into the water, up to my chest, but still felt the threat of coconuts. I decided to go see Caryn at the ice-cream parlor in Kaanapali.

She seemed surprised to see me. I was still using sign language. She asked for a break, and took me outside to a small, round table. She set a sundae glass filled with water in front of me. The morning sun seemed to concentrate all its brilliance inside the water in the sundae glass. Staring into it, I could see Puu Kukui floating upside down in the sky. I told Caryn, inside my head, that the water in Honolua Bay was no longer clear, the way it had been when we snorkeled there in summer, that it was now all stirred up and murky. She took my hand to show that she understood. I told her, still inside my head, that we would find her father. She squeezed my hand. Then I remembered that I had left Becket in peril, and that I had never found my board. I found my voice and said I had to go. She did too, she said, nodding toward her place of work. "*Hana hana.*"

"*Humuhumu.*"

I set off again for Honolua. On the side of the road, near the Kaanapali entrance, Leslie Potts was hitchhiking. I stopped. He had a surfboard and a guitar. I didn't seem to be imagining this. He slid his board into the car, on the passenger side, and sat directly behind me. I drove on. He began to pick out little bluesy riffs on his guitar. We started seeing lines out at sea, marching south, from the swell. Potts whistled quietly. He hummed a few bars, sang a few lyrics. He had a keening, breathy singing voice, well suited to country blues. "How's the board?"

"It went in the cave."

"Ouch. Did it come out?"

"Don't know."

We didn't pursue the matter.

Back at Honolua, I saw that there were now a dozen guys in the water, and a dozen more waxing up. The surf looked far more organized than it had earlier. Still huge. I parked and hurried to the beach trail. Sitting on the rocks far below, his board beside him, was Becket. I made my way down. He was relieved to see me—not angry at being abandoned, as I expected. If anything, he seemed abashed, preoccupied. Then I followed his glance to a mangled board sitting propped on the rocks behind him. It was, of course, mine. I went over to it. The tail was smashed, the fin snapped off. There were too many dings to count. A flap of fiberglass hung from the underside of the nose. It could all be fixed, Becket murmured. It was amazing it hadn't snapped in half. I wasn't amazed. I felt light-headed and ill, inspecting the damage. The board would never be the same. Becket directed my attention to the lineup, where some of the local heroes were starting to perform. The swell was dropping, the surf improving. Becket, whose board was undamaged, paddled back out.

I watched the show from the narrow beach. It was the worst seat in the house, but it felt right to be down at water level, where wave-roar filled the brain. More guys paddled out. The surf kept improving. Becket came in again, panting, raving. These waves were *insane*. I demanded to borrow his board. He reluctantly let me take it. I battled my way out through the lines of whitewater, relieved to have something to do. The water seemed less interesting at the molecular level than it had before. Now I just wanted a wave to ride. I paddled up to the point, where there were fewer people. There was a light mist—it was aerated seawater, from all the crashing and smashing— and no wind, which left the ocean's surface slickly shiny. Its color was a muted gray-white until a wave reared; then turquoise floodlights seemed to switch on, illuminating the wave's guts from the inside. I cruised the point lineup, constantly paddling, unable to sit still. When a wave finally came to me, I took it. The floodlights switched on in the middle of my first turn. I tried to look ahead, tried to see what the wave had in store down the line and plan accordingly, but I was surrounded by turquoise light. I felt some rapture of the deep. I looked upward. There was a silver, sparkling ceiling. I seemed to be riding a cushion of air. Then the lights went out.

Becket rescued his board before it hit the cliff. That was it, he told me, when I struggled ashore. No more. He had seen my wave. I had disappeared into the tube standing straight up, he said, my arms extended crucifixion-style, face raised to the sky. I never had a prayer of making it. But I reappeared, he said, for a moment, blown through the curtain, somersaulting helplessly. "Rag doll" was the term he used. I couldn't remember the wipeout. All I remembered was the rapture. I lay down on the rocks, shivering. There was speed in the acid, he said. That's why I was cold. He went back out, and he stayed out for hours. I slowly curled into a ball, my arms around my knees. Something seemed to be bending my spine, forcing my head down into my chest. Many things were ending at once, I thought, and for a change I was right.

. . .

CARYN DID FIND HER FATHER. It was the following year, in San Francisco. We had both fled Maui for the civilizing precincts of college. I was back in Santa Cruz, she was living nearby, and we were no longer a couple. My grief over our breakup felt bottomless. I was not always reasonable. Still, Caryn called me after she found Sam, and we went back to see him together. He was living in a hotel on Sixth Street—skid row. We talked our way upstairs. The halls stank of piss, dried sweat, mildew, curry. Caryn knocked on a door. No answer. She called to him. "Dad? It's me. It's Caryn." After several minutes of silence, Sam opened the door. He looked bewildered and unwell. A short, wiry-haired, sad-eyed man. He didn't smile or reach for his daughter. A homemade chessboard, drawn on the side of a grocery bag, was on the bed, set with pieces made from bottle caps and cigarette butts. He appeared to have been playing alone. I left them to it. I walked the tragic warehouse streets, past winos sleeping in alleys. The Jones Hotel, the Oak Tree Hotel, the Rose. This couldn't be Sam's world, after a monastery on Maui. Later, we all went out to a dank cafeteria. Sam and I played chess. Caryn watched, her face a mask of sorrow. I tried to think about the moves. Sam played carefully. His few comments were measured, well chosen. Nobody cried, or said anything barbed. There would be time, I assumed, for that. I wouldn't be there. Still, I wondered what Sam, mental illness and all, might have to tell us about adulthood. Why, for example, did it seem to be always receding as a concept, even as we got older?

ON THIS QUESTION, my professors weren't always a help. I was in awe of Norman O. Brown, a gentle, formidably erudite classical scholar turned social philosopher who took on minor figures like Freud, Marx, Jesus, Nietzsche, Blake, and Joyce and wrestled their work to the ground, declaring victory for "holy madness" and "polymorphous perversity" and Eros over Thanatos, all while living quietly with his family in a ranch-style house near campus. Everybody at UC Santa Cruz called him Nobby; I found the nickname stuck in my throat. Brown did not welcome me back to school. Polite as always, he said he was disappointed to see me. My dropping out to go surfing in Hawaii had evidently represented, to him, a triumph over repression, a vote for Dionysus and erotics and against civilization, which was, after all, just mass neurosis. I made a little joke about the return of the repressed, and we went back to work.

But everything felt different without Caryn: harsher, more jagged. She, for good reason, felt abandoned by her father. I, for less identifiable reasons, felt abandoned generally. The existentialist psychiatrist R. D. Laing—a radical critic, like Brown, of received wisdom, and similarly inclined to see mental illness as a sane response to an insane world, even as a form of "shamanic" journey—described in one of his early books what he called the "ontologically secure" person. That, I thought, was not me. I read and wrote feverishly. My journals were full of anguish, self-excoriation, ambition, overheard speech that tickled me, and long passages from the work of favorite writers copied out by hand. One of the few things that calmed me reliably was surfing.

Bryan Di Salvatore, Viti Savaiinaea, and me,
Sala'ilua, Savai'i, Western Samoa, 1978

FIVE

THE SEARCH

The South Pacific, 1978

CALL IT ENDLESS WINTER. SUMMER IS PART OF THE POPULAR iconography of surfing. Like much of that iconography, it's wrong. Most surfers in most places, north or south of the equator, live for winter. That's when the big storms occur, usually in the higher latitudes. They send forth the best waves. There are exceptions, including, speaking of iconography, Waikiki and Malibu, but summer is most often the doldrums for surfers. An exception that had long interested me was the summer cyclone season in northeastern Australia. Basically, though, when I left Los Angeles in early spring 1978, with a board and a tent and a stack of much-studied nautical charts of Polynesian atolls, I was chasing winter.

It wasn't easy to leave. I had a job I loved. I had a girlfriend. The job was on the railroad. I had been a brakeman on the Southern Pacific since 1974, working local freight in Watsonville and Salinas and mainline trains between San Francisco and Los Angeles. Everything about braking pleased me inordinately—the country we moved through, the people I worked with, the arcane and ancient language we spoke, the mental and physical tests the work imposed, the big iron itself, the paychecks. It felt like I had lucked into a steel-toed, rock-solid version of adulthood. To get hired, I had failed to mention my degree in English. Because most of the Coast Route traffic we handled was agricultural—produce from the Salinas Valley—the work was seasonal, particularly for low-seniority trainmen like me. I used my furloughed winters to earn another degree, which the S.P. also didn't need to know about. The company didn't trust college graduates to become railroaders. It invested time and trouble in bringing young trainmen along, and old heads liked to say that no one with less than ten years' experience could really pull his weight on a train crew. So the company was looking for forty-year men. Braking could be dirty and dangerous, and college grads might decide to move on to something cleaner and safer. I hated to confirm this view by quitting. I believed I would never find another job as satisfying or well paid.

But I had five thousand dollars in the bank, by far the most I had ever saved. I was twenty-five, and I had never been to the South Seas. It was time for a serious surf trip, an open-ended wave chase. Such a trip felt strangely mandatory. I would go west forever, like Magellan or Francis Drake—that was how I thought of it. In truth, difficult as it was, pulling up stakes was in many ways easier than staying. It gave me an excellent excuse to postpone mundane but frightening decisions about where and how to live. I would disappear from the overdetermined, underwhelming world of disco-dulled, energy-crisis America. I might even become another person—someone more to my liking—in the Antipodes.

I told my family I would be gone a long time. Nobody offered any objections. I had a one-way ticket to Guam, with stops in Hawaii and the Caroline Islands. My mother, seeing me off at the airport, gave me her blessing with unexpected fervor. "Be a rolling stone," she said, holding my face and looking searchingly into my eyes. What did she see? Not a career railroader—to her relief, I'm sure. The job had been my base, pulling me back to the West Coast seasonally, but I was still a restless romantic. I had become a prolific writer of fiction, poetry, criticism, almost entirely unpublished. I rambled around and lived in places that took my fancy—Montana, Norway, London—for brief stretches. So I really hadn't been, in my mother's terms, gathering much moss. I had lived with a couple of women, but, since Caryn, had never felt committed heart and soul.

I sensed later—much later—that I might be overdoing the rolling stone bit, even on my mother's terms. She and my father, in the third year of my absence, abruptly flew, uninvited, to Cape Town, where the Southern Ocean was pumping out an abundance of winter swells and I had a job teaching high school. They stayed a week. They never suggested that I consider folding my tents and coming back to the United States, but in the fourth year of my travels they did send my brother Kevin out to fetch me. At least that was how I interpreted his visit. He and I traveled north through Africa together. But I'm getting ahead of my story.

To search the South Seas for ridable waves, I needed a partner. Bryan Di Salvatore said he was game. A piece of serendipity had put us back in touch after I left Maui. The Aloha Airlines ticket folder with his parents' address scrawled on it had surfaced during one of my student-housing moves in Santa Cruz. I wrote to see if he had ever received the payment for his car. He replied from an address in northern Idaho. Yes, the cash had found him. We became correspondents. He was driving trucks—long-distance semis—and working on a novel. On a trip to visit his family in California, he stopped in Santa Cruz. He brought Max with him. It seemed she was living nearby, over the hill in San Jose. Her live-in boyfriend there was a successful pornographer, according to Bryan. That was correct, Max said. She looked, if possible, even more wickedly amused and attractive than she had on Maui.

I took them out to the mouth of the San Lorenzo River, where a rare sandbar had formed after heavy rains the previous winter, creating a mar-velous wave that I patronized daily for the months it lasted. But when I tried to describe the setup to Bryan, Max began rudely interrupting. In a startling imitation of a stoked surfer's drawl, she was completing my sen-tences, usually with the exact cliché I had been planning to use. "The faces were as high as that garage door!" "You could have fit that pickup inside the barrel!" It seemed Max had put in her time with surfers on Maui—"two-minute men," she called them disdainfully—and she believed that we should be able to do better conversationally. Bryan and I agreed to talk surf at a later date.

We talked surf, books, writing. I was working on a novel too. We started exchanging manuscripts. Bryan's novel was about a circle of friends, surfers in high school in Montrose, an inland suburb of L.A. One passage, thirty pages long, contained nothing but words said in the car on the trip from Montrose to a beach north of Ventura. No narration, no stage directions, no attributions. I found it dazzling—the fractured, profane speech was shockingly accurate, sneaky-poetic, and very funny, the story movement invisible but irresistible. This, I thought, was a new American literature. Bryan was from Montrose. His father was a machinist who, as a soldier in World War II, had met his mother in Europe. She was British. Bryan had gone on scholarship to Yale, where he majored in English and wrote for campus magazines. Jack Kerouac had inscribed a book to him, and he had gone to Kerouac's funeral in 1969. I was in awe of such experience, but Bryan wore it lightly, unimpressed with himself. After graduation, he headed for Maui, where he lived and surfed with old Montrose pals and worked as a cook in a hotel restaurant. Few people in Lahaina, it was safe to say, understood his taste. While they were decorating their surfboards with images of Vishnu and badly drawn dolphins, he stuck a picture of the Marlboro Man on the deck of his board. He liked country-western music, demotic American speech, and the collected works of Melville. As a son of the working class, he scorned welfare. He wouldn't even collect unemployment between jobs. Women, meanwhile, seemed unanimously eager to get next to him. He had curly dark hair, a thick mustache, and an air of effortless, old-school masculinity. Max reckoned he was the original brown-eyed handsome man. He was also—more catnip—funny and generous and something of a loner.

We first surfed together in Santa Cruz after he decided to move back to the coast. He was a goofyfoot, meaning he surfed with his left foot back. It's the surfing equivalent of being left-handed. Going right, a goofyfoot is on his backhand—he has his back to the wave. Going left, he is on his forehand, or frontside. For regularfoots like me, rights are frontside, lefts backside. Surfing is notably easier on one's frontside. I was surprised to hear Bryan say he had never surfed Honolua Bay. It wasn't that the wave was a right—plenty of goofyfoots surfed Honolua—but that the crowds had put him off. He and his friends had been fixtures at a country spot a few miles north of Lahaina called Rainbows, which few people checked during swells. I had never surfed Rainbows. And now, talking Maui, I felt like a mindless herd-follower, having been focused while living there only on the most obvious possible wave, the famous Honolua, and quite ready, if necessary, to trade elbows with the mob in the main takeoff bowl, oblivious to the self-defeating meanness of grubbing for waves in that glorious setting. Even Les Potts, the old top dog, had seemed to renounce the battle as demeaning. In Santa Cruz, a busy surf town, Bryan and I went up the north coast looking for empty waves, which could still be found then.

We took long car journeys on any excuse. At a student party in Santa Cruz, Bryan suddenly announced that it was time I saw Rathdrum, the little Idaho panhandle town where he had lived, and we left directly from the party, making a ten-day loop of it, visiting college friends of his in Montana and Colorado. Bryan, loyal to scruffy Idaho, sniffed, "Montana has a hard-on for itself." It was true, but we both later ended up living there—going to graduate school in Missoula, learning to ski, and, in my case, learning to drink. Bryan, after getting a master's, took a job teaching English at the University of Guam. Best known as an American military outpost in the western Pacific, Guam was said to be blown flat annually by typhoons. As a posting, it suited Bryan, I thought—something about its down-home harshness and sheer unlikeliness. Also, it reportedly had good waves. Those reports were soon confirmed by letters and photos. He was surfing his brains out. During his second year on Guam, while I was finishing my studies in Missoula, I proposed the Endless Winter trip.

Bryan was also saving money. And he was up for it, he said. I could check out the Carolines on my way to Guam. Then we could head south.

We should brush up on our Spanish, he said.

I couldn't see why. There wasn't a Spanish-speaking country in the South Pacific.

That was good, he said. We were going to need a language that nobody else understood, for classified communications in dicey situations.

I told him he was out of his mind.

But he wasn't. We ended up using Spanish regularly. It was our secret code. No Tongan could crack it.

My girlfriend's name was Sharon. She was seven years older than me. At that point, she was teaching college in Santa Cruz. We had been together for four years, on and off, and were more deeply attached than we probably looked. She was a medievalist, an enthusiast, adventurous, the daughter of a liquor-store owner in L.A. She had a laugh that went from high to low, drawing you into her confidence, merry eyes, and an eclectic intellectual glamour that wowed people, including me. Underneath all the badinage, though, under her slinky sloe-eyed self-assurance, was a soft and wounded person whose restlessness was, as she would say, molecular. She had a checkered résumé, including a brilliant unemployable ex-husband. She and I had survived long separations, and we had never been especially monogamous—she liked to quote Janis Joplin: *Honey, get it while you can.* We had vague plans to rendezvous after she finished her PhD, which would not be soon. I was ambivalent, I suppose, about my attachment to her, but I didn't give her even a shadow of a veto over my decision to leave.

I had a board custom-made for the trip. It was a 7'6" single-fin. It was longer, thicker, and much heavier than the boards I normally rode. But this travel board needed to float high and paddle fast—we would be in a world of unfamiliar, reef-edged currents—and it needed to work in big, powerful waves. Above all, it could not snap. Where we were going, it would be impossible to replace a broken board. I put a leash on it, which was, for me, a concession. Board leashes had been around for a few years, and in Santa Cruz they had drawn a bright line between purists, who thought they encouraged dumb, sloppy surfing, and early adopters, who thought that having a lost board unnecessarily smashed on the cliffs at spots like Steamer Lane was itself a good definition of dumb. I was a purist and had never used a leash. But even I knew that I couldn't afford to lose my South Pacific board at some Fijian cloudbreak and risk never seeing it again. I rode the board for a few months before we left, and I loved the way it handled bigger days at the Lane. During a scary late-winter session at Ocean Beach, San Francisco, my leash snapped, leaving me in big surf with a long, cold swim that lasted till after dark. After that, I bought a thicker leash and a couple of spares.

HONOLULU WAS MY FIRST STOP. In my overexcited mind, Oahu was all signs and portents. Domenic happened to be there, on a job—he was now shooting TV commercials full-time, with a specialty in tropical ocean action footage. Our friendship had survived, barely, a patch after Caryn and I broke up and he and she became a couple. They hadn't lasted long, but I found the whole business so excruciating that I wrote a thousand-page novel about it, an apocalyptic prose poem that I finished, bashing out the last draft on a borrowed manual typewriter in London, at the age of twenty. (Bryan may have been the only person who read that entire early masterpiece.) Domenic and I had taken a couple of surf trips together since, including one to central Baja California during which he seemed to be always filming me, encouraging me to talk straight into the camera about whatever came to mind. This was a last gasp of the idea that we might be geniuses—his touching faith that I could hold the screen with pure improvisation. I couldn't. Domenic shelved the project in favor of paid work.

Now, as we crossed paths on Oahu, a late-season swell hit and we, obeying dog-whistle orders from the collective surf unconscious, dropped everything and headed for the North Shore. I had by then surfed most of the big-name spots along the famous big-wave coast—I first surfed Pipeline on my nineteenth birthday, not long after that addled huge day at Honolua with Becket. I had had some memorable sessions at Sunset Beach especially. Was Sunset, as we had been told as kids, basically Rice Bowl writ large? Not really. It was a vast wave field, bordered on the west by a roaring rip, with a bewildering variety of peaks swinging in at different angles, producing thick, beautiful waves and regular episodes of terror. Sunset was effectively impossible for the occasional visitor to understand.

On that spring day with Domenic, Sunset was big and clean, and I felt as confident surfing it as I ever had. The leash probably helped. The big, thick board definitely helped. Then a ten-foot west set caught me inside and put the leash, and my confidence, to a severe test. I was trapped in the impact zone, taking each wave on the head, ditching my board, diving deep, getting cruelly rumbled, just trying to stay calm. The leash pulled hard on my ankle, threatening to snap. After half a dozen waves, I was painfully glad to see my board still surfacing near me, though I never had the time to reel it in. By the time I washed into the shallows, back on my board, I was light-headed, breathing raggedly. Domenic found me sitting on the sand, still too tired to speak. The ordeal had felt like a baptism. It was the worst beating I had received in fifteen years of surfing. But I had not panicked.

The next portent was the surprise appearance in Honolulu of a kid named Russell. He and Domenic had been roommates in the early '70s—*Hawaii Five-0* days for Domenic and my family. Russell had been a wide-eyed hick from a tiny sugar town on the Big Island then, but he had spent the intervening years in Europe, mostly in Cambridge, where he had picked up a British accent and large quantities of worldliness and erudition. There was nothing supercilious about this transformation—he was still wide-eyed and soft-spoken, just widely read and widely traveled. Rus-

sell and I spent a couple of long nights talking nonstop about Britain, poetry, and European politics, by the end of which I realized I had been
thoroughly obnoxious to Domenic. I hadn't let him get a word in. When
I nervously suggested as much, he brusquely agreed. "I wanted to catch up
with Russell, find out what's going on with his sexuality," he said. "Maybe
next time." Russell's social affect had, it was true, also changed. It was
now vividly bisexual. But I had been too intent on exchanging ideas about
the decadence of Sartre and situationism even to think of broaching the
obvious personal topic. Domenic's patience with my overwrought erudition had reached its limit, I figured. It was time for me to slip off to Samoa
and grow up.

But there was one more sign. On a balmy blue morning, I paddled out
at Cliffs. There, looking like he had never left, was Glenn Kaulukukui. It
had been ten years, but he headed straight toward me, calling my name
with a gleeful curse, reaching for my hand. He looked older—thicker
through the shoulders, with shorter, darker hair, and a mustache—but the
laughing light in his eyes was unchanged. He and Roddy and John were
all now living on Kauai, he said. "We all still full-on surfing." Although
Roddy did not compete—he worked in a hotel restaurant—his surfing
had never stopped improving, Glenn said. Roddy was now the best surfer
in the family. Glenn himself, as I knew from the mags, was a pro, busy on
the contest circuit, putting in his time each winter on the North Shore.
"I'm a competitor," he said simply. We commenced surfing small, glassy,
uncrowded Cliffs, and I was pleased to see Glenn pausing on the shoulder
of one of my waves, studying me closely, and then announcing, "Hey, you
can still surf." His own surfing, meanwhile, even in soft, chest-high Cliffs,
was glorious. The speed, power, and purity of his turns were on a level I
had rarely seen except in films. And he didn't seem to be pushing himself
at all. He seemed to be playing—intently, respectfully, joyfully. For me,
seeing Glenn surf like that was an epiphany. It was about him, my boyhood idol grown into a man, but it was also about surfing—its depth, or
potential depth, as a lifelong practice. I told him I was off to the South

Seas. He looked at me hard and wonderingly, and wished me luck. We clasped hands again. It was the last time I ever saw him.

I FOUND NO WAVES on Pohnpei, a green speck in the Caroline Islands, then under U.S. administration, now part of the independent Federated States of Micronesia. I did spend long, hot days bumping around in the bush trying to find reef passes that looked promising on my charts, but they were all dauntingly far from shore, the wind was always wrong, the swell always funky. I began to wonder if I had deluded myself about the chances of finding ridable waves in random tropical locales. (As it happens, a luminous righthander was later discovered on the northwest corner of Pohnpei. I was there in the wrong season for that wave.) I was reading, between fruitless forays, Claude Lévi-Strauss's *Tristes Tropiques*, which has a nice first line: "I hate traveling and explorers." The paterfamilias of structural anthropology goes on, about his profession: "We may endure six months of traveling, hardships and sickening boredom for the purpose of recording (in a few days, or even a few hours) a hitherto unknown myth, a new marriage rule or a complete list of clan names." This sounded, in my little surf-skunked corner of Micronesia, ominously familiar. Would it take months of hard searching to find even some mediocre wave—the surfing equivalent of a new marriage rule?

SPEAKING OF ANTHROPOLOGY, I found on Pohnpei a collision of local tradition with modernity—and this would turn out to be an inescapable theme everywhere in the Pacific—over how to get drunk. In the evenings the men either drank, in a slow, ceremonial, communal ritual, using coconut shells as cups, a mild indigenous liquor called sakau—it's called other names on other islands, most commonly kava—or else they drank imported alcohol. Imported alcohol, whether spirits or beer, cost money and was associated with colonialism, fighting, bars, general dissipation, and domestic violence. I hung with the sakau crowd, on principle, even though I found the stuff, which was viscous and gray-pink and medicinal-smelling, vile. It numbed the mouth, though, and after eight or ten cups it tilted my brain to an angle from which I began to understand, or believe I understood, a complex form of checkers that was the local pastime. The game was played with cigarette butts and little cylindrical coral pebbles, and it went fast, with an abundance of muttered commentary, some bits of it in English. "What's this, Christmas?" "You crazy dude!" I never gained the confidence to actually play, but I became a passionate kibitzer.

We drank under a dilapidated thatch pavilion in somebody's backyard, by the light of a naked yellow bulb stuck up on a post. Deep in their sakau cups, my companions would start mumbling to themselves, bowing their heads to drool great careful white streamers into the mud. In this romantic setting, I managed to meet a girl, Rosita. She was a tough, pretty nineteen-year-old from Mokil Atoll. She said she had been thrown out of school for stabbing a girl. But she wasn't all bravado—she was very concerned, at least, that no one see her stealing into my hotel. One of my secret ambitions for this just-begun journey was to consort with women from exotic lands, and young Rosita seemed like an auspicious start. (*What's this, Christmas?*) She had traditional-looking tapa-pattern tattoos on her thighs and, on one shoulder blade, a heart-and-scroll design that looked like it belonged on a U.S. Marine circa World War II. The sex was comically terrible, as I struggled to figure out what might please her. Nothing seemed to, at least not as I understood pleasure. But then she cried, in her green skirt and white blouse, when I left Pohnpei. I knew that my secret ambition regarding women was profoundly unoriginal. It took me a while to figure out that it might also be no fun.

GUAM WAS MILSPEAK, I was told—short for Give Up and Masturbate. The etymology was bogus, but the place was impressively bleak. Heroin addiction seemed to be the leading form of entertainment, followed by shopping, fighting, robbery (a traditional way to fund a heroin habit), television, arson, and strip joints. On an island surrounded by warm turquoise seas, no one seemed to use the beaches. There were almost no trees—a disastrous oversight at 13 degrees north. The island's trees had been blown down by typhoons, people said, or destroyed in World War II, after which the U.S. military, hoping to prevent erosion, scattered tangan tangan seeds over much of the land from airplanes. Tangan tangan is a tall, dense, colorless brush. Not native to the Pacific, it nonetheless thrived on Guam. To travel the island's roads was to pass between long gray-brown walls of tangan tangan. The local architecture was squat and concrete—built to survive typhoons. The economy was sustained by low-end Japanese tourism and the vast U.S. military presence. When I told Bryan that my *World Almanac* listed copra (dried coconut) as Guam's major export, he laughed. "Most Guamanians think copra is a TV show—'What time's *Copra*, 8:30 or 9?'"

Bryan seemed to be having a ball. He had a delightful, serious girlfriend, Diane—a schoolteacher and single mom. He had a jolly crew of guys he surfed with, and after surfing drank beer with. Most of his friends seemed to be teachers from the U.S. mainland. His students were nearly all island kids—indigenous Chamorros, Filipinos, other Micronesians—who had to figure out what to make of a professor who wore baggy shorts and vintage aloha shirts and exhorted them all year to see the magic in language and literature, and then, on their final exam, gave them a multiple-choice question about which famous personage their teacher most closely resembled, with every choice the same: "Clint Eastwood."

The surf during my Guam stay was AWOL—"flat as piss on a board," in Bryan's words. All the great spots I had heard about and seen pictures of—Boat Basin, Meritzo—didn't show a ripple for weeks on end. Worse, Bryan seemed less than elated to see me. Had he turned ambivalent about our plan? I hung around, waiting for him to wrap up his Guam life. I stewed and spent a lot of time alone in his bare-bones, cement-walled apartment while he hung out with Diane and her son. I decided that

Diane and I were locked in a silent battle for Bryan's soul. She and her son were moving back to Oregon. What were Bryan's intentions? He didn't confide in me, but he was obviously struggling. He was also under fierce pressure from his mother, who, from Los Angeles, was making her disapproval of his job-quitting plans known. Was this why he had gone to Yale, to become some kind of bum? I didn't really know her, but Bryan's mother had always seemed formidable, dour, and very tightly wound in a North West England sort of way. Her golden American son's highly developed sense of fun seemed never to have infected her. I decided that she and I were locked in a silent battle for Bryan's soul.

I also decided that the disapproval gene had been, subtly but successfully, transmitted intact, and that I was now feeling its lash. The smallest things about me seemed to irk Bryan. I had stopped shaving when I left California; he made it clear that he disapproved of my scraggly beard. Then he told me that I needed to start using deodorant. I took that friendly advice hard. Encouraged by girlfriends, and by the Age of Aquarius in which we had grown up, I had always thought of myself as naturally sweet-smelling. On the phone to Sharon, I mentioned this very personal insult, expecting gentle reassurance, and instead got a long pause. Well, she said finally, he might be right about that. So, I thought, now I was facing a conspiracy. My surf partner and my girlfriend had both decided, possibly in concert, that it was time to rein me in, to tame the wild child, to crush the fresh-smelling free spirit they had once loved. Next they would have me wearing a coat and tie to work in an office park.

I was clearly going Guamshit—a malady much discussed among Bryan's teacher friends—although I had the sense to keep my more lurid paranoias to myself. The truth was that Sharon was being wonderfully open-minded about my taking off on this open-ended trip. The fact that I was immature and headstrong (and Sharon, being older, had all too much perspective on my self-absorption) didn't mean, however, that I was physically still a boy. They were undoubtedly right: I'm sure I reeked like a hostler.

I had a novel in progress to keep me busy during the Guam dog days. The main characters all worked on the railroad in California, a milieu I knew well, but the plot wandered off the rails, as it were, and got lost somewhere on the coast of Morocco. (Sharon and I had traveled in Morocco, after a long winter in England.) Bryan read what I had, and pronounced it a mishmash. He was right, and a couple of long talks about where I had gone wrong convinced me to chuck it all. The railroad was still the world I wanted to write about, but I needed new protagonists. And I still trusted Bryan above all readers of my stuff. As for my doubts about his commitment to this Endless Winter plan, they were at least half projections, I realized, of my own fears and misgivings.

In the end, we went. Or tried to go. We had bought cheap tickets to Western Samoa on Air Nauru, an airline that turned out to operate at the whim of the king of a miniature Micronesian country called Nauru. The king commandeered our plane just as we were waiting to board, and the ticket agent told us to come back in a week. I complained, to Bryan's embarrassment, and the Air Nauru rep quickly started handing out hotel and meal vouchers to those knocked-back passengers who hadn't already left the airport. We ended up staying at the Guam Hilton for a week. The other Air Nauru refugees staying free at the hotel kept trying to buy me drinks, and Bryan thought the incident illustrated a fundamental difference between us, although the moral of the story seemed to change each time he told it. Sometimes it was about his passivity, other times my obnoxiousness. We took, for the folks back home, poorly lit photos of one another styling like Frankie Avalon, balancing carefully on our boards, in our hotel room. Check it out, everybody: the first stop on our world surf tour. Bryan and Diane got to spend another week together. Then we really left.

WITHIN WEEKS, it felt like we had been knocking around the South Pacific for half our lives. We traveled by local bus and truck and ferry, by canoe and freighter and open boat, by small plane and yacht and taxi, on horseback. We walked. We hitchhiked. We paddled. We swam. We walked some more. We bent our heads over maps and charts and strained to see distant reefs, channels, headlands, river mouths. We clambered up overgrown trails and beetling crags and coconut trees to likely vantage points, and were frequently defeated by jungles, bad maps, worse roads, mangrove swamps, ocean currents, and kava. Fishermen helped us. Villagers took us in. People gawked, scythes frozen midswing, as we trudged past their taro patches in the depths of the woods, strange planks under our arms. Children seemed to follow us everywhere, screaming, *"Palagi, palagi!"* (White people!) Privacy became a faded memory, one of those American luxuries left behind. We were curiosities, envoys, entertainment. Nobody understood what the hell we were after.

We wished we had brought a surf magazine. The rain-soaked paperbacks rolling around in our bags were useless as visual aids. (Tolstoy don't surf.)

In Western Samoa we found and rode a powerful, shifty right off the south shore of Upolu, the main island. The wave had great potential, I thought, but was vulnerable to the southeast trade winds, which blew almost every day. Bryan named the spot Mach Two, after the speed of the drop. It had scary, unpredictable, wide-swinging sets and a shallow reef, and it broke half a mile from shore, all of which left me glad I had brought a fast-paddling board. We decided not to camp on that wave, and pushed on to Savai'i, the next island west, where we found, on a coast with lighter winds, a left in front of a village called Sala'ilua.

The challenge, during the southern winter, was simple enough. Big winter swells came from the south, from storms in the Roaring Forties, or from even higher latitudes, down below New Zealand, and the prevailing trades blew from the same general direction. For surfing, that was bad. Onshore winds make a mess of waves—tearing them apart, causing them to crumble, filling the lineup with chop. So we were looking for places where the south swells bent, or wrapped, around a reef or shore, turning

east or west—more likely east, since the trades blew from the southeast—
until they were breaking into the prevailing wind. Offshore winds, as I
hope I've made clear, wreathe waves in glory. They groom them, hold
them up and prevent them from breaking for a crucial extra beat, make
them hollower when they do break, and create little or no chop. But swells
lose their power and size when they turn corners. Steep coasts with quirky
winds could alter the general pattern, but basically we were looking for
reefs perfectly angled to bend south swells into the trades without killing
them. If such reefs existed outside dreams and theory, they also needed,
for our purposes, to come equipped with deepwater channels, also angled
just right, so that the waves breaking on the reefs would have ridable
shoulders and we would have a place to paddle back out after riding them.
It was a tall order.

The left on Savai'i was consistent but undistinguished. We called it
Uo's—*uo* is Samoan for "friend." The trade winds mostly left it alone,
even in the afternoon. Unfortunately, the brunt of the south swells also
steamed past the little bay where we surfed, dropping waves on us daily
but none with much juice. The bigger days were head-high. Uo's had a
promising setup, with a reliable takeoff peak and a long wall. Nearly every
wave was marred, though, by a quick, crossed-up section that broke out
ahead of the hook (the steepest part of the wave) and ended most rides in
frustration. At low tide it was extra-quick, and getting in and out of the
water got nasty. A lava shelf covered with slick, round, ham-sized rocks
was exposed, providing for hilarious-from-shore scenes of slipping, cursing, and ankle-barking, gymnastic attempts to fall down without dinging
our boards. Our boards made big, hollow noises when they hit the rocks.
Worse, there was an outhouse on rickety stilts perched over the lagoon just
west of the break, and its stench got more notable at low tide. Bryan
thought the outhouse would make a great logo for a typhoid prevention
campaign. In the gashes and scrapes accumulating on our soft white feet,
infections bloomed.

Were we the first people to surf this spot? Possibly. To surf this large (roughly forty miles by thirty miles) island? Probably not. But we had no way of knowing. The difficulty, the improbability, of finding good waves on unsurfed coasts was undoubtedly why Glenn Kaulukukui had given me such a searching look when I told him about our plan. Now Bryan and I were completely absorbed, though, in trying to solve the riddles and quirks of Uo's. Surfing a known spot, a mapped spot, with local guys who demonstrate, if only by example, where to take off and what to expect, is an entirely different enterprise. We were making it up ourselves, first trying to identify and then by trial and error figure out new breaks. It was exhilarating, when you looked up from the reef's many oddities and thought about it, to be surfing in such splendid isolation.

And there were, praise the Lord, a couple of sessions, at high tide, when the rogue end-section relaxed and Uo's realized its potential. One of those came at the end of a rainy day after the wind, by some local meterological act of grace, backed around off the mountains and began to blow offshore. The clouds were low and dark, the water a dull gray. Bryan said that except for the palm trees thrashing in the gloom, and the temperature, it felt like northwest Ireland. He was on his frontside—a goofyfoot going left—and he put together a string of long, fast rides, taking a high line through the shut-down section and threading it cleanly. The surf was shoulder-high and pulsing. The wind added drama to the approaching sets and a faint blue light high in the faces just at the moment of breaking. We surfed till after dark, then walked back into Sala'ilua through a warm, thick, gentle rain.

The village had no hotel. (The whole island of Savai'i, as far as we knew, had no hotel.) We were staying with a family, the Savaiinaeas, who had several adjoining *fales*—open-walled, thatch-roofed traditional houses. Staying with a family was a delicate business. We had showed up in Sala'ilua one afternoon, after a long ride in the back of a dump truck. The truck, with a bed of old rubber sandal forms recycled as padding, doubled as an open-air bus. Our boards were jammed between baskets of taro and fish. The truck dropped us next to a cricket pitch covered with green cocoa beans laid out to dry in the sun. The village was neat, all thatched roofs and well-spaced breadfruit trees, and very quiet. It felt shy. We couldn't quite see the waves. We had a letter of introduction to the Savaiinaeas from a cousin of theirs whom we'd met in Apia, the Samoan capital. We could hear children yelling, then see them gathering at a safe distance. Finally, a young man wearing a black lavalava approached. We murmured our business, and he led us to Sina Savaiinaea. She turned out to be a handsome woman in her thirties. She read our letter, ignoring a breathless crowd that had gathered around us. Sina glanced at the long, filthy canvas bags under our arms—they contained our surfboards—but did not miss a beat. "You are welcome," she said, taking the wraps off a thousand-watt smile.

Sina and her husband, Tupuga, and their three daughters deluged us with an embarrassment of hospitality. Meal after lavish meal, cup after cup of tea. Our sweat-stained T-shirts would vanish and reappear in the morning washed and pressed. Bryan, who smoked, said ashtrays seemed to be emptied ten times a day. We tried to observe the basic local manners we'd learned—never sitting with a foot pointed at someone, never declining anything offered, greeting every guest with a handshake and a "*Talofa*." But there was no escaping our pampered, privileged role as clueless guests. We even slept inside mosquito nets we'd brought, like little sheikhs with backpacks. Conversations were surprisingly cosmopolitan. Every grown man in Sala'ilua seemed to have traveled and worked all over—New Zealand, Europe, the United States. (Samoa has a large diaspora relative to its size; there are said to be more Samoans living overseas than at home.) There was a *matai*, or chief, who had been to the United Nations. There was even a guy in a denim jacket with a big American flag on the back who had made a pilgrimage to Lourdes.

And yet Savai'i felt like a world unto itself, a universe complete, out of time. There was no television. I never saw a telephone. (Cell phones and the Internet were many years away.) There were imported goods, mostly from China, in the tiny makeshift shops—shovels and flashlights, Golden

Deer cigarettes, Long March transistor radios. But daily life was very largely a do-it-yourself affair. People farmed, fished, and hunted for their meals. They built their own houses and boats, made their own fishnets, mats, baskets, fans. They improvised endlessly. I was enchanted. I had set off from the United States with an ignorant ambition to see more of the world before it all turned into Los Angeles. There was no danger of that happening, of course, but fetching up in rural Polynesia caused my vague discontent with industrial civilization to snap into sharper focus.

Seen from a certain angle, everything in Samoa—the ocean, the forest, the people—had a kind of noble glow. This glow had nothing to do with picture-perfect beaches or grass shacks, those worn-out ideas of paradise, nor with my old storybook dreams—my Umi-and-his-brothers days were long behind me. I didn't even have bare-breasted-maiden fantasies, or none worth writing about. I also doubted, after surveying the Samoan teenagers we met, that there was a preneurotic adolescence to be had here—apologies to Margaret Mead. (Gauguin, for that matter, was disappointed in Tahiti—he reckoned he got there a century too late.) No, Samoa was thoroughly Christianized and literate. Global pop culture flourished with its usual virulence. Every little kid's hero seemed to be Bruce Lee. The inescapable tune that year was Boney M's cover of "Rivers of Babylon." What enchanted me was simply that people were still living so close to the land and sea, and so communally. To my Western eyes, they were paragons of graceful competence and imagined wholeness.

Sina's brother, Viti, was a short, well-built guy in his late thirties. He had spiky hair, long sideburns, a shy smile, and a modesty that almost hid his quick mind and cool ingenuity. He had lived in New Zealand, where he worked, he told us, in the Hellaby Corned Beef Factory, the Bycroft Biscuit Factory, and the New Zealand Milk and Butter Factory. He had sent money home, but he was happier here, he said. "There, you must wear a cardigan, and you can see your breath in front of your face while you wait for the works bus." Each morning while we were around, Viti sailed off over the horizon in a homemade one-man outrigger canoe that, according to Sina, he had carved by hand in less than a week—this after single-handedly felling the fetau tree he built it from. In the afternoon Viti brought boatloads of bonito back to the village. At night he took a lantern out on the reef at low tide and speared fish *with a knife*. When he needed cash, he climbed the mountain behind Sala'ilua to his family's copra plantation and brought down a truckload to market. (Samoa, unlike Guam, really did export copra.) When a wild pig got into his taro, he went hunting.

I once asked Viti about pig hunting. He and Bryan and I were sitting in a tiny, open-walled *fale* in the jungle near Sala'ilua drinking homemade beer from an old gin bottle.

"I take a torch and a rifle and some dogs and find his trail, then wait for him, just downwind," Viti said.

It was dusk. The beer was sweet, like apple cider, but as strong as scotch.

"Sometimes I must chase him through the bush. He go up and down the mountain." Viti laughed, miming himself thrashing through the jungle.

"It get dark. Then, after I kill him, I have to wait with him, all night. Only thing I have is my lavalava. I pull it over my head, but mosquitoes are so bad. So bad. It rains. I get cold. Then other pigs come, and all wait around me, because I have killed their brother. The dogs do not stop barking. The pig weigh maybe two hundred pounds. I cut him in two parts. In the morning I find a long stick to carry him, one part each side. But it can be far to a road. So far. You like go pig hunting?"

I thought Bryan would be thrilled to go. We drank another round of Viti's brew.

Now Viti wanted some music. "Give us a song from your country."

Bryan obliged with a round of a cappella Hank Williams.

I got a hot rod Ford and a two-dollar bill
And I know a spot just over the hill

The crowd—a gang of kids grinding garden cocoa beside the *fale*—
went nuts. They hooted and clapped and laughed themselves silly. Bryan's
voice twanged merrily through the jungle. Viti grinned wildly. Now it was
my turn.

But then a long, mournful double conch-shell blast came to my rescue.
"Curfew," I said. "No surfing, no singing."

These curfews came twice a day. They lasted less than an hour, and
people took them seriously. Nobody walked or worked until a second shell
or church bell rang out. We had heard different explanations—that activity ceased out of respect for the chiefs, or for a period of prayer—but the
general message about the strength of *Fa'a Samoa*, the traditional Samoan
way, was clear. On Sundays the curfew was in force all day long. On a
couple of occasions when the surf looked good, I had found the ban hard
to accept. Surely we could slip out for a few quiet rides, far from shore,
and offend no one.

Bryan took pleasure, I thought, in chastising me for these impious suggestions. "You think you're an *iconoclast*?"

No, I did not. I just wanted more waves.

Another pair of conch-shell notes wafted through the trees. My turn to
sing. I closed my eyes and, from deep memory, with no forethought, delivered all five verses of the Fool's Song from the end of *Twelfth Night*. It was
a strange choice, and I was no doubt off-key, but I got into it, the plaintive
philosophical repetitions ("*For the rain it raineth every day*"), the chastened
reflections on marriage ("*By swaggering could I n-e-e-ver thrive*"), and the
applause afterward seemed raucously sincere.

SALA'ILUA HAD A SECOND WAVE. It broke just east of a half-collapsed
waterfront pool hall. We spent a lot of time studying it. The wave was a
bullet-fast left. It was long and hollow and the prevailing wind on it, remarkably, was almost straight offshore. It seemed that a steep mountain
ridge behind the village bent the trades to the west right there, and an

offshore canyon somehow combined with a broken slab of reef to bend swells into the wind. The result was a beautiful but lethal-looking wave, almost surely too fast and shallow to ride. It broke below sea level, into a short, deep trough that the wave itself created, then exploded up across an exposed coral shelf. The wave got better as the surf got bigger, though— more possible, at least, to mind-surf without impossible accelerations through ridiculously fast sections. I walked out on the shelf at low tide to study it more closely. The lagoon was full of both urchins and man-made hazards—fish and crab traps with clear line strung between poles. Set after turquoise, wind-brushed set roared past. The biggest waves were breaking maybe five feet from the rocks. No. Uh-uh. We named the spot Almosts.

Uo's was sloppy and weak by comparison—just a new marriage rule.

On our last night in Sala'ilua, Sina gave us a feast. We had been eating well all week—fresh fish, chicken, coconut crab, clams, papaya soup, yams, and a dozen variations on taro (with spinach, with banana, with coconut cream). Now came pork sausage and banana bread with icing, somehow prepared over an open fire. Also a sharp-tasting black-and-green delicacy from the sea bottom—I missed the name—that toyed embarrassingly with my gag reflex. Bryan and I made heartfelt thank-you speeches and handed out gifts—a glass plate for Sina, balloons for the kids, Schlitz glasses for Viti, cigarettes for Sina's father, a shell comb for her mother.

A proper bus came through the village at 4 a.m. Sina roused us, gave us coffee and biscuits, and, along with Viti and his wife and one of their children, waited with us by the road. The sky was cloudy with stars. A fruit bat flew low overhead; we could hear the leathery flap of its wings. The Southern Cross glistened. The bus arrived, with tinny music spilling through its open door. A silent boy riding on the roof took our boards.

WE MET OUR SHARE of odd bods in Samoa. A young man named Tia led us to a remote beach that turned out to have no surf. As a consolation

prize, I suppose, he told us elaborate stories about each cove and outcrop-
ping and reef we came across. There were fratricides, patricides, and a
vivid cast of Christianized devils. There was a mass suicide—a whole village self-sacrificed. I was impressed. Every rock on the coast seemed to
have a place in a sacred literature. Then Tia said, "You come back in three
years, this beach will be *really* nice place, because I got moneys in the New
Zealand bank, so I buy some dynamites and make it nice."

We fell in with a Presbyterian minister, Lee, and his wife, Margaret.
They were from New Zealand but had just spent nine years in Nigeria.
Now they were living behind a church in Apia, with three small kids. Lee
was eager to show us around. He wore tight red shorts and large gray den-
tures. He had a deeply dimpled chin, thick glasses, and a startling amount
of body hair. He didn't actually know much about Samoa, and his interest
in us soon waned, but Margaret took up the slack and kept inviting us on
outings, or over to their place. Lee had a friend, Valo. Young and studly,
Valo had LOVE ME TENDER tattooed on one bicep. Lee watched Valo constantly, rapturously, and when Valo wasn't around he talked about him. At
a beach, wistfully: "Valo and I could come here and just find a little corner
where no one would ever come across us." I felt sorry for Margaret, who
was dumpy and sweet and, when Lee snapped sarcastically at her, just
widened her eyes girlishly behind her glasses and smiled at us. Valo told
Bryan that Rothman's were his favorite cigarettes because there was a secret message buried in the brand name: "Right on, Tom, hold my ass, now
shoot!" When the next picnic loomed, Bryan and I spoke Spanish to plot
our excuses.

We stayed, on the outskirts of Apia, at a place called the Paradise of
Entertainment. It was partly a motel, with a few modest bungalows, but
mostly it was an aptly named neighborhood boîte, owned and run by an
enormous parliamentarian named Sala Suivai. There was a sunken outdoor stage with a curved bank of bleachers. Some nights they showed
movies. Dance bands played on weekends. Once they set up a boxing ring
and a giddy crowd watched local scientists go at it. Nobody paid us much

attention—the *palagis* with their bandaged feet, their nautical charts spread across the tables near the bar. And being ignored, the urbanity of it, made a nice change.

FINDING RIDABLE WAVES with nautical charts was a long shot at best. We looked for south-facing island coasts that weren't "shadowed" by any barrier reef or landmass farther south. We looked for points and bays and reef passes where the shallow water soundings showed, after one or two fathoms, a sharp drop-off to seaward—places where swells would come suddenly out of deep water into the breaking-wave zone, giving them extra power and hollowness. The angle of any promising patch of reef or beach was critical. The rough line along which waves might be expected to break needed to be canted away from, even curved away from, the open ocean to the south, giving waves a chance to bend, peel, and turn into the wind. We looked for offshore canyons that would focus long-interval swell, and the canyon walls that would cause waves to refract into shallower water. Many stretches of coast—most stretches—could be ruled out for one reason or another. But that left a huge number of places with some abstract surf potential, and actually settling on a spot worth traveling to was, in the end, just glorified guesswork. We had no local knowledge; our charts weren't perfect, and their scale was always too big to account for the individual boulders and chunks of reef that would finally make all the difference. We tried to picture what the swarming numbers meant, as they fell into single digits in the pale blue ribbons of the inshore waters that surrounded the dull yellow splashes of dry land. Looking at the chart of a place you knew, particularly a place that you knew got waves, it was so easy. *This* is why that spot is good, under the right conditions. A two-dimensional chart suddenly became a multidimensional vision of ridable waves. You could isolate half a dozen factors on the chart alone. But studying charts of places we had never even seen? We were flying blind. This was decades before Google Earth. We had to trust in Willard Bascom, the great oceanographer, who wrote, in *Waves and Beaches*, "This zone where waves give up their energy and where systematic water motions give way to violent turbulence is the surf. It is the most exciting part of the ocean."

WE PLANNED TO GO to Tahiti next, or possibly American Samoa. Both places had surfers and known surf spots. Instead, we went to Tonga, about which we knew nothing.

It was a snap decision made during a chance encounter in a waterfront bar with the Australian purser on a freighter bound for Nuku'alofa, the Tongan capital. We boarded the ship, not sober, at midnight. It left Apia at dawn.

The captain only learned we were aboard later that morning. His wrath was reportedly all spent on the purser. With us, he was perfectly pleasant. His name was Brett Hilder, M.B.E. He had a neatly trimmed white Vandyke and wore his uniform well. He gave us a tour of the bridge. That drawing of the king of Tonga on his cabin wall? Captain Hilder had done it himself. The monarch had liked it so much, he signed it. Had we read Michener's *Tales of the South Pacific*? Well, the originals of those stories had all come from Captain Hilder. That's why the book was dedicated to him. (So it was.) But did we know how and why a certain Pacific Island bird had found its way into Herodotus, and into the prophetic books of the Bible? We were about to find out. Incidentally, Captain Cook had dubbed Tonga the Friendly Islands only because he missed by two days the feast at which he and his crew were going to be surprised and made the main course.

Bryan and I found Tonga friendly enough. But the surf was a major tease. On Eua, a solid, tilted lump of an island some twenty miles southeast of Nuku'alofa, I thought we were on the brink of a real discovery. The east coast of Eua was all high cliffs and onshore winds, but the swell sweeping up the southwest coast was highly promising. It looked huge.

On the ferry from Tongatapu, the main island in Tonga, just seeing the lines out at sea made my heart pound. Eua is rugged and has few roads. We rented horses and rode up and down rough trails, through thick bush, checking out likely stretches of coast. Every place we managed to see was a mess—rocky, blown out, closed out, unridable. We kept edging north. Part of the northwest coast had a dirt road, which made life easier, but the swell dropped steadily. At the end of the road, we finally found a ridable wave, in a little palm-lined cove called Ufilei.

It was a wild spot. We paddled out through a gap in the reef that was maybe four feet wide. A short, heaving left was exploding spectacularly at the south end of the cove, just off an exposed lava slab. The waves rose so quickly out of deep water that the faces were still an open-ocean navy blue when they broke. We edged into the lineup. The wave was so fast and thick that it looked more like a sudden drop in sea level than a normal swell. I eventually caught four or five waves. Each drop was critical, airborne, obliging me to throw my arms straight up in the effort to stay over my board. I did not fall. After the drop and one screaming bottom turn, the wave petered out in deep water. The rush of the takeoff was ferocious—the bigger waves were well overhead—but the danger-to-reward ratio, surfing so close to an exposed slab, was absurd. Many months later, on a beach in Australia, we met a guy who said he had surfed Ufilei. He was a well-known board builder, sailor, and filmmaker from California named George Greenough—one of the inventors of the shortboard. By his calculations, he said, a five-foot wave at Ufilei was seventy feet thick. It was an eccentric measurement—I have no idea how one determines the exact thickness of a breaking wave—but a good description of the spot's weird ferocity. After an hour or so, we called it a session.

But we had trouble getting back through the keyhole. There was so much water rushing out of the lagoon through the tiny gap that it was like trying to paddle up river rapids. I gave up, swerved a few yards north, caught a line of whitewater, and bumped and scraped my way across an inch-deep reef. Bryan chose to put his head down and power straight into the current, going nowhere until he was exhausted. My advice, called out from the swimming-pool calm of the lagoon, seemed unwanted. He fumed and struggled. I watched. The sun sank. I don't remember what route he ultimately took, but I do remember how haggard he looked when he finally made it across the reef. He did not say a word to me. I expected him to crawl up the beach, shipwreck-survivor style, and rest, but instead he rushed from the water and set off, board under arm, at a furious clip. We were staying in a guesthouse five miles away. I found him there, still glowering.

THE GIRLS WHO WORKED at the guesthouse were having their fortunes told. Tupo, a sleepy-eyed, broken-toothed teenager in a striped shirt, dealt the cards. Jacks went across the top. The jacks represented, Tupo explained, the four races of husbands: *palagi*, Tongan, Japanese, Samoan. Each time Tupo drew a card, she matched it by suit with a jack, tapped it significantly, and declared, "You know!" The other girls, huddled around a kerosene lamp, listened to her with eyes wide and breath bated. They all had a buttery, slightly stale smell.

To me, Tupo explained, "Girls who are fat and lazy will get Tongan husbands, who only allow them to cook and wash. Girls who are thin and beautiful and work hard will get *palagis*, who will wear watches, and drive them around in cars to moving pictures, and look, look, look at everything. Girls who marry Japanese will go to Japan's land and live very well, smoking cigarettes and only sometimes mopping, but their husbands will become angry with their laziness and one day come home and carve them up with a knife. Girls who marry Samoans will go to Samoa and live like we Tongans do, except they may see TV."

One of the girls sighed. "In Pago Pago I see television. Very beautiful!"

Tupo predicted that within a month I would get a letter with money from my family. I would marry a *palagi* girl, but I would leave someone weeping in Tonga.

Hanging out with the guesthouse girls, joking and passing the kerosene-lit evenings, I couldn't help but notice that I had abandoned, at least temporarily, my ambition to sleep with women from many lands. Rural Polynesia was not a place for the casual hookup, never mind old sailors' tales of wanton Tahiti—or, in a movie version seared in memory, the island princess burning up the screen with Brando's Fletcher Christian. Captain James Cook's sailors had actually found a wanton Tonga, I learned later (from Tony Horowitz's *Blue Latitudes*). One of Cook's crewmen described the local women as "to the last degree obliging"—willing to sleep with a visitor in exchange for a single iron nail. And a Dutch surgeon on a seventeenth-century voyage reported that in Tonga the women "felt the sailors shamelessly in the trouser-front, and indicated clearly that they wanted to have intercourse." Such stuff was a long way, alas, from the exceedingly Christian women we met. Most of them wore a stiff woven mat called a *ta'ovala* around their midsections, tied closely over their other, already cumbersome clothes. These were small, conservative societies that we passed through on our oddball quest. Many of the women we encountered were wonderful flirts, but the boundaries were clear, and they seemed essential to respect. I did not want to leave someone else weeping. Neither did I want to get my ass kicked by her uncles.

"IT LOOKS GOOD," Bryan said. "You look like a really liberal priest."

He was talking about my beard, which had become increasingly scruffy. But of course he was talking about more than that, I thought. We were starting to get on each other's nerves. Moving through unfamiliar worlds, we carried a world together, full of shared understandings, into which we could retreat. But it was crowded in there, with two big egos jostling. We were so dependent on each other, so constantly together, that any little difference chafed and inflamed. I found myself copying into my journal a passage from *Anna Karenina* about Oblonsky and Levin and their strained friendship. Was Bryan smiling ironically at me? I thought so, and I took little gibes like that priest remark too much to heart.

That was because I knew he was on to something. Bryan was a stick-in-the-mud sophisticate, skeptical of all things nouveau. In college at the height of the student antiwar movement, he had held the fury of his class-mates at arm's length, once carrying a sign at a protest march with the un-gung-ho message, WAR IS SPACE—GO METS. He still found the phrase "world peace" hilariously inane. I was more earnest. In high school I had marched against the Vietnam War, fervently believing it must be stopped. I had been raised on coffeehouse protest music—Joan Baez, Phil Ochs— and it still had a secret place in my heart. Bryan loathed such stuff and all the sentimental, suburban self-congratulation it represented. I never heard him quote Tom Lehrer, whom I knew slightly from Santa Cruz, but I was sure he would dig Lehrer's sly lines:

We are the folk song army
Every one of us cares
We all hate poverty, war, and injustice
Unlike the rest of you squares

I admired Bryan's stubborn dissent from liberal orthodoxy. I had also ac-quired, while braking on the railroad, some of the workingman's gimlet eye for soft cant.

But bumming around in the South Pacific was bringing out something else in me, something more troubling, from Bryan's perspective, than fa-cial hair. I was getting interested in self-transformation. I was straining to understand the worldview of the islanders whom we moved and lived among—and I had been doing so since before Guam, when I let myself sink deep into the coral-pebble speed-checkers subworld around the sakau bowl in Pohnpei. I had come here to learn, I figured, and not just a few things about some far-flung places and people. I wanted to learn new ways to be. I wanted to change, to feel less existentially alienated, to feel more at

home in my skin, as they say, and in the world. This was a hopelessly New
Age wish, and I would never have mentioned it to Bryan. But it came out
in my quickness to pick up local expressions, local lore, wherever we found
ourselves, and in my wholehearted admiration for subsistence farmers and
fishermen, and the ease with which I fell into a kind of intimacy with
many of the people we met. I had that facility with strangers, but it had a
new intensity now, and I wondered if Bryan sometimes felt abandoned by
me, or disgusted.

Then there was the self-disgust, which we each wrestled with differently. Being rich white Americans in dirt-poor places where many people,
especially the young, yearned openly for the life, the comforts, the very
opportunities that we, at least for the seemingly endless moment, had
turned our backs on—well, it would simply never be okay. In an inescapable way, we sucked, and we knew it, and humility was called for. But we
had different ways of interpreting this obligation. Bryan's conservative instincts thrilled, I thought, to the heavy patriarchy of the Samoan chief
system. My romanticism, meanwhile, filled village social interactions with
a prelapsarian warmth and psychic health.

Surfing, under the circumstances, was a godsend. It was our project,
why we got up in the morning. After we ran across a group of Western
backpackers in Apia, I grumbled, according to Bryan, that they "were
nothing but goddam sightseers." I didn't remember saying that, but it was
in fact how I felt. We did plenty of *palagi* looking-looking-looking ourselves, and there was something obscene about that, but at least we had a
purpose, an objective, however fleeting, pointless, idle, and silly it might
seem to anyone else.

WE FOUND A SURFER on Tongatapu, an American named Brad. Actually, he heard we were there, staying at a beach hostel northwest of Nuku'alofa, and one day he appeared, on a horse. He was twenty-three, with
very short hair. He seemed to be a missionary of some kind. He said he

was living in a village nearby, where he was helping to build a Pentecostal church and was engaged to marry a local girl. He was from Santa Barbara, California, via Kauai, and had been in Tonga eight months. He had an odd, deliberate manner that I found entirely familiar. I guessed he had traveled the same path that a great many surfers took, from California beach town to Hawaiian outer island, ingesting an overload of hallucinogens along the way, and then arriving, somewhat fried, at the feet of their Lord and Savior. People called them Jesus freaks.

But Brad did not preach. He just wanted to talk surf. We were the first surfers he'd seen in Tonga.

We had only one question: Were there waves?

Oh, yes, he said. Oh, yes.

But not this time of year.

He had a north swell spot, Ha'atafu, up at the north end of the Hihifo peninsula. It broke from November to March or April, on long-period swells from the North Pacific. There were several rights, all reef passes, that Brad compared favorably with the best spots on Kauai. That was a high standard indeed. He had been surfing these passes completely alone. This time of year, he said—it was now June—there were a few lefts wrapping around from the south, but they were small and insanely shallow.

I insisted that we go immediately to Ha'atafu. It was a long walk. Brad took us as far as a trailhead, deep in the woods, and gave us directions to the spot. By the time we reached the coast, it was late afternoon. The reef was far from shore, across a broad lagoon, and the sun was blazing behind what looked like chopped-up waves. But the glare was too fierce to tell anything, really. I wanted to paddle out to get a better look. Bryan demurred. The wind was onshore. The sun was going down. There wasn't enough time to discuss it. I stuck my flip-flops under a bush and struck off paddling.

Bryan turned out to be right. It wasn't worth it. The waves were awful. And it was indeed insanely shallow. The worst part, though, was the currents. The Hihifo peninsula is five miles long, and I was near the tip of it, being swept seaward and sideways like flotsam. I had to fight my way back into the lagoon, grabbing coral heads to hold position, getting dragged and sliced and, though I had no time to think about it, scared. Once I escaped the surf zone, having caught no waves, I had zero chance of hitting shore anywhere near where I had started. There were short, nasty coral cliffs lining much of the coast. I ultimately reached land at some tiny cove far to the east at dusk. Then I had to hike through the woods barefoot in the dark, a long, uncomfortable slog. Bryan was frantic, understandably. This was a regular chafing point between us. I thought he worried too much. He thought I took stupid risks. Neither of us was wrong.

SOMEBODY HAD PERSUADED the king of Tonga that he was sitting on billions in offshore oil and gas. An American company, Parker Oil and Drilling, had generously agreed to help him find the stuff, and a few of its employees and their dependents were staying at the same half-built beach hostel we were. It was called the Good Samaritan. The owner was a Frenchman named André. He had half a dozen small tourist *fales* finished, with more in the works, and a funky little outdoor restaurant with a limited but excellent menu (fresh-caught fish, essentially), for which André was the chef. Tables at André's were limited. I found myself sharing one with Teka, a Parker Oil person. She was slim, sharp-featured, nineteen, from Texas. Her dad was doing something important for the king. Teka had just flunked out of Sam Houston State University in Huntsville, she told me, and was on her way back to Singapore, where her family lived, and where she worked as a model.

Teka took a sort of anthropological interest in Bryan and me. We were surfing Ha'atafu every day now, striking off early while the winds were light and usually returning, famished and sun-fried, to the Good Samaritan in the afternoon. The waves had been frustratingly small but well shaped and vicious. My hands and feet were a *salade russe* of coral cuts, and Bryan had a large raw scrape on his back, the dressing on which I changed twice a day. The water was so shallow at the reef passes we surfed, I even managed to smash the nose of my precious board on the bottom. Teka had watched me elaborately patching the ding on a makeshift rack in the shade of a breadfruit tree.

Bryan and I, Teka announced, were exactly like every other "beach bum" in California, Florida, and Hawaii. We had no goals, no cares for tomorrow. Our type could be found "especially at Waikiki Beach," she said. "If there was an earthquake, you wouldn't worry about your house or your car. You'd just say, 'Oh, wow, a new experience.' All you care about is finding a perfect wave, or something. I mean, what will you do if you find it? Ride it five or six times and then what?"

It was a good question. We could only hope that at some point we'd be forced to answer it. In the meantime, without disputing that we were highly typical bums, I wanted to know who Teka knew who had worthier goals than we did. Her mother, she said. Her mother, Cherie, intended to "write a book, actually three," this summer. Cherie was on the premises. She rose late and was drunk by noon. Her main occupations seemed to be sunbathing, putting on makeup, smoking dope with her daughters, and changing her "outfit" many times a day. But then one evening she told me, "I put you in my book today. It says, 'I love you.'" So there was a book being written. That was more than Bryan or I could claim. Teka had another example: her boyfriend, who was managing a disco, she said, in Huntsville, but who had his sights set firmly on someday "owning *and* managing a men's clothing store."

One of Parker Oil's field managers was a big, thick-spectacled Texan named Gene. He had a face like turkey wattle, a scary smoker's voice, and a local girlfriend who was seventeen. Gene was pushing sixty. His girlfriend was a knockout but not happy. I overheard her telling the wife of a Parker executive that she was a half-Fijian orphan, and therefore a social outcast in homogeneous Tonga. She had turned to prostitution, she said. She was now desperate to get away from Gene. "Help me! Help me!" she pleaded.

The executive's wife looked stricken. I couldn't hear what she said to the girl, but I was standing there when she approached Gene. She timidly tried to make conversation, mentioning that she had heard that his young friend was half-Fijian.

Gene snarled, "I don't care what she told you, honey, she's a nigger."

Brad came by that night on his horse. I asked him if the police could be trusted to enforce the law against Parker Oil's employees. He gave me a long, thoughtful look, and then shook his head. "They're with the king," he said. Gene's desperate girlfriend would be the one arrested if charges were laid.

I asked Brad about his life in Tonga. He rarely left this area, he said. Nuku'alofa, which is a small, drab town, had come to seem like the bright lights. He was the only *palagi* in his village, which was farther out the peninsula and deep in the woods. His neighbors and future in-laws were nonplussed by surfing, he said. "They see me head off into the bush toward the sea with this flimsy craft. Then I come back hours later empty-handed. They think I'm a very poor fisherman. All I do, they think, is float."

It was remarkable to think that this mild, unprepossessing kid had been surfing Ha'atafu alone, month after month. On northwest cyclone swells, he said, he had ridden it double-overhead—ridden waves, that is, twice his height. This was electrifying news. It was also, at ultra-shallow Ha'atafu, a scary idea. Had he ever hit the bottom hard? I asked. He gave me a little sideways look that meant, *Every session, dude. You've surfed it.* But if he got badly hurt, I thought, the distance between that reef and help would be enormous. There were the waves, the coral, the howling rip, the wide lagoon, the cliffs, at least a mile of jungle to the nearest village, and at least an hour on a very infrequent bus to town, where the medical facilities were probably sketchy. None of this needed saying.

Brad's immersion in rural Tonga far outstripped, of course, anything I was likely to do in the South Pacific, unless I joined the Peace Corps or married a village girl or both. I had to laugh at myself. Was Brad feeling less existentially alienated as a result of his experience? I didn't know him well enough to ask.

I was curious about the king, Tupou IV. He was an absolute monarch who weighed, reportedly, 440 pounds. But Brad blanched when I asked about him. He obviously didn't know me well enough to feel safe discussing the king. I asked if it was true that all the fruit bats in Tonga were the official property of the king, and that only he was allowed to hunt them, which was why the woods were so thick with bats at night. A fisherman on Eua had told me about the king and the fruit bats. Brad declined to confirm or deny the story. He mentioned that he had a Bible study session to go to. He retrieved his horse and rode away down the beach in the moonlight.

I SAW A GRAFFITO in Nuku'alofa, ALL OUTER PROGRESS PRODUCE CRIMINAL. At the post office I tried to send my father a telegram. It was his fiftieth birthday. But I couldn't tell if the message actually went. The guy behind the counter, who looked like Stokely Carmichael, had little colored postal stickers pasted all over his face. He was friendly, but he fiddled with his ancient typewriter in a slack-handed way that did not inspire confidence. I had not heard from my family, or from anyone else, since Guam— more than a month. There was no way for them to contact us. Did anyone back home even know what country we were in? I wrote lots of letters—to my parents, to Sharon—but they would take weeks to arrive. Phoning never occurred to me. Among other things, it was too expensive.

I wandered down a road of half-built cinderblock houses—their construction presumably on pause until the next batch of remittances arrived from family members in Australia. I passed a graveyard. There were slim brown beer bottles—Steinlager, from New Zealand—stuck neck down in the sand around some of the graves. Steinlager bottles were everywhere in Samoa and Tonga. Local fruit drinks came in them, relabeled. They were used as borders for gardens and school yards. In the cemeteries in Tonga, late in the day, there always seemed to be old women tending the graves of their parents—combing the coral-sand mounds into the proper coffin-top shape, sweeping away leaves, hand-washing faded wreaths of plastic flowers, rearranging the haunting patterns of tropical peppercorns, orange and green on bleached white sand.

A shiver of secondhand sorrow ran through me. And an ache of something else. It wasn't exactly homesickness. It felt like I had sailed off the edge of the known world. That was actually fine with me. The world was mapped in so many different ways. For worldly Americans, the whole globe was covered by the foreign bureaus of the better newspapers—the *New York Times*, the *Washington Post*, the *Wall Street Journal*—and, at that time, the big newsweeklies. Every place on earth was part of somebody's beat. Bryan understood that map before I did, having gone to Yale. But when I'd found an old copy of *Newsweek* on Captain Brett Hilder's bridge, and tried to read a George Will column, I'd burst out laughing. His Beltway airs and provincialism were impenetrable. The truth was, we were wandering now through a world that would never be part of any correspondent's beat (let alone George Will's purview). It was full of news, but all of it was oblique, mysterious, important only if you listened and watched and felt its weight.

On the ferry back from Eua, I had ridden on the roof with three boys who said they planned to see every kung fu and cowboy and cop movie playing at the three cinemas in Nuku'alofa until their money ran out. One boy, thin and laughing and fourteen, told me that he had quit school because he was "lazy." He had a Japanese comic book that got passed around the ferry roof. The book was a bizarre mash-up: cutesy children's cartoons, hairy-armed war stories, nurse-and-doctor soap opera, graphic pornography. A ferry crewman frowned when he got to the porn, tore each page out, crumpled it, and threw it in the sea. The boys laughed. Finally, with a great bark of disgust, the sailor threw the whole book in the water, and the boys laughed harder. I watched the tattered pages float away in a glassy lagoon. I closed my eyes. I felt the weight of unmapped worlds, unborn language. This was what I was chasing: not the exotic, but a broad-beamed understanding of what is what.

The sadness of the obscure graveyard, of unforgotten elders buried under sand, made my chest tight. It seemed to mock this whole vague enterprise. Still, something beckoned. Maybe it was Fiji.

OUR FIRST EXPEDITION in Fiji was a botch on several fronts. First, we went east from Suva, the capital, which is itself on the wet side of the main island, Viti Levu, which meant that we just went deeper into the mud. Our charts showed a major river mouth with a nicely curved bay and a well-angled gap in the barrier reefs that otherwise stopped most swell coming into southeastern Viti Levu. The bay was in fact there, and the swell did sneak through, but the wave was just a long muddy close-out. It took us a couple of days to figure that out, though, partly because we took the wrong grog.

Bryan and I had learned not to show up in remote villages empty-handed. Ballpoint pens and balloons for the kids were optional, but something for the chief or the coastal landowners really wasn't. The best gift, the traditional offering, was an armload of the root from which kava is made. In Fiji it's called *waka*. We had planned, leaving Suva, to buy a batch at a farmers' market near the bus station, but suddenly our early-morning bus was leaving and, in haste, we dodged into a shop and bought a fifth of Frigate Overproof Rum instead. The rum would be welcome, we figured, and we were right. The problem was that when we reached Nukui, a village near the bay we wanted to check—this was after a long ride in an outboard-powered canoe through a maze of impressively dense mangrove swamps—the headman, Timoci, who greeted us warmly, insisted on opening the rum immediately and passing the flagon around the small circle of men who happened to be on hand. We polished off the bottle in fifteen minutes. It was still early afternoon. We were now kneewalking. We never made it to the beach that day.

Kava is a much more civilized beverage. It needs to be pounded and prepared and is usually consumed only after nightfall. A group, normally men-only, sits cross-legged on mats around a great wooden bowl, known in Fiji as a *tanoa*. A coconut cup is passed around. In Fiji the group claps three times, hollowly, and the drinker claps once and says, *"Bula"* (hello, or life), before taking the cup, which is known as a *bilo*. After draining the cup, the drinker claps once and says, *"Maca"* (pronounced *matha*—it means dry, or empty), and everyone claps three times together. The ceremony can go on for six or seven hours and innumerable *bilos*. Guitars get played, stories told, hymns sung, often with a stunning soprano harmony part.

The closed-out waves at Nukui were at least good for shoving kids into the whitewater on our boards. Some of them were extremely quick learners. One group of boys, getting impatient, dragged two coconut logs into the water and actually caught waves on those. Smaller kids ran up and down the sand with coconut shells on strings under their feet, making a sound exactly like clopping horseshoes. The children in Nukui had a great many homemade toys: round nuts that they used in a never-ending game like marbles; tin-can tops on a string that somehow spun and whistled; a coconut leaf twisted on a stick into an elegant wind-spinner. Amid all this tender ingenuity, I found myself staring one evening, after a great deal of kava, into the ceiling of a hut and suddenly seeing on a crossbeam a pair of child's rubber boots. The boots were dusty and cut in a vaguely cowboy style, and the sight of them pierced me unexpectedly. They were a talisman both from the manufactured world and from my own Lone Ranger boyhood.

In the canoe weaving back through the mangroves to the landing where the bus stopped, I sat opposite a chubby teenage girl. Her T-shirt had on it a drawing of a cat sprawled drunk in front of a television, under the caption HAPPINESS IS A TIGHT PUSSY. I had to assume that no one, starting with her mother, got the joke. The low gray skies of the river delta—we had not seen the sun once in Nukui—now opened and drenched us with

cold rain. We spread ponchos over our packs. We were definitely in the
wrong part of Fiji. The place had three hundred islands.

SUVA IS A RAIN-GREEN, bustling city, the biggest in the South Pacific.
It straddles a hilly peninsula above a broad blue harbor. We stayed in an
affable dive—half brothel, half dormitory—called the Harbourview. The
owners were an Indian family. Half the population of Fiji (and most of the
business class) is ethnically Indian. Sailors of every known nationality
reeled into the Harbourview's bar at night, got into old-fashioned fistfights, and took the bargirls upstairs. We slept and stored our gear in a
stifling room with many bunk beds for a few bucks a night. Downtown
Suva was full of tourists, expats, cruise-ship passengers. We each lucked
into brief flings with Australian lasses on their way through.

Our plan was to head west, and maybe back south to some promising-
looking islands out in the swell window. Suva is a popular stopover for
cruising yachts, so we scoured the noticeboard at the Royal Suva Yacht
Club for sailboats looking for crew. While we waited for something to
come through, I started spending my days in the Suva City Library. It was
in a fine, airy colonial building on the waterfront. At one of its wide ma-
hogany reading tables, I made a new start on my railroad novel, in longhand, with new main characters.

There were a couple of surf yachts docked in Suva. One belonged to an
American with a Tahitian girlfriend. He was heading west but his boat,
Capella, was small. The other was a fifty-five-foot Australian ketch called
Alias. It had a rust-streaked hull and a salty, heavy-weather look, with
frayed, old-fashioned fittings and bicycles and surfboards lashed to the
bow rails. I guessed the boat was eighty years old. It turned out to be two.
A surfer commune had built it from scratch near Perth, in Western Aus-
tralia, with stolen wood and parts and scavenged tools. The women in the
group had waitressed to keep the workers fed. The hull was ferrocement.
A tall, sun-wrecked, curly-haired character named Mick told us the boat's

story. *Alias* had barely survived its maiden voyage, he said, after its novice
sailors, impatient for wind, took it far south, into the Roaring Forties, and
got clobbered by a gale. "Seas were as high as the mast," Mick said. "Got
knocked down once. We were all down below, praying. Thought we were
going to die." When they limped into South Australia, half the group dis-
embarked, swearing off sailing forever. Four people—two couples—had
stayed. Now Mick's girlfriend, Jane, was heavily pregnant, so *Alias* would
be going nowhere until after she delivered.

One morning, while I happened to be visiting, the marine radio on
Alias crackled with a fragment of electrifying news. I missed it, but Mick
did not. He yelled as if he'd been shot. "Graham!" Graham was the other
surfer aboard. He appeared in the companionway, two narrowed bright
eyes surrounded by a blond lion's mane. "'A perfect three-hundred-yard
left,'" Mick said. "That's what I just heard. I think it was Gary, calling his
mate here." What he meant, he explained to me later, was that a third surf
yacht, skippered by an American named Gary, was in Fiji. Gary had been
traveling with *Capella*, but he had gone ahead alone a few weeks before.
The radio call was clearly about a discovery somewhere to the west. Mick
went to work on the guy who had received the call. He was a plump, wary
fellow named Jim, and he was not happy to be getting the third degree
from a tall, determined Aussie. He eventually allowed that Gary was sailing in the Yasawa Group, in northwest Fiji, and had apparently found
waves up there. That made no sense. The Yasawas were blocked from re-
ceiving south swells by an archipelago called the Mamanucas and by a
very large, reef-encircled area west of Viti Levu known as the Nadi Waters.

A NOTICE WENT UP: a yacht seeking crew. While I wrote down the particulars, a young Englishman also checking the noticeboard told me that
he had just left the yacht in question. "Don't do it, mate," he said. The
skipper, he said, was a maniac. An American. His entire crew had deserted
here in Suva, after one short crossing, and the same thing had happened to

the same skipper plenty of times before. "Once you're at sea, he starts shouting abuse nonstop," the Englishman said. He gave a persuasive little shudder. "Just another New Yorker battling his way through paradise."

We ended up leaving Suva on a westbound bus. The south coast of Viti Levu was dense with small towns and fishing villages. As we left the wet zone, rain forest gave way to small sugarcane farms. There were signs for tourist resorts tucked away in sunny bays. Craning to catch glimpses of waves, we saw nothing too encouraging. There was swell, but the reef was mostly quite far out, and the trades were still onshore.

The obvious place to start looking for surf was in the southwest corner of Viti Levu. That region comprised a lacuna, unfortunately, in our chart collection. At the chandlery where I got the charts, in California, the clerk had said that this one chart had, absurdly, remained classified since World War II, when the Allies, concerned about a Japanese attack—Fiji would have made a good staging ground for assaults on New Zealand and Australia—didn't want maps of the shipping entrance to the Nadi Waters in free circulation. So we were employing even more guesswork than usual. Still, it was clear from any land map that we should check out the mouth of the Sigatoka River, which drained most of west Viti Levu, and then work our way west from there.

The Sigatoka River mouth turned out to be a spooky patch of coast. For a start, there were huge sand dunes. I had never seen anything like them in the tropics, and the villagers we met in the neighborhood were unanimous: the dunes were unnatural. Indeed, they were haunted. The surf breaking off the dunes was also, in my experience, a tropical first. It was a big, cold, foggy beachbreak. It belonged in Oregon or Northern California, not Fiji. The water was cold because the mighty Sigatoka debouched at the east end of the beach. And the big river brought not only chilly, brown, semifresh water from the mountains but a steady supply of dead animals, muddy reed mats, plastic bags, and other garbage. All this stuff came swirling and bobbing through the lineup. The waves, however, were good, particularly in the mornings. They were shifty, powerful A-frames.

Aboard *Alias*, Suva Harbor, Fiji, 1978

Pig corpses aside, these were the best waves we had surfed in the South Pacific. There was no village near the surf—see haunted dunes, above—so we hiked west until we found a small grove of trees in a gully behind a high dune. It was a well-protected spot, both from the trade winds and from intruders, who could approach from only one direction. We camped there.

The tent we carried was too small for both of us to sleep in comfortably. I preferred sleeping outside anyway. But the gully where we camped had an unusual amount of ground-level night life—rats, crabs, snakes, centipedes, and I didn't want to know what else. I strung up a hammock and slept better there. For supplies, we hiked inland to a village called Yadua. We made tea on a little cooking ring fired by a blue Gaz propane cartridge. For bigger productions, like oatmeal or canned corned beef, we built a fire. One night, heavy rain chased me into the tent. I didn't like being crammed against Bryan, and I imagined he didn't care for it either. I crawled out at first light. The garbage in the surf was thicker than ever, with the runoff from the downpour, but the swell was clean and had built overnight.

Down toward the river mouth there was a reliable channel running out to sea. We used that to paddle out. But when the surf got big—over six feet—there were outer sandbars that started breaking, and the wisps of dank fog that drifted out from the dunes over the dun-colored water— perfect clammy products of the weird Sigatoka microclimate—made it feel like there might be something much larger lurking out there, a huge set preparing to mow us under. As it was, I took some memorable beatings after going left, surfing away from the channel. I kept telling myself to take only rights, but then a big, sweet left wall would appear, and I would find I lacked the willpower to say no. Did I mention that the place felt sharky? Fishermen in Yadua, when they heard we were entering the ocean there, told us, with something between disgust and alarm, that we were nuts. That beach was a shark pit. With all the offal in the water, we had already assumed that. But shark attack was a distant third on my own list of Sigatoka worries, after, one, drowning under a rogue set and, two, contracting some hideous illness from the waterborne filth.

Bryan turned thirty while we were camped there. He only told me about it later. I was a bit stunned. It seemed like such a strange secret to keep. Or maybe "secret" was the wrong word. It was just silence, really, a form of privacy, a refusal of some obvious, conventional sentiment, and as such, very Bryan. For all the intensity of our friendship, and despite our now constant companionship, I always felt, in some basic way, shut out. Was it me in particular, or the world in general, that he seemed to keep his guard up against habitually? The old-school masculinity that so many people, including me, found attractive carried with it no small loneliness. Then Bryan double-surprised me by saying that he could not think of a better way to spend his thirtieth birthday: surfing good waves at an un-mapped spot in the South Seas, gone from the known world.

Was he really happy? I wasn't, especially. I was intent on our search, determined to keep pushing, and I could feel deeply satisfied by a good surf session. I was also interested in Fiji, which presented not only an abundance of the preindustrial village life I wanted to lose myself in but also more social complexity, livelier politics, and many more women of interest than Tonga or Western Samoa had. (Australians counted.) Still, I was anxious frequently, and given to lacerating self-doubt. And I obviously didn't see Bryan the same way he saw himself, which I found disorienting.

To me, he seemed to be going troppo. He said he was delighted to be here, but that wasn't how it looked. Tiny hassles, and all kinds of innocuous people we met, annoyed him, I thought, unduly. He had taken to pacing, with hunched shoulders, furrowed brow, hands locked behind his back, and to sighing, and pronouncing, with exaggerated precision, on the idiocy of various people and things. That bus driver who told us we could walk from Sigatoka town to the coast? He didn't know where the ocean was any more than he knew where his side of the road was. That walleyed lady who ran the Harbourview? She was a crook and a menace. I actually thought Bryan was getting scary. He was certainly making me nervous.

We started drinking kava with some guys in Yadua. They had a shack on the edge of the settlement, which was near a paved artery called the Queens Road, making it feel more like a little highway town than a traditional subsistence village. And yet the kava ceremony proceeded much as it did anywhere else. It started in the late afternoon. We would head over there after the surf blew out. We sometimes stumbled back to camp at midnight. The regulars at the kava shack were fishermen who kept their boats in a cove just west of the dunes, but other men from Yadua also came. The only woman around was the wife of a guy named Waqa. She helped prepare and serve the grog. People were curious, of course, about the camping *palagis*—*kaivalagis*, in Fiji—but they were also remarkably cool, I thought, with us, letting us explain ourselves at our own pace, or not.

I loved watching people chat, even when I understood nothing, which was often, since they usually spoke Fijian. They seemed to have an enormous repertoire of gentle, intricate social expressions. They used their mouths, hands, eyes—all the usual communication apparatus—but also chins, brows, shoulders, everything. Watching people listen was even better. There was a lovely, widely shared mannerism that I couldn't recall seeing before: a slight, jerky shifting of the head from side to side; a constant cocking of the neck, notch by notch, the way a bird does. I read it as a gesture of extreme tolerance. The listener was continually resettling his mind at different angles in order to take in different speakers, different impressions, with maximum equanimity. We *kaivalagis* provoked a visible speedup of this mental-spinal repositioning, I thought, but that might have been paranoia.

Bryan, meanwhile, was assailing my equanimity with his testiness to a degree that no amount of head-bobbing would let me tolerate. One night, lit with kava courage, I announced that I was sick of walking on eggs around him. He announced, astonished, that *he* was sick of walking on eggs around *me*. We hiked back to camp under a gibbous moon in a jolly mood. I said I hoped his tent was full of scorpions. He hoped I fell out of my hammock. The expression, anyway, was walking on eggshells, not eggs.

THE MORE WE STARED at the Yasawas on the map—these were the islands where the American yachties had supposedly found waves—the dumber the idea seemed. They were blocked from south swells, period. Still, we went up to Lautoka, a port in northwest Viti Levu. Boats ran from there to the Yasawas. We dithered on the quay, pricing ferries, asking questions. Nothing we heard changed our minds: going out there with surfboards was silly. We gave up on the whole west Fiji idea, defeated, and booked an early-morning bus back to Suva. But we got only as far as the station. Bryan had a bellyache that was getting worse. An all-day bus ride was not on. We returned to our hotel. Bryan went back to bed. I strolled around Lautoka.

That afternoon I saw a strange thing on the street: blond hair. A young white woman, no less. I followed her into a café and introduced myself. She was from New Zealand, named Lynn, and happy to chat. Over coffee, she said that she was on a yacht with a couple of American guys, including her boyfriend, and a Tahitian woman.

Where had they been sailing? I asked.

They had been anchored off a little uninhabited island for weeks, she said, "so the boys could surf."

Oh.

She knew she was spilling a secret. But she seemed to relish the mischief. Her boyfriend was a schoolteacher in American Samoa, she said, John Ritter.

I knew him, I said. In truth, another surfer-teacher on Guam had told us to look up Ritter in Pago Pago, but we had never made it there. This was fantastic, I said. Take me to him, I said.

She did.

Ritter was startled when I turned up with Lynn, and visibly alarmed when I started rattling off the names of surfers he knew on Guam and insisting he come to our hotel to meet Bryan. Ritter was soft-spoken, watchful, in his late twenties. He had bushy, sun-whitened hair and granny glasses patched with duct tape. He didn't try to hide his irritation with Lynn. But then he seemed to decide that the jig was up, and he agreed to come have a beer.

The wave, he told us, was not in the Yasawas. That was a ruse. It was in the Mamanucas, which made way more sense. Actually, it was out on the Malolo barrier reef, which protected the Mamanucas, on the southern edge of the Nadi Waters. The island was called Tavarua. It was roughly five miles off west Viti Levu. The wave wrapped all the way around the west side of the island and broke back into the trades. Ritter drew a rough map on a napkin. It could be fickle, he said. It needed the right swell. He didn't seem to want to say more.

The next day, while we were getting ready to go investigate, I found the missing chart. Bizarrely, it was in a rack of tourist brochures. The prohibited chart had been used as the backdrop for a placemat-sized ad for a "three day magical lagoon cruise" on a yacht running out of a resort down the coast. The ad was on heavy browned paper, with ragged, scrolled edges drawn to look like a pirate-age treasure map. The chart, evidently pulled from somebody's prewar library, was the real thing, however, the missing piece in our collection. Tavarua was on it, and the long barrier reef running northwest from the island, with "Blind Rollers" and "Breaks Heavily" and "Awash" written along its billows. The closest village to Tavarua on Viti Levu was called Nabila.

We took a bus there. The village was several miles from a paved road. There was a miniature sugarcane railway running under burnt brown hills. Mangroves grew in dull profusion along a waveless coast. The bus stopped under a breadfruit tree. "Nabila," the driver said. The village was hot, silent, sleepy. There seemed to be nobody around. We climbed a big hill that rose behind the village, slowly winding past thatch-roofed, mud-walled huts into which surprised-looking children scampered. They didn't see a lot of tourists here. The trail was dusty and very hot. A few hundred feet up, we came to a good lookout spot. We turned and trained our binoculars on the tiny island across the channel. We were looking straight into the wave. It was coming from the northwest, having wrapped nearly 180 degrees. It was a long, tapering—a very long, very precisely tapering—left. The walls were dark gray against a pale gray sea. *This was it.* The lineup had an unearthly symmetry. Breaking waves peeled so evenly that they looked like still photographs. There seemed to be no sections. *This was it.* Staring through the binoculars, I forgot to breathe for entire six-wave sets. This, by God, was it.

THE FISHERMEN WHO TOOK US across from Nabila had never seen a surfboard before. They had never seen even a photo or a drawing of one. They refused to believe that we rode waves on them. They figured our boards were little airplane wings. Did we use them for fishing? When we got to Tavarua, coasting in with outboard engine lifted through a coral-studded channel on the northeast shore, we could see that the swell had dropped sharply from the day before. It actually looked too small to ride now. But our companions would be confirmed in their doubts if they didn't see some surfing, so I quickly paddled out. The water over the reef was absurdly shallow, less than a foot deep, and the waves were knee-high and weak and really too quick to surf. But I managed to snag one, and when I jumped to my feet I could hear shouts and whistles coming from the beach. I rode for a few yards, then bellied in. The swell we had seen from the hillside was dead.

Tavarua Island, Fiji, 1978

By staying for even that short demonstration, our friends had been trapped by a dropping tide. They tied their boat to a tree. It was soon left high on the sand. There were four of them, all ethnic Indians. Bob was the leader. Stout, voluble, middle-aged, he liked to shout orders at Peter, his nephew, who was twenty-nine. Then there was an eight-year-old boy, Atiljan, and a thin, quiet, very old man with a white mustache. Bob and Peter were full of instructions for us. First, the snakes. Banded sea snakes, highly poisonous, would come ashore by the hundreds each night in search of freshwater. "Play with the snake, you will have to suffer," Peter said. He went down the beach, quickly found a snake, grabbed it behind the head, and held it up. It was about four feet long, striped black and white, with a paddlelike tail. Peter returned it gently to the water. We had heard that this snake (*Laticauda colubrina*), whose name in Fijian is *dada-kulachi*, was nicknamed the three-step snake, since that was how far you were likely to get if it bit you. It was supposedly the sixth-deadliest snake in the world, firing a fatal cocktail of neurotoxins and myotoxins through its fangs. The good news was that its mouth was very small. Peter showed us how to make a fist while handling one, or while paddling past one, so that it could not bite between one's fingers.

And between one's toes?

Peter shrugged. They were normally not aggressive.

Bob showed us three big piles of dry wood at the edge of the jungle on the eastern shore. These, he said, were for signal fires. Fishermen used them to communicate with their families on Viti Levu. One fire meant you were fine—just staying the night to avoid rough water. Two fires meant you were not fine and would need help. "Maybe the engine not working." Three fires meant an emergency. If one of us got badly hurt, we should light three fires at nightfall. A boat would come, "even if bad weather."

They showed us where wild papaya trees grew, not too far into the bush, and where good eating fish tended to run near shore at high tide. The tide was coming in now, and would soon be full enough, I thought, to let them cross the reef, but Bob said the wind was blowing too hard. They would spend the night. He would light one of the signal fires later to let their families in Nabila know they were here. Peter took a handline to the fishing spot and quickly caught a string of a dozen grey mullet. We grilled them on sticks, ate with our fingers, and washed the meal down with green coconut milk. Bob inspected our supplies. He was not impressed with our unused fishing gear. He ordered Peter to leave us some stouter line and better hooks. High above us, the wind thrashed in the coconut trees. The sun dropped into the western Mamanucas.

Our campsite, which was at the edge of the jungle, facing the wave, was well sheltered from the trades and included what the Nabila men said was the only man-made structure on Tavarua: a fish-drying rack. The rack, which consisted of six short wooden poles driven into the sand and a thatch netting, was about two feet off the ground. It was the size and shape of a single bed. I tested the strength of its thatch. It seemed sturdy. Bob nodded approvingly. That was a good place to sleep, he said. The snakes, which were fast in the water but inept on land, could not climb those poles. Bryan planned to sleep in the tent. He had it pitched and zipped tight, and he let me know, with sign language, that if he ever found the zipped mesh left open I could expect to be tortured with sharpened stakes and Bob's machete and our can opener. A brain fork—a popular Fiji tourist souvenir, purportedly used in cannibal days—might also come into play.

The moon rose. Peter, staring into the fire, told us that his hair was cut short and strangely because he had recently lost his father. Peter had a cheerful, innocently confiding manner. He was tall, toothy, unshaven. His personal life sounded complicated. He talked about a girlfriend toward whom his intentions were unsettled. "If I leave her, she must marry," he said. "She cannot stay home. You know the peoples, they cannot stay without sex." Bob ordered him to go check on the boat, which now needed an anchor set. Peter jumped up and threw off his clothes. Bob said, "Get on, you bloody bastard, he doesn't want to look at your dirty prick!" Peter loped off into the dark.

Bob rolled up in my board bag. Peter used Bryan's like a sleeping bag, draping the end flap over his head like a hood. The old man kept the fire going. Each time he threw on a dry palm frond, Peter would wake up and whip out a paperback and read a few lines by the light. His book was a detective novel in Hindi with a garish, worn cover. Little Atiljan slept in a nest of green leaves he had made. The old man did not sleep. He quietly prayed and sang, and his songs and prayers threaded through my dreams. He had a very thin face and high, sharp cheekbones. Whenever the fire flared, I could see he was gazing east, out into the night, at Nabila, across the channel.

. . .

ON THE FIFTH DAY, or maybe it was the sixth, we surfed. It was still too small, really, but we were so surf-starved by then that we scrambled out at the first hint of a swell. Thigh-high waves zipped down the reef, most of them too fast to make. The few we made, though, were astounding. They had a slingshot aspect. If you could get in early, top-turn, gather just enough speed that the hook didn't pass you by, and then set the right line, the wave seemed to lift the tail of the board and hurl it down the line, on and on and on, with the lip throwing just over your back continually—a critical moment that is normally no more than a moment but that seemed to last, impossibly, for half a minute or more. The water got shallower and shallower and even the best rides didn't end well. But the speed runs were dreamlike. I had never seen a wave peel so mechanically.

As the tide peaked, something very odd happened. The wind quit and the water, already extremely clear, became more so. It was midday, and the straight-overhead sun rendered the water invisible. It was as if we were suspended above the reef, floating on a cushion of nothing, unable even to judge the depth unless we happened to kick a coral head. Approaching waves were like optical illusions. You could look straight through them, at the sky and sea and sea bottom behind them. And when I caught one and stood up, it disappeared. I was flying down the line but all I could see was brilliant reef streaming under my feet. It was like surfing on air. The wave was so small and clear that I couldn't distinguish the wave face from the flats in front of the wave from the flats behind the wave. It was all just clear water. I had to surf by feel. This was truly dreamlike. When I felt the wave accelerate, I crouched for speed, and suddenly I could see it again— because the waist-high crest, seen from down there, was higher than the horizon.

The trades puffed, the surface riffled, and the hyperclarity was gone. The tide dropped and we were back on the beach.

Our hands, feet, knees, forearms, and Bryan's back all streamed bright blood from brushes with the reef. Even medium tide seemed to be out of the question.

I HAD WRITTEN BY HAND eight pages of first-aid instructions in a small all-purpose notebook. Infections, fractures, shock, burns, poisoning, head wounds, heat exhaustion, even gunshot wounds—the basics of field treatment were spelled out in careful lists, extensively underlined. I had no training, and neither, as far as I knew, did Bryan. But I showed him where the instructions were, between drawings of Nuku'alofa and notes for my railroad novel, and I sometimes reread them myself, trying to commit the material to memory. Not much stuck. Near-drowning, splinting, tourniquets, unconscious victim—it felt, to my primitive mind, like bad luck to picture this stuff too clearly. Bryan mused that something common, like appendicitis, could quickly finish off one of us out here. We'd have to wait till nightfall even to light the signal fires. True enough, I thought, but, again, bad luck to imagine.

It took twenty-five minutes to walk around the island, if you didn't rush. Bryan counted the fresh snake tracks across the beach one morning: 117. The snakes were, as Bob said, ungainly on land. It took them minutes to cross the ten yards of sand between the high-tide line and the jungle. They were easy to spot and, indeed, not aggressive. Away from the campfire at night, a flashlight was useful to avoid stepping on one. But most of my close encounters with *dadakulachi* were in the water, where they were plentiful, both on the surface and in the depths, both on the reef and in the lagoon.

Everything was plentiful on the reef: urchins, eels, octopus, and, by my conservative estimate, eight million species of fish. I swam out every day at high tide, drifting with mask and snorkel but no fins or spear, following schools of ridiculously beautiful creatures through shallow coral canyons, around great crimson fans and stolid greenish brain-lumps and wicked-looking staghorn. I recognized a few familiar faces: parrot fish, goatfish, triggerfish (*humuhumu!*), grouper. There seemed to be a hundred different types of wrasse. There were angelfish, goby, puffer fish. I thought I saw sweetlips, tilefish, surgeonfish, snappers, blenny, coral breams, Moorish idols. I did see barracuda and a small whitetip shark. And yet, to me, most of the countless fish going about their business on the Tavarua foreshore were nameless, mysterious. Some were so pointlessly gorgeous I found myself groaning in my snorkel.

Our fishing was pitiful. Even with the hooks and line the guys had left, and knowing the best spot and tide, we couldn't seem to catch a thing. I pried an octopus off the reef, pounded and boiled it to a fare-thee-well, using way too much freshwater, and it was still too tough to eat. (I should have used salt, I learned later. That was if we had salt.) We did a piss-poor job generally of living off the land and sea. We soon picked and ate all the ripe papayas we could find. I climbed the shortest, most wind-bent palm trees for green coconuts, but I was defeated by the taller, straighter trees. There were lots of beefy bats with yellow-striped faces—they hung like gray seedpods in the upper story of the jungle by day and swooped overhead at night—that would probably have made great fruit-bat soup. We had no notion how to catch them. There were crabs of various types, but the ones that looked like the best eating lost their allure when we saw how efficiently they excavated and devoured human excrement.

We had brought food, in any case. Cans of pork and beans, beef stew, corned beef, packaged soups, ramen, crackers, jam. And just enough water. There was no potable water on the island. The *dadakulachi* drank, apparently, dewdrops and tiny mud puddles in the bush. We wished we had thought to bring something sweet. We reminisced about favorite meals back in the world—fried chicken, big American hamburgers. Even the goat chow mein in Suva came to seem delicious in memory. We made a list of every bar in Missoula, Montana, where either of us had ever had a drink, coming up with fifty-three. We were becoming characters, we knew, in a desert-island cartoon. "Do me a favor, will you—stop saying 'entre nous.'" At night we saw airliners flying overhead, and ships passing

into the Nadi Waters, headed for Lautoka, all ablaze with lights. We were
like cargo cultists, agog at the idea of electric lights. I particularly missed
chairs.

Bob and the gang returned, as arranged, after a week. We left our
boards and most of our gear on the island, went into Nadi, a market town
south of Lautoka, bought more supplies, and were back on Tavarua the
next afternoon.

THE FIRST SOLID SWELL hit the next week, around the first of August.
There were head-high days. There were overhead days. Oneiric, highly
charged, the sessions run together in memory. On August 24, according
to my journal, it was double-overhead.

The wave had a thousand moods, but in general it got better as it got
bigger. At six feet it was easily the best wave either of us had ever seen.
Scaled up, the mechanical regularity of the speeding hook gained soul, its
roaring, sparkling depths and vaulted ceiling like some kind of recurring
miracle, the tracery on the surface and the ribbed power in the wall full of
delicate, now visible detail, each wave suffused with the richness of a one-
off. Sometimes the wind swung east, blowing into the hook and sending a
hard chop up the face, particularly in the last hundred yards to the channel. When the wind blew south or southwest, it came around the west side
of the island, making a mess of the waves as they approached us on the
half-mile-long wrap from the southern edge of the reef. But then they
cleaned up suddenly as they made the last turn into the lineup, and the
slingshot aspect of the wave was doubled by a trailing wind that slipped
under your board and whispered, *Go.*

We slowly figured out the takeoff. There were extra-tall trees that, tri-
angulated, worked as lineup markers, and reliable boils over big coral
heads near what seemed to be the uppermost takeoff spot. The current
ranged from slack to fierce, and it ran both up and down the reef, depending on the tidal flow. As the surf got bigger, breaking out in deeper water,

being dashed on the reef receded as an issue. But it was still important to get in early. Catching the wave, even at the optimal spot, was like jumping on a train that was not slowing down. It helped to paddle deep, stroke hard against the grain of the water drawing off the reef, and then angle left as the wave began to lift your board, digging extra-hard into the bottom of the face, jumping up early, finding the speed in the wave's belly with a quick pump before picking a line—before setting, that is, an initial course, to be intricately adjusted as the wave unfurled. When it got bigger and more consistent, deciding which wave to go on was a challenge in itself. What I struggled with then was adrenaline overflow. Paddling over the first wave of a set, seeing the lines stacked up behind it, with the next wave already cracking and peeling far up the reef, I would find myself gasping, heart slamming, mind juddering. What to do? I had never, in a lifetime of surfing, been confronted with such abundance.

It was, for me, as a regularfoot, a considerable irony that the wave was a left. I could surf it only half as well as I might have surfed a comparable right. My backhand technique improved, though. Esoteric questions of rail unweighting that I had never considered were suddenly illuminated in the endless screaming run under the endlessly pitching lip. I began switching rails straight off the bottom turn, keeping my outside rail, my toe rail, down on the water even as I tracked up the face, thus staying ready to bank downward on an instant's notice, and not letting the offshore breeze get under my board and blow me up higher than I wanted to be. My board went faster than I thought a board could go. I learned to relax, to a degree, in critical positions where my instincts shouted that it was time to brace for impact. Again, it seemed that, on this wave, that last-second moment could go on for a very, very long time.

Bryan was on his frontside. He could rise to his feet on the drop and watch the whole thing come to him. He didn't have to twist and look over his shoulder. He could let his left hand trail on the face. He refused to hurry, even when I thought he should. The first part of the wave, where you had to quickly get up to speed, sometimes picked him off when a couple of scrambling pumps near the top after the takeoff might have let him escape and set sail. But he didn't appreciate my saying so, and the stylishness of his attack was unimpeachable—the casual entrance, the bullfighter's calm as the wave stormed around him, then climbing and dropping in long arcs at hull speed. Bryan was still surfing Rainbows, I thought, back on Maui, drawing his own idiosyncratic lines far from the madding crowd, and I was still surfing Honolua, high-amping because I thought the wave demanded it.

Paddling back out after a long ride was a nerve test. Exalted and depleted both, I found I could not calmly watch another set pour through unridden. I was hardwired to grab a wave, even just an end-section. The idea that there would be more, that in ten minutes we would very likely be looking at another, equally good set from a much better takeoff spot far, far up the reef, simply had no traction in the psychology of scarcity, which was still mine. Bryan laughed unsympathetically as I hesitated, moaning, hyperventilating.

Our conversation changed. It usually had a busy, must-say-everything edge to it, even during the long, lazy days of waiting for waves on Tavarua. But out in the lineup, once the swells started pumping, large pools of awe seemed to collect around us, hushing us, or reducing us to code and murmurs, as though we were in church. There was too much to say, too much emotion, and therefore nothing to say. "Look at this one" felt like grandiloquence. And it was only inadequate shorthand for "My God, *look* at *this* one." Which was in turn inadequate. It wasn't that the waves beggared language. It was more like they scrambled it. One overcast afternoon, with a southwest wind scrawling small-bore chop like scrollwork across the approaching faces, I realized I was seeing long German words in Gothic script, *Arbeiterpartei* and *Oberkommando* and *Weltanshauung* and *Götterdämmerung*, marching incongruously across the warm gray walls. I had been reading, in my hammock, John Toland's biography of Hitler. Bryan had read it before me. I told him what I was seeing. "*Blitzkrieg*," he muttered. "Molotov-Ribbentrop."

I rode a wave one evening, long after the sun had set, with the first stars already out, that stood up and seemed to bend off the reef toward open water, which was impossible. There was a dark, bottle-green light in the bottom of the wall and a feathering whiteness overhead. Everything else—the wind-riffled face, the channel ahead, the sky—was in shades of blue-blackness. As it bent, and then bent some more, I found myself seemingly surfing toward north Viti Levu, toward the mountain range where the sun rose. *Not possible*, my mind said. *Keep going.* The wave felt like a test of faith, or a test of sanity, or an enormous, undeserved gift. The laws of physics appeared to have been relaxed. A hollow wave was roaring off into deeper water. Not possible. It felt like a runaway train, an eruption of magical realism, with that ocean-bottom light and the lacy white canopy. I ran with it. Eventually, it bent back, of course, found the reef, and tapered into the channel. I didn't tell Bryan about it. He wouldn't believe me. That wave was otherworldly.

Surfers have a perfection fetish. The perfect wave, etcetera. There is no such thing. Waves are not stationary objects in nature like roses or diamonds. They're quick, violent events at the end of a long chain of storm action and ocean reaction. Even the most symmetrical breaks have quirks and a totally specific, local character, changing with every shift in tide and wind and swell. The best days at the best breaks have a Platonic aspect—they begin to embody a model of what surfers want waves to be. But that's the end of it, that beginning. Bryan had no interest in perfection, it seemed to me, and his indifference represented, among the surfers I've known, a rare degree of realism, maturity, and philosophical appreciation of what waves are. I didn't have much interest in the perfection chimera myself. More than he did, though.

Another last-wave-of-the-day, this one at the end of the longest single session we had on Tavarua. The surf was big—this may have been August 24, the day my journal said was double-overhead—and we had abandoned our established policy of surfing only at high tide. The wave was ridable at lower tides, perhaps even at low tide, provided it was big enough, we saw now. I had been out nearly all day, from sketchy midtide when only the brawniest turquoise screamers cleared the reef by a reasonable margin, through peak tide and the peak of the swell, when the biggest sets actually swung wide, breaking out so far and in such deep water that they sometimes lost the reef and shouldered, rumbling straight in for five or ten seconds, big solid walls of foam with no breaking hook, until they felt the reef again and the walls stood up and resumed their wailing progress. A couple of sets had scared me, not because I took any especially bad beatings, or because I was held underwater extra-long, but simply because the waves were now stepladdering into serious size and I had brief, unpleasant visions of finding something from another realm behind the big wave I was already scratching to get over. Maybe we had no idea what this place was capable of, and the price for all this joy and good luck was about to be exacted? It was the first time I had been afraid of the waves on Tavarua. My fears were unnecessary. Nothing too heavy came. Instead, I caught and rode so many waves, through four or five distinct phases of the day, that I felt absolutely saturated with good fortune, and more deeply connected to the rhythms of the wave than ever before.

And so came that last wave. The tide was dropping. Bryan had already gone in. The swell was also dropping. The wind had clocked around and gone light northeast—onshore—making for messy conditions and a hard-looking, army-green surface that resembled Ventura more than it did the tropics. A very solid set appeared, backlit and thundering far up the reef. I paddled over a couple, having learned a measure of patience, and took the third wave. It was bumpy but beautifully shaped, and I hurried because the onshore wind was likely to make it crumble quickly. That happened. The wave also swung around harder than most, so that the long wall ahead seemed to be hitting the reef all at once, peeling even faster than usual. I began to wish I had not chosen this wave, but it was too late to pull out or even, I realized, dive off—the tide seemed to have dropped two feet since my previous wave, and coral heads were suddenly boiling up everywhere. Worse, the wave seemed to be growing as it ran down the reef. It was now several feet overhead and the face was not clean. There were weird little sections and chandeliers falling and throwing. But it was extremely fast and I was low in the face and now it was dredging, sucking all the water off the reef. I had, again, no exit, no choice but to drive, pedal smashed to the floor. After a rapid-fire series of critical sections, surfing blind, things happening too fast for me to react except instinctively, I came skittering out into the channel. I lay down on my board, shaking. Then I struggled in, paddling against the current. On the beach, I got only halfway up to our campsite. On my knees in the sand, in the twilight, absolutely spent, I was surprised to find myself sobbing.

WE DIDN'T ALWAYS SURF ALONE. John Ritter and his friends came back and anchored outside the channel. There was no swell at the time, though, and they left without surfing again. *Alias* and *Capella* also came, and they got waves. Bryan and I actually served as pilots on *Alias*. We took that bus, finally, from Lautoka to Suva, got mail from home for the first time in months at General Delivery—our loved ones seemed to be fine, carrying on in a parallel universe—and then, finding that Mick now had mostly correct coordinates for the wave, we sailed back west on the cement ketch. *Alias* anchored off Tavarua, and we went back to camping on the island. A swell hit the next day, and Mick and Graham, both goofyfoots, were gobsmacked. They surfed themselves silly. Graham, in particular, was a lovely surfer. When the swell dropped, they sailed to Nadi. *Capella* also left. Then, as soon as the yachts were gone, more waves arrived, with a light southwest wind, the trailing wind that slipped under your board and whispered, *Go.*

We went.

By the time we left Tavarua that year, we figured nine surfers knew about the wave. That number included a couple of Aussie crew guys and it assumed that Ritter and Gary were the first to surf there. In the small world of surfing, the wave was a major discovery. In the scarcity logic of that world, it was essential to keep it a secret. We all swore a vow of silence. Bryan and I got in the habit of saying "da kine," Hawaiian pidgin for whatchamacallit, when we meant Tavarua, even with each other. Mick and Graham, with whom we ultimately sailed away on *Alias*, called it Magic Island—an uninspired name, I thought (but there were worse to come).

From a vine on the island I took a handful of tiny, bright red-and-black seeds. On the night after we left, we got roaring drunk on *Alias* while at anchor off a resort near Nadi. I woke up with a freshly pierced right ear and one of the bright seeds hanging on a fishhook from the hole. Within days, the ear was horribly infected. I sent the rest of the seeds to Sharon, suggesting she string them on a necklace. She did, but later told me that she never wore the necklace because the seeds gave her a rash.

Bryan Di Salvatore and Joe the swagman,
between Coober Pedy and Alice
Springs, Australia, 1979

SIX

THE LUCKY COUNTRY

Australia, 1978–79

SOMEONE SENT US A COPY OF *OUTSIDE* MAGAZINE WITH AN AR-
ticle by an old professor of mine. It was about a lost weekend of skiing and
carousing in Montana. I remembered the weekend, though differently. I
was surprised that anybody would be interested in our grad school revels.
Maybe my grasp of American amusement was weakening with distance.
The article mentioned that I was now "living the unexamined life in Australia." Except for the Australia part, that was news to me.

Bryan and I had landed in a beach town called Kirra, in Queensland,
near the New South Wales border. We were the proud owners of a 1964
Falcon station wagon, bought near Brisbane for three hundred dollars,
and had car-camped and surfed up and down the east coast, from Sydney
to Noosa. It was dazzling to be back in the West, with all its comforts and
conveniences, and to be surfing known spots—there were even road signs,
SURFING BEACH. It was great to have wheels. Food and gas were cheap.
Still, we were nearly broke. And so we rented, with our last funds, a moldy
bungalow at the back of a ramshackle complex misnamed the Bonnie
View Flats. Most of our neighbors were unemployed Thursday Islanders—
Melanesians, from the Torres Strait, up near Papua New Guinea—and

some of them possibly had views. We didn't. But the beach was just across the road, and we had not chosen Kirra randomly. The place had a legendary wave. And the southern summer was starting up and, with it, we hoped, northeast cyclone swells.

Bryan got a job as a chef in a Mexican restaurant in Coolangatta, the next town south. He told the owners he was half-Mexican, but fumbled it when they asked his name. He said McKnight when he meant to say Rodriguez. He didn't have a valid work visa under any name. They hired him anyway. I found a couple of backbreaking jobs, including ditchdigging, which deserves its reputation as the worst sort of donkey work, for cash paid daily. Then I got hired as a pot washer in a restaurant at the Twin Towns Services Club, a big casino just over the New South Wales border, fifteen minutes' walk from our place. I told them my name was Fitzpatrick. The manager said that as a condition of employment I had to shave my beard, and so I did. When Bryan came home that night, he took one look at me and shrieked. He looked genuinely distressed. He said it looked like half my face had been burned off. I was pale where the beard had been, dark brown everywhere else.

There, there, I said, it'll grow back.

I blew my first wages on surfboards. Kirra is on the Gold Coast, a surfing center, and there were cheap used boards everywhere. I bought two, including a 6'3" Hot Buttered squashtail that turned on a dime and, when necessary, went outlandishly fast. It was a sports car of a surfboard, and a nice change after months of riding my sturdy travel board. Bryan also got new, much smaller boards. The year-round neighborhood spot was called Duranbah. It was a wide-open beachbreak immediately north of the Tweed River mouth, very near my casino job. Duranbah always seemed to have waves. They were often sloppy, but there were gems scattered among the mush. On my twenty-sixth birthday, I got a sweet barrel on a shining right and came out dry.

The pointbreaks—Kirra, Greenmount, Snapper Rocks, and Burleigh Heads, the spots that put the Gold Coast on the world surfing map—

would light up after Christmas, people said. They would start breaking, in fact, on Boxing Day, December 26, we were assured by a nonsurfing neighbor. We laughed at the not-likely specificity but looked forward to the waves.

In the meantime, I was falling hard for Australia. The country had never interested me. From a distance, it always seemed terminally bland. Up close, though, it was a nation of wisenheimers, smart-mouthed diggers with no respect for authority. The other pot washers at the casino, for instance—they called us dixie bashers—were a weirdly proud crew. In a big restaurant kitchen, we were at the bottom of the job ladder, below the dishwashers, who were all women. We peeled potatoes (which we called idahos), handled the garbage, did the nastiest scrubbing, and hosed down the greasy floors with hot water at the end of the night. And yet we made an excellent wage (I could save more than half my earnings) and, as employees, we had entree to the casino's private members' bar, which was on the top floor of the building. We would troop up there after work, tired and ripe, and throw back pints among what passed for high rollers on the Gold Coast. Once or twice, my coworkers spotted the owner of the casino in there. They called him a rich bastard and he, properly chagrined to be rich, bought the next shout.

I had never seen the dignity of labor upheld so doughtily, not even on the railroad. Australia was easily the most democratic country I had encountered. People called it the Lucky Country. This epithet was coined by a social critic, Donald Horne, whose 1964 book of that title decried the mediocrity of Australia's political and business culture, arguing, "Australia is a lucky country, run mainly by second-rate people who share its luck." But the phrase had lost its meaning over time, and it had been widely adopted as a sunny national motto. That was fine with me.

The usual class markers from other places seemed wonderfully scrambled. Billy McCarthy, one of my fellow dixie bashers, was hale, well-spoken, forty, married with a couple of kids. I quizzed him one night over beers and learned that he had been a professional saxophonist in Sydney, with a day job as a foreman in a perfume factory. He had followed his parents to the Gold Coast, where he went into business with a friend mowing lawns and washing windows, growing bonsai plants to sell at flea markets, potting palms to sell on consignment at shops. He was still working as a nurseryman but needed the steady restaurant wage. He played golf, often with musicians up from Sydney to play the casino's nightclub or other local venues. If Billy felt embarrassed to be working as a kitchen hand, I could not detect it. He was hardworking, cheerful, politically conservative, usually whistling some corny tune, always ready with a quip. Effortlessly, he made me feel welcome. Once, as I was coming into work, I heard him call out, "There he is, the man they couldn't shoot, root, or electrocute."

The head chef, meanwhile, called me "Fitzie," to which I always failed, suspiciously, to respond. The chef was the boss in the kitchen. When I once gave him shit about a garishly decorated fish being sent out, he glowered at me and said, "Don't come the raw prawn with me, cobber." I couldn't tell if I had gone too far. But McCarthy and the other dixie bashers got a kick out of the exchange. They took to calling me Raw Prawn.

Local surfers were less welcoming. There were thousands of them. The ability level was high, the competition for waves acute. Like anywhere, each spot had its crew, its stars, its old lions. But there were full-blown clubs and cliques and family dynasties in every Gold Coast beach town—Coolangatta, Kirra, Burleigh. There were also hordes of tourists and day trippers, and Bryan and I would be assumed to belong to that low stratum of surf life until we could establish otherwise. The guys we began surfing with regularly were fellow expats—an Englishman we called Peter the Pom, a Balinese kid named Adi. Peter was a cook at the casino, a solid surfer, married to a local girl. They lived in a flat in Rainbow Bay, overlooking the wave at Snapper Rocks. Adi had also married a local girl. He was a talented surfer, working as a waiter, sending his wages home. One night I took Adi and his cousin, Chook, to a drive-in to see *Car Wash*. Chook had hair down to his waist and was the skinniest grown man I'd ever met—"chook" is Aussie slang for chicken. He and Adi got drunk on sparkling wine and laughed themselves sick at the movie, which they called *Wash Car*. They thought African Americans, whom they called Negroes, were the funniest people on earth.

The casino threw a fancy staff pre-Christmas party, giving me the chance to relive a painful part of high school that I had missed by being a hippie surfer who would sooner have gone to jail than to the prom. All the young women in the kitchen—waitresses, dishwashers, pastry chefs— were excited about the party. I could hear them giddily reviewing their dresses, dates, hairdos, the band, their after-party plans. I found that I very much wanted to go, perhaps even with a pretty waitress on my arm. But I didn't own a long-sleeved shirt, let alone the tuxedo that I gathered was de rigueur. More to the point, it was clear that to these girls I didn't exist. Their swains were all local bravos whom they had probably gone to high school with. I spent the night of the party in my tiny, grotty bungalow room trying to work on my novel. How I hated being a foreigner, always on the outside. The intensity of my shame and self-loathing was unsettling.

Sharon and I wrote letters, many, and hers were usually a comfort to get, but I could hardly tell her everything. She was undoubtedly being similarly discreet. The true parameters of my loneliness were mine to cope with.

BRYAN AND I WANTED TO WRITE an article for *Tracks*, a surf mag published in Sydney. *Tracks* was nothing like its glossy, clean-cut American cousins. It was a newsprint tabloid. Editorially, it was rude, witty, aggro. It actually seemed to be the main Aussie youth mag, like *Rolling Stone* in its U.S. heyday. Huge bundles of it appeared at the newsstands every two weeks. Our notion was to make fun of the domestication of surfing in Australia. *Tracks* and its readers already hated Americans. When being polite, they called us seppos, short for septic tanks, rhyming slang for

Yanks. More commonly, we were just dickheads. We figured we could rile them. The editors invited us to have a go.

The target was almost too easy. Surfing was fully mainstreamed in Australia—all the clubs and contests and school teams and well-marked Surfing Beaches, complete with car parks and hot showers. I actually half liked the wholesome hoopla—and surfing's mass appeal was, to be sure, the only reason a niche mag like *Tracks* could double as an all-purpose national youth paper—but culturally it was screamingly lame. Bryan and I had grown up in a Southern California where most beach towns, and beach cops, loathed and harassed surfers. My high school would have expelled us before they supported us. Surfers were bad boys, outlaws, rebels. We were, that is to say, cool. Surfing wasn't some tamed, authority-approved "sport." Bryan and I figured we could play up that stuff for *Tracks*.

The hard part was the writing. Neither of us had ever cowritten anything, and our assumption that we shared a sensibility proved wildly wrong. We agreed on the idea for the piece, but Bryan couldn't stand my drafts, and I despised his. Why was I being so ordinary, so predictable? Why was he being so purple, so over the top? When was he going to grow up? Was I *aspiring* to mediocrity? I didn't want my name on the self-admiring juvenilia he was producing. Etcetera. I got so mad I crumpled up the pages we were arguing over and threw the paper ball at him. He later said that he nearly punched me before storming out instead.

We had known each other for eight years at that point, and our flat, fierce disagreement over virtually every line of this ditty for *Tracks* made me wonder when our literary differences had become so pronounced. When we first met, in Lahaina, what drew us together was discovering we loved the same books. In fact, the first words I ever spoke to Bryan were, "What are you doing with that book?" He was crossing a post office parking lot with *Ulysses* in hand, and the familiar prongs of the big "U" on the Random House paperback cover had caught my eye. We stood there in the sun talking about Joyce, and then the Beats, for an hour or two—

while Domenic waited impatiently in the shade—and it seemed inevitable that we would meet again. Of course, our tastes had never been exactly the same. I was the more dedicated Joyce fan—I later spent a year studying *Finnegans Wake* with Norman O. Brown, an exercise in masturbatory obscurantism that Bryan would never have undertaken—and he had an eye for genre fiction, including westerns, that I lacked. I liked Pynchon; Bryan thought his prose awful. And so on. But we were always turning each other on to new writers and, more often than not, finding the same virtues in their stuff. Bryan tended to be years ahead of the reading public—he was extolling Cormac McCarthy's work long before most critics had heard of him—and I was glad to follow his leads. In Australia we were digging into Patrick White and Thomas Kenneally and turning up our noses at Colleen McCullough. So why did every sentence he wrote about Aussie surfing annoy me, and vice versa?

We were headed in different directions, clearly. I had started as a teenage lyric surrealist, language-drunk à la Dylan Thomas, and had been slowly trying to sober up. I was now more interested in transparency and accuracy, less enamored of showy originality. Bryan remained enchanted by the music of words—what he once called "the incredible foot-stomping joy of a well-turned phrase." He loved pure captured dialect, cracked vernacular humor, vivid physicality, and a knockout metaphor, and he disliked nothing more than a lazy stock expression.

I voted to abandon the article, or at least to have it carry only his byline. But Bryan was determined that it should have both of our names on it. So we dialed back his stuff to the point where I could agree to sign it. We used our real names, which was lucky, because the piece caused an unexpected stir. Peter the Pom, who knew us only by our fake work names, actually asked me if I had read it. Some local guys were seriously irritated, he said, by all the exuberant insults from these American wankers. Bryan and I quietly decided to deny authorship, if pressed. We had hoped to piss off readers. We did not want to get hounded off the Gold Coast. *Tracks* traditionally published wonderful abusive letters, and we got ours. I liked

"I wouldn't spit on you mongrels if you were on fire." Bryan liked "May your earlobes turn to assholes and shit on your shoulders."

I MET A WOMAN, SUE. She told me I was "as mad as a two-bob watch." She meant it as a compliment. I liked her enormously. She was a big-mouthed, bosomy, bright-eyed mother of three. Her husband, a local rock musician and heroin addict, was in jail. We lived in fear of his release. Sue and her kids lived in a high-rise beach town called (talk about mainstreaming) Surfers Paradise. Sue was a bon vivant. She loved avant-garde music, art, comedy, Australian history, and all things Aboriginal. She knew lots of Gold Coast gossip—which cokehead surf star had shopped his mates to the cops, which cokehead surf star was rooting his sponsor's wife. She also knew the beautiful, eucalyptus-forested highlands behind the coast, where cattle grazed and kangaroos bounded and scruffy back-to-the-landers lived in a cannabis-soaked version of the Aboriginal Dreamtime. We passed days up there when the surf was flat. Sue's kids, who ranged in age from eight to fourteen, made me a great jokey collage, with cute koalas skeptically surveying the strutting of Gold Coast flaneurs. Then I got a midnight phone call. The husband had been released. Sue had received a heads-up, bundled the kids into her rattletrap car, and was already hundreds of miles from Surfers Paradise. "Off like a bride's nightie," she said. "Off like a bucket of shrimp on a hot day." She sounded chipper, all things considered. They were en route to her mother's place in Melbourne, more than a thousand miles away. She would catch me on the flip side. I should watch out for her husband.

Sue was not really an example of this, but a lot of Australian women seemed to be sick of Australian men. "Ockers," as they were called—the name came from a popular TV show—drank too much beer, loved their mates and football first, and treated women shabbily. Whether this generalization was true or fair, I could not say, but Bryan and I, once we had been in Kirra long enough to make it clear to the natives that we were resident, began to feel like the innocent benefactors of a mass sexual disillusionment. Compared with your typical ocker, we were sensitive, modern guys. Gold Coast women had time for us. Even when we behaved caddishly, we seemed to be an improvement on the local brand. I missed Sue, and was happy to continue not meeting her husband, but my heartsick wallflower phase passed, thank God.

I got a new job, as a barman at the Queensland Hotel in Coolangatta, which was an old-fashioned pub during the week and a rock and roll club known as the Patch on weekend nights. (Sue and I saw Bo Diddley there.) I learned to pull pints of beer properly under the close supervision of a career barman named Peter. Peter told me that if I got anything wrong, the customer had the right to throw the beer (but not the glass) in my face and demand a repull. The list of punishable errors was long: too much head, too little head, flat beer, warm beer, too little beer, any hint of soap in the glass. This news had its intended effect: I pulled scared and carefully. Weekday nights were slow and easy. Friday and Saturday nights at the Patch, which was in a big, dark, barnlike building out behind the old pub, were madness, with screaming customers six deep at the bar, blasting punk rock, and ten thousand rum and Cokes. The summer tourist season was starting. After work, I would walk down the beach road back to Kirra, grateful for the silence, stopping at the top of the point where the great wave was said to break, peering into the sloshing blackness beyond the base of the jetty. All the Gold Coast waves we had surfed so far had been sweet, warm, soft, a little sloppy. People said Kirra, when it broke, was a rocket-fueled pointbreak with crazy, hammering power. That was hard to picture.

THE FIRST CYCLONE SWELL HIT, of course, right on Boxing Day. Kirra woke up. The hard-to-picture became the can't-look-anywhere-else. But the wave was a strange, ungainly beast, nothing like a California pointbreak. Large amounts of sandy water were rushing around the end of the jetty, forming a torrent down the coast. It was overcast and glary that first

morning, the ocean surface gray and brown and blinding silver. The sets
looked smaller than they were, seeming to drift almost aimlessly onto the
bar outside the jetty, then suddenly standing up taller and thicker than
they should have, hiccuping, and finally unloading in a ferocious series of
connectable sections, some of the waves going square with power—the lip
threw out that far when it broke. It was hard to believe that this wave was
breaking on a sand bottom. I had never seen anything like it. The crowd
was bad at dawn and rapidly getting worse. We got amongst it, as the
Aussies say.

I probably caught three waves that day. Nobody would give me an
inch. The downcoast current turned the whole place into a paddling contest. Nobody spoke. The paddling was too grueling, and the least pause or
inattention meant yardage lost. I was in good shape, but the top locals
were in obscenely good shape, and this was what they lived for. Near the
top, near the takeoff, the current got even stronger. As a set approached,
you had to sprint upriver at a precise, not obvious angle, somehow putting
just enough distance between yourself and the flailing, growling pack so
that you were the one person in the pit as the water dredged off the bar,
and then swerving and, with a last few hard strokes, catching the wave
before it pitched. Then, assuming you stuck the takeoff, you had to surf it,
speed-pumping like crazy on one of the fastest waves in the world. It was
a lot like work. If you made a wave, though, it felt worth it. It felt worth
anything. This, I thought, was a wave I could get serious about.

It didn't have the open-ocean size or broad-faced beauty of a Honolua
Bay. It was a far more compact, ropier wave. The first hundred yards
had an amphitheater feel, with spectators lining the jetty at the point,
the guardrail along the coast road, a steep green bluff that rose behind the
road, and even sometimes a parking lot in front of the Kirra Hotel, a large
plain pub tucked under the bluff. Beyond that it was open beach, and
when the swell was big and the angle was right, a ride could run on for
another two hundred yards, unobserved, an empty, ecstatic racetrack. It
wasn't a mechanical wave. It had flaws, variety, slow patches, close-outs.

Concussion wavelets off the jetty or the inside bar often ran back out to sea, marring the third or fourth waves of a set. But the cleaner waves had a quality of *compression* that was, sometimes literally, stunning. The heaviest waves actually seemed to get shorter, they gathered so much force as they began to detonate across the main bar, a shallow stretch known as the Butter Box section. Even with a sand bottom and a makable-looking wave, it was a deeply intimidating section. You had to come into it fast but stay low on the face, be ready to duck when the thick lip threw horizontally, and then somehow stay over your board through an ungodly acceleration. The Butter Box section gave new meaning to the old surf imprecation, "Pull in!" There was only one way to make it—through the barrel, pulling in.

I had surfed my share of frontside tubes, from that reliable inside section at Lahaina Harbor Mouth to a slabby mutant wave in Santa Cruz called Stockton Avenue, where I snapped boards in half on three-foot days and was lucky not to get hurt on the shallow rock reef. But Stockton was a short, freaky wave—a one-trick pony. Kirra was just as hollow, and it was a pointbreak. It was as long as Rincon or Honolua, and hollower than either one. And the bottom, again, was sand, not coral or cobblestone— an unprecedented setup, in my experience, at a great pointbreak. The sand was not especially soft, I learned. I hit it so hard once, in the Butter Box, that I came up with a concussion, unable to say what country I was in. Another time, also in the Butter Box, and not on a big wave, I got my leash wrapped so tightly around my midsection that I could not breathe. On yet another occasion, same section, my leash tore through my rail and ripped half the tail off my favorite board. So the sand was a blessing, certainly, but the violence of the wave remained—inseparable, as always, from its fierce appeal. That steel thread.

The pecking order at Kirra was disconcertingly long, and the guys on top tended to be national and world champions. Michael Peterson, a two-time Australian champ, ruled the lineup when we started surfing there. He was a dark, brooding, brawny character, with a thick mustache and a crazy look in his eye. He took any wave he wanted, and he surfed like a

Paul Stacey, a Kirra local, heading into the Butter Box, Kirra

demon, with a wide power stance and savage hacks. One morning, I noticed him staring at me. We were near the takeoff spot, and I was paddling
hard, as always, trying to beat the pack to the next set wave, but Peterson
stopped paddling. "Bobby!" he cried. I shook my head no and kept going.
He looked like he'd seen a ghost. "You're not Bobby? You look exactly like
my mate who's in jail! I thought they'd let him out. Bobby!" After that
incident, I often found Peterson staring at me in the water. We became
nodding acquaintances, even though I spooked him, and I felt the pecking order ease around me when other guys noticed me and the legendary
Peterson exchanging little g'days. I was happy to take the break. Like everybody else, I just wanted more waves.

   Bryan and I had the advantage of living about as close to Kirra as it was
possible to live—unless you lived at the Kirra Hotel, which had no rooms.
I checked the jetty every night on my walk home from work, and if there
was any hint of a swell, we would hit it before first light. It turned out to
be a great surf season, one of the best in memory, people said, with at least

one solid swell virtually every week in January and February. One cyclone, Kerry, smashed through the Solomon Islands and then seemed to drift around the Coral Sea for weeks, pumping out powerful northeast swell. Our early-morning go-outs were often fruitful, yielding fresh waves with, for an hour or two, relatively few people. There was a regular predawn crew, not all of them especially hot surfers. There was a gawky, friendly, bearded guy who rode a big-wave gun, hardly turning at all, and who always yelled, as he jumped to his feet and set his line, "*I got a lady doctor.*" I happened to know the next line in that song: "*She cure da pain for free.*" She did.

KIRRA, BEING A CROWDED, famous right, was not Bryan's kind of wave. He surfed it faithfully, and managed to find the seams in the mob, the uncrowded early sessions, the inflection points in the series of sandbars where he could get his waves, but he was not committed to the dogfight in the same way I was, or to chasing the grail that on great days was made incarnate over and over in the vortex of the Butter Box (which we took to calling simply the wild section). He seemed to like Australia as much as I did—the incorrigible cheekiness of Aussies, the amazing wages, the rich slang, the sunshine, the girls. But he wasn't writing, which was worrying. He had finished, on Guam, a novel set in a small town in the Idaho panhandle. It was terrific, I thought, even better than his Bildungsroman about his surf buddies in high school. He had sent it off to an agent in New York. This was the kind of grown-up follow-through I had never dared. (I now had two novels sitting in a drawer, read only by friends.) The manuscript hadn't yet found a publisher. Bryan wasn't discouraged by the delay, he said, but he seemed to have entered a fallow phase.

He read insatiably—fiction, biographies—sitting in an old wicker chair that he propped by the front door of our bungalow. I found, in a junk shop in Coolangatta, a tall stack of old *New Yorker*s selling for a penny apiece, bought a few hundred, and gave them to him for Christmas.

He put the pile on one side of his chair and started methodically working his way through them. They became an hourglass of our time in Kirra—a hundred mags down, two hundred to go. Meanwhile, I was banging out chapters of my railroad novel, having finally found a story line. We shared an ancient typewriter, donated to us by Sue. Bryan typed long, droll letters to friends back home about our adventures in Oz, some of them nonfictional. Occasionally he read out passages that he thought would amuse me. One that stuck in my mind, but did not amuse, described the two of us as a physically improbable pair of traveling surfers. He was too fat, he wrote, and I was too skinny. It was true that I was skinny, and that he was a bit plump, but my vanity recoiled at this expanded self-deprecation. My reaction was odd, partly because I had always tried to ease tensions with Bryan—and I had done this even more with Domenic—by compulsively making myself the butt of jokes and stories. But my body, apparently, was off-limits for mockery, at least in any way that suggested weakness or, God forbid, unmanliness. Bryan had a better attitude. He gave his students no choice except Clint Eastwood, whom he did not remotely resemble. This shtick was, of course, part of his ladykilling charm.

Speaking of bodies, the Gold Coast was an open-air object lesson in how I was destroying mine through surfing. Looking around at Australians who spent a lot of time in tropical sun for which they were genetically unprepared—most were of Northern European ancestry—I could see my own sorry medical future. Every other surfer, even teenagers, seemed to have pterygia—sun-caused cataracts—clouding their blue eyes. The scabby ears and purple noses and scarily mottled arms of the middle-aged were fair warning: basal-cell carcinoma (if not squamous-cell, if not melanoma) ahead. I already had pterygia myself, in both eyes. Not that I took any preventive measures, or that surfing in colder places was necessarily any less damaging. My years in the freezing ocean in Santa Cruz had given me exostoses—bony growths in the ear canal, known as "surfer's ear"—which were now constantly trapping seawater, causing painful infections, and would eventually require three operations. Then there was the usual run of surf injuries: scrapes, gashes, reef rashes, a broken nose, torn ankle cartilage. I had no interest in any of this at the time. All I wanted from my body was for it to paddle faster and surf better.

I DID BECOME, AT KIRRA, a paddling machine. My arms basically stopped getting tired. Getting to know the downcoast current helped. It was constant, but it had vagaries, weak spots, eddies—sometimes, at different tides, even deep slow troughs slightly outside—and its patterns changed with the swell size and direction and the movement of the sand. There were relatively few guys exploiting those vagaries, and we got to know each other. We competed so hard, trying to make each stroke count, that we rarely spoke, but a rough wave-sharing arrangement emerged nonetheless, out of some combination of necessity and respect. I began to get more waves. And I began to learn what to do with them.

It was the opposite of surfing Tavarua, in most ways. That was an empty, immaculate coral-reef left, breaking in Edenic abundance. This was an ultra-crowded, sand-bottom right in the Aussie Miami Beach. And yet both were long, demanding, superlative waves that required fast, fine edgework and rewarded close study. The key to surfing Kirra was entering the wild section at full speed, surfing close to the face—pulling in—and then, if you got inside, staying calm in the barrel, having faith that it just might spit you out. It usually didn't, but I had waves that teased me two, even three times, with the daylight hole speeding ahead, outrunning me, and then pausing and miraculously rewinding back toward me, the spilling lip seemingly twisting like the iris of a camera lens opening until I was almost out of the hole, and then reversing and doing it again, receding in beautiful hopelessness and returning in even more beautiful hope. These were the longest tube rides of my life.

Which raised the question of claiming. The best thing to do, by far, if you came flying out of a deep tube was nothing. Keep surfing. Act as if such things happened to you all the time. This was difficult, if not impossible. The emotional release of some little celebration was practically a physical necessity. Maybe not an obnoxious fist pump, or arms thrown up touchdown-style, but some acknowledgment that something rare and deeply thrilling had just happened. On one of the bigger days we got at Kirra, when the sets were swinging wide and breaking in slightly deeper, much bluer water than usual, I pulled into a tube that was oblong, not cavernous, and saw the ceiling ahead begin to shatter—to chandelier. I bowed my head, crouching low, expecting the ax, but held my line and squeaked through. As I came out, astonished, rising and trying to stay cool, I noticed Bryan among the paddlers going over the shoulder. I heard a few hoots, but nothing from him. Later, I asked him if he had seen the wave. He said he had. He said I had overclaimed it. I had come out with my hands raised in prayer, he said. Pretty lame. That wasn't praying, I said. It was just a little thank-you. My hands had been clasped, not raised. I was mortified. Also angry. It was a childish thing to care about, but his disdain for my elation seemed mean. Still, I vowed never to claim again, no matter how great the wave.

Greatness is relative, of course. On that same big swell, perhaps that same afternoon, I was walking back after an extra-long ride that had carried me halfway to Bilinga, the next village north—carried me so far that paddling back seemed silly. I had decided to walk to Kirra and try to punch through up near the point. I was alone on the beach. The swell was peaking, the wind offshore, the waves now seemingly nonstop. Far outside, I saw a tiny surfer in red trunks pull into a big blue barrel, emerge, disappear, and emerge again. It was a guy I had never seen before, surfing at a speed I had rarely, if ever, seen before. He kept doing it—disappearing, emerging. He seemed to be riding in the wrong place on his board—too far forward—but somehow turning from there, making small adjustments that kept him in the barrel for ridiculous amounts of time. He kept going, and his stance, I could see as he got closer, was casual, almost defiant. He claimed none of the barrels he threaded. He was getting one of the best rides I had ever seen, and he was acting as if he deserved it. I actually couldn't understand, technically, half of what he was doing. Nose turns inside the tube? It reminded me of the first time I saw a shortboard in action—Bob McTavish at Rincon. What I didn't know was that this kid in red trunks was the newly crowned world champion, Wayne "Rabbit" Bartholomew. He was a local boy, just home from the international contest circuit. Physically slight but fearless in big waves and absurdly talented, he was the Mick Jagger of surfing, endlessly lauded in the mags for striking rock-star poses in heavy situations. He had grown up surfing Kirra, and the ride I saw was a master class in how it could be done, if you happened to be the best surfer in the world.

THE SUMMER TOURIST SEASON was winding down at the Patch. Bryan and I had saved enough money to push on. We were keen to take a big drive around Australia. Our car, however, was not. The water pump was on the blink, causing the car to overheat. Bryan found a spare pump in a junkyard. We installed it, quit our jobs, said our good-byes, and, in half an hour, moved out of the Bonnie View Flats. Bryan paused as he shut the door, and said, with studied casualness, "Let's call it an era." Ten miles down the road, the Falcon's temperature gauge swung back to Hot. I stuck a piece of masking tape over the gauge, blocking out the bad news. Then I wrote on the tape, "She'll be right." It was the unofficial Australian national motto.

In Sydney we met up with *Alias*. Mick and Jane and their Fiji-born baby boy were moored in a quiet corner of the harbor, near Castlecrag. Graham and his girlfriend were off working. Over shrimp and beer, Mick described a moneymaking scheme they had cooked up. There were lots of rich yuppie surfers in Sydney, he said. The plan was to persuade a small group of them to pay thousands for a surf safari to Magic Island on *Alias*. They would not be told where they were going—only that it was "the world's most perfect wave." If the first trip was a success, the passengers would tell their wealthy friends, and the charter business would take off by word of mouth. The secret would be kept, basically. The trick would be to persuade the first group to cough up the brass and get on a plane to Nadi. Photos would be a big help. He and Graham had been too busy surfing Tavarua to get any decent photos. Did we by chance have any good ones?

Bryan and I mumbled that we too had been busy surfing, and had few photos, none of them good, which was true. It was also true that we had no wish to see this scheme succeed.

We headed south, surf-camping our way around southeast Australia to Melbourne, where we found Sue and her kids (her husband seemed to be firmly out of the picture now) living with Sue's mother. They had a full house, so we stayed with Sue's younger sister. She was a university student, living with a group of punk rockers in a burned-out squat in a bad part of town. By night, we drank and danced with the punks and watched old movies (*Sergeant York*) on a clapped-out black-and-white TV they had scavenged. By day, we went to a marathon international cricket match, Australia versus Pakistan, with Sue's mother, eating cucumber sandwiches and sipping Pimm's Cup. Bryan, in a moment of late-night why-not, let the punks shave his head. They wore his dark curls as adornment, hanging off their much-pierced ears, and he, after sobering up, announced ruefully that his new stage name was Sid Temperate.

We headed west, toward the Great Australian Bight, which has the world's longest line of seacliffs, and the Nullarbor Plain, which is the world's largest hunk of limestone. It was hot, bright, treeless, unpeopled. We drove through salt flats and sand dunes on dirt roads and camped at a remote, flyblown surf spot known as Cactus, where the water was cold and a deep Southern Ocean blue. There were two long lefts, one called Cactus, one called Castles, breaking off a rocky headland, and a heavy right a few hundred yards west called Caves. The swell was solid, day after day. Some days it was more than solid. The wind was hot, full of dust, and offshore, blowing out of the great central desert. Bryan rode the lefts. I was riding a new board now, a pale blue 6'9" rounded pintail that I had bought in Torquay, a beach town in Victoria. I had left my South Pacific board, not without regret, for sale on consignment at the shop where I found the pintail. I hoped the pintail, which was built in New Zealand, might work as my new all-around board. It was light and fast and on bigger days at Caves seemed able to handle a serious drop without side-slipping.

The other surfers at Cactus were a hardy mix of travelers and transplants. The transplants were all from other, more populated parts of Australia—blokes who knew a great, uncrowded wave when they saw it and didn't mind living in the back of beyond. They surfed and scraped by on the dole, or fished, or found something to do in Penong, a truck stop up on the paved highway thirteen miles inland. Some lived in scrap-built shacks in the desert. These characters ruled the lineup, naturally, but it was still uncrowded, and we found them surprisingly generous with waves. Some could even be garrulous. One told me a cautionary tale featuring his mate, Moose, who one day found himself faded into a wipeout by a visiting camper. Moose came up smiling, but then paddled in, got in his truck, and drove several times back and forth over the tent of the offending visitor before returning to the lineup, still all smiles. I was careful not to drop in on Moose.

There was another local known as Madman. He had a crew cut and an unusual amount of energy, churning back and forth in search of the gnarliest takeoff spots in the broad, boil-filled expanse of heaving, eight-foot Caves. My informant said that Madman had once broken a leash on a big day out here, but, too rabid to go in and repair it, had kept surfing, simply clamping the broken cord in his teeth and holding on to his board that way. Then a bad wipeout tore the leash out of his mouth, along with his two front teeth. Madman later grinned at me, for no apparent reason, confirming that the teeth in question were gone.

Cactus, like the rest of the Nullarbor coast, is known for great white sharks—people called them white pointers. I met a guy in the water who said that he had been attacked by a white pointer five years before in the exact spot where we were sitting. He was a mild person—no Madman or Moose—and I was inclined to believe him. He said that the shark had really only bitten his board, but that he had been injured in the thrashing, sliced up mainly by the broken bits, the sharp fiberglass edges, of the board. It had happened in midwinter and his wetsuit, he said, had saved his life. Even so, he had needed 150 stitches and had been out of the water for eighteen months. He reckoned that lightning never struck in the same place twice, so he surfed here without fear now. Try as I might, after hearing his tale, I couldn't feel the same karmic safety zone.

Cactus didn't tempt me as a place to live, but it reminded me of other surf-exile scenes I had run across, in Hawaii and Oregon and Big Sur and rural southwest Victoria. People came for the waves and stayed. They learned the place, and found ways to survive. Some became, over time, members in good standing of the local community; others stayed on the margins. I had surfed a few spots, notably Honolua Bay, where the wave commanded such devotion that I could see renouncing all other ambition than to surf it, every time it broke, forever. There were other beauty spots with good, uncrowded waves, places where the living was cheap and, at a glance, looked easy. I might end up, I guessed, in one of those. Then there was Tavarua. Bryan and I still never spoke the name. It existed out of time. I never thought about going back to live in Fiji.

BUT I DID WONDER what I was doing with my life. We had been gone so long now that I felt unmoored from all possible explanations for this trip. It was certainly no longer a vacation. What was I vacationing from? I had wangled a one-year leave of absence from the railroad, which had run out while we were in Kirra. Officially resigning my job as a trainman, and my precious seniority date—June 8, 1974—had been unexpectedly difficult emotionally. I still believed I would never find another job so satisfying and well paid. But it was done. I panicked sometimes, convinced I was wasting my youth, aimlessly wandering on the dark side of the moon while old friends, classmates, my peers, were building lives, careers, becoming adults back in America. I had wanted to be useful, somehow, to work, to write, to teach, to accomplish great things—what had happened to that? Yes, I had felt compelled, almost required, to take a big surf trip. But did it really need to last this long?

Our plan was to go to Bali next. Great waves, dirt cheap. Sharon had written that she could probably meet us in Asia in a few months' time. Maybe she knew what it was that I was supposed to be doing out here. But she didn't surf. In fact, she was terrified of the ocean. Was "surfing" even what I was doing? I chased waves instinctively, got appropriately stoked when it was good, got thoroughly immersed in working out the puzzle of a new spot. Still, peak moments were, by definition, few and far between. Most sessions were unremarkable. What was consistent was a certain serenity that followed a rigorous session. It was physical, this postsurf mood, but it had a distinct emotionality too. Sometimes it was mild elation. Often it was a pleasant melancholy. After particularly intense tubes or wipeouts, I felt a charged and wild inclination to weep, which could last for hours. It was like the gamut of powerful feelings that can follow heartfelt sex.

On good days, I still thought I was doing the right thing. The particulars of new places grabbed me and held me, the sweep of new coasts, cold, lovely dawns. The world was incomprehensibly large, and there was still so much to see. Yes, I got sick sometimes of being an expatriate, always ignorant, on the outside of things, but I didn't feel ready for domestic life, for seeing the same people, the same places, thinking more or less the same thoughts, each day. I liked surrendering to the onrush, the uncertainty, the serendipity of the road. And I generally liked being a stranger, an observer, often surprised. On the day we crossed from Victoria into South Australia, passing between tall rows of Norfolk pines, deep green under low clouds, we spotted a country racetrack, parked, slipped into the grandstand, and watched from the rail a terrific horse race, then watched the jockeys in their bright silks holding their saddles on the scales. Behind the racecourse pub, we found a rugby ball and started running old football pass patterns, throwing funky spirals and snagging them at full stretch while a group of barefoot kids hooted. Our Australian visas were running out and I, at least, would be sorry to leave.

Bryan and I had our own domesticity, of course, and it was often strained. Being friends as in writing letters was so much easier than being friends as in living together. We bickered and, every few months, fought bitterly. I resented the fact that it felt dangerous to do anything out of the ordinary, anything outside the rut of habit. One morning at Cactus, when the wind was sideshore and the waves poor, I rose early and took a walk along the waterline, westward. The limestone tidepools were shiny in the rising light. The ubiquitous outback flies were absent, perhaps because of the hour, perhaps because of the wind. I ended up walking a long way, and saw not a soul. By the time I made it back to camp, it was midmorning and Bryan was pissed. Where had I gone? He had cooked and eaten breakfast without me. My oatmeal was stiff and curdled. I didn't feel like accounting for myself. I was munching an apple. He continued to grouse. I exploded. How dare he tell me when I could go where? Unfortunately, I spat a mouthful of half-chewed apple onto our tent, more or less deliberately. Bryan stalked away in disgust. Thankfully, he never mentioned the Apple Spat (or Spat Apple) again. It was almost as bad as a similar row we had in Western Samoa, when I shouted at him to never again tell me what to do, and he seriously considered, he later told me, pulling the plug on our South Pacific trip, which was then barely two weeks old.

WE SET OFF for the Never Never—the Northern Territory. Australians had been warning us not to try to cross the Center since we first started muttering about doing so, back on the Gold Coast. We should especially not try it in an unreliable car. "Bush rangers" lay in wait for unwary travelers. It was many days' drive between way stations. That, we could see from the map, was an exaggeration, but we did buy a jerry can to carry extra gasoline, and a water bag, and a few extra hoses, and our car was undeniably unreliable. It overheated daily, and often wouldn't start. We had taken to parking it only on inclines, however slight, for the jump starts it frequently needed. When we pulled into gas stations, radiator steaming and hissing, attendants usually wanted to check the temperature gauge. They'd stick their heads in the driver's window. "She'll be right" always got a laugh.

We headed northeast from Cactus on a dirt road so obscure that we saw just one vehicle—a cattle truck—in two hundred miles. The washboard road caused the car's back window to rattle so hard that it fell down into the door. We tried to raise it and fix it in place, but no fix we attempted lasted more than ten minutes. We drove on, with white salt-dust, and later red bulldust, pouring in through the open back window. We wrapped bandanas around mouths and noses, and were thankful we'd filled the "esky"—a cheap styrofoam cooler—with Crown Lager in Penong. Distances between outback towns are sometimes measured in "tinnies"—how many cans of beer it takes to traverse them. It was at least a dozen tinnies to the main road north, also dirt, which we met in a village called Kingoonya, where a tumbledown roadhouse offered the world's most welcome steak burgers, served by Australia's most beautiful waitress.

Even the main road through the Center was rough. We saw no pavement for six hundred miles. We did see an unnerving number of burned-out vehicles lying on their sides in the saltbush, and decided to heed much-heard advice that without a "roo bar"—a cowcatcher for kangaroos—driving at night was inviting disaster. We saw enough kangaroos by day, both in the road and bounding along in the desert. So we camped at night. A huge flock of galahs, pink-and-gray parrotlike birds, wheeled above us one morning while we struggled to jump-start the Falcon.

We picked up a swagman, Joe, who was marching along with a knapsack fifty miles from a building. Joe was tiny, as if shrunken by the sun, deeply wizened, not young, and I would not have called him jolly, but he talked volubly all day about boreholes, billabongs, and sheep stations he had worked on. And he methodically guzzled our beers. I asked him about the crazy flies. He said you never got used to them. Even the blackfellas didn't get used to them, he said. Then he asked to be dropped at a faint track that ran off to the east. We filled his water bottle and gave him five dollars.

We crossed into the Northern Territory. At a dust-choked hamlet called Ghan, I peeked inside a filthy board bag strapped to the car's roof. My new pintail was in there. Shiny, pale blue, the board was a vision, so cool and sleek. It conjured another world, an unimaginable freshness. Our plan was to drive to Darwin, a town on the north coast, sell the car, and find a way to Indonesia from there.

Bryan had not finished reading his entire stack of *New Yorker*s before we left Kirra, and the fifty or so remaining had been stuffed under the front seat. We sometimes pulled them out and read from them aloud—short stories, poems, reviews, humor pieces, essays, long reported pieces. Many of these, one or both of us had read before, but hearing them in the outback was different. It was a test. How would the stuff hold up in the harsh, no-bullshit desert light? Some of it did fine. The writing was still strong, the stories still funny. But pretension and flab came up fluorescent in this merciless scan, and certain writers suddenly seemed like hothouse poseurs. They became unintentionally hilarious.

We were feeling pretty full of ourselves. This was like long road trips we had taken in the West back home, but with less pavement and more beer. Mailer's *A Fire on the Moon* failed the outback test, which distressed me, since he was one of my heroes. It didn't help that he was up against Patrick White's *Voss*, an utterly convincing novel about a Prussian natural-ist on a nineteenth-century expedition across the middle of Australia. We bantered and read and took potshots at wombats with cheap green plastic water pistols. I liked the way Bryan drove. He did it with a long-distance trucker's posture, upright. On straightaways, he left one hand on his leg. He read with a similar relaxed, long-haul attentiveness. We rarely ran out of things to discuss. Mick and Jane had laughed at us on our way out of Sydney. We had driven in convoy with them down to Wollongong to look for waves. When we got there, they said that they had been watching us for an hour straight, both gesticulating, particularly me, nonstop. I had been developing, on that drive, an early version of a theory about Patrick White, having just read *The Eye of the Storm*. It had been the same on *Alias*, they said, the two of us constantly ear-bashing one another, privately amusing the Aussies.

On the north side of Alice Springs, we picked up two hitchhikers, Tess and Manja (pronounced mun-yuh). They were graduate students, they said, from Adelaide, going to a women's conference in Darwin. They said they didn't mind the deep bulldust drifts that now filled every corner of the Falcon. They put on bandanas, and we traveled with them for five days. Tess was a bantam lass, wearing a man's plaid shirt. She was slight, pale, butch, incisive, with short dark hair and a wicked dry wit, which she deployed at the expense of the hearty, unsuspecting fellows whom we met at petrol stations and in the far-flung pubs where we hid from the midday heat, which was now too much for the struggling Falcon. Tess was relatively easy on Bryan and me and our water pistols, even after we insisted we were Vietnam vets, unrepentant but mentally damaged. "Poor boys," she cooed. We said our surf scars were war wounds. "Blimey, that must have hurt. Buy us a pint."

Manja was tall, soft-voiced, warm-eyed, slim. She laughed, or at least smiled indulgently, at all the right places. She was earnestly political, but wore it lightly, in the diffident Aussie way. At night, she and I would slip away and find a quiet place to lay our sleeping bags. She told me about her childhood. She had grown up on a farm on the Murray River. Hunters there used to shoot kangaroos and wallabies, she said, and if they found a little jocy still alive in the pouch, they would give the baby to a farmkid as a pet. They were great pets—gentle, loyal, intelligent. She used to dress up her young wallaby in a hat and coat and the two of them would walk and hop, holding hands, to town.

· · ·

OUR IDYLL WENT TO HELL in Darwin. Tess and Manja had a house to stay in, a feminist commune of some kind, no men allowed. Tess was happy to see the back of me. It seemed I had interrupted a preexisting idyll—something Manja had neglected to mention. Bryan and I stayed in a campground outside town. There wasn't much to Darwin. It had been blown flat by a cyclone a few years before. Rebuilding was proceeding slowly. The town was allegedly on the coast, but all we could find was mud and scrub and poisonous-looking shallows. It was hot, flat, plug-ugly. There was an airport, though, with cheap weekly flights to Denpasar. We sold the car for two hundred dollars to a bunch of Yugoslavian bauxite miners. By some miracle, it started when they came to inspect it. We changed campgrounds, not certain that the miners fully grasped the meaning of "as is."

I longed for Manja. We managed to rendezvous at an old hotel that had survived the cyclone. Suddenly, I didn't want to leave Australia. It would be better, she said, if I went.

She was right. I turned up that night, uninvited, at the commune. Nobody answered the door. I let myself in. I could hear festive noise in the backyard. I got as far as the back door. On a concrete deck, under a bright porch light, Manja was getting a haircut. Most of her long blond locks were already on the ground. Tess was merrily clipping off the rest. Manja's new crew cut was light brown, her head very round and vulnerable-looking, like a baby's. Four or five women were applauding her transformation. She was grinning goofily, drinking a beer—a stubby of Toohey's, I noticed, while a wave of despair rose in my throat. I must have made a noise. Manja screamed. Others bellowed. Scuffling and shoving and shouting occurred. I half thought Manja might leave with me. Instead, I left with the police.

Weeks later, in Bali, I got a letter from Manja. She apologized for calling the cops. They were fascists, and she hoped they had not abused me.

They hadn't. In fact, being good ockers, they had turned me loose with off-color oaths of gender solidarity. Her misadventure with me, Manja wrote, had only strengthened her resolve to have nothing more to do with men. I hadn't respected her boundaries, which was so typical. I couldn't argue with that. I still liked her, though. If she had written that she was coming to Indonesia, I would have met her plane.

Bryan, me, and José from Ecuador, Grajagan, Java, 1979

SEVEN

CHOOSING ETHIOPIA

Asia, Africa, 1979–81

BRYAN LOATHED BALI. HE WROTE AN ARTICLE FOR *TRACKS*—IT
carried, by tradition, both our names, though I only gave it a light edit—
mocking the notion, then widespread among Australian surfers, that Bali
was still an unspoiled paradise of uncrowded waves and mellow Hindu
natives. In fact, he wrote, it was overrun with surfers and other tourists. It
was a place where one could "see topless and bottomless Europeans of
both sexes," "listen to the lies of surfers from all over the world," "hire a
board carrier and experience the dizzying thrill of colonialism," and "tell
people you're from Cronulla when you're really from Parramatta," the latter being a less cool Sydney suburb than the former.

I agreed that Bali was overrun, and the collision of mass tourism and
Indonesian poverty was grotesque, but the place suited me nonetheless.
We stayed in a cheap, clean *losmen* (guesthouse) in Kuta Beach, ate well
for practically nothing, and surfed daily. I found a good writing spot in a
college library in Denpasar, the provincial capital, catching a bus there
each morning. It was a cool, quiet refuge on a hot, noisy island. My novel
was rocking along. A street vendor with a little turquoise cart would show
up outside the library at midday, my signal to knock off. He served rice,

soup, sweets, and satay through the opened windows of campus offices. I liked his *nasi goreng*—fried rice. In the afternoons, if there was swell, Bryan and I headed out the Bukit Peninsula, where a brace of great lefts broke off limestone cliffs. There were good waves around Kuta too, even on small swells, and, when the wind blew southwest, in a resort area on the east coast, Sanur.

The spot that sank its hooks in me the deepest was a sweeping, already famous left called Uluwatu. It was out on the southwestern tip of the Bukit. There was an eleventh-century Hindu temple, built of hard gray coral, perched on the edge of a high cliff just to the east of the wave. You entered the water, at high tide, through a sloshing sea cave. Uluwatu got big, and on bigger days, when the wind was light offshore, the long blue walls did something I had never seen elsewhere. In discrete, well-separated places along the swell line, they gently feathered far, far ahead of where you were surfing—hundreds of yards ahead, and hundreds of yards from shore. There were apparently a series of narrow rock ridges running out to sea from the inside reef, formations shallow enough to make a big wave feather but not, at least on the swells we surfed, to make it break. It was unsettling at first, but then, after a few screaming rides on massive waves that did not close out, the sight of those distant feathering sections just heightened the joy of rocketing around in the breaking part of the wave, since those strange wafts of spray out in the bay would soon become, you came to trust, solid sections on the inside shelf.

Inside Uluwatu was known, unoriginally, as the Racetrack. It was shallow and very fast, with sharp coral that left its claw marks on my feet, arms, and back. One afternoon, it scared me badly. The crowd, which could be thick at Uluwatu, even in 1979, had thinned out, which I found mysterious, since the surf was excellent. There were maybe five of us still out. The tide was low. The waves were big and quick. I could see twenty or thirty guys on the cliff, all squinting into the dropping sun, which should have caused me to ask, *Why are they watching and not surfing?* I got a couple of sweet rides, and then a wave that answered the question I had neglected to ask. It was well overhead, dark-faced, thick, and I, sky-high on testosterone, made the mistake of driving hard and low into the Racetrack. All the water drained off the reef. The tide was too low to surf down here at this size. That was why everyone had left. I could not pull out. It was too late for that. I could not dive off. There was no water. I got the deepest backhand barrel of my life. It was very dark, very noisy. I did not enjoy it. In fact, even as it became clear that I might actually make it, I wished, with a weird bitter awareness of the irony of it, that I could be anywhere else on earth. It should have been a moment of satori, a thunderbolt of enlightenment after long, patient practice. Instead, I was miserable because fear, entirely justified, filled my heart and brain. I made the wave, but I escaped horrible injury, if not worse, by pure dumb luck. Pulling in had been a low-odds survival move. Stupidity had put me inside that tube. If I had a chance to do it over again, I wouldn't.

There were so many surfers in Kuta, it was like attending a world conference of the wave-obsessed. They might all have been lying, but there were people talking surf on beaches and street corners, in bars and cafés and *losmen* courtyards, 24/7. Max, who had once mocked me and Bryan, would have had a field day with this mob. But I found it oddly moving, the intensity with which a group of guys could talk about the lines of a board standing up against a wall—its release points, its rocker—or the way that surfers often dropped to the ground to draw in the dirt the layout of their home breaks for guys from other places, other countries. Their stories, they felt, would make no sense if their listeners didn't understand exactly how a reef back in Perth caught a west swell. They lost themselves in diagrams more detailed than anyone wanted. Some of this strange ardor could be put down to homesickness, or simply to the countless hours spent surfing and studying that particular reef, but a good part of it was also, it must be said, dope-fueled. Surfers in Bali, together with the legions of nonsurfing Western backpackers, smoked daunting quantities of hash and pot. Bryan and I were the rare abstainers. Cannabis had started making me anxious in college; I hadn't smoked any in probably five years. Bryan liked to call everything except alcohol "false drugs."

I had begun trying to interest magazines in travel pieces. My first assignment came from the Hong Kong edition of a U.S. military publication called *Off Duty*. I had never seen the magazine (I have still never seen it), but the $150 they offered sounded grand. They wanted a story about getting a massage in Bali. Massage ladies were everywhere in Kuta, with their pink plastic baskets of aromatic oils. I was too shy to approach one on the beach, where pale bodies were being kneaded by the dozen all day long. But as soon as I mentioned my interest, the family that ran our *losmen* produced a sinewy-armed old woman. The children of the establishment laughed as she eyed me with sadistic pleasure and ordered me down on my belly on a cot in the courtyard. I was actually frightened as she dove into my back muscles with her powerful hands. I had torn an upper back muscle on the railroad, while yanking on a rusted cut lever in Redwood City, and it had never properly healed. I imagined this macho masseuse tearing into the sore spot and doing more damage. I wondered uneasily if such an episode might at least make good article copy. The injury had a bittersweet history already. When it happened, my fellow trainmen advised me to take no money, and sign no papers, from the company. This could be my million-dollar ladder, they said—the piece of defective equipment that allowed me to sue the railroad, get rich, and retire young. I considered such thinking contemptible, and so a few days later, when my back felt better, I cashed a check, signed a release, and returned to work. Of course, my back started hurting again the next day, and had ached ever since. But the masseuse didn't hurt me. Her fingers found the messed-up muscle, explored it, and worked it long and gently. It stopped aching that day, and the old throb didn't resume for weeks.

At some point I got sick. Fever, headache, dizziness, chills, a dry cough. I was too weak to surf, felt too awful to work. After a day or two, I dragged myself to Sanur, lying in the back of a minibus, and found a German doctor in one of the big hotels. He said I had paratyphoid, which wasn't as bad as typhoid. I probably got it from street food, he said. He gave me antibiotics. He said I would not die. I had almost never been sick before, which meant I had no experience of debility to draw on. I sank into a fretful derangement, sweating, listless, self-despising. I began to think, more desperately now, that I had wasted my life. I wished I had listened to my parents. (Patrick White: "parents, those arch-amateurs of life.") My mother had wanted me to become a Nader's Raider—one of the idealistic young lawyers working for Ralph Nader, exposing corporate misdeeds. Why hadn't I done that? My father would have liked me to become a journalist. His hero had been Edward R. Murrow. As a young man, he had worked as a gofer for Murrow and his buddies in New York. Why hadn't I listened to him? Bryan came and went from the room, looking dubiously at me, I thought, as I sloshed in self-pity. No, he said, the waves weren't much good. Bali still sucked. Where was he sleeping? He had met a woman. An Italian, I gathered.

We were getting mail—poste restante, Kuta Beach. But I had not heard from Sharon in weeks. I began to feel forgotten, angry. One morning, when I was slightly stronger, I walked slowly to the post office. There were cards and letters from family and friends but nothing from Sharon. I thought about sending a telegram but noticed a group of tourists gathered by a set of old wall phones under a sign, INTERNASIONAL. The telephone—what a concept. I called her. It was only the second or third time we had spoken in a year. Her voice was like music from another life. I was entranced. She and I wrote a great many letters, but the vast, delicately balanced distance between us collapsed when she murmured in my ear in real time. She was alarmed when I said I was sick. I should get well. She said she would meet me in Singapore at the end of June. This was major news. It was mid-May.

I got well.

. . .

INDONESIA IS A BIG PLACE, with more than a thousand miles of coast exposed to Indian Ocean swells. Only Bali had been much explored by surfers. Bryan and I were ready to look for waves elsewhere. On the south-eastern tip of Java, there was a fabled wilderness left known as Grajagan. An American, Mike Boyum, had built a camp there in the mid-'70s, but nothing had been heard from him recently. It seemed like a logical place to start. We sold our extra Aussie boards. From among the hordes in Bali, we found two accomplices—an Indonesian-American photographer from California named Mike, and a blond Ecuadorean goofyfoot named José.

It was a difficult expedition. We bought supplies in an East Java town, Banyuwangi, a long way from the coast. Vehement haggling seemed to be the local norm for every transaction, at least with *orang putih*—white men. Mike's command of Bahasa Indonesia, which we had thought at first was good, disintegrated under pressure. I became chief haggler. (Bahasa Indonesia is an easy language to learn if you don't mind speaking it badly. It has no verb tenses, and in much of the country it is—or at least was then—nobody's first language, which helped level the field for a foreigner.) At the coast, in the village of Grajagan, we needed a boat to take us ten miles across a bay to the wave. More wild, sweaty haggling, many hours. The villagers had seen surfers before, they said, but none in the past year or so. I drew up a contract in my journal, which a fishermen named Kosua and I signed. They would take us across for twenty thousand rupiah (thirty-two dollars), and come back for us in a week. They would supply eight jerry cans of freshwater. We would leave the next morning at 5 a.m.

The boat we sailed in was nothing like the delicate, colorful little *jukung* outriggers that fished off Uluwatu. It was a broad-beamed, heavy-bottomed beast, powered not by a patch of sail but by a large, noisy, ancient outboard with a strangely long propeller shaft. It carried a crew of ten. Five minutes into our voyage, it capsized in the surf in front of the village. Nobody got hurt but everybody got upset, and a lot of stuff got wet. Kosua wanted to renegotiate our contract. He tried to argue that this trip was more dangerous than we had let on. That was rich, I thought, after crashing on a sandbar that he had to negotiate every time he took out his boat. So we haggled for another day or so, until the surf got smaller. Then we went.

Grajagan the surf spot, known locally as Plengkung, was way out on a roadless point where the thick jungle was said to be one of the last redoubts of the Javan tiger. Kosua dropped us in a cove about a half mile down the beach from some ramshackle structures that had been Boyum's camp. It was low tide, and there were great-looking waves breaking off a wide, exposed reef beyond the camp. We started humping our gear in the heat, as Kosua motored away. The jerry cans were hideously heavy. It was all I could do to drag one along the sand. Mike couldn't even manage that. Bryan carried two at a time. I knew he was strong, but this was ridiculous. Even more impressive: after we got to the camp and all fell prostrate in the shade, gasping for water, Bryan opened a jerry can, tasted the water, spat it out, and said calmly, "Benzine." What was impressive was his calmness. He went down the line of plastic cans. Six of eight were undrinkable. They had been used to carry fuel, and had not been properly cleaned. Bryan dragged the two cans of potable water to the base of a tree. "Looks like strict rationing," he said. "Want me to be in charge?"

Mike and José appeared to be in shock. They were silent. I said, "Sure."

The whole Grajagan misadventure went like that. Screwups, mishaps, constant thirst, and Mike and José half-catatonic. Bryan and I seemed, by comparison, seasoned and resourceful. The pattern had started in Banyuwangi. As they got daunted, we divided tasks and took care of business. Bryan and I had been traveling together for more than a year now, and it felt good—redeeming, even—to know how completely we could rely on each other. The division of water, for that matter, would be fair, I knew, down to the drop.

Boyum had built several bamboo tree houses, all but one of which had collapsed. We slept, gingerly, in the uncollapsed one. We saw no tigers,

but we heard large beasts at night, including wild bulls known as banteng
and angry-sounding boars rooting around the trunk of our tree. Sleeping
on the ground was out of the question.

Our bad luck continued during our first surf session, when Bryan came
up from a wipeout holding the side of his head, his face white with pain.
We suspected a burst eardrum. He was out of the water for the rest of the
week.

I tried to assure him that the waves were not as good as they looked,
and they really weren't. They looked incredible—long, long, long, fast,
empty lefts, six feet on the smaller days, eight-feet-plus when the swell
pulsed. I now think that José and I were surfing the wrong place. For me,
it was natural to move up the line, toward the top—to the first place
where a wave was catchable. At Grajagan it was big and sectiony and
mushy up top, but that's where I went, and José followed my lead. I figured I could connect some of the racier parts of the wave farther down.
Except I rarely could. There were always flat spots, then unmakable sections. I was misreading the reef completely. It apparently never even oc-
cured to me to move down inside, to try to find a corner in there where a
makable takeoff led to a cleaner, better-peeling wave. On the biggest day,
José wanted no part of it, and Mike, who had rarely left his mosquito net,
convinced me to paddle all the way up to where it was genuinely huge. He
even talked me into wearing a little white wetsuit vest he carried. It would
make a nice contrast with the turquoise water and my brown arms, he
said. I caught one monster wave, against my better judgment, barely making the drop on my trusty New Zealand pintail. Mike said he got the shot,
though I never saw it.

In fact, the only time that I knew for sure that he even had film in his
camera was a year or two later, when someone sent me a full-page photo,
shot by Mike, from an American surf mag. There was empty low-tide
Grajagan, with me standing in the foreground, pintail under arm. The
waves, as usual, looked magnificent.

Frustration is a big part of surfing. It's the part we all tend to forget—

stupid sessions, waves missed, waves blown, endless-seeming lulls. But the fact that frustration was the main theme of my surfing during a week of big, clean, empty waves at Grajagan is so improbable to other surfers that I haven't forgotten it. Bryan never believed it either.

My parents had sent us a pair of baseball caps from a TV movie they had worked on, *Vacation in Hell*. People would ask what the phrase meant. My Bahasa Indonesia was not up to a good translation. Bryan took to saying, "You're looking at it, friend."

Mike, when we parted—he and José went straight back to Bali—had solemnly advised us, "Indonesia is a death trap." That was melodramatic, but it was not easy traveling, on the super-cheap, up through Java and Sumatra, with surfboards. Every bus and van we caught was uncomfortably, insultingly overcrowded, as operators tried to squeeze more profit, literally, out of passengers. Still, I had to admire the heroics of the boy conductors, their incredible feats of balance, agility, and strength, clinging to doorframes at hair-raising speeds, their rapid-fire bargaining over fares, and in some cases their adroit public relations, keeping the customers at least half-satisfied. Barefoot, dressed in rags, these brilliant kids made American trainmen, always carefully dismounting locomotives and freight cars per our detailed instruction manuals, always wearing our steel-toed boots, look like pikers.

We caught a train across part of Java. Hanging out the window to catch the breeze, I was struck by how, for somebody seeing Indonesia from a train, the main business of the nation seemed to be defecation. Every stream, river, weir, and rice-paddy canal that the tracks crossed seemed to be lined with farmers and villagers placidly squatting. It was a tour of the world's biggest, most picturesque toilet, and it reminded me that I had vowed to be more careful about what I ate and drank after my Bali paratyphoid follies. I was still eating at street stalls, though, and we were still staying in dives. I had contracted malaria, in any case, at Plengkung. But

I didn't know that yet. Bryan's eardrum, meanwhile, was indeed burst, said a doctor in Jakarta. He gave him some drops, and said it would heal.

Rural Southeast Asia, in its intense tropicality, bore a superficial resemblance to rural Polynesia. But the differences between the two regions were far more pronounced. Vast civilizations had risen here on the surplus created by rice-based agriculture. Hundreds of millions of people lived and jostled here, in incomprehensibly complex caste societies. I took to interviewing people, semiformally—it was an odd thing to do, with no particular project in mind, but I was curious and they often seemed pleased to be asked—about their family histories, income, prospects, hopes. A rice farmer near Jogjakarta, who was a retired army captain, gave me a detailed account of his career, his farm's operating expenses, his oldest son's progress at university. Across nearly every story I heard, however, a thick veil fell around the period of 1965–66, when more than half a million Indonesians were killed in massacres led by the military and Islamic clerics. The main targets had been communists and alleged communists, but ethnic Chinese and Christians had also died or been dispossessed en masse. The Suharto dictatorship that emerged from the bloodbath was still in power, and the massacres were suppressed history, not taught in schools or publicly discussed. A pedal-taxi driver in Padang, a port city in western Sumatra, told me quietly about spending years in prison as a suspected leftist. He had been a professor before the great purge. He liked Americans, but the American government, he said, had aided and applauded the killing.

Sumatra was for us a refreshing change from Java. More mountainous, less crowded, more prosperous, less stifling, at least in the areas we traversed. We had a treasure map, given to us in the South Pacific by an intrepid Australian kneeboarder who said she had surfed a great wave on Pulau Nias, an island west of Sumatra. It was no longer a secret spot, apparently, but a key threshold had not yet been crossed—no photos had been published. We caught a small, spartan, diesel-powered ferry from Padang. It was about two hundred miles to Nias, and a storm clobbered

us the first night out. We wallowed in total darkness. At times, terrify-
ingly, we seemed to lose steerage. Waves washed across the deck. The only
cabin was a small, grimy plywood hut for the helmsman. Most of the
passengers were sick. But people were amazingly tough. Nobody screamed.
Everybody prayed. We were lucky no one went overboard. We were lucky
the old tub didn't sink. We putt-putted into Teluk Dalam, a little port on
the south end of Nias, on a muggy gray morning. There was nothing
about Teluk Dalam, I thought, that would have been out of place in a Joseph Conrad novel. Nias had a population of five hundred thousand and
no electricity.

The wave was about ten miles west, near a village called Lagundri. The
kneeboarder was correct. It was an immaculate right. It broke off a point,
but it was really a reefbreak, since the wave did not follow the shoreline. It
stood up distinctively, a ruler-straight wall, when it hit the reef, but then it
peeled across, away from the shore, without sections, for probably eighty
yards, barreling beautifully into the wind, before it hit deep water. A small
company of tall coconut trees on the point leaned out over the water, as if
they wanted to get a better look at the wave. It was a splendid sight, truly.
Lagundri Bay was horseshoe-shaped and deep. The village, roughly a mile
down from the point and separated from the beach by a palm grove, was a
modest collection of fishermen's shacks except for one imposing, rather
ornate three-story wooden house with an elaborately peaked roof. This
was the *losmen*. There were four or five surfers staying there, all Aussies. If
the other surfers were dismayed that we showed up, they hid it well. We
hung our mosquito nets on a second-floor balcony.

It was on that balcony that Bryan told me he was bailing. I remember,
when he said it, that I was reading a biography of Mark Twain, by Justin
Kaplan, that we had traded back and forth. It was a hot afternoon. We
were waiting out the worst of the heat before a late-day go-out. The news
was not a complete surprise. Bryan had been muttering about meeting
Diane in Europe during her summer vacation.

Still, it hurt. I kept my eyes on the book.

It wasn't me, he said, after I asked. He was just tired. And homesick. And sick of traveling. Diane had given him an ultimatum, but he was ready to go. He would look for a cheap flight in Singapore or Bangkok, probably head out in late July. That was six or seven weeks away.

WE SURFED. The swell was remarkably consistent for the first week or so. The brilliance of the wave seemed only to increase. It was ridable at all tides. It never seemed to blow out. There was a little reverse current running out to sea from the bottom of the bay that helped keep the surface groomed in all conditions. Paddling out was absurdly easy. You walked to the point, beyond the wave, slipped through a keyhole in the reef, and arrived in the lineup with hair dry. Except for being a world-class right, it was the categorical opposite of Kirra. There was no demonic current to fight. If every surfer within five hundred miles had been out at the same time, there would still have been no crowd. And where Kirra's essential quality was breathtaking compression, the wave on Nias felt like pure expansion. It invited you to move farther up, get in earlier, take a higher line, pull in deeper. The takeoff was steep but straightforward. You just had to get over the ledge and be on the wave when it jacked. There was no time to carve big turns on the main wall. It was a run-and-gun wave, with a glorious tube if you took a high line and timed it well on a wave that opened up. It wasn't a top-to-bottom barrel—it was what is known as an almond-shaped barrel—although it broke hard enough to snap boards. The wave wasn't extremely long, like Tavarua, but neither was it dangerously shallow. And the wave on Nias had an extraordinary grace note. The last ten yards of the main wall, just before it hit deep water, stood up extra-tall. The face there was, for no obvious reason, often several feet taller than the rest of the wave. This great green slope, particularly the top third of it, begged for a high-speed flourish, a maneuver to remember, a demonstration of both gratitude and mastery.

I peaked, in some ways, as a surfer on Nias, although I didn't know it at the time. I was twenty-six, probably stronger than I had ever been, as quick as I would ever be. I was on the right board, on the right wave. I had been surfing consistently for a year-plus. I felt like I could do almost anything on a wave that occurred to me. When the surf got bigger, late that week, I doubled down and surfed with more abandon. The extra-tall end-section let me bank off the top from a height that I had never before attempted, and mostly I came down cleanly on my board. I did know that I had never surfed so loosely in waves that size. I felt immortal.

ALTHOUGH IT WAS THE DRY SEASON, a two-day rainstorm flooded the village and filled the bay with brown freshwater, which seemed to kill the waves.

I went to bed feeling weird and woke up with a fever. I assumed it was a paratyphoid relapse. More likely, it was malaria. I started feeling less immortal. Maybe Indonesia was a death trap. Three Australian surfers had discovered the wave at Lagundri in 1975, and one of them, John Giesel, after repeated bouts of malaria, had died, reportedly of pneumonia, nine months later. He was twenty-three. One of the two guys who first surfed Grajagan, an American named Bob Laverty—the other guy was Mike Boyum's brother—died only a few days after returning to Bali. He drowned at Uluwatu. Mike Boyum survived Indonesia but got into cocaine smuggling, went to jail in Vanuatu, and later died, while living under an alias, at a great wave he found in the Philippines.

I was also tired, and homesick, and sick of traveling. I wasn't tempted to quit Asia with Bryan, but I was having trouble remembering exactly why I was here. There was surfing, but it wasn't going to get any better than Lagundri. I simply couldn't picture returning to the United States. I copied out a passage from *Lord Jim*: "We wander in our thousands over the face of the earth, the illustrious and the obscure, earning beyond the seas our fame, our money, or only a crust of bread; but it seems to me that for each of us going home must be like going to render an account." I was

not ready for that accounting. For one thing, I couldn't return to the
United States without finishing this novel. I thought about it constantly,
filling journals with plotting, rethinking, self-castigation, and exhorta-
tions to greater efforts, but I hadn't written any new material since Bali.
Where could I hole up and get back to work? Writing felt like it justified,
barely, my existence—this extremity of obscurity I had perversely chosen.
But I was also starting to worry about money. We were living on a few
dollars a day, but cities like Singapore and Bangkok would be a different
story. Bryan had enough to get home. Running out of money in Southeast
Asia could be grim. I doubted that Sharon had much saved. We would
need to be frugal.

But it was farcical, gross, I knew, for me to be fretting about money in
Lagundri, where the ambient ironies of the Asia Trail were never far away.
The Asia Trail was the great snaking overland route from Europe to Bali,
slogged down by thousands of Western backpackers since the '60s. It was
being broken into pieces in 1979 by the Iranian revolution, and the So-
viet invasion of Afghanistan was about to remove another poverty-ridden,
dope-rich Shangri-la from the itinerary. But the trail, which included a
main stop at Lake Toba, in north Sumatra, also had a tiny tributary that
ran out to Nias. This had little to do with surfing as yet. It existed, apparently, because of the local culture, which had developed in relative
isolation and included stone megaliths, spectacular ironwood architecture
known as *omo sebua*, war dances, and hilltop villages with houses mod-
eled after the Dutch galleons of slave-trading days. And so an odd collection of European hippies and tourists wandered up the coastal road
through Lagundri. The villagers looked askance at them all, particularly
the bedraggled backpackers. It was not hard to see why. Here was a large,
awkward member of the global ruling elite who had probably spent more
in an air-travel day than anyone on Nias could make in a year of hard
work, all for the pleasure of leaving an unimaginably rich, clean place for
this desperately poor, unhealthy place. Here he was struggling blindly
down the road under an enormous pack, disoriented and ignorant and

sweating like a donkey. He wanted to see Asia from the ground, not from the Hilton height of some air-conditioned resort that any sane person would prefer. The complex ambitions and aversions that brought the poor backpacker seven thousand miles to struggle and suffer from dysentery, heatstroke, or worse in the equatorial jungle—anything to be a "traveler" and not a "tourist"!—were perhaps impossible to untangle, but it was well known that he brought so little money that he was hardly worth hustling.

Bryan and I were in the same economic bracket, of course. And being a rich *orang putih* in a poor brown world still sucked irredeemably. We, that is, sucked.

The family that ran the *losmen* in Lagundri was Muslim, which made them unusual on Nias, which is predominantly Christian. In the nearby villages, the churches shook with fervent song. On the jungle paths, small unsmiling men with machetes tucked in their waistbands carried enormous jute bags of coconuts. Our hosts were affable, and relatively cosmopolitan—they came from Sumatra—and they warned us against going beyond the village at night. The local Christianity was strictly nominal, they said. During World War II, when the island was cut off from the outside world, congregations had swiftly reverted to precolonial practice and eaten the Dutch and German missionaries among them. I was unable to verify this gory gossip.

My fever alternated with chills. A headache was constant. I was taking chloroquine, a popular malaria prophylaxis, unaware that it was useless against many local strains of the disease. Indonesian villagers often asked for pills without specifying what kind. Vitamins, aspirin, antibiotics— there seemed to be a general faith in pills. At first I thought the requests might be for sick relatives or friends, or for stockpiling against illness, but then I saw perfectly healthy-looking people pop whatever was handed over, no questions asked. It would have been funny if it weren't so ominous. Now that I was sick, people left me alone. Babies wailed. I listlessly read a collection of Donald Barthelme stories. Lines stuck in my head.

"Call up Bomba the Jungle Boy? Get his input?" Boney M's execrable, inescapable "Rivers of Babylon" wheezed from a village teenager's tape deck.

I listened to Bryan and the Aussies shooting the breeze. Bryan was on a roll. He had them blowing Sumatran coffee through their noses. I heard him say, "Oh yeah, if a surf spot's too far from town in the States, we just call up the Army Corps of Engineers and they move it. Takes two or three days, a lot of trucks, they have to close the whole highway. Sometimes they bring the whole bay, other times just the reef and the wave. You should see it going down the road—guys still surfing it and everything. They have to go really, really slow. It's quite an operation."

I would miss him unspeakably. He said it wasn't me, but I knew it partly was. We pulled together nearly effortlessly now, and we hadn't quarreled in months, but the subterranean dynamics of our partnership had not changed. I was after something, whatever it was. And the chemistry of my brashness and what Bryan called his passivity, which he had been noting since Air Nauru and the Guam Hilton, was not doing him any good. He did not want to feel like he was along for the ride. He had to get away. But what would this long, strange trip be like without him? He and I spoke a language no one else understood. "Oh, wow, a new experience"—that was what we were supposed to say after an earthquake, or if someone stole our car, according to Teka of Tonga. But we said it after smaller fiascoes—hell nights on leaky ferries, days of unslaked thirst brought on by dirty jerry cans. "Radio Ethiopia"—that was an unlistenable Patti Smith song, some secondhand Rimbaud trope. But it stood for all faux-exotic hipster posing—names dropped in New York of places never visited, let alone lived through. We felt superior to, if also vaguely threatened by, all that. Those were the people getting on with careers in the arts, having what Bryan sometimes called Suckcess. Now he was going back to the United States. I was staying in Ethiopia. I was silently envious.

I started feeling stronger, started taking little walks. On a jungle path I met an old man who reached out and silently patted my belly. It was his way of saying good morning.

"*Jam berapa?*" What time is it? That was the question kids loved to ask, pointing at their watchless wrists.

"*Jam karet.*" Rubber time. It was a stock joke answer, meaning that time was a flexible concept in Indonesia.

People I met would often demand, "*Dimana?*" Where are you going?

"*Jalan, jalan, saja.*" Walking, walking, only.

Everybody in Indonesia always wanted to know if I was married. It was rude to answer, "*Tidak*"—no. That was too blunt. It disrespected marriage. Better to say "*Belum*"—not yet.

I wondered what Sharon would make of Nias. She had been dauntless in Morocco, game for any casbah detour. I began telling people in Lagundri that I was going to Singapore but would be back in a few months. They put in their orders: a man's silver Seiko automatic watch; a Mikasa volleyball; a guestbook for the *losmen*. I started a list of things I wished we'd brought: honey, whiskey, duct tape, dried fruit, nuts, powdered milk, oatmeal. More protein would be welcome. Meat and even, oddly enough, fresh fish were rarities in Lagundri. Our meals were mostly rice and collard greens, with hot chilies to help fight bacteria. Like everyone, we ate with our hands. A fisherman in Java had taught me the best way to eat rice with your fingers. You used the first three fingers as a trough and the back of the thumb as a shovel. It worked. But I needed more food, more vitamins. My boardshorts were falling off my hips.

The sun came back out. The mud in the bay cleared up.

I caught a ride into Teluk Dalam on the back of a motorbike. I had heard that there was a shop in town with a generator and an icebox. I found the shop, and put two large bottles of Bintang, the Indonesian version of Heineken, in the icebox. I wandered around town, sent Sharon a telegram reconfirming our plans to meet. Then, when the beers were cold, I packed them in sawdust and raced back to Lagundri. I presented them to Bryan on the second-floor balcony, still icy. I thought he might weep with joy. I nearly did. Few things in my life have tasted better than those beers. Even we were speechless.

Everything had a valedictory feel. Bryan asked me to take a picture of him "for the grandkids." He stood on the beach with his board, looking mock-heroically into the sunset. He was wearing a sarong, which everybody, including both local men and foreigners, normally did, but Bryan normally didn't.

The surf got good again. But it always seemed to be late afternoon, the golden hour. On our last evening, without any discussion, Bryan and I took off on a wave together—something we never did. We rode for a while, then straightened off and rode the whitewater on our bellies, side by side, across the reef, giving each other a fist bump as we glided into the shallows.

SINGAPORE WAS A SHOCK after three months in Indonesia. It was so orderly, rich, and clean. Sharon, when we met at the airport, was shocked by how aggressive Bryan and I were with cabdrivers and street porters. I tried to explain that we were suffering from post-Indonesia stress syndrome, and didn't know how to act around people who weren't trying to haggle us into the ground. It was true, but she seemed unconvinced.

Our hotel room was air-conditioned. Sharon had brought an old-fashioned nightgown, elaborate, white, with a Victorian number of small buttons down the front. The gown could be simply thrown off upward, but the buttons were genius.

Bryan went to Hong Kong to see friends, and we stole off to Ko Samui, an island in the Gulf of Thailand, where we stayed in a bungalow on the beach. It was quiet, lovely, Buddhist, cheap. (Later, I heard, hundreds of hotels got built there. At the time it was just fishermen and coconut farmers.) There were no waves, no electricity, good snorkeling. Sharon, fresh from Northern California, seemed a bit dazed by rural Southeast Asia— the ferocious heat, implacable insects, the lack of creature comforts. And yet she was in high spirits: relieved to have finished her doctorate, happy to have flown the academic coop. When we first met, she had been a

Chaucer specialist, but she had ended up writing a dissertation on the samurai figure in recent American fiction. "The latitudes of tolerance are immense," she liked to say, quoting Philip K. Dick—referring here to her flexible dissertation advisers, there to arcane sexual practice, and most often to a general philosophical effort to comprehend the unfamiliar. She had deep reserves of adaptability herself, and a kind of romantic interest in preindustrial life that I knew well, although in me, I realized, it had faded. I was glad, and very grateful, she had come. She announced that she was keen to go to the hill country in northern Thailand, and to Burma— Rangoon, Mandalay—and she said yes to Sumatra and Nias. Her skin began to lose its fogbound pallor. Her laugh kicked back in—that high- low laugh, with its throaty, theatrical ending that drew you in.

I felt somewhat lost, truth be known. After Indonesia, I found the absence of hassling, the unbegrudged privacy on Ko Samui, unnerving. There was almost too much time and space in which to concentrate on each other. I was accustomed—deeply accustomed, by that point—to a different type of companionship. Also to constantly chasing waves, or at least slogging toward them. So this was my new life. We were both being careful—if anything, too polite. But we had brought a bottle of whiskey from Singapore, and when we broke that open we got more reckless. I had changed, apparently, become leaner and darker, and not just physically. I was more measured, even reserved, which Sharon found discomfiting. She, meanwhile, made pronouncements I found annoying. "These people have a very special love for children," she said one day, watching a family pass down a dirt track. It was a sweet, or at least an innocuous, thing to say, but it gave me heartburn. She seemed to mean the Thai people—all forty-six million of them, perhaps three of whom she had met. It was just a style problem, I told myself. I had been speaking a different language— more cutting, ironic, masculine, permanently on guard against sounding silly—for a long time. I was fluent in that dialect, which had its lecherous crudities. I just needed to learn, or relearn, a new shared language. Sharon demanded to know why I got so particular with her—"hypercritical" might have been the word she wanted—after she had a few drinks. Was I so intolerant with Bryan when he got tipsy? The answer was no. So I bit my tongue when I had mean thoughts. It didn't help that I was feeling vaguely unwell. I had been felled briefly in Singapore by another fever, which a doctor had said was malaria. It must have been a mild case, I figured, when the symptoms passed. Sharon urged me to eat more rice and noodles. I was all ropy muscle. A body needed some fat reserves. And it was lovely, I realized, to have somebody looking after me, looking *at* me, like that.

We headed to Bangkok, where we reconvened with Bryan, staying in a big, seedy place called the Station Hotel. The city was hot, chaotic, exciting, exhausting, with bright river taxis racing up and down the canals, stunning Buddhist temples, great street *satay*, and a rather European-looking palace. An impressive amount of drug consumption and petty drug trafficking seemed to be taking place at our hotel, among both Westerners and Asians. The presence of multiple criminal underworlds was palpable in certain quarters of Bangkok. I had a couple of assignments from *Tracks*—pieces about Indonesia beyond Bali—and I worked on those. Bryan's byline would also be on them—Australian youth expected no less—after he gave my copy a light edit. But the fees would be meager, whenever they found us, and I was increasingly worried about money. With an income tax refund received, incredibly, from that worker's paradise, Australia, I had just over a thousand dollars. Sharon had less than that. A cherubic German hustler in Sibolga, Sumatra, had offered to buy all my traveler's checks for sixty cents on the dollar—all I had to do, he said, was report them stolen and I would get a complete refund—and I now wished I had thought more seriously about doing it. The Station Hotel had more Asia Trail hustlers per square foot than any place we'd been. Maybe I could sell my traveler's checks here. Bryan and Sharon both rejected the idea. It was risky and wrong and I would be out of my league. All true, of course. But our stints as illegal alien laborers in Oz had worked out well, had they not?

The news was full of a humanitarian crisis on the Thai-Cambodian border. The Vietnamese army had driven the Khmer Rouge from power early that year, and a large number of refugees had been driven over the border. The Khmer Rouge had gone back to the bush and had forces in the same area, fighting the Vietnamese and increasing the general misery. I found myself poring over maps and news stories, wondering what it would take to get down there as a relief-agency volunteer. It was only a day's drive away. Two young Frenchwomen I met at a café were going. One was a photojournalist, the other a nurse. There would be no money in it for me, and I hadn't broached the idea yet with Sharon, but she had read Robert Stone's *Dog Soldiers*—indeed, it was in her dissertation. The literary action was in Vietnam, or at least in its endlesss aftershocks. Amid this scheming and war dreaming, I made up my mind and went to the local American Express office, where I reported that I'd lost my traveler's checks. The clerk who took my false report seemed skeptical, causing my mouth to go dry with fear, but the German hustler turned out to be right. I had a full refund in a day or two. Still, I had no idea what to do with the original checks, which were now hot goods. Defrauding American Express apparently seemed to me a fine, Robin Hood–ish thing to do. I was sticking it to a corporation that normally stuck it to everyone else. Indeed, it seemed wimpy compared with the derring-do of some of my literary idols. Dean Moriarty stole cars for kicks. William Burroughs! Bryan and Sharon were unimpressed when I told them about my caper. They suggested I flush the old checks down a toilet if I didn't want to end up in a Bangkok jail.

All this went away the following night, in any event, when I ended up instead in a Bangkok hospital. It was an excellent little garden hospital, the best my friends could find. My memory of that night, and of the subsequent days, is watery and dim. I know I developed a high fever, began to rave, and was too weak to walk across a hotel room, let alone resist the decision to hospitalize me. I know I was horrified by the fanciness of the place they took me to—it was a clinic for foreign diplomats, apparently—

but was told firmly to shut up. The doctor was German. She said that my blood was "black with malaria" and that I should be flown immediately to the United States. At that point, my friends hesitated. I was able to make my absolute opposition to such a drastic measure understood, and they were reluctant to overrule me. There was discussion of my survival chances, and of all the malaria cases the doctor had seen in forty years in Asia. They did not put me on a plane.

Dark days ensued. Wild, aching fevers turned into rattling, arctic chills. I lost a startling amount of weight, bottoming out at 135 pounds. (I'm six foot two.) The old doctor—her name was Dr. Ettinger—was severe but kind. She said that I was a lucky boy and would survive. Small nurses gave me big shots in both hips. I was so listless that I did not leave my bed for a week. Paranoia and depression annexed my brain. I couldn't bear to think about the unpayable bill that was mounting up. Bryan and Sharon came daily and entertained me with stories from the Bangkok beyond the quiet lawns and hedges I could see. But it was hard for me to laugh or smile. I felt lost, spiritually, and the growing suspicion that I was wasting my life came back with a vengeance. I wished my father would appear and give me some concrete, comprehensive advice. I would follow it to the letter. Not that I wanted my parents to know I was ill. And they didn't know.

Then Bryan stopped coming to visit. Sharon was vague about his reasons. He was meeting with some people. I decided that the two of them were sleeping together. I went over in my mind, many times, an incident at the Station Hotel. Bryan had been sitting in our room. Sharon was taking a shower. She had strolled out of the bathroom naked, and Bryan had bellowed and covered his eyes. She laughed and called him a prude, while he groaned and begged her to put something on and kept his eyes covered. At the time, I had thought it was funny. She knew she looked great nude, and she got a kick out of shocking him. They were good friends and she knew that under his macho bawdiness was a certain primness and a strict sense of boundaries. So she enjoyed teasing him. That was all. There was no sexual tension between them, I thought.

But maybe I was wrong. Or maybe she was having her revenge on me for being a selfish jerk, leaving her hanging forever while I chased waves. Once, exasperated by my travels with Bryan, she had shocked me by saying, "Why don't you two just fuck each other and get it over with?" It was so off the mark and, in its fatuous literalism, not like her. But how well did I really know her? How well, for that matter, did I know him? I had never told him she said that, but I could imagine his reply if I had—"Right on, Tom." It was his go-to quip, which I alone understood, when the subject was male homosexuality. But I had misjudged my friends before, and had been sexually betrayed.

The nights were the worst. I felt trapped in a tropical version of Goya's *Pinturas Negras*. Ghouls seemed to surround my bed, their shadows on the walls. My headache filled the world. I couldn't sleep. I knew, rationally, that Bryan and Sharon had done the right thing by bringing me here. They had probably saved my life. I was getting good care. But the bill was now so far beyond my means, I would be lucky if they—and did that mean the hospital? the U.S. embassy?—let me buy an air ticket home. I would return to the States in disgrace—penniless, my health broken, a failure.

Late one night, long after visiting hours, Bryan showed up at my bedside. He was carrying a large shopping bag. He didn't say a word. He turned the bag upside down and dumped its contents—many fat, dirty bundles of Thai baht, the local currency—on my lap. It was a lot of money. It would be enough to cover most, if not all, of my hospital bill, he said. He looked exhausted, triumphant, angry, a bit crazed.

I never got the full story, but I got the gist from Sharon. Bryan, seeing that my situation was desperate, had looked through my bags in our room and found the checks I had reported lost. (I had long forgotten, in my delirium, that they existed.) Then he had gone out and sold them, for sixty cents on the dollar, to Chinese gangsters. It had not been a straightforward transaction. He had refused to hand over the goods until he had payment in full in hand. The whole thing had taken days, and had turned into the haggle to end all haggles. It was all totally unlike Bryan, from beginning to end, and yet he had prevailed. For the two of us, it was a full role reversal. He took a huge risk, freed me from the hospital, and in the process freed himself from me.

SHARON AND I did make it to Nias eventually. It was monsoon season by then, though, and the rains messed up the waves. There were also fifteen surfers in Lagundri, and the reason why was presented to me on arrival: a ravishing photo of the ravishing wave had appeared in an American surf magazine. The era of semisecrecy was over. Fifteen guys would soon be fifty guys. Many people in the village, including children, seemed to be sick. It was endemic malaria, the *losmen* owners said. People begging for random medicines was even less funny now. I was taking a new prophylaxis for malaria—two, in fact—and still hobbling from the big injections the little nurses had given me months before in Bangkok. There were a few days of good waves. I found I had regained enough strength to surf. The volleyball, guestbook, and watch were graciously received. But these little tokens of exchange now felt, to me, gruesomely beside the point.

We pushed on, always edging west. We caught a ship from Malaysia to India, sleeping out on the deck. We rented a little house in the jungle in southwest Sri Lanka, paying twenty-nine dollars a month. Sharon was ostensibly quarrying articles from her dissertation. I resumed work on my novel. We got Chinese bicycles, and each morning I rode mine, board under arm, down a trail to the beach, where a decent wave broke most days. We had no electricity and drew our water from a well. Monkeys stole unguarded fruit. Sharon learned to make delectable curry from our landlady, Chandima. A madwoman lived across the way. She roared and howled day and night. The insects—mosquitoes, ants, centipedes, flies—were relentless. At a Buddhist monastery down the hill, young monks held rowdy parties, blasting taped music and banging on cowbells till dawn. I heard a lot of anti-Tamil talk—we were living in a Sinhalese district—but this was before the civil war.

I wonder now if Sharon had any interest in my grand travel plan, or if she even knew what it was. It was corny, so I never mentioned it, my ambition to go, without too many shortcuts, around the world. I remember, back on the morning I left Missoula, telling a friend there. We were standing on the sidewalk, surrounded by dim snowy mountains, outside the café where she worked. That day, I said, I was heading west, to the coast. When I came back—pause for hokey effect—it would be from the east. She cocked her head and laughed and dared me to do it.

Sharon was interested in Africa, so our notions were still in step. We kept going west. We looked for a ship to Kenya or Tanzania, but both countries required visas that weren't available in Sri Lanka. We ended up flying to South Africa. In Johannesburg we bought an old station wagon and made our way to the coast at Durban. We car-camped down through Natal and the Transkei to Cape Town. I surfed. This was 1980, still the heyday of apartheid. I continued to do my informal interviews of randomly encountered people. Here those yielded great hauls of weirdness: inscrutable evasions from polite black workers and country folk; the most relaxed and profound racism from white fellow campers. Sharon and I were on a steep learning curve, reading Gordimer, Coetzee, Fugard, Breytenbach, Brinks—their unbanned work, anyway. Every surfer was white, which was no great surprise. For the next leg of our rambles, we had a bold idea: a huge tack to the north, "Cape to Cairo," overland. But we were running out of money.

In Cape Town we heard that the local black schools suffered from a perennial shortage of teachers, and that the academic year was just beginning. Someone gave me a list of township schools. At the second school I visited, Grassy Park Senior Secondary, the principal, a blustery fellow named George Van den Heever, hired me on the spot. I would teach English, geography, and something called religious instruction, starting immediately. My students, who wore uniforms and ranged in age from twelve to twenty-three, seemed gobsmacked to find a clueless white American standing in their classroom, wearing brown plastic loafers from Sri Lanka and a three-dollar striped tie bought that morning at Woolworth's, but they swallowed their doubts and called me "sir" and were for the most part helpful and kind.

Sharon and I rented a room in a damp old turquoise house overlooking False Bay, on the Indian Ocean side of the Cape of Good Hope. The Cape Peninsula is a long, spindly finger pointing south at Antarctica. At the peninsula's base—its north end—sits a spectacular high massif, and the city of Cape Town wraps itself around that. The north face of the massif is Table Mountain, which overlooks the city center. The black people of Cape Town had been banished en masse from the city to a scrubby wasteland to the east called the Cape Flats—one of apartheid's signature acts of rabid and remorseless social engineering. Grassy Park was a "coloured" township on the Flats—a poor, crime-ridden community, and yet far less wretched than some of the shantytowns that surrounded it. We lived, by law, in a "white area." Since Grassy Park was only a few miles from the False Bay coast, my commute actually wasn't bad. Out in front of our dank mansion, there was a wide, shapeless beachbreak, which I surfed when I wasn't too busy grading papers or planning lessons.

My job became all-consuming. Sharon considered teaching too, but she had paperwork problems with the bureaucracy. Then word came that her mother was seriously ill. She threw her things in a bag and flew to Los Angeles. I muttered about going with her, but I didn't seriously consider it. It had been a year since she came to Singapore. We had found a good rhythm together—our curiosities overlapped; we rarely quarreled. But I had projects: a novel, a circumnavigation, places I wanted to surf, and, now, teaching in Grassy Park. Sharon's goals were less immediate, less evident. With my usual one-eyed thoughtlessness, I never asked her what she wanted. We never talked about the future. She was nearly thirty-five. The truth was, we were mismatched. I had somehow kept her interested for years, but I wasn't what she wanted. Meanwhile, I took her for granted. We made no plans or vows when she left Cape Town.

. . .

ONE OF THE REASONS teaching became so engrossing was that it was impossible to teach using the textbooks we were given. They were rank with apartheid propaganda and misinformation. The geography curriculum, for instance, included a section on South Africa's neighbors that depicted them as peaceful Portuguese colonies. Even I knew that, in fact, Mozambique and Angola had both fought long, bloody wars of national liberation, had thrown out the Portuguese some years before, and were both now fighting desperate civil wars in which South Africa was arming and training the rebels. Our curriculum's version of South African urban geography was, in its way, worse. It treated residential racial segregation, for instance, as if it were a law of nature, peacefully evolved. Presenting this regime-serving fiction as fact in a community that existed only because of violent mass evictions from downtown neighborhoods designated "white" was clearly not on. So I buried myself in research, trying to quickly learn up these and other topics, which turned out to be harder than expected. Many of the relevant books were banned. I found my way to a special section of the University of Cape Town's library where some banned publications could be consulted, not checked out, but I was still, of course, playing hapless catch-up when it came to local and regional politics and history.

Not that my students seemed particularly concerned about my expertise or lack thereof. They nearly all declined to be brought out on political subjects—whether from indifference or wariness of me, I couldn't tell. The exceptions were among the seniors I saw, ostensibly for religious instruction. At their insistence, we never cracked the Bibles that were our sole textbooks, but passed our class time in free-ranging discussion. Their favorite topics were careers, computers, and the pros and cons of premarital sex. Among the seniors not averse to talking politics was a brooding, worldly boy named Cecil Prinsloo. He knew somehow about my efforts to teach my academic classes something other than the government syllabus.

Some of my students, Grassy Park High School,
Cape Town, 1980

He started staying after class to talk, questioning me closely about my background and views, testing my feeble grasp of the situation in South Africa. The only real resistance to my efforts to end-run the syllabus came not from my students but from my more conservative colleagues. They too had heard that I wasn't simply preparing my classes for the standard examinations they would eventually face, and they let me know that this was unacceptable. I couldn't see what to do. Luckily, none of my students in the exam subjects I taught were facing standardized national exams that year. Those were another year or two away for them. So my abandoning the toxic syllabus wasn't putting them in immediate academic peril. I tried to reconcile myself to the good chance that I would soon be fired. I had no job security—just the principal's goodwill. And the principal was quite conservative himself. But I really, really didn't want to stop teaching.

Everything changed one April morning when our students suddenly started boycotting their classes, protesting apartheid in education. I say it was sudden because it stunned me. In truth, the boycott had been long and carefully planned. The school was plastered with banners: DOWN WITH GUTTER EDUCATION; RELEASE ALL POLITICAL PRISONERS. The students were marching, singing, fists raised, roaring the Zulu call-and-response of the liberation struggle:

"*Amandla!*" (Power!)

"*NGAWETHU!*" (To the people!)

At a mass meeting in the school courtyard, Cecil Prinsloo told the crowd, "*This is not a holiday from school.*" He emphasized every word. "This is a holiday from brainwashing."

Other Cape Flats high schools were also boycotting, and the protest quickly went national. Within weeks, two hundred thousand students were refusing their lessons, demanding an end to apartheid. At Grassy Park High, the students continued to come to school each day, organizing, with the help of sympathetic teachers, an alternate curriculum. I was among the sympathetic teachers. With revolution-minded students now in charge, my previous deviations from the syllabus no longer seemed like derelictions, and I stopped fearing for my job. My classes on the U.S. Bill of Rights were packed. It was a chaotic, exhilarating period.

But the exhilaration was short-lived—a matter of a few weeks. The authorities had been wrongfooted. The prime minister, P. W. Botha, blustered and threatened, but the state's enormous machinery of repression seemed slow to lurch into gear. Once it did, however, the atmosphere darkened fast. Student leaders, including some from our school, and revolution-minded teachers, including my colleague Matthew Cloete, who taught in the classroom next to mine, began to disappear—some into hiding, most into the regime's jails. It was called detention without charges, and the number of known detainees quickly soared into the hundreds.

The confrontation escalated. In Cape Town it climaxed in a general strike in mid-June. For two days, hundreds of thousands of black workers stayed home. Factories and businesses were forced to close. The police, now armored and fully mobilized, attacked illegal gatherings—and all gatherings of black people were effectively illegal now, under something called the Riotous Assemblies Act. Burning and looting began, and the police announced that they would "shoot to kill." The Cape Flats became a battlefield. Hospitals reported hundreds of maimed and injured. The press reported forty-two dead. Many of the dead and injured were children. The schools were all closed now, along with all the roads into Grassy Park. Information was hard to come by. When the roads reopened, I drove to Grassy Park. The destruction in some areas of the Flats was extensive, but our school was fine. I found three of my students. They said that they had stayed inside their houses throughout the violence. It seemed that none of our students had been hurt, which felt like a miracle.

Three weeks later, classes resumed. We were only halfway through the school year and, as the principal kept reminding us, there was a great deal of extra work to do now.

DID I SURF while my world abruptly compacted into a township high school and a few dozen teenagers there? Some. There were good waves on the Atlantic side of the Cape, where the water was surprisingly cold—my parents sent me my wetsuit. Heavy swells rolled in from the Southern Ocean as winter commenced. Most of the better spots were in rocky coves, some of them right in the city, hard by swanky apartment blocks. Others were farther down the mountainous, windswept Cape. My favorite spot was a quiet country righthander called Noordhoek. It broke at the north end of a magnificent sweep of empty beach: an A-framed peak with a lovely inside wall, good on southeast winds. The water was often a luminous blue-green. I sometimes surfed it completely alone. One afternoon I climbed the hill back to my car and found it full of baboons. I had left a window open. The monkeys had made themselves comfortable and did not scare easily. I ended up having to use my board as épée, club, and shield when they staged frightening mock attacks, teeth bared, before ambling off.

The place I was waiting on, though, was in the Eastern Cape, some four hundred miles up the Indian Ocean coast from Cape Town. It was called Jeffreys Bay, and no circumnavigation on a surfboard would be complete without a stop there. *The Endless Summer*, a 1964 film that warped the career goals of many young surfers, including me, climaxed near Jeffreys, when two American surfers found "the perfect wave" at Cape St. Francis. The spot featured in the film turned out to be a fickle creature, not often ridable, but Jeffreys Bay was the real thing: a long right point of the highest quality, with heaps of swell in the winter and frequent offshore winds. I tried to keep my eye on conditions, and I made a couple of quick trial runs from Cape Town without catching it especially good. Then, in August, I went for a week on a promising weather map: two big low-pressure spirals in the Roaring Forties. They looked like wave-generating storms spinning right in the window for Jeffreys.

And they were. The surf pumped all week, peaking on a day so big that only one guy made it out—a number of us tried and failed—and he caught only one wave. Jeffreys Bay was a tiny, tumbledown fishing village with a few stucco summer houses scattered through the aloes. I stayed in a weatherbeaten boardinghouse in the dunes east of the village. There were four or five Australians also staying there, and it was comforting, I found, to be back in the easy company of Aussie surfers. The great wave was just down the beach, farther east. There were few people around— rarely more than ten surfers in the water—and with the size of the waves and the length of the rides we were generally scattered up and down the point. On a couple of mornings I was the first one out, slipping through a keyhole that I'd seen the locals use near the top of the point. There was often an icy offshore wind, and at sunrise the waves approached out of a blinding sea. As soon as you caught one, though, the wave threw a deep green-and-silver shadow inside which, as you rose to your feet, everything became radiantly clear.

It was an astoundingly long ride. Longer even than Tavarua. And it was a right—on my frontside. The two spots are not actually similar. Jeffreys is rocky but not especially shallow. It's a facey wave, a broad canvas for sweeping long-radius turns, including cutbacks toward the hook. It's fast and it's powerful but it's not particularly hollow—it has no bone-crushing sections à la Kirra. Some waves have flat sections, or weird bumps, or go mushy; others close out. The rule, however, is a reeling wall, peeling continuously for hundreds of yards. My pale blue New Zealand pintail loved that wave. Even at double-overhead, dropping in against the wind, it never skittered. Some of the biggest sets that week nobody wanted, at least not out at the main takeoff spot, where the walls on the big days were massive and intimidating. You want it? No, you go! And the moment would pass, the beast unridden. Farther down the line, at a less scary juncture, somebody might jump aboard. These were the best waves I had ridden since our first trip to Nias, more than a year before. It was different, surfing in a wetsuit, and the famous Jeffreys was nothing like the equatorial obscurity of Lagundri, but technically it was as if my board and I picked up almost exactly where we had left off. Big right wall, power over the ledge, jump up, pick a line, pump for speed, run and gun. Try to keep from screaming from joy.

In the evenings we threw darts, played snooker, drank beer, talked surf. The owner of the guesthouse was an older man, a British colonial blowhard who had been chased south from East Africa by decolonization. He liked his gin and loved to boast about all the Africans he had "taken down from the tree" and taught some useful skill—boot polishing or how to use a broom. I couldn't listen to him. The Aussies didn't mind him, though, which reminded me of my least favorite thing about Australia. In the casino kitchen where I had worked, the other dixie bashers all talked disdainfully of "wogs," a vast category of humanity that included southern Europeans. Refugees were pouring out of Southeast Asia then—"boat people"—and the caustic racism that suffused the subject in nearly every discussion I heard in Oz was startling.

As things turned out, I made it back to Jeffreys the following winter—1981—and caught it good again. By then, I had been in South Africa eighteen months—far longer than I had ever expected to be. And yet I never found anyone in South Africa to surf with. I got to know surfers in Cape

Town, but their familiar obsession with scoring waves felt, under the apartheid circumstances, vaguely embarrassing, almost ignominious. I had no right to judge how South Africans, black or white, dealt individually with their extraordinary situation, but working on the Cape Flats, seeing the workings of institutionalized injustice and state terror up relatively close, was deeply affecting me—was making me impatient with, among other things, myself. There was simply no escaping politics, and I found no common political ground with any of the surfers I met. So I chased waves alone.

My PARENTS CAME TO CAPE TOWN, on short notice, uninvited. I didn't want them to come. I was exceptionally busy at school, but it wasn't that. I was homesick, chronically, particularly now that Sharon was gone, and I was worried that seeing my mother and father—seeing their faces, hearing their voices, particularly my mother's laugh—would shatter my resolve to stay on this lonely expat track and complete my chosen projects: teaching, the novel.

It was also the cognitive dissonance between the world I was living in now and what I imagined to be their world. Not that I had anything like a clear view of their lives. They wrote letters faithfully, and I did too. So I knew the outlines, even the details, of my family's projects, mishaps, interests. My siblings were in college now, and they also wrote. But my parents' reports of movies made, vacations taken, sailboats bought, seemed to arrive from a particularly distant planet. My father had been on the ropes, professionally, a few years before. He and my mother had started their own production company, and then had shows canceled, deals fall through, financing vanish. I only understood how bad it was when I discovered that they were attending trendy neo-Buddhist "est" seminars offered by an authoritarian charlatan named Werner Erhard, who briefly charmed much of Hollywood. This discovery had frightened and, I am ashamed to say, disgusted me. It suggested desperation and seemed so egregiously L.A. (Actually, "est" was popular in New York, Israel, San Francisco, and many other places—even white Cape Town!) My parents' New Age nadir now seemed to have occurred very long ago, though. In the intervening years, their company had prospered, their horizons widened. They were making pictures they were proud of, working with people they liked. This was all to the good, of course. The problem was, I had been gone so long, their lives now sounded very glossy and foreign, while my life in Cape Town was so funky and modest. I was not ready for some spiffed-up jet-set version of my parents to come crashing into my humble schoolteacher's daily slog. They understood that, I'm sure. But enough was enough—it had been two and a half years—and I didn't have the heart to ask them to stay away.

That was lucky. It was unambivalently terrific to see them. And they seemed elated to see me. My mother kept grabbing my hand and kneading it between hers. They both seemed younger, more bright-eyed and spry, than I remembered them—and there was nothing spiffed-up about them. I showed them around the Cape. They seemed fascinated by every Cape Dutch gable and WHITE PERSONS ONLY sign, every shantytown and vineyard. I was living at that point in a room near the university, on the eastern slopes of Table Mountain. With two of my housemates, we climbed the mountain—not a small hike—and picnicked on top. From up there, we could see, out in Table Bay, Robben Island, where Nelson Mandela and his comrades were imprisoned but not forgotten. (Their words and images were strictly banned.) Then we descended the western slopes to the coast.

My folks insisted on visiting Grassy Park High. My students double-insisted that I bring them. And so we went, on a day that I had taken off. The principal was an enthusiastic host—he loved Americans. He took my parents on a campus tour, and I made sure that we stopped in on my students, whose schedules moved them always in a group. Each time we entered a classroom, they all sprang to their feet, staring, bellowing, *"Good afternoon, Mr. and Mrs. Finnegan."* I didn't know what to do, so I introduced them individually, running up and down the rows—Amy, Jasmine, Marius, Philip, Desiree, Myron, Natalie, Oscar, Mareldia, Shaun—eliciting grins and blushes as I went. After five or six classes of this, the principal claimed he had never seen such a prodigious feat of memory, but it actually was effortless and, I realized, an easy way to show my parents, without belaboring it, the extent of my involvement with these kids. My own classroom, New Room 16, had been taken over by a group of senior girls who had prepared a banquet. There was a huge pot of curry, and a great array of Cape Malay specialties: *bredie, samoosas, sosaties, frikkadels,* yellow rice with raisins and cinnamon, roast chicken, *bobotie, buriyani.* School had let out by then, and the other teachers were invited. June Charles, my youngest colleague—she was only eighteen yet teaching high school—guided my father through the strange and tasty dishes. My mother, meanwhile, hit it off especially with a math teacher, Brian Dublin, and complimented him more than she knew when she said that with his beret and his beard he reminded her of Che Guevara. Brian was an activist whose seriousness and dedication I had come to admire.

My parents, it occurred to me, were proud of me. Okay, it wasn't the Peace Corps—my mother's early ambition for me—and it certainly wasn't Nader's Raiders. But I had become their son-who-was-helping-oppressed-black-kids-in-South-Africa, which was not bad. They were particularly taken with an ad hoc career-counseling project I had started, which they heard all about from my biggest fan, the principal. The project had grown from my first conversations with seniors, who were full of big career dreams but seemed to have almost no information about colleges and scholarships. We had written to universities and technical schools all over South Africa and received armloads of booklets, brochures, and applications, including a great deal of encouraging news about financial aid and "permits" that would allow black students to attend formerly all-white institutions. The material eventually filled a whole shelf in the library, and proved to be popular reading, and not only among seniors. With the seniors, I had worked out applications plans and strategies that seemed to me quite promising. What I didn't know was that the "permits" we needed were fiercely controversial in the black community and had become, indeed, the object of a liberation-movement boycott—nobody could bring themselves to tell me. Actually, what I didn't know was far more than that. Very few of our seniors, for instance, would ultimately qualify after their final exams for entrance to most of the universities we were interested in, including the University of Cape Town. There were already, of course, existing networks, invisible to me, for graduating seniors to make their way into the worlds of work or further study. In the end, I came to see my careers program as an enormous American folly, even in some cases quite destructive, where it encouraged false hopes or encouraged kids to defy boycotts that I knew nothing about.

But my parents, who were even more clueless than I was, thought my work looked grand. Which felt great, in a rueful sort of way.

THE REMEDIATION of my cluelessness—my ground-level education in progressive South African politics—came largely from activists like Brian Dublin, Cecil Prinsloo, and others who eventually decided to trust me. My main interlocutor turned out to be a senior from another high school. Her name was Mandy Sanger. She was a friend of Cecil's, and she had been one of the regional boycott leaders. She took special pleasure in puncturing what she considered self-serving liberal illusions. As the school year wound down, and I saw nothing—after the ragged and violent end of the great student boycott—but discouragement and retrenchment for what everybody called the Struggle, Mandy set me straight about lessons learned, commitments deepened, and national organizations strengthened. "This year was a big step forward, and not only for students," she said. She was only eighteen, but she had the long view.

There was no graduation ceremony, no end-of-year ritual. My students drifted away after their exams, wishing me happy holidays, hoping to see me next year. I wasn't going to teach another year, though. I had saved enough to resume, on the super-cheap, my travels—but only after I finally finished, I decided, my poor old railroad novel. Before I buckled down to that, I planned to spend Christmas in Johannesburg with friends. My ancient car wasn't up to the long drive, so I would hitchhike. To my surprise, Mandy asked to come along. It seemed that she had business, unstated, in Johannesburg. I didn't see how I could say no. The trip took us several days. We dodged cops, slept out in the veld, squabbled, laughed, got burnt by the sun, chapped by the wind, and met a wild miscellany of South Africans. After Christmas, we hitchhiked to Durban, where Mandy had more student-activist business, again unstated. The phones, the mail were no good—the Special Branch, as it was called, tapped phones and opened mail. Resistance activists needed to meet face-to-face. After Durban, we hitchhiked down the coast. In the Transkei, we camped on the beach. I borrowed a surfboard and pushed Mandy into gentle waves. She cursed nonstop. But she was athletic, and she was soon popping to her feet unassisted.

Mandy was interested in my plans—whether I would just keep traveling around forever. Not a chance, I said. I would soon head back to the United States. But I asked her advice. Did she think there was anything useful that I could write for American readers about the situation in South Africa? She had, I knew, a hardheaded, utilitarian view of what foreigners could do to help the Struggle, and I had taken on enough of that view myself that the idea of entertaining my compatriots with appalling tales of "apartheid" now felt inadequate, or worse. Obviously, my readers would do nothing. The cause would not be advanced. Maybe I would do better just to write about—hell, something I actually knew about. Surfing. We debated this question intermittently on our long looping hitchhike from Cape Town to Cape Town. Mandy complained that I had complicated her view of America, which she normally thought of as a capitalist ogre hell-bent on destroying progressive movements around the world, with my stories of the brakeman's life on the railroad in California. Then, on a sun-drenched point in the Transkei, watching Xhosa fishermen pull in *galjoen* with bamboo poles, she encouraged me to return to the United

States and figure out there what I could usefully write. I could probably write about subjects other than surfing. "And I say that as one surfer to another!"

I RETURNED TO MY NOVEL. It took me another eight months to finish. I realized that my interest in the kind of fiction I was writing was fading. South Africa had changed me, had turned me toward politics, journalism, questions of power. The only sour note during my parents' visit to Cape Town had come when my father asked what I was writing, and then seemed impatient to hear that I was still basically an amateur. At the end of the school year, I found myself vowing to take no more day jobs. I would write for a living, period. I started writing essays, short features, for American magazines. I wrote nothing about South Africa—though I had a pile of overflowing notebooks. I yearned to go home—wherever exactly that might be. I clung to a line in one of Bryan's letters. He had moved back to Missoula. There was a spot on the softball team for me, he wrote. *A spot on the softball team.*

Sharon and I finally broke up, decisively. Her mother had died, and Sharon had taken a job in Zimbabwe, running a school for disabled ex-guerrillas. Zimbabwe's long war of national liberation had recently ended, and "building socialism" had begun. The decisiveness of our breakup was all Sharon's. I was more upset than I had any right to be. Our dissolution had been overdue.

My brother Kevin showed up in Cape Town. I had encouraged him to come. Still, I had the paranoid idea that our parents had sent him to get me. If so, the timing was good. I was ready to leave at last. Maybe Kevin and I would go Cape to Cairo. My surf odyssey was over. I tried to ship my blue pintail to the United States—I was extremely fond of that board. But sending it cost money, and I needed every cent, so I sold it instead. My old station wagon was failing. We traded it for an equally old but somewhat sturdier Rover.

Saying my good-byes around Cape Town, I called Mandy. Her mother answered and, when I asked to speak to Mandy, burst into tears. The Special Branch had detained her. Her mother did not know where she was being held. Mandy was still in prison when we left South Africa.

Kevin and I drove north, camping, through Namibia, Botswana, Zimbabwe. We saw a lot of big game. Kevin seemed enthusiastic, engaged, and not like he was on an onerous errand, which was a relief. He seemed to know an awful lot about everything—African history, politics. When had that happened? He had studied history in college, earned a degree in art. He was working in film production. He could drink me under the table. We left the car in Zimbabwe with Sharon—a miserable scene for me, since she was already on to the next man: a young Ndebele ex-guerrilla, now an army officer.

We continued slogging north, traveling the length of Lake Malawi on a crowded old ship, the MV *Mtendere*, calling in at forlorn villages, sleeping on the deck. Zambia, Tanzania, Zanzibar. We reached Masai country by local bus and camped on the rim of the Ngorongoro Crater. Then, at the foot of Mount Kilimanjaro, I lost my passport to a pickpocket in a bus station, and we could not cross into Kenya. We backtracked to Dar Es Salaam. I was feeling pretty beat. I was ready, I announced, for the West. Now Kevin seemed relieved—he had a life to resume in California. We abandoned Cape to Cairo and took the cheapest flight north: Aeroflot to Copenhagen, via Moscow.

I made my way alone through Western Europe. I was sleeping on the couches of friends, grateful for every creature comfort. In London I caught a plane to New York. The joy of each American thing. By then it was late autumn. My brother Michael was at New York University. I slept on the floor of his dorm room. Michael was studying French lit, playing cocktail-lounge piano with remarkable finesse. When had *this* happened? I hitchhiked to Missoula—a long, cold, magnificent trip. A truck dropped me on the interstate, and I staggered into town. For what it was worth, I was coming, as promised, from the east.

Author, Noriega Street, Ocean Beach, San Francisco, 1985

EIGHT

AGAINST DERELICTION

San Francisco, 1983–86

The ocean has the conscienceless temper of a savage autocrat spoiled by much adulation.

—JOSEPH CONRAD, *The Mirror of the Sea*

BY THE TIME I MOVED TO SAN FRANCISCO, I HAD BEEN SUCCESS-fully confining surfing to the sidelines of my life for a couple of years at least. It was 1983, early fall. I'd spent the previous summer in a roach-infested basement in the East Village, banging out a screenplay, sleeping on the floor. My railroad novel was still bouncing between publishers. The few interested editors wanted me to unpack the technical language, the railroad jargon, for the general reader, but that was where the poetry was, I thought, the elusive genius of place and workplace that I hoped to capture. I passed. In truth, I didn't want to dive back into the manuscript for any purpose. I was afraid of what I might find—infelicities, corniness, yet more juvenilia.

I had been ricocheting around the country. Unable to afford rent, I stayed with Bryan in Montana, with my parents in Los Angeles, with Dom-enic in Malibu. My accounting, in Conrad's sense, upon coming back to America had been neither triumphant nor disabling. There were Rip

Van Winkle moments. I was unfamiliar with the telephone answering machine—now everybody had one. But I was really just glad to be back, and eager to work. Missoula had been splendid, everything exactly as I remembered it. Bryan was ensconced there, writing hard, back in the American swing. Not surfing. He seemed burnished, confident, older— the higher latitudes agreed with him. Nobody else could understand where I had been these last years. He and I could still talk all night. I went deer hunting in the mountains above the Blackfoot River on my twenty-ninth birthday. Still, I didn't stay. Something told me I belonged in a city. Some hardheaded sprite of ambition, no doubt. I even considered L.A. But my old prejudices were too strong. I freelanced. Assignments trickled in, including that screenplay, which did pay the rent, even in New York. I still felt mentally flayed by my time in South Africa. But my reservations about American readers, about writing about politics—even writing about South Africa—passed.

I had a glorious new girlfriend: Caroline. She was from Zimbabwe. We had met in Cape Town, where she was an art student. Now she was a graduate student at the San Francisco Art Institute. She had joined me in New York, on that basement floor—it was the first place we shared. Caroline worked as a hostess at a restaurant on lower Fifth Avenue. We did not leave Manhattan once that summer. Our block was popular with junkies, drug dealers, and prostitutes. It was hot and grimy and we often fought. We were both hardheaded and short-tempered. But when she went back to school, I followed her.

THE FACT THAT San Francisco gets some of the best waves in California was for many years a secret. Santa Cruz, seventy miles south, was already a crowded surfing center when I went to college there, but among the thousands of people who surfed Santa Cruz only a handful ever ventured up to San Francisco. I had surfed Ocean Beach, the main spot in the city, a few times while I was railroading out of Bayshore Yard, which was near

Candlestick Park. So I knew. Still, I didn't understand what I was getting into by moving there. I had a contract to write a book—about teaching in Cape Town. We rented a flat in an unfashionable, foggy, mostly Asian neighborhood called the Outer Richmond. The room I used as an office had flocked lime-green wallpaper. I could see the north end of Ocean Beach from my desk.

From up there, on most days, Ocean Beach looked reasonable. Four miles long, perfectly straight, lots of swell, many promising sandbars. Prevailing winds were northwest, onshore, cold, the standard California afternoon sea breeze. But there were plenty of happy exceptions—mornings, fall, winter—when it was glassy or blowing offshore. The whole four miles was beachbreak, meaning it had no point of land or built obstruction—no reef or river mouth, no pier or jetty—to define it. The shape and whereabouts of the waves depended mainly on the configuration of the sandbars. That configuration changed constantly. All waves are too complex to diagram in detail, but beachbreaks are, among surf spots, an especially unpredictable species. And Ocean Beach, which receives an unusual amount of groundswell, mainly from the North Pacific—and is also raked by great tidal currents because San Francisco Bay, all four hundred square miles of it, fills and empties twice a day through the Golden Gate, just around the corner to the north—was as complicated a proposition as any surf spot I've seen. Had it been a book, it would have been something dauntingly difficult—continental philosophy, theoretical physics. Besides being complex, Ocean Beach got big. Not California big but Hawaii big. And it was cold-water, unmapped, and, once you got amongst it, frequently unreasonable.

I STARTED SURFING IT at the north end, a wind-protected, relatively gentle break known as Kelly's Cove. Kelly's had deep spots and some random wishwash outside but regularly produced thick green wedges that broke quickly across an inside bar. The waves were not things of beauty, but they had guts, and if you could decode some of their eccentricities, they offered occasional pitching backdoor barrels. Kelly's was the most popular spot along the whole of Ocean Beach, but even it was never crowded. Heading south, the next stretch, known as VFW's, was a broader field, with bigger waves and a wide array of bars. VFW's was off the west end of Golden Gate Park. A graffiti-covered seawall stood above the beach.

The next three miles of Ocean Beach abutted on the Sunset District, which was a seedier version of the Richmond—low-rise, sleepy, a sloping grid of streets built in a hurry on sand dunes as wartime worker housing. The seafront there was a rough embankment pierced by dank pedestrian tunnels and topped by a battered coast road known as the Great Highway. Except on rare warm days, the beach was mostly deserted. Winos sprawled in the few sun traps; the homeless sometimes camped there briefly, before the wind and cold drove them away. At high tide, Korean fishermen in rubber boots wrestled with surf-casting rigs. The surf, as you moved south, got generally bigger, more intimidating, with the outer bars farther from shore. Seen from the water, especially when the surf was big, the streets running inland became lineup markers—they told you where you were. In the Sunset, they were named in alphabetical order, from north to south: Irving, Judah, Kirkham, Lawton, Moraga, Noriega, Ortega, Pacheco, Quintara, Rivera, Santiago, Taraval, Ulloa, Vicente, Wawona, and then the oddball, Sloat. You didn't say you surfed Ocean Beach—you surfed Judah or Taraval or Sloat. South of Sloat Boulevard was the city zoo, beyond which sandy bluffs began to rise and the urban oceanfront—Ocean Beach—ended.

I found myself getting in the water most days that first fall. I was riding a secondhand 7'0" single-fin. It was a plain vanilla board, stiff but versatile, a good wave-catcher, stable and fast. I had an old custom-made wetsuit, now fraying and leaky, a relic from my prosperous brakeman days. I found a few sandbars that produced fine peaks, for a few days at least, on certain tides and swell angles, before the sand moved on. I was getting to know the board. It was well suited to the big open faces, knifing through the offshores, responsive at speed. But it was difficult to duck-dive—it was thick, and therefore hard to sink deep enough to escape incoming whitewater. Paddling out at Ocean Beach was nearly always an ordeal—yet another reason so few people surfed it—and my board's extra volume did not make it easier. I tried to keep my go-outs short. I worked better after surfing, though. The icy water, the exertion, then thawing under a hot shower, left me physically quiet, able to sit without fidgeting at my desk. I slept better too. This was before the first big winter swells.

THERE WAS A SMALL CREW of local surfers. They were effectively invisible to the rest of the city. Indeed, native San Franciscans would tell you that there was no surfing in San Francisco. There was surf, of course, but the ocean, I was more than once informed, was too cold and stormy for surfing. In truth, it was usually too rough for *learning* to surf—the nearest beginner breaks were outside the city. And there was a contingent among the Ocean Beach regulars who had learned their chops elsewhere—in Hawaii, Australia, or Southern California—and had moved to the city as adults. These newcomers, who tended to be professional types, and who now included me, remained distinct in some ways from the homegrown surfers, most of whom grew up in the Sunset.

But both groups bought their wax and wetsuits at Wise Surfboards, a bright, high-ceilinged place on Wawona, a few blocks from the beach. Flanked by a Mexican restaurant and a Christian day-care center, it was the only surf shop in town. There was a long row of shiny new boards along one wall and racks of wetsuits in the back. If you were looking for someone to surf with, Wise's was the place to start.

Bob Wise, the proprietor, was a tightly built, sardonic James Brown fan in his early forties. He ran, from behind the counter, a permanent bull session on the peculiarities of Ocean Beach, and of the guys who surfed it. It was a sort of surf-story jukebox, featuring a well-worn collection of tales: the time Edwin Salem found himself facing, in waist-deep water, a wave pushing before it the trunk of a redwood tree; the time the resin barrel blew up, burning off Peewee's eyebrows. Business was usually slow, except when rich dope growers from up north came in loaded with cash and saying to their friends, "You want a board? Lemme buy it for you. You think Bobby might want a board? Let's get him one too."

One afternoon when I walked in, Wise was midstory, regaling a couple of customers. "So Doc, who can see the surf from his window, calls me up and says, 'Come on, let's go out.' So I keep asking him, 'But how *is* it?' And he goes, 'It's *interesting*.' So I go over there and we go out and it's just totally terrible. So Doc says, 'What did you expect?' Turns out that when Doc says it's *interesting*, that means it's *worse* than terrible."

WISE WAS TALKING about Mark Renneker. Renneker was a favorite topic of San Francisco surf banter, even something of a local obsession. He was a family-practice physician who lived a few blocks from Wise's shop, on the oceanfront at Taraval. I actually knew Mark from college in Santa Cruz. He had come to San Francisco for medical school, and he had been urging me to move there for years, extolling the quality of the surf in letters, sending me photos of himself on great-looking waves that he described as merely "average." I couldn't tell if he was joking.

Now that I was in town, Mark and I surfed together often. He was crazy about Ocean Beach, and he had made an unusually thorough study of it. He made an unusually thorough study of everything connected to surfing. Since 1969, I discovered, he had been keeping a detailed record of every time he went out, recording where he surfed, the size of the waves, swell direction, a description of conditions, what surfboard he rode, who his companions (if any) were, any memorable events or observations, and data for year-to-year comparisons. His logbook showed that the longest he had gone without surfing since 1969 was three weeks. That happened in 1971, during a brief stint of college in Arizona. Otherwise, he had rarely gone more than a few days, and he had often surfed every day for weeks on end. In a pastime really open only to the absurdly dedicated, he was a fanatics' fanatic.

He lived with his girlfriend, Jessica, who was a painter, on the top floor of a khaki-colored three-story building on the Great Highway. Across from their apartment, by the tunnel to the beach, was a sign: DROWNINGS OCCUR ANNUALLY DUE TO SURF AND SEVERE UNDERTOW. PLEASE REMAIN ON SHORE.—U.S. PARK POLICE. Mark and Jessica's garage was filled to the rafters with surfboards—there were at least ten, most still on active duty, although on the tour I got, I noticed one collector's item: a 7'0" single-fin, with pink rails and a yellow deck, shaped and originally ridden by Mark Richards, a four-time world champion from Australia. "It's like owning Jack Nicklaus's old golf clubs," Mark said. The Richards was instantly recognizable to any reader of surf magazines. Mark Renneker hadn't ridden it in years. Another five boards stood on their tails in the stairwell. Why did he need so many boards? For riding in different conditions, of course, and particularly for bigger waves, where equipment choice could be crucial. A keen student of board design, he even kept both halves of a cherished 7'4", shaped on the North Shore of Oahu and broken on a big day at Sloat, "for reference." Big waves were Mark's ruling passion.

On the wall at Wise's shop was a framed photo of "Doc" dropping into an enormous, nearly vertical, mud-colored Ocean Beach wall. The face was at least five times his height. I had never seen anyone ride a wave that size in California. I couldn't recall another photo of anyone doing so. The wave was North Shore scale—Waimea, Sunset. Except the water temperature was probably fifty degrees—cold enough to make the surface hard to penetrate, and a falling lip feel like concrete. And the spot was not a famous, well-mapped reef but a shifty, ferocious, obscure beachbreak. I hoped I would never see Ocean Beach that big. Meanwhile, that photo went a long way toward explaining the local obsession with Mark.

He was a hard guy to miss. Six-four, slim, wide-shouldered, with an unkempt brown beard and hair that fell halfway down his back, he was boisterous and imposing, with a big laugh that fell somewhere between a honk and a roar. For someone so tall, he was remarkably unselfconscious. He carried himself like a ballet dancer. Before he paddled out, he ritually performed a series of yoga stretches at the water's edge. With people he liked, he was endlessly garrulous. There was always something going on with the waves, the wind, the sandbars, the lineup markers at Santiago that required detailed, spirited comment. Everybody knew when Mark was in the water. "Don't you know the law of the surf movie?" he yelled to me, one morning, in mediocre waves.

I didn't.

"There will never be good waves on the day after the night that a surf movie, or even surf slides, are shown!"

We had looked the night before at slides from a surf trip to Portugal that he had taken with Jessica.

Later that morning we were sitting in his study, warming up with coffee. Mark's desk looked out on the ocean. His bookshelves were filled with medical texts (*Cancer Epidemiology and Prevention*), nature guides (*Mexican Birds*), books on the ocean, the weather, and hundreds of murder mysteries. On the walls were photos of Mark and friends surfing, along with faded posters for old surf movies—*The Performers, The Glass Wall*. A collection of surf magazines, going back decades and numbering in the thousands, was carefully stacked and cataloged. A weather radio was barking the latest buoy data. I sat leafing through old surf mags while Mark talked to Bob Wise on the phone.

Mark hung up and announced that Wise now had in his shop exactly the new board I needed.

I didn't know I needed a new board.

Mark was incredulous. How could I be content with just one surfboard? And a battered old single-fin at that!

I couldn't explain it. I just was.

This was becoming a routine with us. Mark was provoked by my per-

ceived lack of seriousness, my casual half-assedness, about surfing. Wasn't
I the guy who had done the big safari, the circumnavigation in search of
far-flung waves? I was. And he was the guy who had stayed put and gone
to med school. But that didn't mean that surfing was as central to my existence as it was to his. My ambivalence about the sport we shared appalled him. It was heresy. Surfing, to begin with, was not a "sport." It was
a "path." And the more you poured into it, the more you got back from
it—he himself was the exuberant proof of that.

I didn't actually disagree. Calling surfing a sport did get it wrong at
nearly every level. And Mark did seem to me to be an overgrown poster
child for the upside of surf obsession. But I was wary of its siren call, its
incessant demands. I was reluctant even to think about it any more than
necessary. So I didn't want another board. Anyway, I was broke.

Mark sighed impatiently. He tapped at the keyboard of his computer.
"You're funny," he said, finally.

I KNEW I HAD GIVEN ungodly amounts of time and heartsblood to
surfing. One of the surf mags published, in 1981, a list of what its editors
reckoned were the ten best waves in the world. I was startled to see that I
had surfed nine of them. The exception was a long left in Peru. The list
included several breaks I had been deeply involved with: Kirra, Honolua
Bay, Jeffreys. I didn't particularly like seeing those names there. They were
famous spots, but they felt like private matters. I did like seeing that the
best wave I had surfed went unmentioned because the world didn't know
about it. Bryan and I, superstitiously, still never spoke or wrote the word
Tavarua. We just said "da kine" and figured we'd get back there in due
time.

One of the many splendid things about Caroline was her skepticism
about surfing. The first time we ever looked at waves together, somewhere
south of Cape Town, a few months after we met, she was appalled to hear
me start jabbering in a language that she didn't know I knew. "It wasn't

just the vocabulary, all those words I had never heard you use—'gnarly' and 'suckout' and 'funkdog,'" she said, once she had recovered. "It was the sounds—the grunts and roars and horrible snarls." She had since grown used to some of the insular codes and cryptic slang of surfers, even the grunts and roars and horrible snarls, but she still didn't understand why, after spending hours studying the waves from shore, we often announced our intention to paddle out by saying things like, "Let's get it over with." She could see the reluctance—clammy wetsuit, icy water, rough, lousy surf. She just couldn't see the grim compunction.

Once, in Santa Cruz, she caught a fuller glimpse of the thing. We were standing on the cliffs at a popular break called Steamer Lane. As surfers rode past the point where we stood, we could see the waves from almost directly above, and then from the back. For a few seconds, we saw an elevated version of what the riders themselves saw, and Caroline's idea of surfing was transformed on the spot. Before, she said, waves to her had been two-dimensional objects, sheer and onrushing, standing up against the sky. Suddenly, she could see that they were in fact dynamic pyramids, with steep faces; thickness; broad, sloping backs; and a complex three-dimensional construction, which changed, collapsing and rising and collapsing, very quickly. The whitewater was concussive and chaotic; the green water sleek and inviting; and the breaking lip an elusive, cascading engine and occasional hidey-hole. It was nearly enough, she said, to make watching surfing interesting.

Caroline was in no danger of becoming an ocean person. She had been born and raised in a landlocked country, Zimbabwe. I sometimes thought that her cool, critical take on various American enthusiasms (self-improvement, self-esteem, some of the rawer forms of patriotism) came from having grown up in the midst of a civil war in then Rhodesia. She had fewer illusions about human nature than anyone else I knew. I later realized I was wrong about the war's impact on her thinking. She just had uncommonly good sense and a deep, easily embarrassed modesty. What was important to her was making pictures—etchings, in particular. The cop-

With Caroline, San Francisco, 1985

perplate process she used was elaborate and outrageously labor-intensive, almost medieval, and her classmates at the art institute seemed to be in awe of her draftsmanship, her technical knowledge, her obsessiveness, her eye. I certainly was. She often worked all night. She was tall, long-waisted, pale. She had a Pre-Raphaelite stillness to her, as if she had stepped out of a Burne-Jones painting into scruffy, postpunk San Francisco. With people she liked, she could be jolly, even bawdy, tossing a wicked impasto of British and African street slang. She knew, and found a surprising number of occasions to use, a Gujarati expression for masturbation. *Muthiya maar!*

In the late afternoons, we took to walking in the hills just north of our place. The park up there was known as Lands End, and the hills looked west into the ocean and north into the Golden Gate. Cypress, eucalyptus, and tall, gnarled Monterey pines helped break the cold sea breeze. There was an old public golf course, never busy, up there too. Somebody gave me three or four rusty clubs—I could carry them all in one fist—and I started playing, for laughs, during our walks, the few holes near our place. I knew nothing about golf, and we never saw the clubhouse, but I liked whacking the ball off the deep-shadowed tees, down the lush fairways, while the low sun made the hills glow before it fell into the Pacific. Caroline wore baggy sweaters and long, beribboned skirts that she sewed herself. She had enormous eyes and a laugh that pealed thrillingly in the twilight.

I was becoming domesticated. Not at Caroline's behest—she was an expat art student, twenty-four, with no discernible interest in settling down—but by my own wary choice, with concessions small and extra-small to stability and convenience. I opened a checking account, the first of my life, at the age of thirty-one. I started paying U.S. taxes again, happily—doing so meant I was really back. I got an American Express card, ruefully vowing to be a model customer—my weak private reparations program for defrauding the company in Bangkok. I realized that in the thirteen years since high school, the longest period I had ever kept the same address was fifteen months. That was in Cape Town. *Basta*. Enough with itinerancy. I was writing my book in longhand, but if I ever had the money I would get a computer, just like everyone else, at least in the Bay Area, seemed to be doing. I had developed an avid interest in American politics, particularly foreign policy. I got an assignment that sent me to Nicaragua to profile a Sandinista poet for a magazine in Boston, and I came back feeling sick about the war we were funding there. I wrote a short piece for the *New Yorker* about Nicaragua and was electrified when the magazine ran it the following week.

Mainly, my head was in South Africa. I lived in my journals and memories, in thick piles of books and periodicals that I had never managed to read while living there—so much was banned—and in correspondence with friends in Cape Town. Mandy had been released from jail not long after I left, though not before she had missed her exams and failed her first year of college. In her letters, she sounded fine. She sent her sympathies to me and to everyone living in Reagan's America. There were a fair number of South Africans in the Bay Area, some of them scholars, some of them dedicated anti-apartheid activists, and I fell gratefully into their company. I started to do a bit of public speaking—a college, a high school. I was painfully nervous, and unsure where to draw the line between journalism and activism when it came to something as patently unjust as apartheid. I wrote. My first plan for the book called for nine chapters. It eventually had ninety-one. I covered the lime-green walls of my study with butcher paper, and covered the butcher paper with notes, lists, flow charts, struggling to see the book that might be there.

WHEN THE FIRST early-winter swells began hitting, the Ocean Beach paddle-out got dramatically worse. Most surf spots have recommended routes, shore to lineup; many have channels where no waves break. Ocean Beach had channels, but they rarely stayed put. You could stand on the embankment as long as you liked, painstakingly charting where the waves were breaking, devising a surefire course—all that water rushing in had to return to sea somehow, and it would presumably dig a channel along the course it took, where fewer waves would presumably break—and then rush to paddle out there, only to find conditions so quickly changed that you never got past the shorebreak.

On smaller days, perseverance was usually rewarded. Bigger days were another matter. From the water's edge, looking out across a stepladder of six or seven walls of cold, growling, onrushing whitewater, the idea of paddling out actually carried with it a whiff of lunacy. The project looked impossible, like trying to swim up a waterfall. It took a literal leap of faith to start. You threw yourself into the icy torrent and started plowing seaward. The waves as they approached sounded like bowling balls rumbling down a lane, and then like the crashing of pins as they slammed into and rolled over your bowed head and shoulders, inducing instant ice-cream headache. Long, strain-filled minutes passed. Little or no progress. The frisky, punishing waves came on and on. You tried to present the least possible resistance to the onrushing walls of whitewater, willing them past your body even as they snatched at you, sucking you backward. Breathing turned to gasping, then rasping, and your mind began to play ever-shorter loops, turning over the same half-nonsensical questions: *Is* perseverance rewarded? Is it even recorded? Meanwhile, underneath this aimless, half-hysterical activity, your brain struggled to detect the underlying patterns in the surf. Somewhere—upcoast, downcoast, or perhaps just beyond this next shallow spot—the waves might be weaker. Somewhere, the current must be running in a more helpful direction. The best available route would be obvious from almost any other vantage—from the embankment, or from that pelican's airborne perspective—but from down in the maelstrom, where you sometimes spent more time underwater than out in the visible world, and often got just one foam-edged breath between waves, it merely danced cruelly in the imagination: the theoretical solution to an impossibly complex problem.

In fact, there was a basic structure to the Ocean Beach setup. On any day over five or six feet, particularly south of VFW's, you normally surfed the outside bar, where the waves broke first. To get to the outside bar, you normally had to cross the inside bar, which was where waves tended to break the most relentlessly and the hardest. The guys whom one saw wash up in the shorebreak, defeated by the paddle-out, had usually been stopped by the inside bar. Between the two bars was, usually, a trough—deeper water, where you could sometimes cop a breather, let your vision clear, your sinuses drain, your arms come back to life, and plot a course across the outside bar.

But I wasn't always happy to reach the trough. Crossing the inside bar sometimes took me to the limit. If you gave up soon enough, you would just wash in, but if you pushed past a certain point, that option vanished. If I started getting seriously worked, I usually abandoned my board entirely, relying on my leash. I simply clawed my way along the bottom, fistful by fistful of sand, coming up for one breath between waves. Frequently, there came a moment when I thought, *No, never mind, this is getting too heavy, I want to go back to shore*. But it was always too late then. The violence in the impact zone on the inside bar at Ocean Beach on a solid winter day was such that one's wishes, one's volition, meant little. It was not possible to turn back. Waves sucked you toward them with monstrous force. Fortunately, the scariest, most powerful wave, the one that seemed truly bloody-minded, always seemed to spit you out the back, into the deepwater trough, once it was through with you. That was why I found the trough increasingly a place of terror. I had suddenly lost all interest in surfing, but I could no longer head toward shore. Indeed, I now faced another test, across a wider field, of much bigger waves.

It helped to remind myself that the waves on the outside bar, however big, were generally softer than the shallow water bombs on the inside. Still, I now had to find an outside channel, which meant craning to read, from the crest of each swell moving through the trough, the horizon. What were the significant patterns in the faint, distant movements of blue-gray water half a mile out? And in the bumps beyond that? Where along the vast, undulating outside bar did the energy seem to be concentrating? Which way should I go? When to start sprinting? Now? Two minutes from now? How to avoid a frightening, deepwater pounding. The fear in these long trough moments was nothing like the concentrated panic I once felt at big Rice Bowl as a kid. It was more diffuse, queasy, contingent. Drowning was just a vague, unlikely possibility, the ultimate unwanted outcome, floating around the edge of things—a cold green specter, nothing more. If I made it across the outside bar intact, it would be time to surf, to find waves to ride. That, after all, was what we were out here for.

A word about bloody-mindedness. For most surfers, I think—for me, certainly—waves have a spooky duality. When you are absorbed in surfing them, they seem alive. They each have personalities, distinct and intricate, and quickly changing moods, to which you must react in the most intuitive, almost intimate way—too many people have likened riding waves to making love. And yet waves are of course not alive, not sentient, and the lover you reach to embrace may turn murderous without warning. It's nothing personal. That self-disemboweling death wave on the inside bar is *not* bloody-minded. Thinking so is just reflex anthropomorphism. Wave love is a one-way street.

Was the surf at Ocean Beach worth the travail of the paddle-out? On some days, certainly. But only for some people. It depended on your tolerance for punishment, the state of your nerves, your ability to read the bars, your ability to surf large waves, your paddling strength, your luck on the day. There might be beautiful waves—big, bowling rights, long-walled lefts—but there were, I found, rarely consistent, well-defined peaks, making it difficult to know where to wait. If there were other people out, you could exchange surmises and lineup markers. As an Ocean Beach newcomer, I eagerly lapped up any tip. I had a ridiculous amount to learn. The camaraderie itself was a comfort. And yet I knew that, in bigger waves, safety in numbers, the "buddy system," was generally useless. In my experience at least, when things got heavy, there never seemed to be anybody around, let alone in a position to help. Particularly at a wide-open, poorly defined break like Ocean Beach, you were emphatically on your own if you got into trouble. And I hadn't even seen it big yet. In those first couple of months, the biggest day I surfed was what the locals might have called ten feet.

WAVE SIZE IS A TOPIC of perennial dispute among surfers. There is no widely accepted method for measuring the height of waves—no method widely accepted by surfers, that is. So the disputes are inherently comic— male-ego opera bouffe, usually, about whose was bigger—and I have always tried to stay out of them. For wave-height descriptions, I try to rely on the visual, with a rider providing the increments: waist-high, head-high, overhead. A double-overhead wave has a face twice as tall as the rider. And so on. But for waves without riders, or waves with deceptive optics, which is to say most waves, it often makes more sense to describe them in feet. Simply eyeballing a wave face, estimating the vertical distance from top to bottom—pretending, for the exercise, that a breaking ocean wave is a flat, two-dimensional object—yields a rough, honest number. But that number is disdained as too high by nearly all surfers, including me. Why? Because underestimation is *más macho*.

Actually, this question of what size to call a wave comes up only in some contexts, not others. I don't remember ever debating, or even discussing, the size of a wave with Bryan, for instance. A wave was small or big, weak or powerful, mediocre or *magnífica*, scary or otherwise, to the exact degree that it was these things. Attaching a number to it added nothing. If a surf report had to be produced for someone who had missed it, some conventional shorthand ("three-to-five") might come in handy, air quotes always implied. The crudity of the description was understood. But that was me and Bryan. At Ocean Beach, wave size calls were taken seriously. Big-wave spots have that effect on people. They induce self-seriousness and magnify insecurities.

Indeed, underestimation is practiced with the greatest aplomb on the North Shore of Oahu. There, a wave must be the size of a small cathedral before the locals will call it eight feet. The subscientific arbitrariness of the whole business is obvious from the fact that among surfers, wherever they live, there is no such thing as a nine-foot wave or a thirteen-foot wave. (Anyone who says there is would be laughed off the beach.) Ricky Grigg, an oceanographer and big-wave surfer, used to phone a friend who lived at Waimea Bay for surf reports when he lived in Honolulu. His friend's wife, who could see the surf from her kitchen, could never grasp surfers' irrational system of wave measurement, but she could estimate with fair accuracy how many refrigerators stacked on top of one another would equal the height of the waves, so Grigg used to ask her, "How many refrigerators is it?"

Wave size ends up being a matter of local consensus. A given wave, transferred intact somehow from Hawaii, where it was considered six feet, to Southern California, would be called ten there. In Florida it would be twelve, maybe fifteen. In San Francisco, when I lived there, a double-overhead wave was reckoned, for no good reason, to be eight feet. A triple-overhead wave was ten feet. A wave four times the height of a rider was twelve feet. Five times was fifteen feet, more or less. Beyond that, the system—if you could call it a system—disintegrated. Buzzy Trent, an old-time big-wave rider, allegedly said, "Big waves are not measured in feet, but in increments of fear." If he said that, he got it right. The power of a breaking wave does not increase fractionally with height, but as the square of its height. Thus a ten-foot wave is not slightly more powerful than an eight-foot wave—because the leap is not from eight to ten but from sixty-four to a hundred, making it over 50 percent more powerful. This is a brute fact that all surfers know in their bowels, whether or not they've heard the formula. Two waves of the same height, for that matter, may differ enormously in their volume, in their ferocity. Then there is the human factor. As a variation on the old maxim has it, "Big waves are not measured in feet, but in increments of bullshit."

When I was a boy, big waves were a big deal. There was a famous crew, including Grigg and Trent, who surfed Waimea, Makaha, and Sunset Beach. They rode long, heavy, specialized boards known as elephant guns—later simply guns. The mags and surf movies celebrated their feats. There were terrifying cautionary tales that every surfer knew, such as the time that two North Shore pioneers, Woody Brown and Dickie Cross, paddled out at Sunset on a building swell in 1943. When the sets got bigger, forcing them to paddle far out to sea, they saw that it would be impossible to return to shore—Sunset was closing out—and decided to paddle three miles west, to Waimea Bay, in hopes that the deepwater channel would still be open there. It wasn't, and the sun was going down. Cross, in desperation, struck for shore. He was seventeen years old. His body was never found. Woody Brown later washed ashore half-drowned and naked. The exploits of Grigg, Trent, and company in the '50s and '60s were mythic sagas to the surfing masses—to gremlins like me. They were not the world's best surfers, but they were intensely dashing. I loved astronauts when I was a kid, but the tiny coterie of big-wave surfers was an even cooler group.

Their heyday passed around the time of the shortboard revolution. People continued to ride huge waves, but they seemed to have hit a performance limit, as well as an upper limit to the size of the waves that could be caught and ridden. Anything bigger than what we called twenty-five feet seemed to move too fast; the physics got impossible. Very few surfers were interested in waves that size anyway. Matt Warshaw, the leading scholar of surfing—he's the author of *The Encyclopedia of Surfing* and *The History of Surfing*, both hefty, authoritative tomes—puts the number of surfers ready to ride twenty-five-foot waves at less than one in twenty thousand. Others think it's far fewer than that. Nat Young, the great Australian champion, a man whom Warshaw considers "perhaps the most influential surfer of the [twentieth] century," and who in his prime was a swashbuckling ripper nicknamed the Animal, had no interest in riding waves over twenty feet. In a 1967 surf film, Young said, "I've only done it once, on one wave, and I don't ever wish to do it ever again. If those guys can enjoy themselves while their hearts and guts are falling down a mineshaft, then I respect them and their courage. I just don't think I could ever express myself while scared out of my wits."

I was with Young, and with the other 99.99 percent. I had surfed alongside a few big-wave specialists on the North Shore, but I thought of them as mutants, mystics, pilgrims traveling another road from the rest of us, possibly made from a different raw material. They seemed bionic, suspiciously immune to normal reactions (panic, fight or flight) in the face of life-threatening peril. In truth, there was a wide middle ground of heavy waves that were not world-ending, not apocalyptically big, and we all negotiated a dark, highly personal fear line whenever a large swell hit. My own upper limit had been edging back for twenty years. I had ridden fairly big waves at Sunset, Uluwatu, outer Grajagan, even Santa Cruz—Middle Peak at Steamer Lane could throw some bombs. I had surfed aggressively, adrenaline-unhinged and unafraid, in big Honolua, in ten-foot Nias. I had even surfed Pipeline, a truly frightening, dangerous wave, a few times, though only on smaller days. But I had never owned a gun, and I didn't want one.

MARK HAD THE COMPLETE BIONIC SWAGGER, in a rare antic hippie-doctor version. He said he had never been afraid of big waves. Indeed, he claimed that the common fear of big waves was unfounded. Just as people are more afraid of cancer, he said, than of heart disease, despite the fact that heart disease kills many more people, surfers are more afraid of big waves than of small waves, despite the fact that small, crowded waves injure and kill many more surfers than big waves do. I thought this theory was tripe. Big waves are violent and scary, full stop, and the bigger they are, generally speaking, the scarier and more violent they are. To anthropomorphize: big waves want, desperately, to drown you. Very few people surf them, and that's the only reason they don't kill more people than they do.

Just as everyone who surfs has a limit to the size of the waves he will venture among, the surfers who live in a place that gets big waves come to know, over time, one another's limits. When I lived in San Francisco, the only other surfer whose range approached Mark's was Bill Bergerson, a carpenter whom everyone called Peewee—an unlikely nickname, left over from the days when he was somebody's younger brother. Peewee was a quiet, intense, exceptionally smooth surfer, probably the best pure surfer San Francisco had produced. His interest in big waves was not, however, indiscriminate. He did not try to surf every big day at Ocean Beach; he paddled out only when it was reasonably clean. Mark, meanwhile, would go out in borderline madness, when no one else would even consider it, and come in laughing. There were people who found this sort of thing annoying.

But Mark trained for big waves with a joyful masochism. One morning I found myself standing on the embankment at Quintara, watching him try to paddle out. The surf was eight-feet-plus, ragged, relentless, onshore, with no visible channels. Even the trough was not in evidence. Getting out looked impossible, and the waves looked not worth the effort anyway, but Mark was out there still, a small black-wetsuited figure in a world of furious whitewater, throwing himself into the stacked walls of onrushing foam. Each time he seemed to be making headway, a new set would appear on the horizon, bigger than the last and breaking farther out—the biggest waves were breaking maybe two hundred yards from shore—and drive him back into the impact zone. Watching with me was Tim Bodkin, a hyrdrogeologist, surfer, and Mark's next-door neighbor. Bodkin was getting a huge kick out of Mark's ordeal. "Forget it, Doc!" he kept shouting into the wind, and then he would laugh. "He's never going to make it. He just won't admit it." At times we lost sight of him altogether. The waves rarely gave him a chance even to clamber onto his board and paddle; mostly he was underwater, diving under waves, swimming seaward along the bottom, dragging his board behind him. After thirty minutes, I began to worry: the water was cold, the surf was powerful. Bodkin, aglow with schadenfreude, did not share my concern. Finally, after about forty-five minutes, there was a brief lull. Mark scrambled onto his board and paddled furiously, and within three minutes he was outside, churning over the crests of the next set with five yards to spare. Once he was safely beyond the surf, he sat up on his board to rest, a black speck bobbing on a blue, windblown sea. Bodkin, disgusted, left me alone on the embankment.

Mark took to calling me at first light. I came to dread his calls. Dreams full of giant gray surf and a morbid fear of drowning would climax with the scream of the phone in the dark. His voice on the other end of the line at dawn was always bright, raucous, from the daylight world.

"Well? How's it look?"

He could see the south end of Ocean Beach from his place; I could see the north end; he wanted a report. I would stumble, shivering, to the window, peering through blurry binoculars at a cold, wild sea.

"It looks . . . hairy."

"Well? Let's hit it!"

Other surfers also got these calls. Edwin Salem, a genial college student, originally from Argentina, and a protégé of Mark's, told me that he used to lie awake half the night worrying that the phone would ring, and then panic if it did. "Doc only called me when it was big and he knew nobody else would go out with him. I usually would."

I usually would too, up to a point not yet determined.

. . .

ON A CLEAR, CHILLY DAY in early November, Mark and I paddled out
at Sloat. It was the first day of a small north swell, and the surf was
confused—lumpy, harsh, inconsistent. He had persuaded me that before
the waves had time to calm down and clean up, northwest winds—which,
according to his weather radio, were already blowing twenty-five knots in
the Farallon Islands, twenty miles offshore—would be here. Those winds,
when they arrived, would wreck the waves completely, so this might be
our only chance to surf this swell. Yes, we were the only surfers in sight,
but that was because the others were expecting it to get better later, on the
outgoing tide. They didn't know about the northwesterlies.

"Or maybe they have jobs," I panted.

"Jobs?" Mark laughed. "That was their first mistake."

It was late morning, still nearly windless. My hands burned with cold.
Even after we got outside, there was no chance to warm them in my arm-
pits because there was a fierce current running north, meaning we had to
paddle constantly just to stay in the same place off the beach. The current
also meant that we were looking only for rights, which carried one south.
I was breathing too hard to argue about employment. Mark had a work
schedule built around surfing, with a variety of gigs and maximum flexibility. He constantly rearranged his practice around swells, tides, and
wind. So he had plenty of work, which he described as highly fulfilling,
and he had no trouble paying rent. I was a convenient person to surf with
partly because my schedule was flexible. His disdain for the convention-
ally employed was in truth mostly a joke, meant to get my goat, which he
enjoyed doing.

Mark's disdain for marriage and children was even more pointed. "The
rule about guys getting married: their readiness to ride big waves goes
down one notch immediately," he liked to say. "And it goes down another
big notch with each kid. Most guys with three kids won't go out in waves
over four feet!"

The waves turned out to be better than they had looked from shore, and we both got a series of short, fast rides on good-sized waves. Their lumpiness gave them odd, unexpected speed hollows. Mark came flying out of one thick-muscled close-out chattering about needing a longer board. He was riding a 6'3". In the moments when the roar of the surf subsided, we could hear monkeys howling in the city zoo, beyond the beach embankment. But really San Francisco might as well have been in another hemisphere. Ocean Beach in the winter is a wilderness, as raw and red-clawed as any place in the Rocky Mountains. We could see traffic on the coast highway, but it was unlikely that the people in the passing cars saw us. Many of them would undoubtedly say, if asked, that there was no surfing in San Francisco.

Mark couldn't resist a large, wrapping left. He took off and in a matter of seconds rode halfway to Ulloa. I caught the next wave, also a left, and was carried even farther north. Paddling back out, we were both driven still farther north by a set breaking south of us. We were now so far down-current that we decided to abandon Sloat for Taraval. The peak breaking over the sandbar at Taraval was shifty and sloppy, though, and we stopped catching waves. A better peak seeemed to be breaking at Santiago. Mark had an idea: let's quit fighting the current. When it was this bad on an incoming tide, it turned into the Sloat-to-Kelly's Express. Let's just ride it north, he said, surfing whatever we found. I was exhausted, and therefore agreeable. We stopped paddling south, and soon the beach started stream-ing past. It was a goofy, hapless feeling, letting the sandbars come to us, instead of struggling to reach a takeoff spot and staying there. Water flows off a sandbar, and can make it difficult to maintain position at the bar's outside edge, where waves will prepare to break, but the rushing, sinuous current was carrying us across all sorts of spots, at all sorts of angles, willy-nilly.

Mark, who loved this kind of half-uncontrolled experiment, provided a running commentary on the bars we were traversing. Here was where that great peak broke last year—at Outside Quintara. And this was the lineup on giant days at Pacheco. See that cross on the mountain? You had to keep it above the church. And you could see that Noriega was starting to do something interesting: "On these pushy swells, it's not really breaking outside and it's not really breaking inside. The inside bar swings out here now, so that it's breaking in the middle, and peeling off in both directions."

He was right about the sandbars at Noriega. Surf was no longer breaking on the outside bars that we had been drifting among. We swirled slowly through a wide, waveless field. An otter popped up ahead of us, swimming on its back. It had a small, shiny red-brown head, with huge dark eyes. Otters weren't common at Ocean Beach; it was as if this one had been summoned by our peculiarly passive behavior.

The current was now carrying us out to sea. I suggested we paddle toward shore. Mark reluctantly agreed to abridge our drifting experiment.

On the inside bar, as we continued our progress toward Judah, we found short, thick waves breaking with surprising power. I liked the quick, steep drops, and caught three straight high-adrenaline rights before stroking into a head-high mistake. My board stuck for a moment in the wave's lip. Then I was launched into space. I tried to get away from my board, but dared not dive straight down—the inside bar was shallow. I hit the water awkwardly, twisted, and hit the bottom, softly, with one shoulder. I felt my board flash past, actually brushing my arms, which were over my face, in the moment before the wave landed on me. I got comprehensively thrashed, and finally surfaced, gasping, with what felt like several pounds of sand inside my wetsuit. I had been lucky—I could have been hurt. I scrambled back out, head ringing, nose streaming.

Mark had started surfing more cautiously. "When it's dredging over a shallow sandbar, that's when you break your neck," he said. It was a paradox—that someone known for taking the most extreme risks was at the same time so prudent—but it was also true that Mark "made" a higher percentage of his waves (that is, exited from the wave still on his feet) than any other surfer I knew. He simply didn't take off on waves that he didn't believe he had an excellent chance of making, and once he committed himself to a wave he hardly ever made a careless or ill-considered move.

We reconvened after Mark caught a right and I got a long left. As we paddled back out, he announced, "November is big and stupid." What he meant was that the surf at Ocean Beach in November was often large but rarely well ordered. But before he could say more we got separated as we rushed to avoid an approaching set. A few minutes later, he went on, "The correspondences between what you see on the weather map and what actually arrives at the Beach aren't really established yet."

In fact, there were great fall days at Ocean Beach, when the first north and west swells of the season met the first offshore winds. Those winds began to blow after the first snowfall in the High Sierras. Of course, fall surf benefited from the inevitable comparison with the months of fog-bound, onshore slop that an Ocean Beach summer entailed. The first large swells of the season actually did arrive in November, though, often before the sandbars were ready to turn them into ridable surf. Winter was when the waves were best. In December and January, the combination of huge winter storm swells and local beach and weather conditions was frequently exquisite.

It would be cold—water temperatures could fall into the forties, and the air on winter mornings could be below freezing. I was considering investing in neoprene booties, gloves, and a hood, all of which some guys were already wearing. A broken leash and a long swim could spell hypothermia. Loss of sensation in hands and feet was already giving me trouble. I sometimes had to ask strangers to open my car door and put the key in the ignition, my own manual dexterity having been deleted by a surf. The passage of time itself could feel distorted: a couple of long sessions in cold water, hard winds, and big waves could make two days seem like two weeks.

We were now coming up on VFW's, where the sandbars were a mess. We had drifted about three miles. But the tide was almost high now; the current seemed to be slackening. We had been out for at least two hours, my hands were numb, and no amount of mashing them under cold rubber wings would bring them back to life now. I was ready to go in.

We decided to hitchhike back to Sloat rather than walk. As we climbed the embankment to the highway, Mark suddenly turned and said triumphantly, "Feel that? Here come the onshores!" He was right. A sharp, dark windline was already moving into the surf on the outside bars, tearing off the tops of the waves. "Those other guys blew it," Mark crowed.

MY OLD PALS Becket and Domenic both seemed to be letting surfing slip. Becket was back in Newport, running construction jobs, doing boat carpentry, delivering yachts. His brand of hide-your-daughters wharf-rat hedonism was ready to be patented, I thought. While his neighbors had I'D RATHER BE SAILING decals on their cars, he drove around Orange County in a work pickup with a bumper sticker that said, I'D RATHER BE PERFORMING CUNNILINGUS. On the wall in his office, when I went to visit, I was startled to find a framed photo of myself. It was the Grajagan shot, clipped from a surf mag, of me standing, board under arm, at the edge of the reef while an empty, backlit, fabulous-looking left roars past. Becket had tacked up a caption, "Chickens Do Surf." The reference was to my ankles, which are skinny. "I know why you had to go around the world," he said while I studied the photo. "It was because you couldn't find enough things to be miserable about in this country."

It was a theory, not without interest, and not so different from Domenic's idea of my self-hating politics. Domenic, meanwhile, had taken his place in the world. He was directing high-end TV commercials. He had married an equally successful French commercial director. They kept an apartment in Paris, a house in Beverly Hills, a condo in Malibu. She had grown kids. Both Domenic and Becket still surfed, or at least owned boards, but neither seemed to be a full-fledged local at any spot. Southern California, with its miasmic crowds, would discourage that, I knew. Once I landed in San Francisco and entered my apprenticeship at Ocean Beach,

I never thought of telling my old surf partners about the great uncrowded waves I had lucked into. I wasn't trying to keep a secret. I just knew they wouldn't be interested. Too much punishment for the occasional sweet ride. Too cold, too gnarly, too hard-core.

My mother had her doubts about San Francisco generally. This made her unusual in Los Angeles, where the natives traditionally wax romantic about their northern counterpart—Baghdad by the Bay, Tony Bennett's lost heart, etcetera. She thought it was a fine place to visit but self-satisfied and somewhat stale, particularly since its hippie heyday. I once heard her call it "an old folks' home for young people," a quip that had some bite since Kevin and I were both living there. Kevin was now in law school, having bailed on the film business. He lived downtown, in a neighborhood called the Tenderloin. Neither of us was exactly slacking, but I did notice, on holidays when we all went home, how L.A. buzzed with a kind of acid élan, an endemic entertainment-industry-ambition frenzy that I had ignored while growing up there but could now safely appreciate. The Bay Area had nothing like it, at least not outside Silicon Valley, which held no interest for me but was obviously fizzing with brainpower.

I knew that my mom had gone back to work, and yet the reality never quite registered with me until I found myself watching a smiling, well-spoken filmmaker, Patricia Finnegan, accept an award in a hotel ballroom in Washington, D.C., for a movie she had produced. Was that my mother? She had started by volunteering at a nonprofit production company, found her feet quickly, and then she and my dad had started their company. They had their start-up struggles, but within a few years my mother was hiring my father as a line producer on movies-of-the-week. She had a sharp eye for story and got on famously—easily, productively—with writers, directors, actors, and network executives, which sounds simple but is actually a rare talent. She and my father were wildly busy. Colleen and Michael each took serious looks at the family business, and then went elsewhere—Colleen into medicine, Michael into journalism, both back east. Kevin, who had strong left-wing politics, would not be returning to

Hollywood after law school. So we had all flown the show-business coop. I couldn't tell if my finally getting some articles published here and there pleased my father, the old newswriter. The book I was writing, I thought, might surprise my parents. They still thought of my teaching in Cape Town as good works. But a large part of the book would be about my failure to help my students and the unintended consequences of my more benighted efforts.

The emotional disarray in which I departed southern Africa had not left me. I still had evil, agonizing dreams about Sharon. I had no contact with her, and I tried to hide my heartache from Caroline. But I sometimes wondered how it might color my account of the struggle for black liberation in South Africa.

Kevin, who had gone to college in San Francisco, was living with a categorically more serious nightmare. The HIV/AIDS pandemic was in its early stages, still poorly understood. In San Francisco young people were falling ill, terminally ill, by the hundreds, soon to be thousands. Caroline and I were new in town, and we didn't know anyone who had tested positive, but Kevin's friends and neighbors downtown were living in terror, and they were being cruelly cut down. San Francisco General Hospital opened the first dedicated AIDS ward in the United States in 1983. Within days, it was full. One of Kevin's closest friends, a sweet young lawyer named Sue, who was his college roommate, and spent Christmas with us, died of AIDS. She was thirty-one. Most of the victims in the city were gay men, of course. Kevin, who is gay, was active in the movement to demand more resources for AIDS research and treatment, but he didn't talk to me much about it. Our travels in Africa felt like they had taken place in another, less stark century. He seemed distracted, at best. I spared him my stories of near drownings on the inside bar at Ocean Beach.

I PADDLED OUT with Mark on a shiny, scary-looking day at Pacheco. It was hard to gauge the size of the surf because there was no one else in the

water. We got out easily—conditions were immaculate, the channels easy
to read—but then we misjudged conditions and took up a position that
was too close to shore. Before we caught our first waves, a huge set caught
us inside. The first wave snapped my ankle leash like it was a piece of
string. I swam underneath that wave and then kept swimming, toward
open ocean. The second wave looked like a three-story building. It, like
the first wave, was preparing to break a few yards in front of me. I dived
deep and swam hard. The lip of the wave hitting the surface above me
sounded like a bolt of lightning exploding at very close range, and it filled
the water with shock waves. I managed to stay underneath the turbulence,
but when I surfaced I saw that the third wave of the set belonged to another order of being. It was bigger, thicker, and drawing much more heavily off the bottom than the others. My arms felt rubbery, and I started
hyperventilating. I dived very early and very deep. The deeper I swam, the
colder and darker the water got. The noise as the wave broke was preternaturally low, a basso profundo of utter violence, and the force pulling me
backward and upward felt like some nightmare inversion of gravity. Again,
I managed to escape, and when I finally surfaced I was far outside. There
were no more waves, which was fortunate, since I was sure that one more
would have finished me. Mark was there, though, perhaps ten yards to my
right. He had been diving and escaping the unimaginable just as narrowly
as I had. His leash had not broken, however; he was reeling in his board.
As he did so, he turned to me with a manic look in his eyes and yelled,
"This is great!" It could have been worse. He could have yelled, "This is
interesting!"

I later learned that, from a record-keeping point of view, Mark had indeed found that afternoon's surf interesting. He stayed out in the water for
four hours (I made the long swim to shore, collected my board from the
sand, and went home to bed), and he measured the wave interval—the
time it takes two waves in a set to pass a fixed point—at twenty-five seconds. It was the longest interval he had ever seen at Ocean Beach. That
didn't completely surprise me. Long-interval waves move through the

ocean faster than their shorter-interval cousins, reach deeper below the surface, and when they break drive more water forward because they have more energy. Mark's journal entry for that session also showed, among other things, that my leash broke on the twenty-first day of that surf season on which Mark had surfed waves eight feet or bigger, and the ninth day on which he had surfed waves ten feet or bigger.

The thing to be feared most, I believed, was a two-wave hold-down. That was a drubbing so prolonged that you didn't reach the surface before the next wave landed on you. It had never happened to me. People survived it, but never happily. I had heard of guys who quit surfing after a two-wave hold-down. When someone drowned in big waves, it was rarely possible to know exactly why, but I believed it often started with a two-wave hold-down. The biggest single reason I was so frightened by the third wave in that monster set that broke my leash was because the wave had two-wave hold-down written all over it. It was a rare slabby specimen for Ocean Beach, like the worst kind of inside-bar dredger—except two or three times the size. I didn't understand where on the bars it was breaking or why—I still don't understand it—but with its ultra-thickness I knew as I swam under it that there would not be much water left in front of it, meaning that it was very likely that if I got sucked over, I would have at least one encounter, possibly catastrophic, with the bottom, as well as an extremely long, possibly fatally long, hold-down. I didn't know about the interval of the swell, but had gathered from the first waves we saw that it was exceptionally long. A two-wave hold-down in extremely long-interval waves would be, for obvious reasons, very long indeed.

Forty or fifty seconds underwater might not sound too bad. Most big-wave surfers can hold their breath for several minutes. But that's on land, or in a pool. Ten seconds while getting rag-dolled by a big wave is an eternity. By thirty seconds, almost anyone is approaching blackout. In the worst wipeouts of my experience, I had no way of knowing afterward precisely—or even imprecisely—how long I had been held down. I tried to concentrate on relaxing, on taking the beating, not fighting it, not burning oxygen, trying to conserve energy for the swim to the surface once the flogging ended. I sometimes had to climb my own leash to the surface, my board being more buoyant than I was. My worst hold-downs were always the ones that I thought had come to an end—one more kick to the surface—before they actually had. The unexpected extra kick, or two, or three, still without reaching the surface, made the desperation for air, the spasm in the throat, feel suddenly like a sob, or a stifled scream. Fighting the reflex that wanted to suck water into the lungs was nasty, frantic.

Nothing physically unpleasant had happened under that third wave in the Pacheco set. And there was no wave behind it, so the two-wave holddown that I feared if I got sucked back over would not have happened. Still, the near miss spooked me. I knew I was not ready for the consequences of getting hit squarely by a wave that consequential. I doubted I ever would be.

IT WAS ASTOUNDING TO ME that anyone learned to surf in San Francisco. I took to interviewing, informally, guys who had. Edwin Salem told me that when he was a kid he built a board rack to hitch to his bicycle, using scrounged plywood, two-by-fours, and wheels off a shopping cart. He would set off from the Sunset District two hours before the tide would be good at Fort Point because that's how long it took to pedal there. Fort Point is a sloppy left under the south end of the Golden Gate Bridge. It gets crowded but is a relatively gentle wave. At twelve or thirteen, Edwin started riding the whitewater at Ocean Beach. Peewee, who was already one of the big guys there, told him that, before he could surf, he had to collect a lot of wood—good dry stuff for a bonfire that would be blazing when he came in. "I collected a *lot* of wood," Edwin said. "And I took a lot of crap." Slowly he became an Ocean Beach local.

Now in his midtwenties, Edwin was a smooth, powerful surfer with curly black hair and merry green eyes. He and I were out at Sloat, catching our breaths after a bruising paddle-out. It was cold, midmorning. The surf was fierce but mediocre; there was no one else out. The smell of fresh doughnuts drifted across the water from a bakery near Wise's shop. On the horizon a container ship was steaming toward the Gate. We decided we were too far out. As we began paddling back toward the takeoff area, gliding watchfully over the swells, I asked Edwin about the surf in Argentina. I knew he still made occasional trips there to visit family. He laughed. "After this place, I couldn't believe how easy it was to surf there," he said. "The water was so warm! The waves were so mellow! There were girls on the beach!"

ON A VERY BIG DAY, the city itself looked different. The streets and buildings seemed glazed and remote, the lineaments of an exhausted sphere: land. The action was all at sea. One January morning in 1984, Ocean Beach was so big that San Francisco felt like a ghost town as I drove the few blocks to the coast. It was a dark, ugly day, drizzling and cold. The ocean was gray and brown and extremely ominous. There were no cars at Kelly's or VFW's. I headed south, driving slowly, so that I could watch the surf. It was impossible to say how big it was. There was nothing—no one—out there to provide any scale. It was twenty feet at least, probably bigger.

Sloat looked totally out of control as I pulled into the parking lot. The waves breaking farthest out were barely visible from the shore. Paddling out was unthinkable. There was no wind, but the largest waves were feathering slightly anyway, from the sheer volume of water they threw forth as they broke. The explosions that followed were unnaturally white. They looked like small nuclear blasts; watching them made my stomach churn. When Mark had phoned me earlier, he had said simply, "Sloat. Be there or be square." But Sloat was out of the question. Mark pulled into the parking lot a few minutes after I did. He turned to me and opened his eyes wide—his way of saying that the waves were even bigger than he had thought. He cackled darkly. We agreed to look at the surf on the south

side of a temporary construction pier that the city had built half a mile
below Sloat. As we were leaving, Edwin pulled into the lot. Mark had also
rousted him at dawn. The three of us drove into the dunes south of Sloat.

The swell was coming from the northwest—it was being generated by
a major storm in the Aleutians—so the pier, which was four or five hundred yards long, was significantly diluting the power of the surf to its
immediate south. The waves there looked barely half the size of the gargantuan stuff on the north side, and almost manageable. There was still
the question of getting out, however. People sometimes paddled out underneath the pier—a regular rip current, carrying water that the surf had
piled up near the beach back out to sea, had dug a deep trench under the
pier, so that waves rarely broke there. But it was nasty under the pier.
There were loose cables dangling, and huge iron sheets sticking up at odd
angles under the water, not to mention the pilings themselves, which were
closely spaced and did not budge when the surf slammed you into them. I
had paddled out under the pier a few times, on days when getting out at
Sloat had been beyond me, but I had sworn not to do it again. In any case,
even paddling out under the pier looked impossible this morning. Broken
waves were rumbling through the pilings like small avalanches through an
iron forest. The only nonlethal way to get out today would be to sneak
past the guard on the construction project, run out on the pier, and jump
off the end, which was safely outside the surf.

"Let's do it," Mark said.

The three of us were now sitting in his van—a brawny, battered,
trek-outfitted 1975 Dodge—parked on a dirt road just south of the pier.
No one had said anything except "Oh my God!" and "Look at that!" for
ten minutes. I had absolutely no desire to go surfing. Fortunately, my
board was inadequate for these conditions; even Edwin's 8'4" gun didn't
look big enough. Mark had two big-wave boards, both over nine feet, with
him. He said that one of us could use one of them.

"This is why I don't own a board over nine feet," Edwin said. He gave
a nervous laugh.

In fact, this was why most surfers didn't own a board over eight feet; it might raise the question someday of actually going out in conditions that required that much surfboard. Once, in Wise's shop, I had heard a surfer mutter as he and his friends studied a 10'0" gun on display, "This one comes with a free pine box." The market for boards that serious was minuscule.

Mark jumped out of the van, went around to the side door, and began changing into his wetsuit. For the first time since I'd moved to San Francisco, I was ready to refuse to go out, and Mark seemed to realize it. "Come on, Edwin," he said. "We've surfed bigger waves."

They probably had, too. Mark and Edwin had a pact, informal but fierce, concerning big waves. They had been surfing together since they met, in 1978. Mark took an interest in Edwin's welfare: counseling him about how to get along in the United States, encouraging him to go to college. Edwin, who lived with his mother—his parents were divorced—treasured Mark's foster-paternal guidance, which came to include a running pep talk on the subject of big-wave surfing. Edwin had the physical equipment for big waves: he was powerfully built, a strong swimmer, a solid surfer. He also had steady nerves and a major endowment of youthful blitheness. Finally, there was the fact that he trusted—even worshipped—Mark. That made him an ideal apprentice in a program that, over several winters, had got him out into bigger and bigger—eventually into some very big—waves. Mark and Edwin's pact consisted mainly of an unspoken understanding that Mark would not take Edwin out on days when he would probably drown.

Edwin was shaking his head lugubriously, unzipping his down-filled jacket. In most company he would make an unlikely Sancho Panza—he is over six feet tall, with square-jawed, leading-man looks—but it struck me, watching the two of them clamber into their wetsuits, that Mark could make any companion seem like a sidekick.

While Edwin fiddled with a leash that he was transferring from his board to the board Mark was lending him—a hefty, pale yellow 9'6" single-fin gun—Mark showed me how to use his camera. Then he took the board that he would ride—a magnificent, narrow 9'8" three-fin—out on the dunes, methodically rubbed wax on the deck, and did a series of deep yoga stretches, all without taking his eyes off the surf.

"Why do we do this?" Edwin asked me. His nervous laugh rose and fell.

Finally, Edwin was ready, and the two of them set off, trotting lightly past the guard's trailer, disappearing behind stacks of mammoth sewer pipe, then reappearing a minute later out on the pier, still jogging—two lithe silhouettes, their big boards dramatic against a whitish sky. Beyond the pier I could see waves breaking off Sloat where I had never seen them break before. Farther north still, the ranges of gray-beige swells and white walls were a scene out of my surfing nightmares. The waves scared me even as I sat, warm and dry, in the van.

At the end of the pier, Mark and Edwin climbed down a ladder, flopped on their boards, and started paddling back toward shore. Their approach gave scale to the waves, which turned out to be less monstrous than I'd imagined. When Edwin quickly took off on a meaty left, it stood up about three times his height. The wave was mud brown and hungry-looking; I started snapping pictures. Edwin pulled into it well, but the wave suddenly lined up all the way to the pier, fifty yards north, closing out, and he was forced to straighten off. The whitewater exploded and engulfed him. A moment later, his board came cartwheeling out of the whitewater; his leash had snapped. The waves were breaking close to shore—there was no outside bar on the south side of the pier—and Edwin washed in quickly. He came chugging up the dunes, and he grinned when I told him that I'd got several shots of his ride. "It's not too hairy out there, I don't think," he said. "Kind of closed out, maybe." He wanted to borrow the leash from my board. I gladly gave it to him. The waves looked more than kind of closed out, and it was not getting any warmer—the air temperature was in the forties.

While Edwin started back out the pier, I noticed a tremendous set breaking on an outside bar perhaps two hundred yards to the north. With people in the water, it was now possible to say that Sloat was indeed twenty-foot-plus. But the set I could see breaking on the outside bar was more than gigantic—it was also phenomenally violent. The waves seemed to be turning themselves inside out as they broke, and when they paused they spat out clouds of mist—air that had been trapped inside the bus-sized tubes. I had never seen anything like it before, even on the North Shore: twenty-foot spitting tubes. Edwin was gesturing to Mark, trying to show him where a set on the horizon on the south side seemed to be planning to break. The thunder of the waves under the pier drowned out the roar of the larger waves farther away, and Edwin never glanced north, where the view would have stopped him cold.

Mark caught a couple of peaky ten-foot rights, both of which he made. I didn't have a good angle on the rights for shooting pictures, though. And, photographically speaking, the situation south of the pier began to deteriorate after Edwin got back out. It started raining in earnest, and Mark and Edwin, whom I could barely see through the mist, caught no waves for half an hour. I stowed Mark's camera, locked his van, and went home.

Shortly after I left, Edwin told me later, he caught another left. He made this one, but the following wave, a fifteen-foot peak that came crashing through the pier, caught him inside. My leash snapped, but this time he did not wash in to the beach. Instead, he was seized and carried by a powerful current straight into the pier. Terrified, he fought his way through the pilings, and came out unhurt on the north side. But there the current turned seaward and began to carry him toward the outside bar— the same bar where I had seen twenty-foot tubes turning themselves inside out and spitting. He swam toward shore, but the current was stronger than he was. He was already hundreds of yards offshore, weak with panic—but still south of the killer sandbar—when a freak deepwater set broke outside him. These were much softer waves than the ones breaking where he was bound, so Edwin stayed on the surface and let them hit him. The set washed him to the inside edge of the rip. There he managed to swim into the path of the whitewater rumbling in from the killer bar, which washed him farther inside. When he reached the beach, somewhere near Sloat, he was too weak to walk.

Mark found him there. Edwin was too shaken up to drive, so Mark drove him home. I don't know whether he mentioned to Edwin what he had been doing while Edwin was fighting for his life in the water and lying gasping on the sand, but Mark later told me that he had grown bored with the long lulls south of the pier and had paddled through to the north side. He had stayed outside the killer bar, but had caught a couple of gigantic waves at Sloat, he said, before heading back south to look for Edwin. He had been worried after he found the board he'd lent Edwin lying on the beach, and very relieved when he finally found Edwin himself. Their pact had survived a severe test. Edwin, after Mark took him back to the apartment he shared with his mother, stayed on land for several days. He surfed little the rest of that winter, and I did not see him out in very big waves again.

ANOTHER COLD DAY AT SLOAT. Half a dozen people are out in eight-foot, high-tide glass. I'm on shore, warm and dry, hors de combat since tearing up my ankle two weeks before in a free fall at Dead Man's, a cliff-side left on the south side of the Golden Gate. I'm back in Mark's van, again with the camera. I almost never take surf photos—I can't sit still if the waves look good—but Mark has seen and seized another chance to put his camera in my hands. Nearly all surfers love shots of themselves in the act of surfing. To say that waves and the rides they provide are inherently fleeting events, and that surfers naturally therefore want mementos, doesn't begin to explain the collective passion for self-portraits. I'm supposed to be shooting two or three guys, Mark and friends, but they aren't getting many waves. The peak shifts south, taking the crowd along with it, and my subjects dissolve in a glittering field of light.

I should move south with them. I drag myself into the driver's seat, start the engine, and feel suddenly like a kid wearing his dad's overcoat: the sleeves fall to my knees, the hem brushes the floor. Mark is actually not much bigger than I am—an inch or two taller—but the seat feels strangely vast, even the steering wheel seems oversized, and the van itself feels less like a car than like some high-bridged, sure-ruddered freighter as I steer it through the puddles and potholes of the Sloat parking lot. From the driver's seat, the van, its bed stacked high with surfboards, seems suffused with a big-cat-stretching sense of power, of rangy well-being and good health. From this surf-rinsed, king-of-beasts view of the world, I think, I too might be inclined to evangelize.

Mark understood the surf-photo compulsion. He not only put on slide shows, and had pictures of himself tacked up all over his apartment; he also delighted in presenting friends with pictures of themseves surfing. I'd seen these photographs hanging in the homes of their subjects, framed like religious icons. He gave me one of myself half crouched inside a slate-gray barrel at Noriega. Caroline had it framed for my birthday. It was a great shot, but it frustrated me to look at, because the photographer, a friend of Mark's, fired an instant too soon. Just after the moment recorded, I disappeared into that wave. That was the shot I coveted: the wave alone, with the knowledge that I was in there, drawing a high line behind the thick, pouring, silver-beaded curtain. That invisible passage, not this moment of anticipation, was the heart of the ride. But pictures are not about what a ride felt like; they are about what a ride looked like to others. This Noriega shot—I am looking at it now—shows a dark sea; my memory of that wave, meanwhile, is drenched with silver light. That's because I was looking south while I navigated its depths, and when I slipped through its almond eye back into the world.

For me, and not only for me, surfing harbors this paradox: a desire to be alone with waves fused to an equal desire to be watched, to perform.

The social side can be competitive or a pure yearning for companionship or, most often, both. It was unusually strong, I found, in San Francisco. The community of surfers was small, and the loneliness of surfing

Ocean Beach when the waves were aroused was huge. Tim Bodkin's wife, Kim, let me know where I stood, community-wise, one fine spring morning. I was waxing my board in front of her place on the Great Highway. Several other surfers were heading through the Taraval tunnel. Kim had her infant son on her hip. She was bouncing him in the sunshine. (Mark had already predicted that Tim would stop surfing big Sloat next winter.) "So is the whole Doc Squad going out?" she asked.

"The what?"

"The Doc Squad," she said. "Don't tell me you haven't heard of it. You're a charter member."

THE NEW ISSUE of *Surfer* lay on the counter at Wise's. Normally I would snatch it up and start leafing. But the cover featured a familiar-looking blue left peeling in the background as a surfer leaped with his board off a boat in the foregound. "FANTASTIC FIJI!!" read the headline. The upper-right corner band screamed, "DISCOVERY!" It was, of course, Tavarua.

I wanted to throw up. And I didn't know the half of it.

The *Surfer* article, it turned out, was not about the discovery of a great new wave but about the opening of a resort. It seemed that two California surfers had bought or leased the island, built a hotel, and were now open for business. They were offering exclusive access to perhaps the best wave in the world to a maximum of six paying guests. This was a novel concept: paying to surf uncrowded waves. Articles about the discovery of a great new spot were a surf-mag staple, but the unwritten rules about disguising its location were strict. Maybe the continent would be revealed, generally not the country, sometimes not even the ocean. People might figure it out, but only a few, and they would have to work at it, and then they would want to keep the secret themselves. Here those rules were all smashed. Crowds at Tavarua would be prevented by the resort and its agreement with local authorities. It would be a private wave. Book now. All major credit cards accepted. There was even an ad for the resort in the same issue of the mag.

Bryan, as it happened, was flying into San Francisco that week from Tokyo. He was freelancing for travel magazines; he had been on assignment in Hokkaido. I met his plane. On the drive from the airport to our place, I dropped the new *Surfer* in his lap. He started cursing quietly. He slowly got louder. Speculating about who had opened their big mouth was pointless. Our shared fantasy had been wrong. Tavarua had not been sitting chastely, transcendent waves roaring unridden down the reef, for six years after all.

Bryan took it harder than I did, or at least less passively—he wrote a cutting letter to *Surfer*. By feeling aggrieved, he told me, we were being dogs in the manger, yes, growling over straw that we weren't using. Still, he thought the whole thing stunk, and so did I. Everything untrammeled in this world gets exploited, he said, and sullied and spoiled. His letter to *Surfer* asked the right questions about financial arrangements between the magazine and the resort, calling the editors pimps or, at best, morons.

It was strange to see Bryan in the flesh. We were still faithful, high-volume correspondents, such that I sometimes felt like I was living a second, more uproarious life in Montana—skiing hard, drinking hard, knocking around with rowdy, talented writers, who always seemed to mass there. Bryan was publishing a lot, articles and reviews, working on another novel. He was living with "a mean skinny woman," as he called her, a writer named Deirdre McNamer, who wasn't mean at all, and who would eventually do him the great favor of marrying him. His travel pieces took him all over the place—Tasmania, Singapore, Bangkok. Deirdre went along to Bangkok, where he showed her the Station Hotel, our old digs. Even he was shocked by its squalor. "How different a city is with money," he wrote—this was on page fifteen of a letter to me from Southeast Asia. "It becomes air-conditioned, manageable, flowing." Bryan's letters were Whitmanic, volcanic, funny—even the ones racked with self-castigation, which were distressingly frequent. He once wrote that he had just realized that the hospitality we received back in 1978 from Sina Savaiinaea and her family in Samoa had cost them a lot of money, relative to their wealth, and that we had repaid them with trinkets rather than the cash that they desperately needed and were expecting but were too polite to mention. He was so horrified he couldn't sleep. And I wasn't at all sure he was wrong.

Bryan hadn't surfed in a while. There was a small October swell. Mark loaned him a board and wetsuit. The wetsuit was too small, and Bryan struggled to pull it on, writhing in the gloom of Mark's garage, with Mark and friends watching with entirely too much amusement. I helped Bryan get the thing zipped. In the water, he struggled again. The Ocean Beach whitewater was, as usual, relentless, and he was out of shape. I duck-dived next to him, making little unwelcome suggestions. We surfed twice during his stay, and he claimed to be elated to be back in the ocean. I waited for a slighting remark from some junior member of the Doc Squad, itching to slap them down. But nobody said anything. Bryan took Mark's measure, and no doubt vice versa. Bryan's least favorite people were the overweening.

Bryan and Caroline, meanwhile, spoke each other's language. I noticed him jotting down throwaway remarks of hers—when she called me a "hyena" for skulking through the kitchen or she indignantly asked why a local fitness buff thought anyone would be interested in his "nasty body." Bryan had brought us English-language tourist decals from Japan—WE MADE A FINE TOUR and WE TOOK A PHOTOGRAPH IN ALL—which we stuck on the fridge.

About a year after that visit, Bryan wrote a short piece about his softball team—the team was called Montana Review of Books—and sent me the manuscript. Did I think the *New Yorker* would want it? It was good, I replied, but not right for Talk of the Town. Too novelistic, too confessional. I was an expert, of course, having sold the magazine one thing. Bryan didn't wait for my advice letter to arrive, though. He submitted the piece. William Shawn, the magazine's editor, read it and called him, full of praise. He flew Bryan to New York, put him up at the Algonquin Hotel, and asked him what else he might like to write. Shawn published the soft-ball piece immediately and gave Bryan an assignment for a two-part piece on—Bryan's idea—the history of dynamite. When I heard from Deirdre that Bryan was in New York and why, I meekly asked that he not open the letter from me waiting for him in Missoula.

A VERY BIG late-winter day at VFW's. Tim Bodkin and Peewee are the only people out. From the beach, the sea is just a blinding, colorless sheet of afternoon glare, intermittently broken by the black walls of waves. Mark was out earlier. When he came in, he called it ten to twelve feet and the northbound current "a killer." A light northwest wind has come up since, marring the surface and rendering the waves a notch more dangerous and difficult to ride. Bodkin and Peewee are catching few waves. Most of the time, they're invisible in the glare. The waves they do manage to catch are all massive lefts, breaking on an outside bar I have rarely seen break and have never before seen ridable. I don't normally think of VFW's as a big-wave spot. On small, clean days, it's usually the most crowded stretch of the Beach. But this is the kind of day when Bob Wise says he gets a lot of phone calls from guys asking hopefully, "Is it small?" And when he tells them, "No, it's huge," they suddenly remember all the business they have in far-flung parts of the Greater Bay Area.

Eight or ten surfers watch from the seawall, nervous and grumpy. All seem to agree that the wind has ruined the surf, that there's really no reason to go out now. An unusual amount of profanity—unusual even for surfers—is being used to discuss the waves, the weather, the world. People pace, fists plunged in pockets, laughing too loudly, dry-mouthed. Then Edwin, who has been silently watching the ocean from behind mirrored sunglasses, erupts. "I have an idea," he announces. "Let's form a support group. I'm not going out there because I'm *scared* to go out there. Why don't we all just say that? 'I'm not going out there because I'm *scared* to go out there.' Come on, Domond, you say it."

Domond, a noisy tough who works in Wise's shop when he's not driving a taxicab, turns away in disgust. So Edwin addresses himself to another homeboy, known as Beeper Dave, but he also turns away, grumbling and shaking his head. Everybody then ignores Edwin, who just laughs easily and shrugs.

"Set," somebody growls. All eyes swing to the horizon, where the blazing sheet of the sea is beginning to lift in sickeningly large gray lines. "Those guys are *dead*."

I DECIDED TO TRY to write about Mark. He was up for it. I sent a proposal to the *New Yorker*: a profile of this amazing urban big-wave surfer and physician. Shawn liked the sound of it. I got the assignment.

Things changed after that between me and Mark. I stopped being mortified that people might mistake me for one of his acolytes. I was his Boswell, don't you know. I interviewed him about his childhood—his father was a psychiarist in Beverly Hills. I cataloged the contents of his van. I followed him around at work, sitting in while he examined patients. He had been a bit of a prodigy when we were in college. After his father developed a tumor, Mark, who was pre-med, started studying cancer with an intensity that convinced many of his friends that his goal was to find a cure in time to save his father. As it turned out, his father didn't have cancer. But Mark kept on with his cancer studies. His interest was not in fact in oncology—in finding a cure—but in cancer education and prevention. By the time he entered medical school, he had created, with another student, a series of college courses on cancer and coauthored *The Biology of Cancer Sourcebook*, the text for a course that was eventually offered to tens of thousands of students. He cowrote a second book, *Understanding Cancer*, that became a bestselling university text, and he continued to lecture throughout the United States on cancer research, education, and prevention.

"The funny thing is, I'm not really interested in cancer," Mark told me.

"I'm interested in people's response to it. A lot of cancer patients and suvi-vors report that they never really lived till they got cancer, that it forced them to face things, to experience life more intensely. What you see in family practice is that families just can't afford to be superficial with each other anymore once someone has cancer. Corny as it sounds, what I'm really interested in is the human spirit—in how people react to stress and adversity. I'm fascinated by the way people fight back, by how they keep fighting their way to the surface." Mark clawed at the air with his arms. What he was miming was the struggle to reach the surface through the turbulence of a large wave.

I asked Geoff Booth, an Australian journalist, surfer, and physician, for his professional opinion. "Mark definitely has the death wish in him," Booth said. "It's some extreme driving force, which I really think only a handful of people in the world would understand. I've only met one other person who had it—Jose Angel." Jose Angel was a great Hawaiian big-wave surfer who disappeared while diving off Maui in 1976.

Edwin's theory was that Mark was driven to surf big waves by the rage and futility that he felt when his patients died. Mark said that was ridicu-lous. Edwin's other theory was Freudian. (He was from Argentina, re-member, where psychoanalysis is a middle-class religion.) "Obviously, it's erotic," he said. "That big board's his prick." I didn't even run that one past Mark.

I FINISHED my South Africa book. While waiting to hear from the pub-lisher, I went to Washington to report a piece on U.S. policy toward south-ern Africa. Civil unrest in South Africa was in the headlines and the anti-apartheid movement was gaining traction globally. A group of con-servative young congressmen, led by Newt Gingrich, judging correctly that apartheid was doomed, had staged a revolt against Reagan administra-tion policy, which was basically pro-apartheid. A wave of Republican infighting ensued, and some of the principals were eager to talk. I had a sharp anti-apartheid ax to grind, but my poker face was getting better (still mixing metaphors, though) and the refinement of my understanding of power proceeded. I wore a cheap black suit, carried a new briefcase Caroline had given me, and tried to act like I knew what I was doing in the offices of congressmen and senators, the State Department, the Heritage Foundation. I found my way into the militarist fringe where Lieutenant Colonel Oliver North, not yet a public figure, operated. I was green and awkward, but I loved the work: chasing leads, making connections, asking hard questions. It was my third or fourth piece for *Mother Jones*, a leftist monthly in San Francisco that was also trying to find its way in the bigger world. The revolt of the young conservatives in Congress succeeded. Reagan suavely reversed field on economic sanctions against Pretoria. His administration continued to rain death, though, on Nicaragua.

My new status as a reporter seemed to dawn slowly on the little community of San Francisco surfers. By then I knew most of the main dudes— and it was still all dudes in the water at Ocean Beach, no women—though few of them knew much about me. When word got around that I was writing about Mark, people looked at me differently, I thought. Some volunteered their takes. "He's the biggest little kid on the Beach," Beeper Dave said. He meant that in a good way. "One thing about Doc," Bob Wise said. "He keeps open the idea that anything is possible." Another view of Mark, until then invisible to me, also began to surface. The most vivid expression of it came from a stranger who paddled up to me purposefully at VFW's. He was a tough-looking guy, long dirty-blond hair, a lot of street in his face, and he got much closer to me than surfing social etiquette allowed. Looking me full in the face, he snarled, "Doc's a fuckin' kook." I said nothing, and after a long moment he moved away. Nice to meet you too. On the face of it, the remark was absurd. A kook, in surf dialect, is a beginner. But the point was the insult, which was about as strong as it gets in surf world, and the seething hostility. Noted.

I saw Mark as a devoted pupil of Ocean Beach. But to some locals, I came to see, he was just a rich kid from L.A., and he was taking up too much psychic space. The social divide between blue-collar natives and white-collar newcomers wasn't actually simple or clear. Many of Mark's buddies were Sunset District homies. And there were plenty of Ocean Beach regulars whose stories didn't fit in any category. Sloat Bill, for instance, was a commodities trader from Texas via Harvard. He got his nickname when, following one of his divorces, he moved into his car and lived for a month in the Sloat parking lot, vowing not to leave until he had mastered the harsh art of surfing Sloat. Whether he had achieved that aim or not, he had certainly made more money, tapping buy and sell orders into a computer plugged into his car's cigarette lighter, than any of the rest of us did while sitting in the Sloat parking lot. Sloat Bill had recently moved back to San Francisco after a stint in San Diego, declaring, "Surfing down there was like driving on the freeway. Totally anonymous."

THE SURFING SOCIAL CONTRACT is a delicate document. It gets redrafted every time you paddle out. At crowded breaks, while jockeying for waves with a mob of strangers, talent, aggression, local knowledge, and local reputation (if any) help establish a rough pecking order. I had competed joyously, on the whole, at Kirra, Malibu, Rincon, Honolua. But most spots, less famous, are subtler, their unwritten rules built on local personalities, local conditions. Crowded days were rare at Ocean Beach. They occurred, though, and the same sensitivities and decorum came into play then as they did anywhere else.

On a February afternoon, I paddled out at Sloat and found at least sixty people in the lineup. I didn't recognize any of them. It was the third day of a solid west swell. Conditions were superb: six-foot-plus, not a breath of wind. Normally the winter bars began to fall apart in early February, but not this year. What had happened, I guessed, was that surfers from up and down the coast who usually didn't want to know about Ocean Beach had decided en masse that with the major winter swells probably over and conditions still improbably clean, the feared O.B. could be safely raided. I understood this selective bravado, of course, because I felt it too, along with an immense relief at having survived another winter—this was my third. Still, I resented the horde. I got pounded on the inside bar, eventually slipped out, and started hunting for a peak to ride. The crowd seemed amorphous, unfocused—there were no conversations in progress. Everyone seemed intent on the waves, on himself. I caught my breath, chose a lineup marker—a school bus parked in the Sloat lot—and took up a risky position straight inside a group of four or five guys.

I was vulnerable there to a big set, but it was important, in a crowd, to make a good showing on one's first waves, and after a long winter I knew the bars here better than these tourists did. As it happened, the next wave to come through held up nicely, shrugging off the efforts of two guys farther out to catch it, and handing me a swift, swooping, surefooted first ride. Paddling back out, I burned to tell somebody about the wave—about the great crack the lip had made as it split the surface behind me, about the mottled amber upper hollows of the inside wall. But there was no one to tell. Two black grebes popped out of the foam beside me, their spindly necks like feathered periscopes, their big, surprised eyes staring. I murmured, "Did *you* see my wave?"

Everyone out here was starring in his own movie, and permission was required before you inflicted your exploits on anyone else. Vocal instant replays and noisy exultation are not unknown in surfing, but they're subject to a strict code of collective ego control. Young surfers sometimes misunderstand this part of the surfing social contract, and brag and browbeat each other in the water, but they generally cool it when older surfers are in earshot. The usual crowd at Ocean Beach was older than most—in fact, I couldn't remember ever seeing a teenager out on a big day—and the unwritten limits on garrulity among strangers here were correspondingly firm. Those who exceeded them were shunned. Those who consistently exceeded them were hated, for they failed to respect the powerfully self-enclosed quality of what other surfers, especially the less garrulous, were doing out here.

I headed for an empty peak slightly north of the school bus. I caught two quick waves, and half a dozen people saw fit to join me. The hassling for waves got, for Ocean Beach, fairly bad. Nobody spoke. Each dreamer stayed deep in his own dream—hustling, feinting, gliding, windmilling into every possible wave. Then a cleanup set rolled through, breaking fifty yards outside the bar we were surfing. Huge walls of whitewater swatted all of us off our boards, pushing a few unlucky souls clear across the inside bar. The group that reconvened a few minutes later was smaller, and now had something to talk about. "My leash leg just got six inches longer." "Those waves looked like *December*." We settled into a rough rotation. Waves were given and taken, and givers were sometimes even thanked. After noteworthy rides, compliments were muttered. The chances of this swell's lasting another day were discussed in general session. A burly Asian from Marin County was pessimistic—"It's a three-day west. We get 'em every year." He repeated his prediction, then said it again for those who might have missed it. The little group at the school-bus peak, while it would never be known for its repartee, had achieved some rude coherence. A light fabric of shared enterprise had settled over all of us, and I found that my resentment of the nonlocals had faded. The tide, which was rising, was unanimously blamed for a lengthy lull. The sun, nearing the horizon, ignited a fiery Z of sea-facing windows along a road that switchbacked up a distant San Francisco hillside.

Then a familiar howl and raucous laugh rose from the inside bar. "Doc," someone said, unnecessarily. Mark was the one San Francisco surfer whom nonlocals were likely to know. He was paddling alongside somebody, regaling him with the plot of a horror movie: "So the head starts running around by itself, *biting people to death*." Mark was wearing a silly-looking short-billed neoprene hood, with his beard jutting over the chin strap and his ponytail flapping out the back, steaming in my direction. When he was still ten yards away, he made a face and yelled, "This is a zoo!" I wondered what the people around us made of that observation. "Let's go surf Santiago."

Mark didn't recognize the unwritten limits on garrulity in the water. He tore up the surfing social contract and blew his great, sunburned nose on the tatters. And he was too big, too witty, and far too fearless for anyone to object. Feeling compromised, I reluctantly abandoned my spot in the rotation at the school-bus peak and set off with Mark for the peaks breaking off Santiago, half a mile north. "'A three-day west'!" Mark snorted. "Who are these guys? It's going to be bigger tomorrow. All the indicators say so."

Mark was usually right about what the surf would do. He was wrong about Santiago, though. The bars were sloppier than those we had left behind at Sloat. There was nobody surfing anywhere nearby. That was really why Mark wanted to surf there. It was an old disagreement between us. He believed that crowds were stupid. "People are sheep," he liked to say. And he often claimed to know more than the crowd did about where and when to surf. He would head down the beach to some unlikely-looking spot and stubbornly stay there, riding marginal, inconsistent waves, rather than grub it out with the masses. I had spent a lifetime paddling hopefully off toward uncrowded peaks myself, dreaming that they were about to start working better than the popular break, and sometimes—rarely, briefly—they actually seemed to do so. But I had a rueful faith in the basic good judgment of the herd. Crowds collected where the waves were best. This attitude drove Mark nuts. And Ocean Beach, with its great uncrowded winter waves, did in fact bend the universal Malthusian surf equation. Freezing water and abject fear and ungodly punishment were useful that way.

I took off on a midsized wave, a detour I quickly regretted: the set behind my wave gave me a thorough drubbing, almost driving me over the inside bar. By the time I got back outside, the sun was setting, I was shivering, and Mark was a hundred yards farther north. I decided not to follow him, and started looking for a last wave. But the peaks along here were shifty, and I kept misjudging their speed and steepness. I nearly got sucked over backward by a vicious, ledging wave, then had to scramble to avoid a monstrous set.

The twilight deepened. The spray lifting off the tops still had a crim-son sunset tinge, but the waves themselves were now just big, featureless blue-black walls. They were getting more and more difficult to judge. There were no longer any other surfers in sight. Now shivering badly, I was ready to try to paddle in—ignominious as that would be. When a lull came, that's what I did, digging hard, struggling to keep my board pointed shoreward through the crosscurrents of the outside bar, using a campfire on the beach as a visual fix, and glancing back over my shoulder every five or six strokes. I was about halfway to shore, coming up on the inside bar, when a set appeared outside. I was safely in deep water, and there was no sense trying to cross the inside bar during a set, so I turned and sat up to wait.

Against the still-bright sky, at the top of a massive wave off to the south and far, far outside, a lithe silhouette leaped to its feet, then plunged into darkness. I strained to see what happened next, but the wave disap-peared behind others nearer by. My stomach had done a flutter kick at the sight of someone dropping into such a wave at dusk, and as I bobbed over the swells gathering themselves for the assault on the inside bar I kept peering toward where he had vanished, watching for a riderless board washing in. That wave had looked like a leash-breaker. Finally, less than forty yards away, a dim figure appeared, speeding across a ragged inside wall. Whoever it was had not only made the drop but was still on his feet, and flying. As the wave hit deep water, he leaned into a huge, elegant carving cutback. The cutback told me who it was. Peewee was the only local surfer who could turn like that. He made one more turn, driv-ing to within a few yards of me, and pulled out. His expression, I saw, was bland. He nodded at me but said nothing. I felt tongue-tied. I was relieved, though, by the thought of having company for the passage across the inside bar, which was now detonating continuously. But Pee-wee had other plans. He turned and, without a word, started paddling back out to sea.

. . .

LATER THAT EVENING, grunts and roars and horrible snarls filled the air in Mark's apartment. Slides from the past couple of winters at Ocean Beach were being shown, and most of the surfers featured were on hand. "That can't be you, Edwin. You hide under the bed when it gets that big!" Mark convened these gatherings quasi-annually. "This was the best day last winter," he said, projecting a shot of huge, immaculate Sloat that elicited a deep general groan. "But I don't have any more pictures of it. I paddled out after taking this one, and stayed out all day." Mark's voice had the nasal, waterlogged quality it got after a long session. In fact, he'd come in from the surf—its steady thunder from across the Great Highway was supplying a bass line for the entertainment—only an hour before. "The moon rose just as it got really dark," he'd told me. "I went back to Sloat. All those kooks were gone. It was just Peewee and me. It was great." I found this scene hard to picture. It wasn't that I didn't believe him—his hair was still wet. I just couldn't imagine how anyone could surf by moonlight in waves as big as those that were pounding Sloat at dusk. "Sure," Mark said. "Peewee and I do it once every winter."

Peewee was there at Mark's that night, along with most of the surfers I knew by name in San Francisco. Ages ranged from late teens to midforties. With only three years' seniority, I was probably the most recent arrival in San Francisco. A slide of me surfing Ocean Beach the previous winter drew a couple of hoots but no insults—I hadn't been around long enough for that. There was a sequence of Mark pioneering a fearsome outer reef in Mendocino County. Local surfers had been watching the place break for years, but no one had ever tried to surf it until, earlier that winter, Mark persuaded two big-wave riders from the area to paddle out with him. The wave broke at least half a mile from shore, on a shallow rock reef, and featured a horrendous drop, along with some troublesome kelp. Mark's slides, taken by an accomplice with a telephoto lens from a mountainside, showed him cautiously riding deep-green walls two or three times his height. The trickiest part, he said, had actually come not in the water but in a nearby town that evening. People at the village hangout had been alarmed to hear that he'd surfed the outer reef, and suspicious, he said, until they learned that he had done it in the company of two locals.

It was surprising to hear Mark mention local sensitivities. They were a real issue—I once saw a clipping from a Mendocino newspaper in which a columnist described Mark as "a legendary super surfer from the Bay Area," adding sarcastically, "I'm sorry I didn't stick around for his autograph"— but I usually thought of Mark as impervious to such matters. Of course, it was also tricky showing these slides to this audience; it required a deft touch, even a measure of self-deprecation. Mark might disregard the finer points of the surfing social contract among strangers in the water, but Ocean Beach was home; here the strong drink of his personality needed sweetening. Earlier in the evening, when Mark complained that his asthma was bothering him, making it difficult to breathe, Beeper Dave had muttered, "Now you know how us mortals feel."

A parade of photographers with their slide carousels followed. There were water shots, some of them good, and many blurry shots of giant Ocean Beach. Some old-timers showed slides from the '70s, featuring surfers I'd never heard of. "Gone to Kauai," I was told. "Gone to Western Australia, last we heard." Peewee showed a handful of slides from a recent trip to Hawaii. Taken at Sunset, the renowned big-wave spot, Peewee's pictures, which were of poor quality, showed some friends windsurfing on a small, blown-out day. "Unbelievable," somebody muttered. "Windsurfing." Peewee, who was one of the few guys from San Francisco actually capable of surfing big Sunset, said little. But he seemed amused by the crowd's disappointment.

THERE WAS ANOTHER PHOTO on the wall at Wise's shop when I first moved to San Francisco. It was flyspecked, curling, captionless, and incredibly beautiful. The photo showed a surfer—Peewee, according to Wise—trimmed very high on a seemingly endless backlit ten-foot left. The wave was lime green and wind-sculpted, and looked as if it must be somewhere in Bali, but Wise said it was at Outside VFW's. The wave was so exquisitely proportioned that it made the 9'6" gun that Peewee was riding look like a shortboard. And the line he was drawing was out of a dream—too high, too fine, too inspired for real life.

During my second or third winter in the city, more photos began to appear on the wall at Wise's. They were all big, wood-framed prints under glass of Mark surfing giant Ocean Beach, with typed captions listing the exact date and place taken and identifying the rider.

Mark and Peewee were the fire and ice of San Francisco surfing, the oversold thesis and the understated antithesis. They were like two opposed theories of character formation. In Peewee's case, experience seemed to be about removing superfluities; in Mark's case, it was all accumulation. More boards, more milestones, more spots conquered. Virtually everything with him hinged on surfing, from childhood to old age. Recalling his L.A. youth, he told me, "Among my friends, there was a strong belief in the surfer's path. Most people swerved from it sooner or later." For his models for aging well, he looked to older surfers—he called them "elders." Doc Ball, a lifelong surfer and retired dentist in Northern California, then in his eighties, was a favorite. "He's still stoked," Mark said. "He still skateboards!"

Peewee agreed that Mark was preternaturally youthful. "He's like somebody who's twenty or twenty-two, with that much stoke about surfing, that much enthusiasm," Peewee told me during a rare conversation. But Peewee disagreed about the long-term benefits of the surfing life. As he put it, "The biggest locals can be the biggest derelicts." We were sitting in a Chinese restaurant near his house, with Peewee warily watching me take notes. "It's such a great sport it corrupts people," he said. "It's like drug addiction. You just don't want to do anything else. You don't want to go to work. If you do, it's always 'You really missed it' when you get off."

As a carpenter, Peewee said, he had some job flexibility, and he tried to take a month off each year to go surfing someplace else, like Hawaii or Indonesia. But there was no way that he could surf as avidly as he had surfed while growing up—not without risking dereliction.

Peewee learned to surf on borrowed boards at Pedro Point, a beginner's break a few miles south of San Francisco. It took him five years to work up to Ocean Beach. He was a Sunset District kid, in awe of the big guys from his era. Eventually he became a big guy himself—over six feet, broadshouldered, with the poker-faced, blond good looks of a B-western gunfighter. But he never managed to ditch his nickname. He also seemed never to have lost the unassumingness of the novice. Getting him to talk, over tepid tea in an emptying restaurant, was the journalistic equivalent of paddling out at Sloat on a mean day. My request for an interview had no doubt startled him. Peewee knew me as a face in the water, a recent Ocean Beach regular, one of Mark's crowd. Now, suddenly, I was a reporter. That didn't mean I was dispassionate. As someone who had been struggling for several winters now with Mark's contention that to miss a swell was a far greater sin than to miss a deadline, I got more comfort than Peewee knew from his simple description of the inevitable conflict between surfing and work. Of course, it was an argument as old as Hiram Bingham—the missionary who saw surfing as barbaric and nearly strangled it in its cradle in Hawaii.

Peewee's self-effacement was so thorough that it was easy to misread him as remote. Even I could see, though, after a while, that his terse exterior hid an acute shyness, which in turn hid an old-fashioned sensitivity. He had been a straight-A student in school—I learned this not from him but from others—and an English major at San Francisco State University. He also took science courses in college, including an oceanography class in which the instructor once averred that the big winter swells that hit the Northern California coast came typically from the south. This notion is solidly false. The instructor refused to be corrected, and Peewee let it slide.

When letting foolishness slide became impossible, though, he was capable of taking a memorable stand. Once, on a crowded day at VFW's during my first winter in San Francisco, a local surfer was behaving badly—stealing waves, jumping the queue, and threatening anyone who objected. Peewee warned him once, quietly. When the guy kept it up, then nearly decapitated another surfer with a clumsy pullout, Peewee invited him to leave the water. The miscreant snarled. Peewee knocked him off his board, turned his board over, and, with small, sharp blows with the heel of his hand, broke off each of his three fins. The guy paddled in. Years later, Ocean Beach regulars who hadn't seen this incident were still asking those who had to tell it again.

Peewee was a locals' local. He was one of those guys who, when you surfed with them at Fort Point, under the Golden Gate Bridge, could look up and tell you how many workers were entombed in its pilings; how long the lines of men waiting for work were during its construction, back in the Depression, and how much they were paid; and how much the present-day maintenance workers, some of whom were friends or relatives, earned. Peewee was a union carpenter, and often served as the job steward on construction sites. When I asked about that, he said simply, "I believe in the construction unions." He was equally closemouthed on the subject of big waves. He preferred them to small waves, he said, because they were uncrowded. "Crowds can get tense," he said. "In big waves, it's just you and the ocean." Peewee was known around Ocean Beach for his iron nerves in big surf, but it took him a number of years, he said, to build up to facing very big waves. "Each new wipeout makes you realize, though, that you're actually safer than you thought. It's just water. It's just holding your breath. The wave will pass." Did he never panic? "Sure. But all you have to do, really, is relax. You'll always come up." In retrospect, he said, the times when he had thought he was drowning were not in fact such close calls.

"Doc's kind of building a reputation here," Peewee conceded, ten years after Mark started surfing Ocean Beach. What about Peewee himself? "I'm kind of maintaining a reputation here," he admitted. Still, he only surfed big waves when they were clean. What was the biggest wave he had ridden at Ocean Beach? "The biggest wave I've taken off on out here, I didn't make," he said. "The wave was perfect—my board was just too small. It was an eight-four. I only got about three-quarters of the way down the face. I fell, and I got sucked up and over. It was the scariest moment I've had. I thought I'd never stop free-falling. But it wasn't so bad." How big was it? "Twelve feet," Peewee said. "Maybe fifteen." He shrugged. "I hardly try to measure waves in feet anymore." That was just as well, I thought, because plenty of surfers around the city believed they had seen Peewee ride waves larger than fifteen feet.

WHILE WE JOUSTED, groveled, and gloried in a world invisible to other San Franciscans, we were still in the city, and it sometimes came to us. One shining day, at low tide, Ocean Beach was wide and full of people. The surf was good, and I was hurrying across the sand, board under arm. Off to my left, two young black men in 49ers warm-up jackets were silently putting a pair of miniature remote-control dune buggies through their paces; they wove and whirled and fishtailed in the sand. Off to my right, a group of white people were beating the hell out of pillows with yellow plastic clubs. As I passed, I could hear screaming and cursing: "Bitch! Bitch!" "Get out of this house!" Some people were weeping. A chubby man in his forties was pounding a sheet of paper laid on a pillow. When it flew off, he chased it down, bellowing, "Get back on there, you bitch!" Near the water's edge, I found another middle-aged man, gazing out to sea, his yellow club at his feet, a beatific expression on his face. He eyed my board as I knelt to strap on my leash. I asked about the pillow beaters, and he said they were engaged in something called the Pacific Process. Thirteen weeks, three thousand dollars. This exercise, he said, was called Bitching at Mom. I noticed he was wearing work gloves. Hey, no use getting blisters while beating the bejeezus out of Mom.

Later, out in the water, I saw a surfer I didn't know drop in late on a big, glassy peak. He was riding a needle-nosed pale blue board and he fought to keep his balance as the wave, which was twice his height, jacked and began to pitch. He didn't fall, but he lost speed in the struggle to keep his feet, and his first turn, now deep in the wave's shadow, was weak. If the wave hadn't hit a patch of deep water and paused for a beat, he would have been buried by the first section. He managed to steer around it, though, and then pull into the next section and set a high line across a long green wall. By the time he passed me, he was in full command, perhaps one turn from the end of an excellent ride. But his face, I saw in the moment he shot past, was twisted with anguish, and with something that looked like rage. Riding a serious wave takes, even for an accomplished surfer, intense technical concentration. But many less selfless emotions also crowd around. Even in unchallenging waves, the faces of surfers as they ride often become terrible masks of fear, frustration, anger. The most revealing moment is the pullout, the end of a ride, which usually provokes a mixed grimace of relief, distress, elation, and dissatisfaction. The face of the stranger on the pale blue board had reminded me of nothing so much as the weeping, contorted faces of the pillow beaters on the beach.

None of this interior Sturm und Drang went with the slap-happy, light-hearted idea of surfing—fun in the sun—that's always seemed widespread among nonsurfers, and now that I was planning to write about it I found myself wondering how much of the actual thing I could hope to convey to outsiders. There were guys who didn't grimace while riding waves, of course, whose style seemed to extend to a serene countenance, even a slight inward smile. But in my experience those individuals were rare.

And then there were great surfers, the fabulously gifted. They were by definition exceedingly rare—although pro surfers were slowly, as the popularity of surfing increased and an international contest circuit matured, getting more common. For them, surfing *was* a sport, with training, competition, sponsorships, the lot. In Australia they were treated like other professional athletes; champions were even subject to public adulation. Not so in the United States, where the average sports fan knew essentially nothing about surfing, and where even surfers paid little attention to contest results and rankings. The best surfers were admired, even revered, for their style and ability, but the important thing we shared with them was esoteric, obsessive, not mainstream but subcultural, certainly not commercial. (Some of this—not much—has changed in recent years.)

The main thing we shared, at every level of talent, was a profound absorption in waves. Mark liked to say that surfing "is essentially a religious practice." But there was too much performance, too much competition (however unstructured), too much appetite and raw preening in it for that description to ring true to me. Style was everything in surfing—how graceful your moves, how quick your reactions, how clever your solutions to the puzzles presented, how deeply carved and cleanly linked your turns, even what you did with your hands. Great surfers could make you gasp with the beauty of what they did. They could make the hardest moves look easy. Casual power, the proverbial grace under pressure, these were our beau ideals. Pull into a heaving barrel, come out cleanly. Act like you've been there before. Make it *look* good. That was the real fascination, and terror, of photos of oneself. Do I look good? If this was a religion, perhaps it didn't bear thinking about what was being worshipped. "*Muthiya maar*," Caroline sometimes trilled over her etching plates as I swapped stories with other surfers over beers.

All surfers are oceanographers, and in the area of breaking waves all are engaged in advanced research. Surfers don't need to be told that when a wave breaks actual water particles, rather than simply the waveform, begin to move forward. They are busy figuring out more arcane relationships, like the one between tide and consistency, or swell direction and nearshore bathymetry. The science of surfers is not pure, obviously, but heavily applied. The goal is to understand, for the purpose of riding them, what the waves are doing, and especially what they are likely to do next. But waves dance to an infinitely complex tune. To a surfer sitting in the lineup trying to decipher the structure of a swell, the problem can indeed present itself musically. Are these waves approaching in 13/8 time, perhaps, with seven sets an hour, and the third wave of every set swinging wide in a sort of dissonant crescendo? Or is this swell one of God's jazz solos, whose structure is beyond our understanding?

When the surf is big, or in some other way humbling, even these questions tend to fall away. The heightened sense of a vast, unknowable design silences the effort to understand. You feel honored simply to be out there. I've been reduced on certain magnificent days—this had happened to me at Honolua Bay, at Jeffreys Bay, on Tavarua, even once or twice at Ocean Beach—to just drifting on the shoulder, gawking at the transformation of ordinary seawater into beautifully muscled swell, into feathering urgency, into pure energy, impossibly sculpted, ecstatically edged, and finally into violent foam.

I HAD TO ADMIT THAT, in part, Mark had succeeded with me. I was surfing more than I would have. I had acquired a couple of new boards—three-fin designs known as thrusters—and a better wetsuit, reducing my hypothermia problem. We made surf runs north and south. When Ocean Beach was big and blown out, we headed to Mendocino County, where Mark knew some sheltered spots. In summer, when O.B. was hopeless, he took me to his favorite south-swell reefbreak, in Big Sur. His generosity seemed effortless, his natural element. He had appointed himself my surf coach, health director, and general adviser. Now he was sitting happily for his portrait. I was thinking more about surfing, if only because I had volunteered to write about it. But was I taking surfing more seriously? Not really. I was taking more notes, but going surfing still felt like something I did basically because I had always done it. Surfing and I had been married, so to speak, for most of my life, but it was one of those marriages in which little is said. Mark wanted to help me and surfing patch up our stubborn, silent marriage. I didn't think I wanted it patched up. Having a sizable tract of unconsciousness near the center of my life suited me, somehow. I almost never talked about surfing except with other surfers. It contributed little to how I saw myself. I was reluctant to think of it as part of my real life as an adult, which I was now busy trying to kick-start. Journalism was ferrying me into worlds that interested me far more than chasing waves.

But something odd was happening. Setting aside my ambivalence, I was letting Mark's exuberance carry me along, letting him become the engine that powered my surfing life. In some ways, I realized, I had let Mark thrust himself *between* me and surfing, antically filling the foreground, haunting my dream life with his fantasies, rending my winter night's sleep with a screaming phone. I even let him preside over primordial moments, his Mephistophelian cackle providing a lifeline from the yawning space of my fear in big waves to some rock face where the psychic crampons held. It was a reporter's passivity, this yielding to an alter ego, but on this story it was disfiguring. I hardly recognized myself in the mirror of the Doc Squad.

Yes, I had been bewitched by surfing as a kid—trotting dreamily down a path at dawn, lit by visions of trade-blown waves, rapt even about the long paddle to Cliffs. The old spell had been broken, at times, or seemed to be. But it always lay there, under the surface, dormant but undestroyed while I knocked around the far world, living in waveless places—Montana, London, New York. I remembered the first time I accompanied Mark up the Mendocino coast, shortly after moving to San Francisco. The swell was big and scary, with a numbing northwest wind ruining every spot except Point Arena Cove, which was protected by a thick kelp bed. I nervously followed Mark out through the channel there, intimidated by the wind, the freezing water, and, especially, by the heavy-gauge waves plunging and grinding down the rock reef. Mark threw himself into the fray, surfing aggressively, and I gradually moved farther out along the reef, taking off on bigger and bigger waves. Finally, I took off on a very big wave, and nearly fell when the nose of my board caught a piece of chop on the takeoff. I recovered, barely, and managed to make the wave. Afterward, Mark, who had seen that takeoff from the channel, said he had actually been frightened for me. "That would have been really, really bad

if you hadn't made it," he said. "That wave was a solid ten feet, and the
only thing that got you down that face was twenty years of experience." It
was true that I had been surfing on pure instinct at that point, too intent
to be scared, although the hold-downs out on that part of the reef did look
to be brutally long. It was embarrassing to admit it but Mark's assessment
pleased me deeply. I was trying to figure out how to live with the disabling
enchantment of surfing—and with Mark's efforts to weave the spell
tighter—but he had said a lot of things, I realized, that I found gratifying.

He also said a lot of things that annoyed me. Once, on another trip to
Mendocino, while we were surfing an exquisite little hidden cove, I had
just ridden a wave rather well, I thought, and Mark had seen it. "You really got a rhythm going on that one," he said as we paddled back out. "You
need to do that more." Giving unwanted advice in the water was a breach
of what I understood as the surfing social contract, and the condescension
of his remark only made it worse. But I held my tongue, which was not
like me. It was ridiculous, I knew, to be so sensitive. But that was not actually why I didn't tell him to shove it up his ass. It was because I was now
planning to write about him. Since getting that assignment, I had changed.
I had become less frank, less spontaneous. For me, this was no longer just
a complicated surfing friendship. It was a writing project, it was reporting,
it was work—indeed, a big opportunity. Speaking hotly could mess that
up. So I tried to remain the unfazed observer. Mark's own manic insouci-
ance insulated him, I thought, from how other people felt. That and his
abiding sense of entitlement and invulnerability.

The seamlessness of his world fascinated me—its willed continuities
and focus, its manifest satisfactions. My own life, by comparison, felt riven
by discontinuities. Surfing, for a start, was like some battered remnant of
childhood that kept drifting incongruously into the foreground of my
days. Surfing bigger waves, especially, felt atavistic—a compulsive return
to some primal scene to prove some primal fact of manhood. Peewee had
also begun to fascinate me. His world, too, seemed seamless, but in a quite
different way from Mark's. The powerful continuities between his past

and present, his childhood and adulthood, were links of place, of community, of character. They were so quiet. They didn't seem to need to display themselves.

SLOAT LOOKED TO BE at least five refrigerators as I pulled up one Sunday afternoon in January. The waves breaking on the outside bar were difficult to see, though. The sun was shining, but the surf was generating a salt mist that filled the air on both sides of the Great Highway—a sharp-smelling haze like some essence from the bottom of the ocean. There was no wind, but gray plumes of spray rose nonetheless from the tops of the largest waves, lifted by the sheer mass and speed of their crests as they plunged. The inside bar was a maelstrom of dredging, midsized killer waves, their dark chocolate faces smeared with drifts of foam. The outside bar looked ill-defined, the swell confused, but the outside waves themselves were smooth and shiny, with clean peaks and sections looming randomly in the mist. Some of them looked ridable—loveliness amid lethality.

I was surprised to see the Sloat lot full. It was Super Bowl day, the 49ers were playing, and kickoff was within the hour. Most of the cars, trucks, and vans were familiar, though: the Ocean Beach surf crew was out in force. Some of its members slouched behind steering wheels, others sat on the hoods of their cars, a few stood on the embankment above the beach. Nobody was in a wetsuit, and no boards had been unsheathed. But everyone was staring out to sea. I looked for a minute, and saw nothing. I rolled down my window and called to Sloat Bill, who was standing on the embankment, heavy shoulders hunched, hands jammed in the pockets of a ski jacket. He turned, regarded me for a moment from behind mirrored sunglasses, then cocked his head toward the surf and said, "Doc and Peewee."

I got out and stood on the embankment, shielding my eyes against the glare, and eventually picked out a pair of tiny figures rising over a massive silver swell. "Neither one of them's taken off for the last half hour," Sloat

Bill said. "It's really shifty." Someone had set up a camera on a tripod, but he wasn't bothering to man it; the mist made photography hopeless. "They're both riding yellow guns," Sloat Bill said. He kept his eyes on the horizon. He seemed miserable, I thought—even more gruff than usual. He was probably agonizing over whether to paddle out himself. Sloat Bill thought of himself as a big-wave surfer, and he did go out on some huge days. But he was a slow paddler, and often never got past the inside bar. He was powerfully built, with a great bull neck—he played competitive rugby, though he was over forty—and he could probably bench-press twice what I could, but fast paddling is not simply a matter of strength. Making a board glide on the surface is partly a matter of artful leverage, and pushing through waves is largely a matter of presenting the least possible resistance to them. Big waves demand a paradoxical combination— ferocity and passivity—that Sloat Bill had never seemed to master. He had only the ferocity. He rolled in the waves like a redwood log, or a canister of pure testosterone. He amused other surfers, very few of whom played rugby. He interested me, although I suspected that I irritated him. He once called me a communist during a poker game at his apartment. Worse, I had sometimes made it out on days when he had not.

Today, I wasn't tempted to try. These waves were far beyond my upper limit. I couldn't see how Mark and Peewee had made it out—or how Peewee had been persuaded to try. It wasn't his sort of surf—not clean. I stood with Sloat Bill a while, trying to keep Mark and Peewee in sight. They disappeared behind swells for minutes at a time. They paddled north constantly, barely holding position against a southbound current. After fifteen minutes, one of them suddenly appeared at the top of an immense wall, paddling furiously toward shore at the head of a peak that looked at least a block wide. A volley of sharp shouts and curses went up along the Sloat embankment. But the wave passed the paddler by; it stood sheer and black across the horizon for what seemed a long time, then silently broke, top to bottom. There were relieved shouts, and strangely bitter curses. The assortment of nonsurfers in the parking lot, on the embankment, on the

beach all looked up in confusion. None of them seemed aware that anybody was in the water.

I had somewhere else to be, across the city—at a friend's house, where
a group of people, none of them surfers, gathered each year to watch the
Super Bowl. I asked Sloat Bill how long Mark and Peewee had been out.
"Couple hours," he said. "It took 'em thirty minutes to get out." He didn't
turn his head.

Twenty minutes later, I was still there, still waiting for something to
happen. The mist was thicker, the sun was lower in the western sky. I was
now going to miss the kickoff. A couple of big sets had come through, but
Mark and Peewee had been nowhere near them. Although there was still no
wind, the conditions were, if anything, deteriorating. Huge rips had started
moving through the outside bars, increasing their confusion. Soon the only
question would be how Mark and Peewee were going to get back in.

Finally, somebody caught a wave. It was a gigantic right, four or five
times overhead, with a wave in front of it that blocked all view of the rider
after the drop. Several seconds passed. Then the rider reappeared, fifty
yards down the line and climbing the face at a radical angle, eliciting
screams of surprise from the gallery. It was impossible to tell who was surfing. He rode all the way to the top of the wave, pivoted against the sky,
then plunged out of sight again. There were appreciative cries and groans.
"Fucker's *ripping*," someone said. The rider was in fact surfing the wave as
if it were a third the size it really was. And he kept it up, wheeling and
carving huge cutbacks, riding from the trough to the crest in unnervingly
sharp arcs as the wave in front of his died down, affording an untrammeled view. It was still impossible to tell who it was, even after the yellow
of his board became visible through the haze. I had never seen Mark or
Peewee surf a wave that size with such abandon. The wave lost half its
height, and all its power, when it hit the deep water between the bars, but
the rider found a stray piece of steep swell that carried him cleanly across
the trough and onto the inside bar. Somehow, as the wave jacked over the
inside bar, he slipped down the face early enough to make a turn, and then

drew a breathtaking line and ran for forty yards under a ledging lip, his arms outstretched against a backlit wall, before he finally straightened out, escaping the lip's explosion by sailing far out onto the flat water in front of the wave. He stayed on his feet when the whitewater, its energy exhausted, finally caught him, and he worked it back and forth all the way to the sand.

As he started up the beach, board tucked under his arm, it was still difficult to tell who it was. Finally, it became clear that it was Peewee. At the moment of recognition, Sloat Bill stepped forward to the edge of the embankment and solemnly began to clap his hands. Others, including me, joined in. Peewee looked up, startled. His face filled with alarm, and then sheepishness. He turned and angled south across the beach, shaking his head, and climbed the embankment where no one could see him.

CAROLINE HAD FINISHED her degree. She was making etchings at night, selling prints in local galleries—images of captivity, wings trussed in boxes, extremely finely detailed. She got a day job as a secretary for a private investigator, then became an investigator herself. She staked out slumlords, interviewed prisoners, impersonated a bank official, a prospective tenant, a United Way canvasser. I went along once or twice as backup to dicey meetings. She tricked people into stating their names, then served them with subpoenas. People kicked the subpoenas down the stairs, believing that if the documents did not touch their hands, they had not been served. (Wrong.) I went along to make sure that they did not kick her down the stairs. (They tried. One bad guy who had been conned by the United Way bit chased her through the hills of Oakland. Luckily, she had been a sprinter at school.) She worked for lawyers. She became interested in American law.

Caroline had come to the United States for the art world. She basically agreed with my mother about San Francisco's mediocrity problem. If she had wanted to live in a pleasant, easygoing city, she could have stayed in

Harare, with her parents and childhood friends. New York beckoned. And yet she was starting to look askance at an art career. A gallery in New York had taken some of her pictures, but to make a living as a printmaker she needed to sell her work for ever-higher prices. It all looked rather airless, precious, too detached for her liking from the basic roil of life. She was also not pleased with the idea that her formal education was complete.

Her father, Mark, came to town on a business trip. He was a minerals trader, now managing Zimbabwe's newly nationalized minerals exporting. He and Caroline stayed up late, drinking a gallon jug of cheap wine to the bottom and banging heads about the war. Their family had been among the few whites who opposed the government in old white-run Rhodesia. But Mark had done some sanctions busting for the rogue regime. Now his daughter wanted to know why. It was a difficult night, and a cruel hangover, but an overdue conversation. At some point, Caroline announced an intention to study American law. Mark offered to help pay for it, confident that with his art-minded daughter it would never come to that. (Wrong. JD, Yale, 1989.)

My book about teaching in Cape Town would soon be published. I wanted to go back to South Africa before that happened. The government was expelling foreign journalists and refusing visas to those who had published work it didn't like. I might not be on their radar yet. I managed to get a tourist visa. The New Yorker gave me an assignment to write about black journalists on a white liberal newspaper in Johannesburg. Shawn, the editor, seemed unconcerned that I still hadn't given him anything about the surfing doctor, though it had been a year at least. New York was calling me too. But it wasn't just serendipity that Caroline and I each wanted to go east. We had survived a rough start, and I could still be a tyrant, but our hearts had enfolded. We found the same things funny.

TOWARD THE END of our third winter in San Francisco, after a series of storms, the sandbar at Outside VFW's began to break regularly for the first time since our arrival. I saw why the wave was a local legend. The bar was unusually long and straight for Ocean Beach, with a deep channel at its northern end. Northwest swells produced clean waves there, but only short rides. The waves hit the bar straight on; one had to take off very near the channel to make them. More westerly swells, on the other hand, struck the bar at a slight angle, making for long, fast lefts of exceptional quality. Since the bar began to break only when the swell was over six feet, Outside VFW's was never crowded. I had watched it break several times, including a couple of frightening days when only Mark, Peewee, Tim Bodkin, and a scatter of other certified big-wave riders paddled out, and I'd actually surfed it a few times on marginal days, when it wasn't breaking with much authority. Then, in early 1986, there came a seriously big and fairly clean day. I didn't have the board for such waves. But Mark did. "You can use my eight-eight," he kept saying, indicating the yellow gun in his van as he scrambled into his wetsuit. "I'll ride my eight-six."

It occurred to me that Mark might be trying to offer my life one last time to the pitiless gods of Ocean Beach. Maybe he already knew what I was trying to find the nerve to tell him—that I had decided to move back to New York. I had mixed feelings about leaving, but one of the biggest was relief. Each winter at Ocean Beach, I had had at least one bad scare—some heavy passage in big surf that troubled my sleep for many nights afterward. Bob Wise understood. "Surfers never do drown out here," he once told me. "It's tourists and drunk bikers and sailors who drown. But even the most experienced surfers get convinced they're about to drown out here at least once a winter. That's what makes Ocean Beach so weird." Mark, who thrived on the weirdness, would not understand, I assumed. But I was glad to be getting away without drowning. I was also glad to be getting out from under Mark's evangelizing gaze. I was tired of being a sidekick. Once upon a time, in Southeast Asia, Bryan had felt compelled to get away from me. But that was different. We were partners. I didn't know how to tell Mark I was leaving. I didn't want to hear about how I was swerving from the surfer's path.

Ten or fifteen guys were hanging out on the seawall. VFW's—Inside VFW's—was the most popular spot along Ocean Beach, and the guys standing around that day, making no move to go out, surfed there regularly. Among them was a beefy housepainter named Rich, who was one of the dominant surfers at this end of the beach. Rich scowled at me as I walked past, the yellow 8'8" under my arm. I realized I had never seen him out in waves over six feet. Today was eight to ten, at least. The swell was massive and fairly west. It was not immaculate—there was a little sideshore wind, and a raging rip—but several stunning lefts roared through, unridden, while we were getting ready to go out. Bodkin and Peewee were already out and each had caught a couple of huge waves, but they were surfing conservatively and letting the ledgier sets go by.

Paddling Mark's board felt like paddling a miniature oil tanker. I kept an old single-fin 7'6" for big days, but I had been riding a 6'9" thruster most of the winter. Thick-railed and sharp-nosed, the 8'8" gun floated me high out of the water, and I had no trouble keeping up with Mark as we started out through the channel. The water was brownish green and very cold; the channel, which ran clear from the shorebreak out to sea, with no inside bar to cross, was choppy and spooky nonetheless, with huge swells sweeping in from both sides, forming fat, unpleasant A-frames that half broke before they vanished. There was a shallow outside bar to the north, where enormous waves leaped up and disemboweled themselves with a horrible growl. To the south, the last section of the long, winding left at Outside VFW's wasn't much more inviting. It too looked shallow and extremely thick. Mark and I paused to watch a smooth-faced wave pitch heavily over the last section of the bar, barely twenty yards from where we lay. Into the great dark barrel it formed, Mark bellowed, "Death!" The idea seemed to please him.

I kept angling out as Mark turned left, cutting across the edge of the bar. Peewee and Bodkin were a couple of hundred yards south, and Mark made a beeline for them, but I circled far around, preferring to look like a coward rather than take a chance on getting caught by a big set. A small set rolled through. It was too far inside for any of us to catch, but even it thundered ominously when it finally broke. I found the scale of things out here thoroughly daunting. I did not look forward to seeing a big set. I checked my position against the shore as I slowly moved south. Huge-lettered graffiti on the seawall—MARIA and KIMO and PTAH—marked my progress. The shore looked, as it often did on big days, bizarrely peaceful and normal. A dark line of cypress trees rose beyond the seawall—a wind-break for the ocean end of Golden Gate Park—and two windmills rose above the trees. Just north, the cliffs were brushed with pink flowers and lined by a stone belvedere, from the ruins of the old Sutro mansion. It all looked so stable. I kept yanking my gaze back and forth, craning to see where I was, then craning to see if anything nightmarish was yet looming out at sea.

Being out in big surf is dreamlike. Terror and ecstasy ebb and flow around the edges of things, each threatening to overwhelm the dreamer. An unearthly beauty saturates an enormous arena of moving water, latent violence, too-real explosions, and sky. Scenes feel mythic even as they unfold. I always feel a ferocious ambivalence: I want to be nowhere else; I want to be anywhere else. I want to drift and gaze, drinking it in, except maximum vigilance, a hyperalertness to what the ocean is doing, cannot be relaxed. Big surf (the term is relative, of course—what I find life-threatening, the next hellman may find entirely manageable) is a force field that dwarfs you, and you survive your time there only by reading those forces carefully and well. But the ecstasy of actually riding big waves requires placing yourself right beside the terror of being buried by them: the filament separating the two states becomes diaphanous. Dumb luck weighs heavily, painfully. And when things go badly, as they inevitably do—when you're caught inside by a very large wave, or fail to make one—all your skill and strength and judgment mean nothing. Nobody maintains their dignity while getting rumbled by a big wave. The only thing you can hope to control at that point is the panic.

I edged south slowly, toward Mark and the others, taking deep, regular

breaths in an effort to slow my heart, which had been pounding unpleas-
antly since the moment I first thought seriously about paddling out. Mark
took off on a wave as I approached the lineup. He screamed as he launched
into a mammoth face and disappeared behind a seething brown wall. The
takeoff spot, I noted, was directly off a big red graffito, PTAH LIVES. Bodkin, who was still sitting with Peewee, shouted my name, grinning widely.
It was a grin that struck me as half wicked amusement at my safety-first
route to the lineup, half congratulation that I was out there at all. Peewee
simply nodded hello. Peewee's blandness in the water was usually a blessing. His poker-faced virtuosity left psychological space for other surfers,
which was something that many of them, I believed, appreciated. Sometimes, though—today, perhaps—I thought Peewee carried surf cool a bit
far. Of course, he probably didn't consider Outside VFW's at this size a
particularly scary place, and maybe didn't realize that for me it was a
stretch.

　　As it happened, luck—and the right board—were with me that afternoon. I caught several big, good waves over the next couple of hours. I
didn't surf them particularly well—it was all I could do to keep the 8'8"
pointed in the right general direction—but they were long, fast rides, and
after each of them I managed to scramble back outside unscathed. Mark's
board was wonderfully stable and allowed me to get into waves early. I
even caught what Mark later called "the wave of the day." On another afternoon, on another board, I would probably have let it pass, but I found
myself at the head of the peak alone, far outside, as a vast wave arrived.
The wall stretched north for blocks, seemingly impossible to make, but by
that point I had great faith in the bar and the channel. I got in early, using
a small cross-chop on the face—what big-wave riders call a chip shot—to
launch myself over the ledge. I had to fight off a little jolt of acrophobia as
I jumped to my feet—the bottom of the wave looked miles beneath me.
Halfway down the face, I leaned back hard into a turn, struggling to stay
over my board as it gained speed across the water running up the face. My
nerve wobbled a second time when I looked over my shoulder at the wall

ahead. It was much bigger than I had expected: taller and steeper and more threatening. I turned away and concentrated, as if wearing blinders, on the few feet of rushing water immediately in front of me, carving long, gradual high-speed turns. The wave held up beautifully, and I made it easily, although the final, house-thick section next to the channel shot me out so fast that I had to abandon all pretense of control, all style, and simply stand there, knees bent, a gratified passenger.

Peewee was in the channel, paddling past as I pulled out. He nodded. We began paddling back out together. My entire body was trembling. After a minute, I couldn't help myself. I asked, "How big was that wave?" Peewee laughed. "Two feet," he said.

WE MOVED TO NEW YORK that summer. It took me seven years to write the piece about Mark and Ocean Beach. More urgent topics—apartheid, war, calamities of different kinds—kept claiming my attention. These were serious matters, consuming as work, self-justifying as projects. Surfing was the opposite. Before I finished the Mark profile, I had published three books—two about South Africa, one about a civil war in Mozambique—plus the first installment of an ambitious book about downward mobility in the United States. I had gone to work full-time for the *New Yorker*, where I wrote, among other things, dozens of opinion pieces. This was another source of my hesitation. Here I was writing, often contentiously, about poverty, politics, race, U.S. foreign policy, criminal justice, and economic development, hoping to have my arguments taken seriously. I wasn't sure that coming out of the closet as a surfer would be helpful. Other policy wonks might say, *Oh, you're just a dumb surfer, what do you know?*

But the biggest reason for my reluctance to finish the piece was a gnawing concern that Mark wouldn't like it. I admired him and found him easy to write about, but he was a complicated character, with a plus-sized self-regard that annoyed, at best, many people in the little surf community

I was also trying to depict. After I left San Francisco, he started editing a medical advice column for *Surfer*. His exploits and epigrams became a staple item in the magazine's regional columns. The surf mags discovered Ocean Beach, partly through Mark's efforts. Then, in 1990, *Surfer* published a phenomenal fourteen-frame sequence of a young goofyfoot, Aaron Plank, on a reeling, double-overhead left at O.B. Aaron was completely hidden from view for seven frames—about four seconds—and came out clean. It felt like the end of an era. The whole world knew about Ocean Beach now. There was even, I heard, a pro contest being held at VFW's.

But the strangest news I had of San Francisco through *Surfer* was a paean to Peewee, by Mark. "Quiet, seemingly egoless, he draws little attention to himself—until he paddles out and goes off," Mark wrote. "Best spot on the beach—Peewee's there. Best wave of the set—Peewee's on it. Best wave of the day—Peewee got it." Mark compared Peewee to Clint Eastwood, and the famous fin-busting incident was mentioned. It was a gracious, unambivalent toast. Had I misread their rivalry? Or was Mark just striking the right high note?

I had been wrong, by the way, to fear Mark's reaction to the news that I was leaving San Francisco. He never missed a beat. We took a last trip to Big Sur together, and he wished me luck. He never seemed to pass up an opportunity, though, once we had landed in New York, to let me know about all the great waves I was missing at Ocean Beach, or on the various surf trips I inexplicably declined to join him on—to Indonesia, Costa Rica, Scotland. In Alaska, he chartered a plane, explored hundreds of miles of coast, and, near the foot of a glacier, discovered and surfed magnificent waves, alone, off a beach marked with fresh grizzly tracks.

I was wrong, too, about losing credibility as a political columnist by revealing that I surfed. Nobody seemed to care one way or the other.

But I was not wrong about Mark's reaction to the piece, when it was finally published. He hated it.

Peter Spacek, Jardim do Mar, Madeira, 1995

NINE

BASSO PROFUNDO

Madeira, 1994–2003

My life had assumed a settled, middle-aged shape. Caroline and I were married. We had been in New York eight years. I was churning out work—columns, articles, books. Journalism. I had turned forty. We had made a world. Bought an apartment. Our friends were writers, editors, artists, academics, publishers. Caroline had set art aside and become, to her own lasting surprise, a defense attorney. She liked matching wits with "the government." I relied more than ever on her warm, unsparing eye. She and I had come to the dance together. Nobody else could know the things we knew, the private language we had built. Before we got married, we had broken up for a while, lived apart. That felt like a near-death experience.

My reporting took me all over, into civil wars and unfamiliar worlds. Some projects swallowed me whole for months and years at a time. Most of the stories I chased were dark with suffering and injustice, but some, like the first democratic elections in South Africa, were hugely gratifying. In the old struggle for my devotion between grown-up work and surfing, work had thrown a hammerlock on chasing waves. Then surfing, ever wily, twisted free. This reversal was abetted, even inspired, by a Rincon-trained regularfoot named Peter Spacek.

He and I met in Montauk, the old fishing village at the east end of Long Island. A surf-magazine editor had given me an address for Peter in a beachfront subdivision known as Ditch Plains. It turned out to be a shingled summer-rental bungalow with a note duct-taped to the front door. There was a Herbie Fletcher longboard, the note said, under the front porch. I should paddle out on that. Below the note was a casual, ex-pert drawing of small, crowded waves. Ditch Plains sits, for surfing pur-poses, at an interesting spot. It's the easternmost settlement on the ocean coast of Long Island. To the west stretch more than a hundred miles of beachbreaks, all the way to Coney Island, in New York City. It's a remark-ably flat, sandy coast. But the sand turns to rock at Ditch, and the last four miles out to Montauk Point are reefbreaks and pointbreaks scattered off a shale-cliffed, roadless shore. In summer, Ditch is a popular family beach, with burrito wagons parked in the dunes and a long, gentle left that breaks along the line where the sand bottom turns to rock. It's a good be-ginner's break. I had never been moved to surf there.

The waves looked chest-high, crumbly, soft. It was a sunny late-summer afternoon. There were probably forty people out, by far the biggest surf crowd I had seen on the East Coast. It was the first time I had been on a longboard in decades. Surfing had endured a longboard revival in the '80s, driven mainly by older guys who could no longer manage short-boards. Longboards require less strength and agility. They catch waves more easily. But longboarders catch waves so early that at many spots they had started crowding out more high-performance boards. For me, it was a point of pride to keep riding a shortboard as I staggered into my forties. Reverting to a longboard would be, I thought, like using a geriatric walker—your dancing days were over. I planned to put it off as long as possible. I knee-paddled around the pack at Ditch and caught a wave out-side. It felt odd, maneuvering a ten-foot board, but the ancient moves came back one by one, and by the end of the ride I was cross-stepping gingerly, mostly ironically, toward the nose. When I kicked out, a guy was sitting on the shoulder studying me. He was a hawk-nosed fellow about my age, with dark blond hair down past his shoulders and a goatee. "They didn't tell me you were a longboarder," he squawked.

Peter was an illustrator, and the editor who had connected us wanted us to collaborate on an article about chasing a hurricane swell up the East Coast. I had surfed a few hurricane swells on Fire Island, but most of my surfing now happened on trips—to California, Mexico, Costa Rica, the Caribbean, France. And most of those trips could also be described, to be brutally frank, as *vacations*. So I was still surfing, but not really. I wasn't even dialed in to the waves around New York City.

After I straightened him out on the longboard question, Peter and I agreed that the swell-chasing article idea was lame. Way too much driving, on a coastline we both found incoherent. Then he started introducing me to Montauk. "It's my little paradise," he said. He didn't mean Ditch Plains, but the uncrowded reef- and beachbreaks in both directions. Peter lived in Manhattan, and had been sharing summer rentals in Ditch for years, but he was still learning the more obscure, fickle spots around Montauk. He was originally from Santa Barbara, and had lived in Hawaii. The first time we scored good waves together, on a solid fall swell at a rock reef east of Ditch, I found the smoothness and power of his surfing startling. It wasn't a style you saw often on the East Coast, where small waves and short rides tend to produce jerky, ungraceful surfing.

That night over dinner he showed me a surf-mag travel piece that had him fired up. The waves in the photos were dreamy: big, deep-hued, knee-weakeningly clean. Their location, following surf-mag convention, was not named, but the editors had not worked hard to disguise the place, and Peter said he knew where it was. "Madeira," he said. "Like the wine." He opened a map. The island sat out in the North Atlantic winter swell window like a bull's-eye, six hundred miles southwest of Lisbon. He wanted to check it out. So did I, suddenly.

. . .

WE MADE OUR FIRST TRIP in November 1994. Madeira was a shock to
the senses—sheer green coasts, tiny cliff-hugging roads, Portuguese peas-
ants studying our boards suspiciously, waves surging heavily out of deep
ocean. We drove through gorges and forests, over high, vertiginous ridges.
We ate *prego no pão* (a garlic steak sandwich) at roadside cafés and tossed
back espressos. We clambered up seawalls and down embankments. There
didn't seem to be any other surfers around. On the north coast, off a village called Ponta Delgada, we found a big left. It was messy and, like every
spot we saw, it broke too close to hungry-looking rocks. But the wave
cleaned up as it swung into the lee of the point, and the inside wall was
long, fast, and powerful. I caught a series of screamers. Peter, paddling
past me, growled, "Would you please stop ripping?" I liked his naked com-
petitiveness. He surfed better than I did, usually, and at Delgada he was
venturing alone out into a windblown, blue-water zone beyond the point,
hunting for monsters that I wanted no part of. But, unlike me, he was
having bad luck with wave selection. He also had, unlike me, a girlfriend
on shore watching.

Alison had been a surprise addition to the trip. She and Peter had only
recently met. She was thin, strong, acerbic, endlessly game, black-haired,
also a commercial illustrator. They both drew constantly—in cafés and
airport lounges, crosshatching away, she reaching over to add ink to his
work in progress. "Don't be afraid of black!" They faxed their work from
hotels and car-rental agencies to clients back in the States. The two of
them were stylish, low-maintenance, nothing-daunted travelers. But they
could be mercurial. The day after we arrived in Madeira, before we had
found waves, they announced that they wanted to go back to mainland
Portugal, which had looked more fun. That was out of the question, I
said. I was silently horrified. What was wrong with these people? Peter
had started sporting a beret—another bad sign. Then we started getting
waves. First at Ponta Delgada, and then, a few miles east of there, we

found a chunky, consistent reefbreak that Peter named Shadowlands. The cliff there was so tall—nearly three thousand feet—that the winter sun never reached the shore. We wore thin wetsuits—long arms, short legs—and slowly worked out how to thread the surprise barrel section at low-tide Shadowlands.

But the main wave region was the southwest coast, where northwest swells swept around the island's western end and were smoothed into long, orderly lines. From our surf-mag source, we knew where to look. There was a village called Jardim do Mar—the Garden of the Sea. It sat out on a small, storybook headland. Off that headland, if the photos were to be believed, a great wave broke. The first time we checked it, the wind was wrong and the surf was small. I went exploring the coast (vertical, deserted, stunning) west of Jardim by surfboard, not expecting to find waves, while Peter and Alison hiked along the rocks. He lugged a board, just in case. At a rugged, boulder-strewn promontory called Ponta Pequena, we stumbled on a surprising setup: clean, fierce little rights wrapping into a shallow cove. Peter and I got amongst it. For chest-high waves, the penalties for falling were unusually high, and Peter left a fair amount of blood on the rocks. I had another lucky outing. Afterward, in his drawings of our first Ponta Pequena session, I saw that Peter had been once again keeping score. He got 1.5 barrels while I got 5, according to a box score included in the drawing. Also, he got hurt and I did not. All while his girlfriend watched.

One reason I liked these little contests Peter devised, it occurred to me later, was that I always seemed to win them. Otherwise, Peter probably wouldn't have mentioned them. Beneath his skater grunge presentation (he still skateboarded, at forty-plus, around his neighborhood, TriBeCa), he had quietly perfect manners. His parents were Czech immigrants who fled Eastern Europe when he was small, and some of his uncommon civility came, I guessed, from them: an Old World upbringing in the wilds of California. The rest, though, was him. But I loved the way he tapped into the showing off and one-upmanship of surfing and turned it into straight-faced gags. I had surfed with too many guys with whom the latent competition was loaded, and therefore never mentioned. Peter's hero at art school had been R. Crumb, and he and the master shared an affinity for lampooning awkward truths.

For Madeira, I had bought a big-wave board, a gun, the first I had owned. It was an 8'0" squashtail thruster, thick and dartlike, built for pure speed. It was ostensibly shaped by an old North Shore hand named Dick Brewer. Brewer was the best-known big-wave shaper in surfing, and I doubted that he had done more than design and sign my board. I had bought it off the rack at a surf shop on Long Island. It was a mystery what the Brewer was doing there—Long Island would probably never see, even on the biggest hurricane swells, waves that required such a board—but I took its appearance as a sign. Peter urged me to get it and I did. He also brought a gun along.

In Madeira, we knew after a few days that we had found something extraordinary. It took us a few forays, though, to grasp its full dimensions.

THE FIRST TIME WE SURFED Jardim do Mar, or the first time we surfed it good, was probably the next year. Even at six feet, it was a serious wave. Heavy, long-interval lines marched out of the west, bending around the headland into a breathtaking curve. They feathered and bowled and broke at the outermost point of the horseshoe, and then reeled down a rocky shore. We paddled out from a primitive boat ramp—a mossy concrete slide off a seawall—far down the point. As we got closer to the lineup, the power and beauty of the waves got more drenching. A set rolled through, shining and roaring in the low winter afternoon sun, and my throat clogged with emotion—some nameless mess of joy, fear, love, lust, gratitude.

A crowd of villagers had gathered on a terrace below the church bell tower. We weren't the first surfers they had seen. Still, they seemed frantically curious about our progress as we tried to figure out the lineup. They cheered when one of us caught a wave. The takeoffs were intense, and must have looked dramatic, with a great ramp of silver face and then a

Jardim do Mar, 1998

broad, backlit, green-gold wall standing up quickly. We both surfed conservatively, picking our waves carefully, then driving hard, using the big faces to carve around sections, showing respect, not pulling in. The speed and depth and scale of the waves were a revelation, a glory. And the villagers clearly knew a good ride when they saw one. They also knew this patch of ocean well, and from their height they could see more than we could. They started whistling us into position. A piercing whistle meant a big wave was coming and we needed to paddle farther out. A more piercing whistle meant we needed to paddle faster. A gentler whistle meant we were in the right spot. We surfed till dark.

That evening we ate *espada preta*—a sweet-fleshed, monstrous-looking deepwater fish—in a café in the village. We wanted to thank the whistlers, buy them a drink, but people were shy, not used to strangers. Peter pronounced the wave "supreme." I started looking for a place to stay.

MADEIRA BECAME MY WINTER RETREAT. Vacations, these were not. They were submersions, some lasting many weeks. The spots we surfed were all dicey, super-complex reefbreaks, demanding the most diligent study and harshly penalizing even small mistakes. For me, with my physical powers dwindling and my work as a journalist in high gear, it was a strange time to take on such a high-stakes, off-the-grid, unforgiving project.

But I found the island a resonant lair. Most of the Portuguese immigrants to Hawaii had come, it seemed, from Madeira. The malasadas (Portuguese doughnuts) we ate as kids had come from here, as had the Portuguese sausage that I once wolfed down uncooked. Even the ukulele had come originally from Madeira, where it was known as the *braguinha*. I could see, or thought I could, in the faces of Madeirans strong traces of the Pereiras and Carvalhos I had known on Oahu and Maui. Madeirans had gone to Hawaii in their thousands to work in the canefields—sugar had been Madeira's first export crop. The island was famous for its wine, but its main export was not wine; it was people. Madeira had been unable to support its own population since the mid-nineteenth century. People, especially young people, were still emigrating in large numbers. South Africa, the United States, England, Venezuela, Brazil—every Madeiran I met seemed to have relatives living overseas.

The African connection was the most intense. When António Salazar, the midcentury Portuguese dictator, tried to export his surplus-peasant problem to his colonies in Angola and Mozambique, a great many Madeirans joined the exodus. Most became farmers (cotton, cashews). Inevitably, many served as soldiers. Even little Jardim do Mar had among its few hundred residents several Portuguese Army veterans of the anticolonial wars. I knew Mozambique, having written about the civil war that broke out there after independence. But I never saw a reason to mention, among the ex-colonists on Madeira, my time in Mozambique. Nearly all the Portuguese had fled after independence.

Now they were fleeing newly democratic South Africa. Shipping containers would show up in the square, the *praça*, in Jardim. The whole village would turn out to unload the loot—ironwood furniture, modern home electronics, even cars, all straight from Pretoria. I became friendly with a Jardim native named José Nunes. He had lived in South Africa. Now he lived with his family above a small bar and grocery that he had inherited from his father. "People come back because they don't feel safe now in South Africa," José said. "Here they're safe. But there's nothing for them to do."

People still fished, actually, and farmed, but the farming was all by hand—grueling work—on little rock-walled terraces. Old men in tweed caps and cardigans, red-faced and bandy-legged, solid-bodied, worked the terraces. Wine grapes, bananas, sugarcane, papayas—small plots and fields were cut into all but the steepest slopes. In Jardim, every porch and wall seemed to overflow with flowers. There was a constant light, gulping music of spring water rushing off the mountain—it ran down through the village, through an intricate system of gutters, watering the lush house-hold vegetable gardens. At the corners of the tiled roofs of the houses were ceramic doves, cats, little boxerlike dogs, busts of young scholars in old-fashioned hats.

I sometimes stayed in a new hotel in the village, and later in rented rooms. I brought work for when there were no waves or the winds were bad. But the surf ruled my days. When it was big, mist and thunder filled the air. At night, during a swell, there was a general roar in Jardim—a deep bass throb that was not the sea but the rocks underneath the point, groaning. Madeira has no continental shelf. It is like Hawaii that way. Giant storm swells from the north and west cross very deep water unimpeded and strike the island full force. But even Hawaii has, in many places, offshore reefs to absorb the impact, and sandy beaches. Madeira supposedly has a beach, somewhere on the east side, but in a decade of chasing waves there I never saw it. The shore was rocks and cliffs, which often multiplied the danger quotient, which was already high, by a large factor. We were mining a rich lode of bliss. But disaster never felt far away.

. . .

OUR FIRST BAD MISADVENTURE came during that second winter. It happened to Peter, at Ponta Pequena. We had paddled out at Jardim, early in the morning. It was glassy and big—twice the size of that first great afternoon session. We were both on our guns. The scale of everything had expanded. There were excellent waves pouring through where we had surfed before, but that zone was now unsafe. The big sets showed far out at sea—darkening bands on a pale blue surface, wide and heavy, steaming silently toward us from the southwest. As they approached, I found it hard to stay in position. I kept sprinting southeast, digging for deeper water, unnerved by the size of the swell. This was as big as anything I had surfed at Ocean Beach, and that had been in another, more physically fit life. A few people seemed to be out on the church terrace watching, but they were not whistling—or perhaps their whistles were being drowned out by the constant boom of shorebreak. Peter was showing more guts, paddling less frantically for the horizon when a set appeared. He angled toward the outer wall, not away from it.

The takeoff was a huge, clean open face, not breaking exceptionally hard, and the wall seemed to hold up reasonably, with no catastrophic sections, all the way down the point. Eventually, Peter caught a wave. With a shout, he jumped to his feet, rode over the ledge, and disappeared for what felt like a very long time. I thought I saw his track once down the line, but I wasn't sure. Then he came flying over the shoulder far, far inside with arms raised. He came back raving. It was doable, he said. It was *insane*. I moved over, into the lineup, heart thudding, and caught a couple. The takeoffs were giddy, almost nauseating, but not overly steep. The faces were maybe twenty feet. (We would call the waves ten or twelve.) I surfed carefully, arms outstretched for balance. The rides were long and swooping, the blue walls like great stretched canvases. Each of my rides ended with a safe, gliding pullout somewhere down near the boat ramp. I was very glad I was on my gun. My confidence began trickling back.

Then Peter surprised me. "Let's get out of here," he said. "It's too much pressure."

I was happy to leave. My hair was still dry. We paddled up the coast, across half a mile of calm water, to Ponta Pequena. It was also big, double-overhead-plus, but unintimidating. The outside takeoff at Pequena was soft—not inconsequential at this size, but easy. Pequena was a strange wave. When it was over six feet, it did not taper down as you rode, as most waves do, but actually got, on the inside, near the shallow cove where we had first surfed it, suddenly more powerful, faster, much more intense. You had to be prepared for the acceleration. It was like surfing from Malibu to the North Shore on a single wave. But there was a pause before the transformation, a pause that gave one just enough time to plan for the shift into hypervelocity, time to decide what line to take, and how to escape. I was starting to love Pequena, mainly for that mutant shapeshift, and on this sunny morning, having survived big Jardim unscathed, I was surfing it hard, happily, unafraid. That may be why it took me too long to notice that Peter had disappeared. We had been riding in a rotation. Then I was surfing alone. I kept watching the channel, kept checking the impact zone. I wasn't worried. Peter was strong and smart. My sense of acute threat from earlier had lifted. Finally, I spotted him. He was on shore, down past the boulders that marked the lower end of Pequena, sitting next to his board, his head between his knees. I headed down there and scrambled ashore.

Peter gave me a nod. He looked out to sea. It wasn't quite the thousand-yard stare, but not far off. It seemed that he had stayed too long on a wave, gotten caught by the next one, sucked into the shorebreak, and then had his ankle leash wrap tight around a rock. At this tide (high), and this size, the Pequena shorebreak was absolutely off-limits. It broke on a steep scree of jagged lava rocks, then smashed against a sheer cliff. Unable to free his leash or even reach his ankle to tear it off, Peter had been trapped—dragged out, flung back. Most of the time, he was underwater. He didn't know how many waves had pounded him. In the end, but not before he had decided he was about to drown, his leash had snapped. "It was a miracle," he murmured. "I have no idea why it snapped."

His board looked to be more banged up than he was. He later made a series of drawings of his predicament in the Pequena shorebreak. With titles like *Undesirable Situation No. 002*, they were semi-comic. But the boulders and cliffs and empty, terraced coast beetled darkly over the tethered, big-nosed surfer.

WE WERE NO LONGER the only surfers around. Shortly after our first visit, a group of Hawaiian pros had come to Madeira. They had scored great surf, and in the lavish magazine spread about their trip they compared Jardim favorably to Honolua Bay. So the secret was well and truly out. Even Mark Renneker, I heard, had paid a visit, wearing a crash helmet to surf Jardim. Jardim was being touted in the global surf underground as not only an A-grade wave but an extreme rarity: a big-wave pointbreak, possibly the best in the world. Nobody knew how big a swell it could handle; nobody had seen it close out yet. The Hawaiians had been wowed by another spot as well, a grinding barrel that broke close to shore in Paul do Mar, the next village to the west. You could see the wave from Jardim—it was beyond Ponta Pequena—but the drive over the mountain to Paul was tortuous.

A big, perspective-challenged mural of the wave at Jardim, painted by a California surfer, had materialized in our absence on a wall in the *praça*. A harlequin crew of Brits, Aussies, Americans, and Portuguese mainland surfers had started passing through the village, lodging here and there. We hit it off with a young couple who had come for the winter, Moona and Monica. He was Scottish, she Romanian. They had met in Bosnia, where they both did relief work during the war. Now they had a new baby, Nikita. Monica was translating *The English Patient* into Romanian. Moona, who had been a pro skateboarder, was fearlessly trying to translate his skater chops into surfing competence, with mixed results, in supremely unforgiving waves. They were a luminous pair, living in a seaside room on next to nothing. I had written about Bosnia, and Moona and Monica said I had to visit Tuzla, the old salt-mining city where they had met. It was an anti-nationalist island in a sea of raging nationalisms, they said. They were so persuasive that, later that winter, back at work, I took their advice and made my way to Tuzla. They were right. It was a ravaged, poignant place from which to look at the war that had just ended in pan-ethnic bitterness.

One morning, half a dozen of us trooped over to Paul do Mar. It was eight feet and rifling. In less than an hour, Peter had snapped his board, gashing his foot, and an American named James had been lip-axed and broken his ankle. They left together for the hospital in Funchal, the capital, three hours away. Two days later, again at Paul, my foot got stuck between two rocks in the shorebreak. I ended up at the same hospital for X-rays (negative), and for the next week surfed with foot and ankle heavily duct-taped for stability. Peter announced that Paul do Mar was not a surf spot, that it was just a picturesque, kamikaze close-out. I disagreed. I found it a mesmerizing wave.

But absurdly dangerous. Besides the raw power, there was the shoreline. The rocks were round, mostly, but the shorebreak borderland you had to cross to enter the water was simply too wide, particularly when the surf was big. Even after timing it carefully, waiting for a lull, letting a shorebreak wave expend itself, then running recklessly with your board over wet boulders, you sometimes didn't make it to water deep enough to paddle on before the next wave slammed you, banging you backward across the rocks—board, body, dignity all battered, sometimes severely. This was not a normal ocean problem. It felt like bad arithmetic—the time and distance did not, for some Madeira-only reason, compute. I had never seen a surf spot with an entrance so daunting. And the exit, getting back onto dry land, could be even worse. The wave we were there to ride was at most only thirty yards offshore, but I sometimes resorted to a very long paddle, around a seawall at the far east end of the village, rather than face that shorebreak.

The glory of the wave was its down-the-line speed. The water was often dead clear at Paul, which made for an unnerving effect on the takeoff. Sometimes, as you caught the wave, jumped to your feet, and, assuming things went according to plan, made a quick edge turn to your right, the bottom did not move at all. The big white boulders underneath the water were stationary, or even inching slightly backward. There was, that is, so much water rushing up the face that no matter how fast your board was moving across the surface, you were, in land terms, standing still. This, again, was not normal ocean behavior. Then, after a few moments of this stomach-turning suspended animation, you would suddenly start rocketing down the coast, with the boulders turning into a long white blur under blue water. You went so fast that on a wave strongly angled from the west, you could ride for a hundred yards without seeming to get any closer to shore. Peter was right, the wave had a strong kamikaze element. It was hollow, shallow, and many waves did close out. But the right wave at Paul do Mar was by itself, to my mind, worth the round-trip airfare from New York.

I GOT THREE OF THEM in quick succession one gray morning. Peter had gone to the north coast at dawn, guessing wrong about what the wind and swell would do. During the previous winter, we had found on the north coast a spot we called, for reasons now obscure, Madonna. We had never seen anyone else in the water there. It was a silky, wind-protected left at the base of a waterfall-striped cliff—a quicksilver wave, sweet and swift. I felt its call, wondered what it was doing, every day. Peter headed that morning, on a hunch, to Madonna. But it was a long trip, and there was a solid swell hitting at Paul do Mar, and the first rule of chasing waves is never to drive away from surf, so I didn't go. He took another guy with him.

The shorebreak at Paul looked too fearsome for me. I made the roundabout slog from the east. The village of Paul do Mar was long, narrow, dusty, and semi-industrial—nothing like the dense tile-roofed hamlet of Jardim up on its sparkling headland. Paul stank, for a start. At the east end of town, by the wharf, it had a strong fish smell. To the west, where the surf was, the stench was lavatorial—people used the shoreline rocks as an open-air toilet. There was primitive worker housing strung along the sea-facing road. Dirty, half-naked children jeered at strange cars. On certain afternoons, roughly half the adults in Paul do Mar seemed to be falling-down drunk. People in Paul, I eventually learned, considered the people in Jardim snobs. Jardimeiros considered Paulinhos riffraff. The two villages faced each other across a mile of sea, with a mountain between them and no other settlements in sight. Their rivalry went back centuries. I got to like them both.

On that gray morning, I paddled far outside and then parallel to shore, trying to see what the wave ahead was doing. It looked big, smooth, peaky, ferocious. There were a couple of guys out, young Portuguese mainland hotshots on tiny boards. I stopped and surfed with them a while. They were excellent surfers but playing it safe, riding the shoulders of waves that were already breaking long before we caught sight of them. Effectively, they were contenting themselves with scraps. Lovely scraps, to be sure. Still, I was on my gun. I was nervous but not weak with fear, even when the heavy sections on the set waves threw out and boomed upcoast. I started moving deeper, paddling west. The usual lineup markers were a pair of brick smokestacks, but those, I could see, wouldn't work today. The main peak today was much farther west.

The peak that I ended up riding was not especially far from shore. It was on the west side of a channel I hadn't seen before—a choppy stretch where a heavy current, a huge amount of water, was hurrying out to sea. I had to angle in and paddle hard to cross the channel, which didn't seem to be following a bottom contour. Evidently, this ocean-bound river had been created simply by the dynamics, the angle, and the sheer volume of this morning's swell. Beyond it, I found a frightening but completely intelligible—unusually intelligible—surf spot: a big, clean, fast-moving, classic horseshoe peak. I knew where to go—out to the place where it stood up tall—and that's where I went.

I caught three waves, just a few minutes apart, each from the heart of the peak. They were textbook waves: huge drops, gaping barrels, reliable shoulders, not very long rides. The water was murky, a stirred-up turquoise-gray, so I couldn't see if the boulders on the bottom were inching backward on the takeoffs or not. Still, I could tell, deep in my chest, that everything was wrong with these waves. The water ran up the face too fast, the lip threw out too hard. To anyone even moderately experienced, the physics of these waves were off. It was obviously too shallow. These waves were far too big for the amount of water they were breaking in. That was why they broke so hard, and why they fired me toward the shoulder like a too-light toy. I corrected for the ominous physics by being extra-aggressive, by overriding my normal takeoff instincts, and by having the right board. Precisely the right board. My third wave had a longer wall than the others. I rode farther down the line, out of the warped chamber of the great takeoff barrel section, onto a relatively flat face, where I got slapped off by a whitewater paw, tumbled a bit, and then came up in a calm area, quite near shore, just inside the big rip current. I saw my chance, sprinted for land, and hit the rocks feet first on the back of a shorebreak wave that chose, after seeming to consider the matter imperiously, to spare me. It drew back not overpoweringly, while I hugged a rock, and a few seconds later I was standing on dry land, in weak sun, waving to a group of kids who had been watching me from a concrete wall, yelling and whistling after each of my rides. The kids were silent now. They waved back noncommittally.

I walked slowly down the coast road through the village. I was barefoot, dripping. To the Paulinhos, I knew, I was one of these new *estrangeiros*, these foreign savages, who washed in from the sea with a flimsy craft, finned and pale. Nobody said, "*Bom dia.*" A high, salt-corroded wall blocked my view of the ocean. Those three waves. I had rarely, if ever, ridden more critical waves. It did not bear thinking about what would have happened if I had misjudged a takeoff, or slipped, or hesitated for an instant. Really, all I had done was surf them correctly, after dialing up my aggression to a level befitting a far better, braver surfer than me. Luck had played a big part, but so had long experience. I recognized those waves as lethal but also as nearly flawless and, with the right equipment and sufficient technique, ridable.

I kept expecting to start shaking, to get hit by some racking adrenaline drain, now that I was safe on land. Instead, I felt fantastic, quiet, light on my feet. I came to a little café. I had been there before, and the owner gave me coffee and a bun on credit. From the raised café steps, I could see the ocean. Great sets were now reeling down the coast, even bigger than earlier. The rip channel had vanished. So I had caught a brief window of big, highly concentrated, well-organized waves at a spot that was no longer there. My luck had been extravagant. I felt like finding a church, lighting a candle, and humbling myself.

What was I doing? Why was I here? I was a grown-up, a husband, a citizen, full of conventional public-spiritedness in my real life. My American life. I was forty-four years old, for Christ's sake. And not a churchgoer. Everything felt unreal, including my sense of disbelief. And yet the cup in my hand did not shake. Indeed, the weak instant coffee tasted sublime.

IN THE EARLY DAYS of our friendship, I sometimes misjudged Peter. I invited him to a gallery opening in SoHo. The work was all by prison inmates. "Yeah, yeah, 'outsider art,'" he said, peering at the pictures. He cocked his head, moved in close, stepped back, frowned. I tried to help. "Looks like that guy's been looking at too much Magritte," I said.

Now Peter frowned at me. "Don't go all art history on me."

I realized that, in his terms, I was probably just thinking in clichés. That was about as brusque as he got.

We repaired to his loft on Murray Street, where he made margaritas ("They don't know how to make 'em in New York") and we watched surf videos with his dog, a bright-eyed toy poodle named Alex. Downstairs, there was a topless bar called New York Dolls. The place made its money from Wall Street guys. Peter, the quiet, funny, aging skater who lived upstairs and sometimes brought his sketchbook in and worked, got special treatment—cheap beer, no hustles—and his house pass extended to his guests. The barmaids fell by to chat between lap dances. They were all, as per cliché, graduate students with heartstopping breasts. It was an unlikely local, but surprisingly relaxed and gemütlich—Peter actually used that word. His New York was full of surprises. He had started out, after art school, working at a big ad agency—quite hard to picture—before prospering as a freelancer. He had been married, divorced. In his day, he had been a nightlifer, and friends from that era still talked about the time he spotted Cher in a club, asked her to dance, and then tore up the dance floor with her.

"It was Cher!" he said, when I expressed disbelief. "It was my big chance!" His irony sometimes had more levels than I could read.

But Peter's big-city days ended abruptly after he and Alison found a tiny old house on a choice piece of land in Ditch Plains. They both sold their lofts and moved out there with Alex. They built a studio across from the house, divided the space, and, working a few feet apart, kept cranking out illustrations. The ocean was across the street. They got a seagoing kayak and fished for striped bass, porgy, bluefish, fluke. They went clamming in Napeague Bay, crabbing in the local salt ponds. Peter installed a commercial smoker in a shed. After a year or two, they seemed to be practically subsisting off their ocean harvest and vegetable garden. They bought an old fishing boat, which Peter refurbished in the yard. When it got too cold to work outside, he built a Quonset hut over the boat. I was a frequent visitor. On hurricane swells, I stayed with them, and Peter and I surfed the obscure, sometimes superb rock reefs and pointbreaks east of Ditch.

They got married during a pumping south swell. The ceremony was out on Montauk Point, on a grassy hillside under the lighthouse. It was

Peter Spacek and Alex, Montauk,
1998—with kayak-caught striped bass

late afternoon, the golden hour, and a pointbreak called Turtles, just south
of where we stood, was firing. The groom's side was lousy with surfers,
many of them from Santa Barbara. The Californians in particular could
not believe what they were seeing at Turtles. It looked like a good day at
Rincon. Everyone tried to attend to the nuptials, but each time somebody
muttered, "Set," many heads turned. There was some glaring, some discreet kicking with high heels, but before it was over, even Alison laughed.

The band played "Up, Up, and Away" at the reception in Peter and
Alison's yard. People (I was one) cringed and thought there must be some
mistake. "It's our song!" Peter squawked as he and his bride danced.
Maybe cheesiness was the new edginess. Peter was wearing an extraordinary outfit—skintight leather pants, laced up in front, sharp boots, some
kind of ruffled pirate blouse. "I don't see why she's the only one who gets
to look hot," he told me. Caroline confirmed that he looked dashing. He
had the lifelong surfer's build: a slim waist under a huge triangle of back

muscles. Caroline watched him dance, and for years afterward called him Ol' Snake Hips. They gave out commemorative coffee mugs that showed a couple, each in waders, each wielding big casting rigs, each leaning back hard, having hooked each other. The image was powerful and slightly disturbing, the drawing style an artful combination of his and hers.

The four of us went fishing on their renovated boat very late that year—after Thanksgiving. It was stunningly cold. We drove out to a deep spot Peter knew, over dark gray water, a few miles northwest of Montauk Point. He told me how much line to pay out. The fish we wanted were on the bottom. The wind kicked up, and each lash of spray coming over the rail turned quickly to ice on the deck. Caroline and Alison huddled in the wheelhouse over a flask of hot spiked tea. Finally, just before dark, Peter and I each hooked up good-sized blackfish. My face was numb. Our hands were useless clubs. We got the fish aboard and then pounded, triumphant, back to Montauk Harbor. That night, at home, I cleaned my fish, which was still twisting and twitching. Too tired to cook, I put it in the fridge. Hours later, we heard the blackfish thumping inside the fridge.

PETER AND I KEPT MAKING our pilgrimages to Madeira. His devotion began to seem suspect to me, though. He kept suggesting that we try someplace new. Why would he even say that? It reminded me of our first Madeira trip, when he and Alison nearly bailed back to mainland Portugal. They now took big-time fishing trips—to Christmas Island, in the central Pacific; to the Bahamas for bonefish—when they had the time and money. Peter said, "It's good to try new things." I found myself saying, No, I want to keep doing the same thing: Madeira. When had I become such a mewling creature of habit?

I actually had good arguments for going back over and over. One was the phenomenal quality of the waves, and their particular spooky allure, quite unlike anywhere else either of us had surfed. And it wasn't as if the surf was easy—a set of challenges that we had now mastered. Not even

close. Moreover, Madeira was becoming famous in surf world. It was get-
ing more crowded each year. It would soon be ruined, overrun, like Bali
and dozens of other surf meccas around the globe. There was already talk
of a big-wave contest to be held at Jardim, with corporate sponsors and big
prize money. I watched these signs, heard these rumors, with rising dread.
We had to surf it now, before it went to hell.

The biggest boosters of Madeira's surf were the mainland Portuguese.
The island had quickly become their Hawaii, their North Shore. Mainland pros flew over on every swell. One young guy, Tiago Pires, was clearly
a rare talent, with balls of steel—he would go on to a respectable career on
the world pro tour, the first (and still the only) Portuguese surfer to qualify for it. The Portuguese surf mags couldn't get enough Madeira. They
splashed the name across their covers, ran huge articles with zero discre-
tion. It seemed to be a size thing. The first Madeira poster I saw, a foldout
in a magazine, showed a mainland pro riding a huge green wall at Jardim,
with a caption calling it "the largest wave ever ridden on Portuguese national territory." The poster was titled *Heróis do Mar*—Heroes of the Sea.

Peter understood the urgency of surfing Madeira before it got, as we
would say, zooed. But he also understood, as I did not, how few surfers
were ever likely to hurl themselves into a solid day at Jardim or Paul do
Mar. He had showed that first article in *Surfer* to a number of guys in
Montauk whom he thought would be interested. They weren't. Too
heavy-looking. I was the only one who bit. But I had thought the photos
made it look idyllic. Now I thought of them as misleading. Without the
rocks and cliffs, without the fear factor, one understood nothing about
these spots. But I felt chained to them now, despite the fear. Peter had a
more arm's-length, less obsessive relationship. And less fear.

Peter was what surfers used to call (some still do) a gnarly dude. There
had always been guys, usually big-wave surfers, who quietly, casually did
things that beggared belief. I remember hearing, on the Hawaiian rumor
mill, that Mike Doyle and Joey Cabell, two surf stars from my youth, had
set off swimming down the Na Pali Coast on Kauai. The Na Pali Coast is

seventeen miles of inaccessible wilderness, facing northwest into the biggest storm-producing expanse of the Pacific. The swim took three days. They wore nothing but trunks and goggles. All they took was a pocketknife, for prying shellfish off the rocks. They did it for fun, to see what they saw. Those two were gnarly dudes, which was both why they did it and why they survived.

Peter was cut from that cloth. He would set off in his kayak for Amagansett, fifteen miles west of Ditch Plains, trolling with a rod propped on his shoulder to see what he could catch, or jump on a cod boat in winter to go fish the shipwrecks off Block Island. He once got a large treble fish hook through his hand and drove that way to the hospital in Southampton, twenty-five miles away. He surfed the biggest days anyone had seen in Montauk, usually alone, and the stories he told, if pressed for details, about those sessions were reliably droll, vivid, self-mocking. He turned terrifying episodes into comic drawings. On a big afternoon at Jardim, he got creamed on a late takeoff and nearly suffered a two-wave hold-down. He was down there so long, he told me, after he finally made it back to the lineup, that he found himself saying good-bye to loved ones. In a drawing I saw later, there was the familiar bewildered, big-nosed, long-haired antihero deep under the monstrous wave, quizzically producing thought balloons featuring Alison and an alarmed-looking toy poodle.

In San Francisco when I lived there, Mark Renneker and Peewee Bergerson had been the gnarliest dudes. That was why other men were obsessed with them. It was boys' own adventure stuff—silly, from most angles. But riding surf that requires serious courage and skill without tooting one's own horn is a keen test of character. In pro surfing, there is a growing niche of gnarly dudes with publicists. That isn't the idea at all.

PETER BROUGHT two old friends along to Madeira. I liked them, but Peter's casual, let's-mix-it-up attitude continued to discomfit me. Hoping to make our trips coincide with good swells, I had begun trying to forecast the surf in Madeira, gathering what I could from marine weather reports, keeping obsessive records of North Atlantic storms—their tracks past Iceland and Ireland and into the Bay of Biscay, their daily maximum wind speeds, and the lowest pressure readings at their cores—creating predictions for what I thought the waves should be doing in southwest Madeira and then phoning José Nunes for reports on what the surf was actually doing at Jardim. José was a busy man, with other things to do than hike out to the seafront and study waves, and he didn't have the specialized vocabulary to tell me much, but he did his best, helping me see that I was consistently getting it wrong. This was before online global surf forecasting came into its own, rendering my primitive efforts irrelevant.

So Peter and I knew nothing about the giant swell that was bearing down on us one winter afternoon at Jardim do Mar in 1997. I had been surfing since dawn, at Paul and at Pequena, and was shaking with exhaustion. Then I saw a series of lovely sets reel through at Jardim. It was late in the day, but not paddling out never occurred to me. I wasn't sure where Peter was. There was nobody in the water, making it hard to gauge the size. I took my gun, which turned out to be the right choice. The waves were quick, powerful, deep green, double-overhead, with offshores gusting up the faces. I caught two or three. My weariness vanished in a flood of adrenaline. Hurrying to make a long wall, I noticed another surfer paddling over the shoulder, craning to peer into the shadows of the pit, where I was trying to hold a high line. It was Peter.

"I knew it had to be you," he crowed. "From the boat ramp, we could barely see this little silhouette."

The glare, looking west into the waves, was indeed blinding. I was extremely happy to see Peter. His company made the surf feel less fearsome. His friends had stayed on shore.

"It looks like there are some big motherfuckers out here," he said.

We both dug hard to the south to avoid a cleanup set. The swell seemed to be building. We edged back into the lineup, and each caught hefty waves. It wasn't classic Jardim—it was too windy—but it was big, fast, soul-stirring stuff. Maybe Peter was right: this place would never get crowded. It was too hairy.

Another cleanup set, and another long, hard scratch to the south. Peter went over the biggest wave first, and I remember seeing him bust sideways through the backlit crest fifteen or twenty vertical feet above me, as I dug for the next flank of the shoulder. It was a close thing, but we both made it over. Outside, a small fishing boat was motoring past. The boat was dangerously close to the surf, and half a dozen fishermen were at the rail, studying us.

"They think we're nuts."

"They're right."

It didn't occur to me that the fishermen, reading their patch of ocean correctly, might have been offering us a lift to a safe harbor, in some town farther east. We waved to them, caught our breaths, and began paddling back to the takeoff zone, trying to line up the church bell tower with a distant pillar of cliff. That was usually the spot. The boat motored away.

Bigger sets kept coming, moving us farther out. They started breaking in a new spot, higher up the point, and heaving with a ledginess I hadn't seen before at Jardim. As we were paddling over the shoulder of an enormous wave, Peter yelled, "What does Brock Little say? Are you supposed to look or not?"

I didn't know what he meant. Brock Little was a Hawaiian big-wave surfer. We were now far outside the normal Jardim takeoff zone. We had made it over the set. The sun was going down. "He either says you should look into the pit, and see exactly what it's doing, so you'll know," Peter said. "Or you should not look, keep thinking positive, don't think about what the wave could do to you, just think about making every fucker you catch."

I favored not looking. The last two waves had been truly frightening. When they broke, they sounded like freight trains colliding.

"We have to move in if we're going to catch a wave," I said. "Look where we are."

Peter agreed. We were ludicrously far from shore. We started paddling in, down the point, glancing back after every stroke. A midsized set appeared. Peter put his head down and dug hard. He pulled away rapidly. My exhaustion was returning, now mixed with the queasiness of fear. I glanced back. There was a very big wave coming. I was more or less in position. I assumed that Peter had caught the one before it, and I did not want to be out here alone. I paddled hard. As the wave began to lift me, a side-chop caught my rail, throwing off my stroke. I kept digging. I heard Peter shouting. I couldn't see him, but I thought I heard, "Go! Go!" The wave seemed to be shrugging me off. I couldn't get it to engage my board. Then I realized that Peter was yelling, "No! No!" I veered right, grabbed my left rail, and went up the big face sideways. I made it over the top, then got whipped by a long downpour of offshore spray as the wave heaved and broke just a few yards inside.

When the mist cleared, I saw Peter off to the southeast, paddling south and pointing, for my benefit, out to sea. The southwestern horizon was dark with a monumental set. It was still quite far away. I started paddling southeast, fighting panic, trying not to hyperventilate.

We made it safely over the set. The waves, however, were the biggest waves I had ever seen from a surfboard. Peter, when we finally stopped paddling, said a strange thing. "At least we know that the ocean can't produce waves any bigger than that." I knew what he meant, because that was certainly how it felt. I also knew that, unfortunately, he was wrong. He undoubtedly knew that too. The ocean could produce much bigger waves, and at this rate it probably would. The idea was simply too horrible to contemplate. Better to pretend that some scientific limit had been reached.

"You know that one you paddled for?"

I did.

"You looked like an ant. You were getting sucked up it backward, like you weren't even paddling. Your board looked like a toothpick. You weren't even looking back."

That was true. I had resolved, overruling basic judgment, not to look back at that wave. Now I knew why Peter had screamed, "No."

Our boards, both 8'0" guns, were as useless as skateboards out here. They were far too small.

The sun was gone.

"Let's just paddle for the boat ramp," I said. "We're never going to catch one of these."

We set off, paddling far to the southeast, away from the surf, and then east, along the coast. Big waves were roaring down the point, but for the moment, at least, there were no more apocalyptic, horizon-blotting sets in sight. We could see people out on the Jardim church terrace, and down on the wall by the boat ramp. It was like old times, except that the crowd now probably included foreign surfers, and if anyone was whistling, the surf was too loud, and we were too far from shore, to hear it. Also, while I couldn't speak for Peter, I was scared for my life.

We started angling in above the boat ramp. Whitewater was slamming into the big rocks below the village. We pointed for those rocks, knowing we would get swept downcoast before we reached them. Even so, we underestimated both the level of continuous violence in the impact zone and the power of the inside current. We tried to time the sprint for shore, moving between midsized sets, but we made poor headway through the swirling currents, and then suddenly the village was streaming past us. We were still at least fifty yards from shore. I could hear shouting. But we were flying helplessly past the boat ramp, with no hope of reaching shore. Then I heard Peter yell, "Outside!" We both spun and started sprinting seaward.

We were in another world now, somewhere east of Jardim. The waves advancing on us were not part of the great pointbreak. They were just giant, shapeless shorebreak, steaming toward a wall of cliff and rocks—a coast unknown to us. The wind wasn't even offshore down here. The surface was choppy and gray and it seemed we were going to take this set on the head. Without speaking, we veered apart. We did not want to get slammed together or entangled underwater. Three waves broke on us. We both abandoned our boards and swam as deep as we could. Our leashes held, and we managed to stay clear of the rocks. When the set ended, we paddled slowly seaward, both too thrashed to speak. My arms felt like lead-stuffed tubes hanging off my shoulders.

I stopped paddling. "Let's head in here," I said.

Peter sat up, turned, and studied the shore.

"Impossible," he said.

"I'm going to try."

"You can't."

"I'll take my chances."

"You'll get killed."

My notion was that I'd get hurt, probably, but not killed. I just wanted to get ashore before it got completely dark. My arms were gone. I didn't even plan to study the shore. I knew it was extremely rugged, empty coast for miles east of Jardim. Hitting the rocks, trying to scramble up a cliff, would be bad, at best. Still, it seemed preferable to drowning.

"What do you think we should do?"

"Paddle back to Jardim."

"I can't. My arms are finished."

"I'll stay with you."

This was not a completely worked-out survival plan. But at that stage I trusted Peter's judgment more than I trusted my own.

"Okay."

We started paddling west, through choppy, heaving, nearly dark water. Slowly, my arms came back. Peter, still much stronger, patiently kept pace with me. It was impossible to tell if we were making progress. The coast on our right was black. The lights of Jardim hove into view, still a long way off. We pointed forty-five degrees above them. Our hope was that we were outside the downcoast current. We were certainly well offshore. Big swells passed beneath us, and then detonated, twenty or thirty seconds later, far inside. It was hard to tell if the village lights were getting closer. But then we noticed smaller lights, lower down, jittering—flashlights. So we were in fact getting closer, and people knew we were out here. There was no coast guard in these parts, but I took some comfort from the flash-lights.

Our plan was half-insane. We hatched it with virtually no discussion. We would paddle far up the point, then separate again, to avoid collision, and this time angle in higher, just under the point. We could no longer see the waves, but when they came, when we heard them, we would take no evasive action. Instead, we would stay on the surface and hope to get blasted shoreward, across the downcoast current. The goal would be to hit the rocks above the boat ramp.

It worked. After a very long paddle, during which we heard set after set bombing past inside, and the flashlights on the seawall kept gamely wav-ing in vertical strokes, trying to guide us in, we turned, wished each other luck, and struck for the church tower. I didn't see what route Peter took. I just dug for shore, taking deep, regular breaths. I noticed the smell of the water change as I entered the impact zone. A foamy, sea-bottom smell. I got farther than I expected before I heard a first set wave thunder outside. There was just enough light left in the western sky to let me see a great dark wall of water above me before it hit me.

Shoving my board away but staying on the surface was profoundly strange, counterinstinctual, and the violence of the wave's impact from that deliberately vulnerable position was shattering. It flipped me very rap-idly and then drove me so deep that I hit the bottom face first. Normally I would have had an arm in front of my face, but I was trying to be a mis-sile, letting the wave propel me where it would. The face-plant in black-ness was a shock, but the blow was to my forehead, and it wasn't particularly fierce, and at least part of the shock was the realization that I was not in very deep water. I was possibly fairly close to shore. When I finally sur-faced, the village lights were above me, and the roar of whitewater hitting the rocks was horribly/encouragingly close. I let the next wave hit me the same unnatural way. It drove me onto the rocks, then hauled me off. The downcoast current now had me in its grip. It carried me quickly down the point, very close to shore, bouncing me across the bigger rocks.

Another wave came and threw me against the seawall just above the boat ramp. Trapped in a surge, I slid across the mossy surface of the ramp, unable to find a handhold, and spilled off the downcoast side into blackness. I could hear people yelling. They had seen me slide past. I could hear my board clonking hollowly—it was still attached to my ankle. Then the current, interrupted by the rock wall of the ramp, lost its hold on me as the shorebreak drained off the rocks. I got an arm around a rock, hung on, and felt the water, weakening, leave me. I turned and, from a sitting position, hauled in my board across the rocks. With it under my arm, I scampered up the lee wall of the boat ramp. And there was Peter, staggering up the same wet-moss incline with his board.

"YOU SURFERS HAVE NO RESPECT for your parents, no respect for your family and friends. To go out there and risk your lives in such a sea—for what? You have no respect for this village, for the generations of fishermen who have risked their lives in the sea in order to feed their families. People here have *lost* their lives, and *lost* their loved ones, in this sea. You have no respect for them!"

These were the imprecations (my translation) of an old woman in Jardim, berating four Portuguese surfers on the seawall next to the boat ramp shortly after they had attempted to paddle out on a big day. They had failed, snapping boards and leashes, and had just washed in, thoroughly whipped. I happened to catch the tirade. This was two years after our sundown Götterdämmerung. Nobody had chastised us that night, but the old woman's feelings were, I had since learned, a common sentiment in the village. There were exceptions—José Nunes talked feelingly about the courage of certain surfers, notably a goofyfoot from New Zealand named Terence. But most villagers had grown bored (if not appalled) by surfing, aside from the few commercial opportunities that surf tourism afforded.

Peter had not come back. Gnarly as he was, he had taken a hint from our close calls. When I asked him about it some time later, he said,

"Things were finally set up like I wanted, and this one slipup was going to ruin it, and make a lot of people sad." I could have said the same thing. In fact, I should have said it. But I lacked his clarity. I wasn't through with Madeira.

I was staying in a room on the point in Jardim. My landlady, Rosa, lived downstairs. She was in her twenties, born in the village. Her husband was in England, working at a fast-food restaurant at Gatwick Airport. Rosa had two rooms that she let to visiting surfers. Both were tiny and bare, but they looked straight down on the great wave. The eight dollars a night I paid didn't seem to brighten the family financial picture much. Rosa's mother lived with her, and the two of them would walk up the mountain to the main road at Prazeres, a grueling one-hour hike, rather than pay a few escudos for the bus. Like all rural Madeirans, they had formidable legs.

Jardim, for all its beauty, was a melancholy and fractious place. There were family feuds. There was a bearded woman, mentally impaired, always barefoot. In her youth she had been, I was told, sexually abused by men and boys. One night she fell off the cliff near the point, landing on the rocks in a sitting position, dead. Some people thought she had jumped. There was a young woman, bright and frustrated with village life, who angrily rebuked me for walking on the shore, under the cliffs, to Ponta Pequena. Her brother, she said, had been killed by falling rocks on that path. A cheap homemade sugarcane rum known as *aguardente* took a toll on the village, particularly on unemployed men.

The only really prosperous family seemed to be the Vasconcellos. They were the traditional overlords of Jardim. The family's members all lived in Funchal now, or Lisbon, but they had run the place for centuries. All of Madeira had been divided up and handed out, complete with serfs and slaves, to factions and individuals on the lower half of the Portuguese crown's long list of toadies. Old Jardimeiros remembered when villagers were required to carry priests and rich people up and down the mountains in hammocks. This was before the road was built down from Prazeres, in

1968. There had been a fat priest whose visits were particularly dreaded. And the island's history only got darker the farther back you looked.

The quinta—the manor house—in Jardim belonged to the Vasconcellos. It was a rambling, crumbling old place with its own chapel, easily the biggest house in town. One year, the village council gathered its courage and asked the quinta family if it could convert some of the family's banana fields into a soccer field. There was no other patch of land in Jardim large or level enough for a field, and every other village—even lowdown, raggedy-ass Paul do Mar—had one. The quinta family, or perhaps its lawyers, said no. "*Não.*" So one night, not long afterward, somebody snuck into the quinta family's fields and chopped down all the banana trees. The following winter, when I came back to Jardim, the fields had not been replanted. Rosa smirked when I asked her about it. She seemed to believe that replanting would just inspire more vandalism. What I couldn't tell was whether she thought the attack on the bananas was a justified peasant revolt or a shameful, destructive act. I could never figure out what people in Jardim really thought about anything political. I despised the quinta family on principle. It probably helped that I never met any of them.

I had spent that fall reporting on the civil war in Sudan. On days without waves, I sat at a card table in my room writing about Nile geopolitics, famine, slavery, political Islam, cattle-herding nomads, and my travels with Sudanese guerrillas in the liberated, terrifying South Sudan. I spent a lot of time staring at wind-torn ocean. We were plagued that year by southeast winds—"the devil's fart," I heard a Cornish surfer call them. At low tide the villagers picked *lapas* (limpets) off the exposed rocks. There was a dwarf, Kiko, who went for *lapas*, but his legs were too short for clambering across big, slippery rocks and his struggles were painful to watch. At high tide, though, Kiko spearfished off the point, and then he was in his element. His swim fins and his masked head looked huge at either end of his muscular, abbreviated body. He would disappear underwater for what seemed like minutes. People said he wriggled fearlessly into crevices where the octopus hid. Born and raised in Jardim, Kiko knew every boulder in the sea off the village. He sold his catch to a local café, the Tar Mar, where his octopus was a house specialty. I often ate it.

I liked to study the movements of the small fishing boats working the steep bank off Jardim. On still nights they would stay out, their yellow lights bravely knitting the blackness under a sheet of stars. The Portugese national anthem is "Heróis do Mar"—Heroes of the Sea. And *The Lusiads*, the sixteenth-century epic poem that enjoys pride of place in the country's literature, is oceanic in both rhythm and subject, celebrating Vasco da Gama's voyage to India in more than a thousand stanzas of ottava rima. The poem is fantastical and too ornate for modern tastes, but it is terrific on the sea and ships. Small details come radiantly into focus, just as they do in the architecture of the Portuguese Empire's golden era—the Manueline style, it's called, after King Manuel I. Even in the stonecarving around church doors of the period, the finest details (bits of perfectly rendered coral, shockingly accurate seaweed) are invariably maritime. Henry the Navigator, King John II—the Portuguese Renaissance was brief but rich and solidly sea-centered. By the time Luís de Camöes, a hard-luck patriot and sailor and the author of *The Lusiads*, wrote his masterpiece, the Inquisition was on and the empire was in terminal decline—already in hock to German bankers.

I wondered if the keening, nostalgic sadness of the fado, the national folk music, which is itself often sea-themed, came from a pervasive sense of lost grandeur. More likely I was just hearing the fado's Arabic taproots. Portugal, like Spain, has always been Western Europe's interlocutor and borderland with Morocco and Muslim North Africa.

Madeira, which is closer to Morocco than to Europe, was uninhabited until 1420, when Portuguese explorers stumbled on it. The island was heavily wooded—hence its name. The settlers cleared the land by burning the primeval forests. One great fire burned out of control, according to legend, for seven years. Madeira became a center of the sugar trade and then the slave trade. Everything came and went by sea, and in that sense Madeira was more Portuguese than Portugal: it was even more pelagic.

These days, the island's economic mainstay is tourism. Cruise ships call in Funchal, a city bristling with hotels, casinos, and tourist shops. Germans, Brits, and Scandinavians ride around the island in enormous buses and tiny rental cars. The more adventurous hike the mountains and gorges.

At one point that winter, I came down with a nasty cold. Rosa's mother, Cecilia, got it too. She blamed her illness on a fruit seller who had failed to wash the pesticides off a batch of custard apples. We went together in my car to a clinic down the coast in Calheta. Cecilia was coughing, her eyes swollen. We kept passing men with big yellow jerry cans strapped to their backs and wandlike nozzles in their hands—pesticide sprayers. Cecilia glared at the men, muttering.

But we each got well in time for Carnival, a local *festa* that runs for four days and ends with a blowout celebrated on Shrove Tuesday. In Jardim people were gathering at the Tar Mar. Rosa and Cecilia and Rosa's little niece and nephew were rigging up party costumes. They dressed me in an atrocious lime-green wig and big disco sunglasses and we all headed over to the café.

At least half the village was at the party. The jukebox was blasting samba, Europop, fados. Most people were in costume—little kids in superhero capes and bunny rabbit outfits, with many adults done up, to my surprise, as ugly, oversexed women with huge breasts, huge pillow-enhanced bottoms, big wigs, and rubber masks with deep wrinkles and too much makeup. A certain hysteria surrounded these flamboyant hags, mainly because one couldn't tell if the person inside the costume was male or female. The painted ladies were dancing and carousing and flirting outrageously, but were careful not to speak. I was no doubt more in the dark than others about who was actually who, but the giddy confusion and sexy buffoonery were general. And a collective delirium seemed to build through the evening as the wine flowed and the music pounded and laughter broke in great waves against the ceiling. It was a brilliant party, and, surrounded by witty disguise, I had never felt closer to the secret, unspoken communal life of Jardim do Mar.

. . .

PETER INVITED ME to a surf slide show in the Flatiron neighborhood in Manhattan. The venue turned out to be a posh office—an ad agency owned by a friend of his. The small crowd was all male, some of them surfers I knew slightly from Montauk. This was after hours, plenty of beer, probably coke for those in the know. There were Montauk surf photos, hooting (no horrible snarls—not a hard-core group), some laughs. Professional-quality shots from a Costa Rica trip. But the main event was a set of Madeira photos supplied by Peter. I hadn't seen most of them before. As usual, I had taken virtually none during all our trips together. Peter had been slightly more conscientious. He had gotten several stunning lineup shots from the mountainside, showing Jardim, Pequena, and Paul do Mar going off. The room rang with sincere curses of appreciation. Otherwise, Peter was like me—unwilling to stay on land when the waves were good.

But several associates and passersby had taken photos of us in Madeira over the years and sent along the results. They were of mixed quality at best, but seeing them made my heart race. There were a couple of shots of me on an unforgettable day at Pequena. These had been taken by one of Peter's old friends who came with us in 1997. The desperate exultation of that session—I surfed for six hours—came back in a rush just seeing those distant, blurry glimpses of a couple of my waves. The waves were big, and I was dancing hard. There was a shot of Peter at big Jardim, taken by James, the American who broke his ankle at Paul and then later that week hobbled out to the point, leg in a cast, to shoot pictures from the cliff.

"Were you guys towing?" somebody asked.

We laughed. "Hell, no."

Tow-in surfing was a then new addition to big-wave surfing, pioneered in Hawaii. Using Jet Skis to whip guys on short, heavy, foot-strapped boards into enormous waves, tow-in surfing had practically overnight doubled or tripled the maximum height of ridable surf. Towing was strictly for specialists—for a small subset, in fact, of the madmen who rode the world's largest waves. Not, that is to say, us. Not even related to us. But looking at the shot of Peter at Jardim, I thought it actually wasn't a dumb question. He was coming off the bottom of a big, dark wave—a twenty-foot face—leaving a strangely long, hot-white wake. He was leaning forward, knees bent, getting maximum speed from his board, and projecting his turn far, far down the line. He did look like he had been whipped into the wave by some force beyond the wave. I knew well the section that had hurled him into that captured moment, and knew why he was driving so hard. He was actually coming into the inside wall, feeling the full catapult power of Jardim. There was a reason people called it the world's best big-wave pointbreak.

Peter also had photos, taken by one of his old buddies, from the night when we were nearly lost. There was one of him on a big, wild-looking wave before the sun went down—probably the last wave ridden that day. Then there were a couple of flash-lit shots of us after we reached land, half-mad, above the boat ramp. They reminded me, oddly, of what Peter's friends had said over dinner afterward. One, a kneeboarder from Santa Barbara, confessed that after we disappeared, he had started planning what he would say to Peter's mother. The other guy, an old art school classmate, seemed thunderstruck. He had been doing the same thing, he said. They had each felt horribly guilty for assuming the worst, and they each still seemed quite upset. Peter and I, though probably in clinical shock, were merry as crickets—guzzling wine, toasting life. In the first photo by the boat ramp, we were both looking dazed. Peter was throwing the camera a shaka sign. I had a streak of blood on my face.

"Ouch," someone in the slide show group said.

We decided, without discussion, not to tell the story. The next shot, the last of the show, would have meant even less to the group. Peter and I, needing to collect ourselves, had turned away from the jubilant crowd at the top of the boat ramp. We retreated to the edge of the seawall and sat for a minute, staring out into the roaring dark. The photo simply showed our backs, our wetsuits shining. It wasn't much of a shot. The house lights went up, with whoops for more beer. I heard Peter say from across the room, "I was going to put my arm around your shoulder, but, you know." I did know.

CAROLINE STARTED COMING ALONG for the first week of my Madeira retreats. We would stay in the new hotel in Jardim—a chilly, mostly empty place built, it was said, with South African money. She was suitably wowed by the natural beauty of Madeira, and loved being beyond the reach of her office. She could spend whole days hiking through the terraces and reading what she called murder books—mysteries—while I surfed. I remember a foggy morning: I was surfing Jardim alone. She was reading on a hotel balcony directly above the break. The waves were head-high, barely clearing the rocks on the sets. After every ride, I would look up. Caroline's nose would still be in her book. I would yell. She would wave. She saw none of my rides. When I finally came in and complained, she tried to explain, not for the first time, how exquisitely boring it was to watch surfing. The lulls between sets seemed to go on for hours. There had been, it was true, some fairly long lulls.

My complaints were trivial, actually, not deeply felt. Caroline indulged my surf fever, even its most juvenile moments, beyond anything I had a right to expect, and I consciously tried never to lose sight of that fact. As indifferent as she was to the ocean and all things surf, our life together was braided with waves. They were a backdrop, a gravitational force, and rarely far away. At our wedding, we said our vows under an apple tree out of sight of the ocean. That morning, however, Bryan and I had gone searching for waves. There were none to be had, but I paddled out anyway at some funky beach on the south coast of Martha's Vineyard, where I took off on a knee-high shorebreak surge just so that Bryan could get a snapshot of me "surfing" on my wedding day—soul-arching in the moment before I hit the sand. Later, at the wedding dinner, he gave an elaborate, finely wrought toast. One of the main themes was a warning to Caroline that she should expect any outing, certainly any holiday, to be ruthlessly, even cruelly, turned into a surf trip. He had been proved right many times over—in France, Ireland, Tortola, later Spain and Portugal. Caroline, who was nobody's idea of a pushover, was a spectacularly good sport about it.

She made the most of the perks: the obscure, often raggedly beautiful spots I dragged her to; the freedom to read; the seafood. For an inlander, she had a remarkable affinity for shellfish. In Madeira, she favored the *espada* at the Tar Mar and the young wine known as *vinho verde*.

How did she put up with my absences, not just when I chased waves without her but, even more frequent and protracted, when I went off reporting? The answer changed as we changed. Caroline sometimes left for weeks herself, to visit friends and family in Zimbabwe, and the separations did us good, I thought, at least in our early years. We needed the breaks. Later, it got more difficult to be apart. Caroline retained a firm vein of self-reliance, though. She was unusually good at being alone. I sometimes thought she got it from her mother, June, who was both deeply attached to her husband and a tough, well-guarded character who listened all night to the BBC's Africa Service and rarely slept. Caroline's father, Mark, who did not particularly like to travel, nonetheless spent a great deal of time on overseas business trips as a minerals trader. Caroline worked extremely hard—she was, as a lawyer, the same perfectionist she had been as a printmaker. My Madeira jaunts were partly redeemed in her mind because they were not just surf trips but writing retreats. I felt the same way, certainly. I got lonely. There was still no Internet or cell phone service in Jardim, so I called home at night from a phone booth in the *praça*. Next to the booth was a communal birdcage, home to parakeets of many colors. In the daytime, the birds sang and pecked at a huge cabbage someone threw in their cage. At night, they fluffed up into little gray silent balls to stay warm. I would huddle in the booth on wet, windy nights, straining to hear the comforting notes of Caroline's voice, her cheerful reports on the luxe life of our daily grind.

· · ·

I MAKE IT SOUND like the surf was always huge. In fact, many sweet shortboard days came my way in Madeira—sessions like that morning with Caroline on the balcony in the fog. Big scary days on the 8'0" were not the rule. Still, everything about surfing had become more serious. After long years of riding pretty much whatever board came my way, I was taking real care with what I surfed on now. I had found a shaper in Hawaii, a North Shore eccentric named Owl Chapman, whose boards I loved. They were sharp-nosed swallowtail thrusters, fast and thick, with very little rocker and unfashionably downturned rails—'70s boards, basically, but with subtler lines, lighter materials, and three fins. I snapped a few Owls in hard-breaking waves (airline baggage handlers also snapped one or two), and not all the replacements worked great—Owl had his own ideas about what I should be riding. Still, most of my Owls were magic boards—responsive, fast-paddling, steady in the barrel. I first rode one in the mid-'90s, on a reporting trip to the North Shore, and I rarely rode anything else for the next ten years.

Why had I become so keen on the finer points of board performance? In a word, Madeira. It had thrown me into big, powerful waves in a new way. The ambivalence that shadowed me at Ocean Beach was gone. Unfortunately, my surfing was in decline. I was getting old. It really hit me on crowded days at Pequena. Crowded in Madeira was still a relative term—there might be twelve people out. Most of them would be red-hot Portuguese guys, probably some of the country's top pros. They paddled and surfed rings around me. Telling myself that they were half my age, or less, and that they probably surfed ten times as much as I did nowadays, should have helped. It didn't. I appalled myself. I missed waves I should have caught, lumbered to my feet when I should have sprung. Getting old as a surfer, I'd heard it said, was just a long, slow, humiliating process of becoming a kook again. I clung to my delusions that I could still surf decently. The Owl boards helped.

My nightmare of an overrun, despoiled Madeira seemed to be slowly coming true. The first Jardim contest had been held. I was careful to be in New York when it went down. The winner was a dreadlocked South African. A second contest was scheduled, with an alarming list of corporate sponsors and well-known big-wave pros. More ominously, the feral denizens of the world surf-paradise trail were increasingly in evidence. Tim, from North Carolina, now shuffled through Jardim's cobbled alleyways in purple drawstring pants, raving from inside a hooded sweatshirt about the "endless barrels" he scored in "Indo" last year. "Bawa, man, unreal. Better than G-Land. Better than Ulu. Better than *this*." I knew I had no right to despise them, but I cringed as the likes of Hatteras Tim began to haunt Jardim, and to make their drawled, snarling claims in the water.

The villagers seemed wary, for good reason, of the more uncouth visitors, and not happy that a couple of local boys were taking up this dangerous sport. Still, the contests were welcome—they brought money into the village—and certainly no local shared my worry about crowds in the water. Surfing was connecting Jardim to the world, and I had to remind myself how deeply the yearning for such connection ran. I understood, or thought I did, about feudalism and isolation. The ancient, despotic order of church and nobles thrived where contact with the outside world was meager. In Jardim the arrival of electricity, of TV, of the paved road from Prazeres—these were each, despite their drawbacks, blasts of spiritual oxygen. On a surfless Sunday morning, I heard a sermon in the village church by a visiting Brazilian priest extolling liberation theology. You would not have heard that when the only way into Jardim was by goat trail or open boat.

One night, the Portuguese national surfing team turned up in Jardim. I wasn't familiar with the concept of a national surfing team. But I was impressed by how impressed the villagers were. This was, by God, *the national team*. They surfed *for Portugal*. They wore official windbreakers, like Olympic athletes—or the beloved national *futebol* squad. To me, of course, they were just another bunch of scruffy young rippers. But I was fascinated by the coach. I never spoke to him. I just watched him climb slowly out of his rental car one morning in the *praça*. He had his wife with him and a toddler in a stroller. He wore his official windbreaker and matching warm-up pants and he looked like a sports administrator, or a phys ed teacher, a soccer coach. What fascinated me was his ordinariness, his ease. I still thought of surfing as a wild thing. You did it with your friends, or you did it alone, but it happened out in the ocean. It couldn't be socialized. Of course, I had seen how pervasive and presentable and clubbed-up surfing was in Australia. It *could* be socialized, and here, in cozy, remote Jardim, I was catching a glimpse of my old anchoritic obsession being integrated into Euro-yuppie team-sport norms. Something similar was happening, haltingly, I gathered, in Southern California and Florida.

Still, there were some engaging people fetching up in Jardim. Besides Moona and Monica, who pushed on to relief work in wartime Liberia, there was a loose group of Brits, not all of them surfers, whose previous vacation destination had been some rural spot in Ireland where they stood a fair chance, on a fair afternoon, of seeing Seamus Heaney on a stroll. He was their idea of a megacelebrity, and they were proud to have never interrupted his thoughts. Two of the women in this bookish group had taken an interest in an American surfer staying in Jardim—an affable blond pro from Long Island. He had brought with him an extensive quiver of his sponsor's boards and he seemed, to his British fangirls, to have nothing but blue sky between his ears. When he was not present, they would pester me, over wine, for details about the hard-core, postverbal American surf samurai mind. I tried to oblige, mostly because I was also interested— sincerely, not ironically—in the guy. He was what is called a Pipeline specialist. He spent his winters in Hawaii surfing one of the world's most dangerous, most beautiful waves. When he pulled a board from his stack and tried to explain how the rocker on this one helped him hold an edge on the foamball—that's the whitewater *inside* a hollowly breaking wave, not visible from the beach—and stay longer in the barrel, I asked questions and listened hard. This kid had been in places on waves where I would never go.

At the center of the British contingent was a couple named Tony and Rose. He was a surfer and landscape painter from Wales. She ran a restaurant there in the summers. They had bought a dilapidated house in Jardim, where they were known as Mr. and Mrs. Estaca. That was because when they first arrived they were given an even more dilapidated house rent-free by the village council in exchange for work, and one of their first tasks was to make hundreds of the sticks that were used to prop up banana trees. The sticks were called *estacas*. Even their dog was called Estaca. The villagers actually cared about Tony and Rose. When the weather turned stormy, with a southeast wind, and Tony and I headed for the north coast, the old women clucked angrily. Didn't we know better than to leave the village in bad weather? There were rock slides. The roads washed out in the mountains. We went anyway. I had to check my silken left, Madonna. Even if we didn't find waves, Caroline and I had found a café in the north that served a grilled parrot fish that justified any expedition.

I HIKED TO PEQUENA on a sunny afternoon. A swell was filling in. The waves looked funky from a distance, with a west wind chopping up the takeoff, which was why there was nobody out, but by now I knew a few things about Pequena—how this wind, for instance, could bounce off the cliffs and blow offshore across the shelf, turning the inside wall into something spectacular. And so it was. I surfed alone for an hour, catching big mushburgers outside, skiing over the ledge, and then red-lining it through the barrel section on my sturdy Owl. Eventually I was joined by three Portuguese pros, including their top dog, Tiago Pires. They had obviously kept their binoculars ready to hand in Jardim. There were still plenty of waves to go around, but Pires ripped so hard that I found him unpredictable, and he and I got tangled up and went over the falls together on the biggest wave that had come through. We were both lucky not to get hurt. It was a long hold-down, and then we got pounded by a heavy set. He seemed none the worse for wear, but I was shaken.

I thought about going in. Caroline was leaving for New York the next morning. I decided to catch one more good one. But it was getting bigger now, and I was surfing sloppily. The takeoffs were intimidating but not difficult, if you knew the wave, which I did. Still, I managed to blow two, and take another set on the head. Now I was exhausted. The sets were stepladdering—each one bigger than the last. It was at least ten feet now. The other guys were somewhere out the back—not in sight. I decided to catch the very next wave I could and go in. I found a nice medium-sized wave, possibly the first of a set. I caught it, shaky with relief. Then I managed to fall off. I popped up, annoyed, and found myself looking at a wall of water that seemed to have marched out of my worst nightmares.

It was already pulling water from the shelf, pulling me toward it, and there was no chance at all that I would escape it. It was the biggest wave I had ever seen at Pequena and it was already starting to break. I swam toward it hard and dove early, but it plucked me out of the depths and beat me till I screamed in hopeless protest. When I finally surfaced, there was another one behind it, just as big, just as malignant. There seemed to be a bit more water on the shelf. I swam to the bottom and tried to get a grip on a rough slab of rock, but was instantly ripped away. Another long, thorough beating. I tried to cover my head with my arms in case it dashed me against the bottom. It didn't. I eventually resurfaced.

There was another one. It was bigger than the others. But the important thing about it was that it sucked all the water off the shelf. Boulders started surfacing in front of me, and then I was standing in a field of rocks in rushing, waist-deep water. I did not understand where I was—a field of rocks had risen out of the ocean, quite far from shore, at a break I thought I knew. In a lifetime of surfing, I had never seen anything like this. The wave mutated into a hideous, boiling, two-story wall of whitewater almost without breaking—it had run out of water to draw from. I had a moment in which to decide what to do before it hit me. I picked a fissure in the wall and threw myself up and into it. The vague hope was that if I wriggled in deep enough, the whitewater might swallow me rather than simply smash me to pieces on the rocks. Something like that occurred, apparently. My feet were sliced up from the leap, but I did not hit the bottom as I rag-dolled shoreward in the bowels of the wave. And when I next surfaced I was in deep water, in the channel east of Pequena, safe.

I slowly made my way back to Jardim. My brain seemed to have shut down. I had, for a moment, expected to die. Not in some vague future, but right then and there. Now it was hard to see quite how to reenter the world. I reached our hotel. Caroline saw that something was wrong. She ran a bath. I don't normally take baths. I lay in the water. Night fell. She lit candles. She cleaned the cuts on my feet. I tried to explain what had happened. I didn't get far. I said that I wanted to go back to New York with her. She washed my hair. I asked why she didn't get angry about all the stupid risky things I did. She knew I was talking about war reporting as much as I was about surfing. She said she assumed I needed to do them.

But didn't she worry?

She took a long time to answer. "When things get bad, I think you get very calm," she said. "I trust your judgment."

That was not how I saw myself, or ever had. Still, it was interesting to hear. She later admitted that she permitted herself some magical thinking, particularly when I vanished into conflict zones and kidnapping hotspots.

I stayed on, too ashamed to leave, whimpering to myself, after Caroline left. I saw a day so big that nobody tried to paddle out. Conditions were clean. Tow-in teams could have ridden it, possibly, launching from some safe harbor. Nobody was towing Madeira, though, at least not yet. I watched it for hours, not remotely tempted. Tony, the landscape painter from Wales, said that he had seen a day so big that waves broke clear across the bay between Paul do Mar and Pequena. Standing on the wharf at Paul, he said, all you saw were stacked mountains of whitewater with the distant peak of the breaking hook of the outermost wave visible high

above all the foam and mist, maybe the top fifteen feet of the wave, moving from right to left—a whole afternoon of mystic behemoths following
each other down the coast.

Tony was red-haired, passionate, maybe forty. Madeira, he said, had
turned his painting upside down. "It's the two-thousand-foot cliffs," he
said. "Suddenly, the horizon is right up in your face and the sea is disappearing into the sky. The clouds are below you, the sea's above you." He
said Madeira had also changed his surfing. "Changed it forever. I don't
surf at home anymore. There's no point. This is deep ocean power. You
know for yourself what it's like. These things chase you down the point
and you just want to get the hell out of there. Head for the greenery, as
they say." Like Peter, Tony wasn't particularly worried about crowds. "People are scared of this place."

For good reason, I thought.

But did I surf to scare myself? *No.* I loved the power, the juice, but only
up to a point. Head for the greenery—that was conservative surfing, not
slam-bam shredding, and it was probably all I was good for at this age. I
paddled out looking for a dopamine rush that was both familiar and rare,
that required nerve and experience but had nothing in common with terror. Similarly, when reporting, I went out looking for stories to satisfy my
curiosity, to try to make sense of calamities—certainly not to get shot at.
In fact, one of my worst days as a reporter had come in El Salvador, on an
election day during the civil war. Three journalists were killed that day,
one wounded. I had been caught in a firefight in a village in Usulután
province. In the next village over, a young Dutch cameraman named Cor-
nel Lagrouw was shot in the chest. The army attacked the car that was
trying to get him to a hospital, pinning it down with aerial fire. Lagrouw
died on the road. I was there when they pronounced him dead. His girlfriend, Annelies, who was his sound technician, did not take her eyes off
him. She kissed his hands, his chest, his eyes, his mouth. She wiped the
dust from his teeth with her handkerchief. After I wrote and filed my
story, I went surfing. El Salvador has a great wave called La Libertad,

which was uncrowded in those days, because of the war. I spent a week hiding out at Libertad. Surfing was an antidote, however mild, for the horror.

These things belonged on opposite sides of the ledger.

The surf went flat and stayed small. I grew a beard. I was working on a story about the global anticorporate movement, which was then in the headlines. I wrote letters, mainly to Bryan. I didn't think Madeira would interest him much, except perhaps on paper. Our last surf trip together had been a few years earlier: a five-day autumn dash to Nova Scotia while he and Deirdre were doing a stint at Williams College. We had lucked into lovely, empty waves.

Bryan had been following his muse deep into American bedrock. He wrote a two-part *New Yorker* piece called "Large Cars," about the life of a long-haul trucker, and then an unforgettable profile of Merle Haggard. He wrote a passionate, scholarly, beautiful book about a nineteenth-century baseball player named John Montgomery Ward. Then he returned to his first love, fiction.

A PREPOSTEROUS IDEA was being tossed around in Jardim. The government would build a tunnel from Jardim to Paul. It was like the setup for an absurdist joke. A highway tunnel, more than a mile long, through a mountain of rock, to connect two tiny fishing villages that hated each other?

Yes. And this was, it seemed, the least of it. The European Union was shoveling money into its "underdeveloped regions." Portugal was getting much of it, and Madeira is to the mainland as Portgual is to Europe—farther south and west and, at least traditionally, poorer. As a result, they were now building bridges and tunnels all over Madeira, furiously spending E.U. grants for "transport infrastructure." These projects would produce, according to the E.U., "time savings." In the meantime, they were producing jobs for Madeirans and windfall profits for politically connected corporations and local contractors. Graft and corruption were rife—that was what people said. But I saw nothing about it in the papers, where the local strongman and regional governor, Alberto João Jardim (no relation to the village), seemed to preside over a ribbon-cutting on some vast new erection every day. There was a rush to build before the E.U. admitted Eastern European nations that would then start getting these grants.

Were the rumors of corruption true? It was hard to know. I was a tourist, not reporting. There was certainly a madness loose on the island. It was a time to make money—in a place where there had been, through the centuries, precious few such opportunities. Plenty of older people seemed stunned, watching the tranquil, terraced hillsides they had known all their lives bulldozed into flyovers for sleek new highways. In Jardim I heard people fret that once the tunnel was finished, drunken louts from Paul would come streaming through, turning Jardim's quiet *praça* into a reeking hangout. Still, men from Jardim would get jobs in the tunnel and their families were thankful for that. It beat emigrating to Venezuela.

WHEN I ARRIVED the following year, the tunnel was under construction. At night, when there was no surf roar, I could hear the machines, the blasting inside the mountain. Sleepless in my dank room, I imagined Adamastor, a sea monster made of rock in *The Lusiads*—"Scowling from drunken, hollow eyes / Its complexion earthy and pale, / Its hair grizzled and matted with clay, / Its mouth coal black, teeth yellow with decay."

We got poor surf that winter. The North Atlantic storms we counted on were tracking lower than usual, battering Madeira itself, and wrecking the waves they did send. When it came time for me to go home, the weather charts showed yet another storm heading our way. This one, I thought, might be different. I decided to stay. The storm hit. It wasn't different, at least not in Jardim, where the surf was huge but unridable.

I drove to the north coast with a young guy from Oregon, André. He was blond, quiet, built square, like a lumberjack. A new tunnel, nearly two miles long, let us whisk through the central mountains in less than an hour. The north was sunny and windless, a different world, and my old flame Madonna was, as they say, on fire. It looked huge. The wave normally ran close to the rocks, locked in cliff shadow. Now it was breaking out in deep blue water, smooth and heavy in the sunshine. I was glad I had brought my gun. We jumped off the rocks far down in the cove. André seemed excessively keen. I was moving tentatively, having trouble swallowing. He was soon a hundred yards ahead. I caught glimpses of him paddling over massive waves. It was even bigger than I'd thought. I was not at all sure I should be out here.

Then André appeared, flailing at the top of an enormous wave. He caught it, free-falling through the drop on his backhand, somehow landing on his board, and then surfing aggressively, carving hard, before sailing over the shoulder. It was a bravura ride. But I saw it—I was seeing everything—through a screen of dread. I found the roar of the whitewater hitting the cliffs to my left nauseating. I kept ordering myself not to look that way. The truck-sized waves exploding up ahead were not better for morale. They made me wish I had stayed ashore. The takeoffs looked impossibly fast and steep and the penalty for blown takeoffs unthinkably severe. Actually, these waves were probably no more difficult than the three beasts I rode on that big day at Paul do Mar. But these were lefts and that had been three years before, on a day when my confidence was unnaturally high. Today I was scared and smelled disaster.

Disaster found André first. He had paddled far up the point, into an absurdly dangerous zone. I had stopped and was using the Madonna lineup markers I knew—a road tunnel, a waterfall—except that I stayed thirty or forty yards straight out from the usual takeoff and sprinted for open water every time a set appeared. I had not caught a wave, or even seriously tried. André caught several, positioning himself so deep that even when he pulled out, I was not within shouting distance. He was on a suicide mission, it seemed to me. A big set could peak up where I was, break all the way across to the point, and trap him horribly. Soon enough, this

happened. He almost escaped. He tried to punch through the lip of a
giant wave, but it sucked him over, snapped his leash, and held him down
for a sickeningly long time. His board had already hit the cliff by the
time the next wave landed on him. He eventually got ashore, down toward the cove. He retrieved his battered board, waved it to me in a signal
that he was done, and hiked back toward the car.

I stayed out for hours. I was too scared to surf properly but could not
face paddling in. I caught a few waves, all just big shoulders, relatively easy
and safe. I had a couple of close calls dodging sets. Rather than try to
punch through the top of the biggest wave of the day—an absolute monster—I abandoned my board and swam under it. The water was clear and
deep and rang with an ungodly hollow banging—the sound, I realized, of
boulders rolling. I could see them down below, rocks the size of file cabi-
nets being lifted off the bottom by the passing of the swell. I had never
seen that before. My leash held and there were no more waves in that set.
I was, if possible, now even more spooked.

Several surf cars arrived. I could see Tony among the small crowd
watching. Having an audience made it worse—the humiliation of surfing
so timidly. But the worst part was the feeling in my chest as I paddled over
large, exquisite waves, over and over, unwilling to risk the takeoffs. It was
such a waste. Such cowardice. My self-loathing spiked insufferably.

THAT NIGHT, back in Jardim, I lay in the dark on a lumpy cot thinking
about quitting surfing. The southeast wind groaned in the eaves of the old
house where I was staying. Various parts of me hurt. My left eye was weeping from too much sun and saltwater. One hand throbbed from a gash
received trying to get ashore at Madonna. The other hand throbbed with
urchin spines picked up in a collision with the reef at Shadowlands the
week before. Both feet ached with infected cuts. My lower back felt like I
had spent the month digging a ditch.

I truly was too old for this. I was losing my quickness, my strength, my nerve. Why didn't I just leave it to guys in their physical prime, like André? Even the guys my age who still tried to ride serious waves—guys in their forties, even fifties—managed to get in the water two hundred, three hundred days a year. Who was I kidding, trying to skate by on a small fraction of that? Why not walk away while I could? Would quitting really leave such a big psychic hole?

IN THE MORNING, Jardim was still a mess. André and I went back to the north coast. I made the trip on autopilot, with no thought or enthusiasm. During the drive, André told me about his divorce. I was surprised he'd been married—he was so young. He and his wife had split up, he said, over surfing, of course. Chicks had to realize, he said, that when they married a surfer, they married surfing. They had to either adapt or split. "It's like if you or I hooked up with a fanatical shopper," he said. "I mean a total fanatic. You'd have to accept that your entire life would be traveling around to malls. Or, really, more like *waiting for malls to open*."

I could see how his marriage might have crashed.

On the north coast, the swell had dropped. It was windy and raining at Madonna. The waves were small, the tide too high. We napped in the car—just a couple of shoppers waiting for the mall to open.

Then, improbably, it opened. The wind dropped, the tide dropped, the sun came out, and the surf began to pump. We paddled out. It was half the size of the day before. The takeoffs were still tricky—many of the drops included little free falls—but I found myself anticipating those weightless moments, actually using them to set up a hard turn off the bottom, which then intensified the acceleration down the line. The smaller waves ran a little too close to the cliff, which, since I was on my backhand, was right in my face, but the rocks flashing past only increased the sense of unholy speed. A few tourists stopped on the road to take pictures, but no surfers appeared. It was just me and some young maniac from Oregon trading beautiful waves, surfing our brains out, hour after silken hour.

. . .

THE TUNNEL TO PAUL DO Mar was finished, unbelievably, before the next winter. Derelicts from Paul did not invade the Jardim *praça*. In fact, the tunnel seemed to be hardly used. It was long, dark, musty. Nobody walked through it. But it was stunningly convenient for surfers. The waves in Paul were now five minutes' drive away. Everything in Madeira was getting rapidly closer. Funchal, which had been a three-hour drive from Jardim when we started coming, was now less than an hour. Madeirans were happy about the convenience, of course. I churlishly feared that the easier access could only mean more surfers. They had held a second contest at Jardim. It had been won by a Tahitian power surfer known as Poto—an international surf celebrity. Not good.

The enormous ongoing transfer of E.U. funds to Madeira—it was hundreds of millions of euros—included, for me, some irony. I was in favor of the whole racket, in theory. It was in rare accord with my idea of the benign (perhaps the only benign) face of economic globalization: richer countries helping poorer countries, directly. Infrastructure, at least in the abstract, was good. In reality, I was horrified by most of the projects. They were hideous and wasteful, and many seemed entirely useless except as temporary job sources and money grabs.

I began to hear rumors that year—this was early 2001—about a "promenade" that the government wanted to build around the Jardim seafront. This made no sense. At high tide, the ocean crashed against the cliffs. I talked to a building contractor in the village about the rumors. He said he supported the project. He was vague about what it might entail. He said it would be modest, if it were even built—just a little paved walkway. I said it would be impossible to build. And who would ever use it? José Nunes told me not to worry. It was probably just talk.

IN NOVEMBER 2001, our daughter, Mollie, was born. We had wanted a child for a while. To say we were besotted would be a grave understate-

ment. Our world got suddenly both much smaller and much larger. A
rascally smile was a universe. I lost interest in leaving New York. Before
Caroline got pregnant, I had been reporting in Bolivia and South Africa.
Now Miami felt like a long way to go for a story. When I went to London
on assignment, Caroline and Mollie came along. I quit war reporting,
even my own mild version of it. I missed two winters in Madeira without
a trace of regret.

But I was hearing things. The "promenade" at Jardim had turned into
a seaside roadway, and by the time I did make it back to Madeira, with
Caroline and Mollie, in October 2003, the thing was under construction.

The project had not been unopposed. A surfer from California named
Will Henry, who had been coming to Madeira, organized protests. Envi-
ronmentalists, geologists, biologists, and surfers from both Portugal and
abroad met and marched in Funchal and in Jardim. The threat to the
great wave at Jardim wasn't the only rallying point—there were other surf
spots being buried under other boondoggles, including marinas. The
E.U.-driven construction boom, the protesters argued, was damaging Madeira's coastal ecology as a whole. It was revealed that one of the beneficia-
ries of the huge new construction contracts was in fact a company owned
by the son-in-law of Alberto João Jardim, the regional governor.

Governor Jardim went ballistic. He called the protesters "communists."
He told a local paper that surfers represented the "kind of barefoot tourism we don't want for Madeira. Go surf elsewhere!" He even mocked their
understanding of ocean waves: "Surfers? They're a bunch of fools who
must think the waves break from land to sea. So what if the waves break
here or fifteen meters further in the water? The waves will always be the
same."

The reception the protesters got in Jardim do Mar was hostile. Local
men associated with the ruling party chased them from the village, hurl-
ing food and abuse. Even a village boy who surfed was run out. Will
Henry got hit in the face. Who were these foreigners, these barefoot fools,
to think they could stop progress in Madeira? Construction went forward.

At Tony's suggestion, we did not stay in Jardim, but up the mountain, at an inn in a seventeenth-century quinta. The inn had a small pool that looked out on the ocean. Mollie, almost two, called the ocean "big pool." Driving down into Jardim with a board on my car, I felt people turning away from me in the *praça*. I imagined they were ashamed. Or maybe they just hated surfers now.

The devastation along the shoreline was hard to comprehend, even while standing beside it. I had said it would be impossible to build a walkway, but that was because I lacked imagination. Vast quantities of rock and dirt had been trucked in and dumped along the waterfront, right around the headland. The job was not complete, but it was already clear that, with enough landfill, they could build an eight-lane freeway along the coast if they chose. Huge yellow earthmovers were roaring back and forth on the landfill, which was not yet paved. In a plume extending from Jardim, the ocean was milky brown with mud. And between the half-built roadway and the water was the most hideous seawall I had ever seen—a chaotic gray heap of giant rectangular concrete blocks. It was aggressively featureless and yet painful to the eyes. The blocks looked like thousands of angrily discarded coffins. This was the new shoreline. Brown wavelets lapped against the blocks.

Governor Jardim, of course, was wrong. For the descendant of a seagoing race, his ignorance of the sea was impressive. Waves don't move offshore when you bury a reef. They simply smack into whatever is where the reef was. Still, I found it hard, staring at the destruction in Jardim, to grasp its finality. Maybe on a very big day, at low tide . . . Even in the rare circumstances under which surfing might still be possible, however, an always dangerous spot would now be orders of magnitude more dangerous. Meanwhile, the ravishing beauty of the shore as seen from the water—the cliffs and terraced fields of bananas, vegetables, papayas, and sugarcane between the point and the cove—had been expunged, replaced by a sinister industrial wall. Accept it: the great wave was gone. Like the tidepools where Jardimeiros had harvested shellfish for generations, and the boulders and shallows where Kiko had speared his octopus, it was now buried under ten thousand tons of crushed rock.

José Nunes was fatalistic. "You think you're living in paradise," he said. "And then . . ." He gave an eloquent shrug—the gestural equivalent of the fado.

Rosa was less diplomatic. She denounced the whole fiasco and she named names—who had profited, who had lied. Her rooming-house business had dried up, of course. Talking to Rosa, I realized that I had finally got what I wanted: there were no other surfers around.

From other villagers, I heard rationales for the new seawall and roadway. They would help protect the village from the sea. More villagers would be able to drive cars closer to their houses. This represented progress—other villages, after all, had such improvements. Tourists, someone even told me, would come to admire the sea from the new road. These comments were offered sheepishly, or defensively, or belligerently, or halfheartedly. There was some truth to some of them, none to others. The brute fact was, the authorities had decided to build the project for their own reasons, financial and political, and the villagers had had no say in the matter.

I mentally composed a report for Peter—he and Alison now had a daughter, Anni, who was a year younger than Mollie. We hiked in the mountains, along a system of irrigation canals, known as *levadas*, that striates Madeira. The *levadas*, many of them hand-built by slaves, were falling into disrepair as the economy shifted from agriculture to tourism. At the refurbished quinta where we stayed, the other guests, who were Danish and German and French, groused about how all the new construction was diminishing Madeira's charm.

SURF SPOTS ARE CREATED and destroyed, both naturally and by human enterprise. Kirra, one of the world's best waves, vanished not long after

Bryan and I lived there. A new dredging regime at the mouth of the Tweed River, a mile or two south, poured sand into the cove where Kirra broke, and in a matter of months the miraculous wave was gone. A new break, known as the Superbank, closer to the river mouth, was created by the same change in sand flow. The magnificent wave that we surfed on Nias, at Lagundri Bay, was violently altered by an earthquake in 2005—not the earthquake near Sumatra that drove the tsunami that killed more than two hundred thousand people late the previous year, but a second one three months later that actually hit Nias harder. The reef at Lagundri was lifted at least two feet—and the wave improved. It got dramatically hollower and heavier—harder to ride, from the looks of it, but undeniably better.

Beyond the loss or gain, I found these sudden changes to established surf spots profoundly unsettling. I remember a winter storm when I was in high school that flooded the lagoon at Malibu and changed the shape of the famous point. I simply could not accept the fact that Malibu was now a different wave. It was one thing for the Army Corps of Engineers to throw up a jetty at some beachbreak or harbor mouth and erase a surfable wave or create a new one. Malibu, I believed, was eternal. It was a fixed point in my universe. I kept surfing it after the big storm. It was now a short, shapeless right. But I was in full denial. The *real* Malibu was underneath all this sand. It would reemerge soon.

As it happened, the old cobblestone point did eventually reappear, more or less the same, in the years after I left L.A. Perhaps, as a child of Southern California, I should have been a hardened catastrophist, understanding that natural history truly goes in only one direction, often violently. Earthquakes, wildfires, megadroughts. But my uneasiness about that 1969 flood remained. The center pole of a stable cosmogony, as far as I was concerned, ran through certain surf spots. (Kirra, after an enormous sand removal effort, has showed signs of resurrection lately.)

Every couple of years, Peter and I still talk about going back to Madeira. We should do it. This next winter. Nobody goes there now. Plenty of excellent spots still break. Maybe even Jardim at the right tide, if it's big enough. But I can't face it, and neither, I think, can he.

ON OUR LAST MORNING in Madeira, the surf was still mediocre. While Caroline and Mollie slept, I dashed to the north coast for a final look. It must have been a true north swell. Not a ripple had arrived in Jardim. The north coast, meanwhile, was gigantic, with lines visible for miles. There were waves breaking out at sea on reefs that I had not known existed. The winds were light offshore. The shorebreak near the road looked at least ten feet.

I drove west, to Madonna. I parked in the old roadside spot. The high black cliffs, the gauzy waterfalls—nothing had changed. There was no one around. The surf was clean and huge. The outside boil, where I had once heard boulders rolling on the bottom, was breaking on every set. I knew the water was deep out there, but the waves were black-faced and doubling up as if it were shallow, as if they needed even more water to fully express their rage. They looked too mean to surf. But then they shouldered and ran down the reef in a fairly orderly way. Those big left walls were actually surfable, on the right board, by the right person, doing everything right, surfing balls-out.

I watched it for at least an hour. I walked back along the road, studying the shorebreak, trying to time the sets and lulls. The shorebreak, incredibly violent, seemed to have no lulls. It was more forbidding than the worst days I had seen at Paul do Mar—my benchmark for unreasonably dangerous shorebreak. You would simply have to jump in somewhere else, perhaps down at the harbor in Seixal, a few miles east. And paddle back there afterward too. There was no coming ashore near Madonna.

Did I seriously consider trying to surf? If there had been someone else there, pulling on a wetsuit, waxing up, I would probably have done the same. I know I felt the gears spinning, turned by ancient compulsion. Parts of me were already anticipating the shock of the water, envisioning the line of approach. It was more reflex than thought. That was my most heedless, least reasonable self down there. It did not weigh risks and probabilities. It didn't deserve to be called decision making. I wasn't proud of it. Still, I felt hot shame and regret as I drove away.

Author, Tavarua, Fiji, 2002

TEN

THE MOUNTAINS
FALL INTO THE
HEART OF THE SEA

New York City, 2002-15

A LONGBOARD BECKONS. IF I LIVED IN A HOUSE NEAR THE BEACH, or in a house at all, or had a van, I would probably own one by now. But I live in jammed Manhattan, and I can stuff my shortboards in closets and corners, under beds, in homemade ceiling racks. I can jump on trains and buses, even the subway, with a shortboard, run through airports with relative ease, and lock boards inside cars, where a longboard wouldn't fit. So I keep putting off the inevitable. In small, weak waves, I struggle to my feet now, especially if I'm wearing a thick wetsuit. A longboard would be a blessing on those days—easy, graceful gliding rather than blown waves and frustration. Instead, I avoid small, weak waves. In waves even slightly bigger, my shortboards still work fine. The stronger push, the vertical dimension—the board drops away on takeoffs, leaving room for my feet to get under me properly. I'm not riding tiny, up-to-the-minute boards, which are now mostly under six feet. I am, however, still riding boards that, by my standards, are loose and quick and fit nicely in the barrel—in those rare, electric moments when I manage to find my way there.

I've become, strange to say, over the last decade, a New York City day

surfer. Coastally, the city sits in the crotch formed by the sprung legs of
Long Island and the Jersey Shore. While it took me years to discover Montauk's waves—partly because I was busy but mostly because of a deep-
dyed West Coast snobbery toward all things Atlantic—it took me longer
still to see that there was surf of real interest practically on the city's door-
step. The opaque screen behind which the best waves broke—I should
have known it—was winter. Not only are winter days short and punish-
ingly cold, but the window of good conditions—solid swell, offshore
winds or no wind—is often brief. East Coast summers are dismal for surf.
Fall is hurricane season, which can bring good swells. But it was winter
that hooked me on chasing waves on short notice from the city. Storms
known as nor'easters charge up the coast, not infrequently producing
combinations of swell and wind of shockingly high quality. You just have
to know where to go when.

You also need to have work that can be done at night, a tolerant family,
a state-of-the-art hooded wetsuit, and, in my experience, the Internet.
Without online buoy data, real-time wind readings, precise wind and swell
forecasts, and "surf cams," it would be impossible for me, at least, to know
where to go when. The cams are online video feeds from cameras mounted
here and there—on deck railings, burglar bars—and aimed at the ocean
in places known to get waves. On days when the window of good surf is
only a couple of hours, the cams tend to tell you what you missed. If it
looks good, that is, on your screen, it's probably too late. Conditions will
deteriorate before you get there. You dash on an educated guess.

Chasing waves remains for me a proximate cause of vivid friendships.
My education in the vagaries of local jetties, sandbars, wind patterns,
shore-town cops, and desperate wetsuit-changing spots around New York
has come mainly from a goofyfoot dancer named John Selya. He and I
met when Mollie was small. Selya lived just a few blocks from us, on the
fuddy-duddy Upper West Side, but he was also renting a house, with a
bunch of other surfers, in Long Beach, on Long Island, in the wintertime,
when rents were almost nothing. Long Beach gets waves. It has a train

station. It's less than an hour by car from Manhattan. If we surfed there, or anywhere nearby, the house was a place to change, dry wetsuits, leave boards, even sleep in the event of a two-day swell. But the house wasn't essential. If the winds blow out of the west, as they often do, we go to New Jersey, not Long Island. Selya's main surf buddies were another dancer named Alex Brady and a goofyfoot geophysicist whom they called the Lobbyist. I didn't even notice when they let the house go. By then, I was in the rotation, permanently on call, dropping everything when the planets (and the buoys) lined up, going alone half the time, in borrowed cars.

Still, Selya makes me look half-committed. "This surfing once a week is no good," he says. "It's barely maintaining." Selya has one of the worst cases of surf fever I've encountered. He's insatiable; he'll chase any hint of swell. He's a binge-watcher of surf videos, an exacting connoisseur of great surfers and great waves, a student of advanced technique. He actually expects his own surfing to improve. And it does, perceptibly, each year. I've never seen that before in anybody beyond their teens. Selya was in his midthirties when we met, and already an excellent surfer, with a style that

John Selya, New York, 2015

manages to be both muscular and delicate, but when I compliment him on a wave well ridden he says things like, "Thanks. It was sweet. But I need more verticality."

This must be a dancer thing.

"And a Jewish thing," he says. "You gotta suffer."

But not, in his case, whine. Selya joyfully surfs junk waves that I wouldn't consider leaving my desk for. He's an old-fashioned craftsman— he works hard to make things look easy. One December afternoon, we were out in an ice storm off Laurelton Boulevard, Long Beach. The surf was big: meaty, long-walled lefts, way overhead, pouring out of the east, all gray-black and ragged, with a hideous westbound current. Selya and I seemed to be the only people in the ocean. There was a hard north wind, dead offshore. We had to paddle ceaselessly against the current. When one of us veered to catch a wave, the ice pellets coming off the land were blinding. You had to stare down at the deck of your board, push over the ledge by feel, and then surf with gaze averted. Selya got a long one, riding for a block or more. He battled back outside. I asked him how his wave was. *"Like buttah,"* he yelled. That became the catchphrase for the session. We were too tired to say much more. The waves were actually splendid, more than worth the toil and trouble. And there was something perfect, in that stormed-out, ugly North Atlantic winter ocean, about pretending it was easy.

When we finally washed ashore, incipient hypothermia was having its way with my sense of time and space. Trudging, board clamped under arm, head down against wind, past the hulking nursing homes of Long Beach, I wasn't sure what day it was, or if we were on the same ice-covered street where we had left the car. We were. Selya couldn't afford a surfed-out daze. He had a show that night. In fact, he was the star of a long-running Broadway hit—Twyla Tharp's *Movin' Out*. We changed in the car (this was after the rental house) and dashed back to Manhattan. I dropped him at the stage door. He panthered in with minutes to spare.

. . .

MY PARENTS HAD MOVED to New York in the mid-'90s. Moved *back* to New York, I should say. I saw it as a triumphant return, a big "Blacklist *this*" to the ghost of Joe McCarthy. But when I said so they seemed nonplussed. That was ancient history. They had come because their kids were here. Michael was an investigative reporter at the *Daily News*. Kevin was a labor lawyer in Manhattan. And Colleen was nearby—she and her family lived in western Massachusetts.

My parents were both still producing movies and TV, which meant they were often in L.A. or on location. But their apartment on East 90th Street became the new clan gathering spot, especially once the grandkids started arriving—Colleen's two daughters and then our Mollie. For me, it was a middle-aged second chance, to be enfolded again in the family I had left too young. Moll had a seat on the back of my bicycle, and it was a short ride across the park to my parents' place, where we always felt intensely welcome. We ate in the kitchen, dogs underfoot, TV news grumbling in the background. I couldn't possibly fit in the place that part of me yearned to reinhabit. There was, of course, no going back. Still, I was shocked by the comfort I took from hanging out with these lively, doting, terribly familiar people, my parents.

They had a mysteriously rich social life immediately. Some of their new friends were actually old friends—film and theater people they had worked with. But they also seemed to reinvent themselves with unnerving ease. When Frank McCourt had a hit with *Angela's Ashes*, it turned out they were buddies from the Irish Arts Center—or maybe it was the American Irish Historical Society. I had never known my parents to take the least interest in things Hibernian, but hey, they were new in town, and they had a fine old-sod name. They went to concerts and plays and readings at a furious rate. My mother, especially, had a formidable cultural appetite. My father parked his sailboat on Long Island and started exploring the local waters. I imagined he missed California, but the more we sailed together, the more I saw that I was wrong. He loved poking around new bays and reaches. My mother, meanwhile, soon insisted she barely remembered L.A. (She didn't call it L.A. All her life she called it "Los Angeles," on some obscure point of principle or hometown pride.) Nearly seventy years of living there did a quick fade now, into the fog of memory. New York was home. I make her sound like a diva. She wasn't. She was forward-looking. Although she had been taking French classes for years, now she started taking Italian too.

CAROLINE AND I SANG Mollie to sleep, first in our room, where her crib stayed for a couple of years, and then in her room. We made up a song, which named every aunt and uncle and cousin and grandparent, celebrating how much each one loved her, and ending with our own declarations. It was a soporific, deeply felt lullaby, and it always came first. After that, we each had our own songlist. I would hear Caroline's high, clear voice from down the hall, slipping sleepily through "The Holly and the Ivy." My repertoire was mostly folk music from the LPs my family owned when I was a kid—old American tunes, or latter-day imitations, sung by Joan Baez, Pete Seeger, and Peter, Paul and Mary. Also some early Dylan and, of course, the Fool's Song from the end of *Twelfth Night*.

> But when I came to man's estate
> With hey, ho, the wind and the rain
> 'Gainst knaves and thieves men shut their gate
> For the rain it raineth every day

This stuff had lodged deep, obviously, beyond all critique. I sang until Moll was asleep, then tiptoed away.

I wondered, as she got older, if she listened to the lyrics. We sang her to sleep, ritually, until she was eight or nine. I once asked her, just to see what she would say, about a line in the fourth verse of "Autumn to May." It

Mollie, Long Island, 2009

seemed she knew every word. The downy swan's hatchling went from snail to bird to butterfly, she said. *"And he who tells a bigger tale would have to tell a lie."*

I WENT LOOKING, as a reporter, for the place in Los Angeles where I grew up. It no longer existed. The hills were covered with houses. Mulholland Drive was paved. New-tract saplings had turned into redwoods. Woodland Hills had become a mature suburb. I interviewed Mr. Jay, my favorite English teacher from high school. He said the school had gone to hell. Ethnic gangs fought in the parking lot. (Armenians versus Persians, he said.) Shakespeare classes were long extinct. Families who had the money now sent their kids to private schools. If I wanted to write about growing up in a newly minted bedroom community, which I did, I would need to go at least two valleys farther out.

I made my way to the Antelope Valley, in northern L.A. County. All the discontents of sprawl were concentrated there, along with the fallout from a busted housing bubble, shrinking defense and aerospace industries, and shrinking public budgets for everything but prisons. There was a suffocating racial tension in the schools and an epidemic of methamphetamine abuse. I ended up writing about a number of teenagers who were washing around, trying not to drown, in this toxic exurban pond. My story focused on two warring skinhead gangs, one antiracist, the other neo-Nazi. It was difficult stuff, even before one of the kids I got to know stabbed one of his rivals to death at a party.

This was not the place where I grew up, nor any kind of updated facsimile. This was a cold new world, all stark downward mobility. I found the reporting, which took several months, deeply disturbing, and I tried to take occasional breaks, and to time those breaks to coincide with promising surf forecasts. I would drive late at night to a little condo that Domenic kept then in north Malibu, let myself in, sleep, and in the morning ride a borrowed board at a nearby pointbreak. Those mornings were both cathartic and Edenic. Bougainvillea spilled down chalky cliffs. The kelp, the eelgrass, the gentle blue waves. Seals barked, gulls cried, dolphins breached. I felt spiritually poisoned—some acrid cocktail of anger, sadness, hopelessness—by the story I was working on. Surfing had never made more sense.

It traces a bright memory thread through a motley of assignments. In 2010, when I needed a morning off from debriefing police torture victims in Tijuana, I knew a wave, a glossy left, just across the border, and that was where I ran. In 2011, I was in Madagascar with a team of reptile experts who were trying to stop poachers from driving a rare, golden-shelled tortoise into extinction. The team members could talk turtles, snakes, and lizards all day, all night. They could bushwhack, it seemed, indefinitely through killing heat if they thought a good specimen might be hiding under a rock out there. I realized at some point that Selya and I were much the same, minus the science and conservationism, about surfing. We could talk waves until any nonsurfers in earshot, starting with our wives, fled in horror. We did it on surf runs, over surf mags and videos, at sidewalk cafés on Broadway, trading shots of tequila, which Selya called "loudmouth soup." The topic was inexhaustible, in our view, its finer points effectively infinite. In Madagascar, my companions decided to launch yet another expedition to see yet another tortoise, and I bailed out, going off the clock in a coastal town called Fort Dauphin, where I found a board—a beat-up but serviceable 6'6"—and surfed myself to exhaustion in rowdy, wind-ripped waves for three days until they returned.

In 2012, a story took me to Australia. It was the first time I had been there since Bryan and I ducked out of Darwin. I was writing about a China-driven mining boom, and a mining magnate named Gina Rinehart. She was the richest person in Oz, floridly right-wing, and something of a national obsession. My reporting was partly in Sydney and Melbourne but mainly in Western Australia, where the iron ore and Rinehart were. I found Australia changed, less cheeky, less "Jack's as good as his master," more preoccupied with its billionaires—or maybe that was only because I was writing about one of them. I looked up Sue, my old pal from Surfer's Paradise, who was living on the coast south of Perth. She, at least, was as cheeky as ever, bless her larrikin soul. She was a besotted grandmother now, living in a house full of books on a gorgeous bay. "Bet you never thought I'd make a quid," she said, which was true. She had somehow turned an abalone license into a comfortable life. She advised me to remember that Rinehart, who impressed me as a paranoid bully, was the only woman in the man's world of mine bosses, which I tried to do. Sue's son, Simon, who lived nearby, loaned me a board and wetsuit and gave me directions to a beachbreak called Boranup. It was a country spot, with cold, clear turquoise water, white sand, big, brushy hills with no buildings in sight, and a scatter of surf trucks parked on the beach. The waves were four-to-six, peaky and clean, the wind offshore. I surfed for hours, slowly figuring out the bars. My last ride felt like a reward for effort: a long, smoking overhead left all the way into the shallows.

. . .

SURFING BLEW UP, I'm not sure when. It was always too popular, in my narrow view. Crowds were always a problem at well-known breaks. But this was different. The number of people surfing doubled and doubled again—five million estimated worldwide in 2002, twenty million in 2010—with kids taking it up in practically every country with a coastline, even if it was only a big lake. More than that, the *idea* of surfing became a global marketing phenomenon. Logos identified with surfing, slapped on T-shirts, shoes, sunglasses, skateboards, hats, backpacks, flew off shelves in shopping malls from Helsinki to Idaho Falls. Some of these billion-dollar brands started out as back-of-the-van boardshort vendors in California and Australia. Others were latter-day corporate concoctions.

Actually, surfing imagery has long been used to flog product. Fifty years ago, Hamm's beer signs showing Rusty Miller dropping in at Sunset were an American bar and liquor-store staple. In the industrial wastelands of New Haven, Connecticut, I once saw a billboard depicting a guy deeply tubed—also on a wave recognizably Sunset—with SALEM stamped in smoke rings on the wave face. Alcohol and tobacco companies, keen to have their names affiliated with a healthy, picturesque sport, were prominent contest sponsors in the early days of pro surfing. But the spooky and incongruous ubiquity of surf imagery today is something new.

There are five blood-red surfboards bolted to a granite wall in Times Square. I've been cutting through Times Square in all weathers since 1987, when I first went to work for the *New Yorker*. But I only started feeling *furtive* there in the last few years. It's partly those boards. They're all single-fin pintails with an elegant, exaggerated, needle-nose shape. They're not actually surfboards, they're just décor—shop frontage for a Quiksilver outlet—but for me their stretched-teardrop outline recalls, viscerally, a time and place (Hawaii, my late teens) when boards with a very similar shape were all the rage in larger waves. Then there's the video running on multiple big screens above the same shop. For anyone else on the street, I assume, it's just more flashing eye candy. That turquoise wave reeling from screen to screen? I know that wave. It's in eastern Java, off a jungle wilderness. Bryan and I camped there, in a rickety tree house, in another life. Why do they have to show *that* wave? And the young guy slouching in its depths? I know who he is. He's an interesting character, mainly because of the things he declines to do with his talent. He doesn't compete, or pull the obvious big maneuvers in the obvious situations. His sponsors, including Quiksilver, pay him to slouch stubbornly, stylishly, a postmodern Bartleby admired in the world of surfing for his refusals. So why does it matter that I know at a glance just who that slacker threading a familiar Indonesian barrel on a video in Times Square is? Because I sometimes feel like my private life, a not-small corner of my soul, is being laid out for hawking, anything from consumer loans to light trucks, on commercial surfaces everywhere I look, including, lately, taxicab TVs.

Surfers hope bleakly that surfing will one day become, like rollerblading, uncool. Then, perhaps, millions of kooks will quit and leave the waves to the die-hards. But the corporations selling the idea of surfing are determined, of course, to "grow the sport." Some underground panache may be useful for marketing, but really, the more mainstream, the merrier. Meanwhile, thousands of entrepreneurs, most of them underemployed surfers, have opened beachfront concessions to teach surfing in dozens of countries. Coastal resorts now include surf lessons among their amenities. "Cross surfing off your bucket list." It's unlikely that surf schools for tourists will add many new faces to the crowded lineups where seasoned surfers battle for scarce waves. Still, I find it unsettling when random Manhattanites jauntily announce that they surf. Oh yes, they say, they learned how on vacation last summer in Costa Rica.

SURFERS AROUND HERE—Long Island and Jersey locals—are strangely genial. I've never gotten used to it. There was a baseline reserve in California and Hawaii, an idea of cool in the water—what was worth saying, what level of ride or wave or maneuver merited a hoot of approbation—that I internalized as a kid and can't unlearn. On this coast, people will hoot anyone, friend or stranger, for almost anything that looks halfway decent. I like the unpretentiousness, the lack of snobbery, and yet some unredeemed part of me recoils. Greater New York lineups are, against stereotype, mellow. I have never seen a threat or even an angry exchange, let alone a fight, in the water here. That's partly because the crowds are never maddeningly terrible à la Malibu or Rincon, partly because the waves are usually not worth fighting over, but mostly it's culture. A certain superciliousness and self-absorption that long ago became the norm on more celebrated coasts and islands in surf world have never taken root in these parts. It's easy to strike up a conversation in the lineup with a stranger here—I've done it a hundred times. People are even eager to share detailed knowledge of their local breaks. Another transplant surfer I know calls it "urban aloha." But it's really more suburban or shore-town. At least I've never met anybody in the water who said they live in Manhattan. Brooklyn, a few times, yes.

Selya is a local everywhere we go. He was born and raised in Manhattan, but he lived for a critical adolescent surfer-development period on the Jersey Shore, and he's consummately at home on Long Island. In fact, *Movin' Out* is a musical about blue-collar kids on Long Island, set to Billy Joel tunes. Selya played a prom-king type, Eddie, who ships out to Vietnam and comes home damaged. Heavily muscled, high-strung, charismatic, not tall, he looked the part, and became the character, and his dancing shot out the lights. When we first met, he asked if I knew the *New Yorker*'s dance critic, Arlene Croce. I didn't. "I gotta put that lady on my payroll," he muttered. I looked up her review of *Movin' Out*. It called him "an utterly remarkable dancer." Selya had spent much of his career at American Ballet Theatre, initially under the direction of Mikhail Baryshnikov, before moving to Broadway. He still had the ballet dancer's duckwalk. I noticed that in an interview with the *New York Times*, he compared dancing and surfing. With music as with waves, he said, you are "yielding to something more powerful than yourself." I thought he had that right.

Chasing waves with Selya is like diving under the surface of this octo-megalopolis we call home. He knows shortcuts, in-jokes, dive bars, lore. He slips into a Broadway diner at dawn, orders an egg sandwich with the kind of regular-customer byplay you normally see only in a tightly edited movie. "Make it nice." He listens to obnoxious two-guy sports talk radio with a faraway grin. I suspect he can talk each Mets pitcher's mechanics as long as the shock jocks can. Like Peter, he's a pleasure to surf with. He's competitive and self-critical. He's a much stronger paddler than I am these days, and he catches a ton of waves. His surfing is precise, aggressive, explosive—balletic. He's also an unusually astute audience. On a cold winter afternoon in New Jersey, we're surfing big, shifty waves at a spot we rarely ride. Our regular spots are too big today, all closing out. Late in the session, I paddle for a warbling, lurching set wave. I get hung up in the lip—cursing my heavy wetsuit, my weak arms—and then barely stick the drop, bottom-turning in a pressure crouch under a surprisingly tall, dark, heaving wall. I make the wave, pulling out in cliff shadow far inside. I've lost track of Selya. As I start back out the channel, wondering if he saw that drop, I get a glimpse of him way outside, bobbing over a swell in a last slanting column of sunlight. He has his back to me, but one arm raised high, fist clenched. That answers my question. He saw it.

On another Jersey winter day, even bigger, and sloppier—the swell's too east; our educated guess on this dash was not so smart—Selya says, "I'm not feeling it." He stays on shore. He's not a big-wave surfer. Neither am I. But I can't face returning to the city completely skunked. So I suit up and paddle out. Water in the thirties, air in the thirties, an icy west wind. Evil brown ocean. I have an awful session—missing waves, getting blasted. The surf's huge, by East Coast standards, but it's not good. I wash in. Back at the car, Selya says, "Sorry about the stench of defeat in here." I manage to convince him, I think, on the drive home that he missed nothing but punishment. As the Manhattan skyline lifts into view across the salt marshes and docklands of Newark Bay, Selya says, "Look at that. It's like a giant reef. The rock and coral sticking up, all the sea life down in the cracks."

Selya's work takes him all over, and he contrives to surf between shows on tour. In Brazil, in Japan, he's found boards and waves. He once dashed from London to Cornwall, a five-hour drive, to surf. Last year, from Denmark, he texted me cell phone shots of tiny gray, horrible-looking North Sea slop: he was all over it, clambering across jagged rocks. He does an annual gig with Ballet Hawaii, in Honolulu, in December—the heart of the surf season on the North Shore. He and his wife, Jackie, who's a Broadway singer, flee to Puerto Rico when they can. In 2013 they rented a house in the northwest corner of the island, which is surf country, during surf season. I bunked with them there during a swell so solid that I was very glad I'd brought my 8'0" Brewer gun.

We sometimes chase waves far from home. A few years ago, with a bunch of other surfers, we chartered a boat out of West Java. Surfwise, the trip was a bust. We anchored for ten days off an uninhabited island in the Sunda Strait that's known to get great waves. It was the height of the swell season in Indonesia, but the surf stayed small. Selya brought a bag of DVDs—some Steve Buscemi movies and a complete set of *The Office*, the British original, with Ricky Gervais. He screened them at night, on a tiny portable player, in the sweltering hold where we all slept, and Gervais became the unlikely trip mascot. Selya knew the scripts by heart. You could hear him in the lineup, cracking himself up with favorite lines, nailing the bumptious provincial accent of David Brent, the office manager played by Gervais, while we paddled in circles, chasing mediocre waves. Selya is a connoisseur of cringe. He loves the ingenuity of desperate efforts to maintain dignity in the face of humiliation. "I identify," he explains. Toward the end of the trip, I came down with an apparent malaria relapse. I've had them, infrequently, over the years. Fever and severe chills. There were no thick blankets on board—we were anchored at six degrees south. So Selya loaned me, when the chills got bad, a velour leisure suit—black, with red piping—that he'd brought for the plane rides. I curled up in my bunk, freezing, groaning, dressed as a Jersey wiseguy. I sweated through the leisure suit. It was okay, Selya said. We could burn it if we ever got back to land.

Peter Spacek was on that trip. When I got sick, he kept an eye on me. He hardly surfed—the waves weren't worth it—but he did a lot of sketching: close studies of reef life, boat life, and the many species of fish he caught. He and I collected broken chunks of bright blue and red coral for our daughters.

MY FATHER SAILED HIS BOAT to Florida for the winter. It wasn't necessary—most boat owners in the Northeast just haul out—but he was mostly retired now, he had the time. I joined him in the spring for a northbound leg, starting in Norfolk, Virginia. We sailed the length of the Chesapeake Bay, then down the Delaware River, around Cape May, and up the Jersey Shore. Rounding Cape May, coming out of Delaware Bay, we had our traditional near disaster. A large fleet of small white-hulled fishing boats appeared to be working the shoals off the cape. It was a cold, clear morning. We wondered what could be running, to attract so many boats. The "boats" turned out to be breaking waves. We were nowhere near shore, but the depth sounder started reading twenty feet, fifteen, ten, and suddenly the breaking waves were all around us. I was at the helm, dodging waves, frantically trying to find deeper water. That boat drew six feet, and I saw the sounder's reading drop to five, four, three. At that stage, I had the boat heeled hard over, wallowing in the troughs just to keep the keel out of the sand. The waves weren't big, but they weren't whitecaps—they were breaking waves in chest-deep water. We could see the bottom. It was pale. It would have been a very bad place to run aground, in forty-degree water, miles from shore. Somehow, we got off the shoal. We motored out to sea, reviewing our charts. Yep, there they were. Horrendous hazards. The shipping channel hugged the Delaware shore. After a week of sailing carefully through shallow bays and narrow canals, we had seen open ocean and, idiotically, relaxed. We were too shaken to laugh. We sailed slowly to Atlantic City, tied up the boat, and took a Greyhound bus to New York.

It had been a sweet week. Nosing up the Chesapeake, we put into hamlets you would never find by road. We ate hard crabs, soft crabs, blue crabs, she crabs. Shot the breeze with waitresses and tackle shop owners. My father and I had always shared an affection, bordering on compulsion, for checking out obscure places. Each of our wives kidded us about all the aimless detours taken on family trips. My dad's favorite part of making movies and TV was location scouting. My favorite part of my work is following my curiosity around the bend, over the next ridge, into the souk, hunting facts and asking questions, going where the story seems like it

Bill and Pat Finnegan, Yosemite,
California, 1990s

might be rich. One evening, moored to a can under an oak-covered bluff, sipping the one vodka tonic he allowed himself, Dad asked me about Somalia. He had read my piece about it, but he wanted to know what the place looked and felt like, how ordinary people got by, what they ate, how I got around. So I told him, and he listened so hard, in the deepening shadows of that peaceful cove, to my descriptions of bombed-out Mogadishu, and the long scarves the women wore, and the teenage gunmen I had to hire as bodyguards, and the heavy-weapon battlewagons known as "technicals" that they drove around and fought from and slept on at night. He took in the tragedy and every detail of this far-flung world with such unfeigned wonder, I felt honored to bring him the news. It was a place he knew he would never go, and I had gone, and he wanted to hear about it. If he had any worries about my safety, he kept them to himself. We had always been lucky—dumb but lucky, he liked to say. We had this unappeasable curiosity in common.

The strangest place we found that week was called Delaware City. It was a small town at the Delaware River end of a canal that once ran to the Chesapeake—connecting Philadelphia and points north to Baltimore and Washington—before it was supplanted by a bigger, deeper canal built on a different route. Delaware City's sleepy main street was a monument to its heyday: an impressive row of big, brick, nineteenth-century buildings. We ate dinner at a grand hotel built in 1828. We were the only customers in the place.

That whole sail felt like time travel, down through layers of an older country, down through our own shared and not-shared history. I asked my dad if he had stayed in touch with anyone from Escanaba, his hometown. He shuddered, literally, at the thought. No. But wouldn't it be interesting to turn up at, say, his sixtieth high school reunion, which would be coming up? *No.* He would rather cut off his right arm, he said. Why? "Because I would have to account for myself," he said. "And what am I going to say, 'Hollywood producer'?" I didn't see what was so terrible about that. But I'm not from the Upper Midwest.

At one point, tacking out of Annapolis, he said, "You've got the habit of leaving things unsaid, of shoving things under the rug." I was startled, unnerved. "Maybe it's inherited," he added.

I wondered what things he had in mind. He seemed to mean resentments. Did I have so many? Once upon a time, I had secretly blamed him for my miseries, for the anguish that plagued me through my college years after Caryn left. My notion was that his devotion to my mother, his emotional dependence on her, had set me a bad example, had given me a model for love that ended up devastating me. But I had abandoned that idea, that ludicrous resentment, long ago. There were plenty of things I was actually glad I had left unsaid. Still, the comment haunted me. It haunts me today. All the things I wish I had said when I had the chance.

A moment recurs. We were motoring through the Delaware and Chesapeake Canal—the big one that does not come out at little Delaware City. A tremendous oceangoing tugboat thundered past us, pulling a barge. Dad, in a hooded slicker, stood at the rail, arms straight down at his sides, staring up at the boat as it passed, seemingly transfixed by the towering bridge and its red-and-white brightwork. I remember the boat's name, *Diplomat*, gilded on its stern. On the aft deck, a brawny redheaded sailor was smoking, a young guy, with enormous arms folded across his chest. He seemed to be striking a pose as his gaze flicked across us. Dad seemed frozen in awe. I was struck by his raptness. Amused, touched. I admired his unselfconsciousness. But there was also something alarming about his motionlessness, his arms straight down like that.

TAVARUA HAD A LONG RUN as a dream wave. It was famous—famous in surf world, anyway—for its near perfection, but also for its exclusivity, for the fact that it was private. It was the one great wave on the planet that did not succumb to the tragedy of the commons. It didn't become hideously crowded, effectively ruining it for everyone. The American-owned resort prospered. To surfers who objected to having a wave reserved for paying customers, the arrangement was a travesty. In principle, I sided with them. I had reported on privatization in different contexts, including municipal water in Bolivia and the maintenance of the Tube in London, and I was generally against it. I also had my own feelings about the resort, rooted in those prelapsarian days on the island with Bryan.

As a surfer, however, I was as susceptible as the next fiend to the fantasy of great uncrowded waves. We all live in a fallen world, I rationalized. I yearned to surf it again. As things turned out, the Fijian government, by then a military dictatorship, killed the Tavarua fantasy in 2010 when it abruptly canceled its long-standing "reef management" agreement with the resort. The waves were thrown open to the public, which meant, in effect, surf-tour operators. Boats packed with surfers soon began racing to Tavarua from nearby hotels and marinas on any hint of swell, turning the lineup into the familiar Malthusian feeding frenzy.

Before that happened, though, I became a regular resort guest. It started in 2002. The way the resort worked, groups of about thirty rented the whole place for a week, with most groups returning year after year, and that year a California-based group invited me to fill a spot. I didn't think too hard about it. I was turning fifty, and Tavarua called to me from well outside the range of my convictions, such as they were, about privatization. I wanted to surf it again while I still could.

The resort was low-key. Sixteen bungalows, communal meals. It seemed that the owners had done some blasting on the reef to open up the boat channel, but the wave out front was the same. Same rifling, too-good-to-be-true left flaring down the reef at hull speed. Surfing it was a sense-memory barrage. The blue swell breaking far up the reef, the intricate scrollwork on the face, the unforgiving coral. The critical moment that seemed to go on forever, the sensation of impossible abundance. I had lost a step or two in the twenty-four years since I last rode it, and the wave, particularly the takeoff, was as quick as ever. But I was crafty from long experience, and I could still make the wave, still ride it respectably. The lineup was no longer empty, of course. One had to share with fellow guests. But that was easy enough. The takeoff spot, which we had once found by using a crossed pair of extra-tall coconut trees, was now established by the reflection of a bar mirror in the resort's restaurant.

On the island, I gravitated to our old camping spot. The fish-drying rack where I had slept was gone, but otherwise the spot was unchanged. The view into the wave, the islands beyond. The rough sand, the soft air. The deadly snakes, the *dadakulachi*, were a rarity now. I felt delivered to a pampered new world. There was cold beer. There were *chairs*. There was a helicopter landing pad where the fishermen had once stacked dry wood for signal fires. I wondered what little Atiljan, who had slept in a nest of green leaves, was doing now. Was he a fisherman with kids of his own? Most of the workers at the resort were villagers from Nabila, but only one or two were ethnic Indians. Fiji's democracy had been smashed by a series of military coups mounted by ethnic nationalists from the Fijian side. Ethnic Indians had been turned into second-class citizens. The Tavarua resort had curried favor with the military regime by staging a professional surf contest at a time when Fiji's sporting links to the world had been largely severed by international sanctions. When I asked a gentle young bartender from Nabila what she thought about the government's moves against democracy and ethnic Indians, she shyly said that she supported the government. "They are for the Fijians," she said.

After I asked around about Bob and Peter, our onetime ferrymen—I learned nothing—a couple of older fellows from Nabila, now working on Tavarua, figured out who I was. They treated me like a long-lost cousin, and they had a good laugh at my expense. I was the American who had failed to start a hotel. Each week, the resort put on something it called "Fiji Night," with drumming and kava and speeches in Fijian by village elders for the guests. I found myself threaded into these speeches, made part of the history of the island and the coming of surfing. None of my fellow guests noticed, but the Fijians in the show all nodded knowingly, chuckling, and then gave me sympathetic pats on the shoulder when we met on the island's trails. I imagined that they knew at a glance that I really didn't have the right stuff for starting and running a business in Fiji. One of the American surfer-founders had apparently provided the capital. He had long since withdrawn, selling out to other investors. The other founder was the tough guy, responsible for building this little empire in the tropical wilds. He now lived in California and visited only occasionally. He had a big house carved out of the jungle on the south side of the island.

I dreaded writing to Bryan about my visit. He was waiting for a report. As it turned out, he did not object, as I thought he would, to my availing myself of the resort's privatized, commodified, and expensive waves. (Room and board ran about four hundred dollars a night.) He didn't even seem to retch at my description of Fiji Night. What disgusted him most, strangely, was an image of a volleyball game between staff and guests. "I imagined 'smile on face' and pure venom inside," he wrote. But his reaction to my report was complex and thoughtful, full of anger, jokes, jealousy, awe, and, as always, self-criticism. He vowed to make more frequent trips to the Oregon coast, where he occasionally went to surf.

The resort's owners had discovered a second wave, also a long left, out on an open-ocean reef about a mile south of Tavarua. They called the spot Cloudbreak, and it was actually what made the resort viable. The island wave, though world-renowned for its flawlessness, was too fickle to support a carriage trade with a one-week turnaround. It could easily go a week without breaking properly. (The owners had dubbed it, unforgivably, Restaurants.) Cloudbreak, which caught every passing swell, was far more consistent. Boats ran out there all day long, anchoring in the channel while guests surfed. Cloudbreak was bigger, shiftier, more rough-edged than the island wave, with many more imperfections. It had a number of different takeoff spots, and plenty of unmakable waves. But Cloudbreak had its own magnificence. I started rising in the dark, catching the first boat, and riding Cloudbreak at dawn, slowly figuring out lineup markers. The hills of Viti Levu, five miles east, could tell you, once you got some basic triangulations, where on the long, flat, brilliant reef you were.

Author, Cloudbreak, Fiji, 2005

I snapped a brand-new Owl out there that first week. The pieces went onto a large pile of broken boards rotting in the jungle behind the boat-mens' shack on the island. All those boards, I assumed, were Cloudbreak wreckage. The wave had bottomless reserves of deepwater power. It was like Madeira that way. But it didn't scare me like Madeira did, partly be-cause it was far more mapped out by other surfers in all conditions, but mostly because it had no rocks and cliffs. You could hit the bottom, par-ticularly on the inside section, where it got as shallow as the island wave, but when you wiped out or got caught inside, you could always wash in across the reef. The violence dissipated, as it does most places, the farther you were swept in. At extreme low tides the reef came out of the water and you could actually stroll across it to a likely jumping-off spot. For that matter, there were lifeguards—the boatmen, who kept an eye on the guests. On big days they ran Jet Skis in the channel, swooping into the impact zone to pick up people in trouble. During that first week, a ski came for me twice. I waved it off both times—I was fine. I took Cloud-break seriously, but my decade of Madeira trips, surfing places where washing in was often not a survivable option, had inured me, I realized, to more normal ocean perils.

I would never spend the kind of time on Tavarua that I had on Madeira. With Mollie now the center of our lives, I had no wish to. We could barely afford the trips I did take. Still, I became a regular, hitting it year after year, spending six, eight hours a day out at Cloudbreak. The groups I went with were a mix. There were Republican contractors from Florida, with their hard-charging sons, and film-business people, with their hard-charging sons. Young hotshots from Hawaii traveling on their sponsors' dimes. Some of the world's top pros were frequently there. Domenic came a couple of times in the early years. He was living in Malibu, in a happy second marriage, with four young children. He still cackled at my self-mockery, and it was dreamy to trade waves with him in the South Pacific. Surf-centric trips without his family soon stopped making sense for him, though. Bryan and I never even broached the idea of his going back. I made some friends on Tavarua, notably two Californians, Dan Pelsinger and Kevin Naughton, who were nearly my age and, like me, still could not get enough. We started taking lower-budget surf trips together—Mexico, Nicaragua, Indonesia. But the trips I trained for, saved for, lived for, were Fiji.

"PEOPLE I KNOW in New York are incessantly on the point of going back where they came from to write a book, or of staying on and writing a book about back where they came from." Thus A. J. Liebling, in "Apology for Breathing," a short, terrific essay. Liebling was pretending to apologize for being from New York, a city he loved lavishly and precisely. Now I'm one of those New Yorkers incessantly on the point of going back where I came from. But with me it's not a matter of packing up or staying on, but rather of being always half poised to flee my desk and ditch engagements in order to throw myself into some nearby patch of ocean at the moment when the waves and wind and tide might conspire to produce something ridable. That cracking, fugitive patch is where I come from.

Indeed, this is a book about that myth-encrusted place.

A Web editor at the *New Yorker*, having marked my many sudden desertions of my post, suggested I try a blog about surfing around New York. I thought that sounded good. Truancy and production shortfall could be turned into salty copy, introducing readers to, as a deck-line might put it, an underworld of urban wave-chasers. Our queer devotions, frustrations, little triumphs, and large peculiarities, plus a few waterfront characters, plus photos, could probably keep a blog burbling along. I saw myself mentally composing pithy, arcane posts while straggling home, half-frozen, on the Van Wyck Expressway.

As a courtesy, I ran the blog plan past the guys I surf with most. "No," said one. "Absolutely not," said another. They didn't want our spots exposed. They didn't want to be outed as my sidekicks. Blogs were lame. Objections sustained, plan shelved.

I generally let people know when I'm working as a journalist. Memoirs are morally blurred that way. Most private citizens don't expect to be written about, particularly not by their intimates. I've always, more or less, kept journals. But the notion of a book about my surfing life, particularly about the unsuspecting people I've chased waves with, is relatively recent. Few of my companions were warned.

Already embarked on the writing, I ran the idea, expecting the worst, past my New York surf crew. We were crawling home on the Van Wyck. They were surprisingly enthusiastic. For some reason, a book was to them less objectionable than a blog—less present tense, perhaps, less inherently privacy betraying.

"Will John be in it?" asked the Lobbyist.

He meant Selya, who was driving.

"I am a mere footnote," Selya said.

Not true, as it turns out.

But here's a true footnote: Barack Obama didn't believe me when I told him where I went to junior high school. This was in early 2004, before he was very famous. I was writing a story about him and I had been teasing him about his having gone to Punahou School, which is the top prep academy in Hawaii. We were sitting in a Caribbean-themed restaurant in a small shopping center in Hyde Park, Chicago. "No effing way," he said, laughing. (He didn't actually say "effing." But we weren't on the record.) I did, of course, go for a while to Kaimuki Intermediate. But nobody there knew that I would write about them. Our lives were off the record. That's the tricky part. Facts are easy.

MY DAD'S RAPTNESS at the boat rail wasn't just raptness. It was Parkinson's. The symptoms came on slowly, then not slowly. The disease carried him away from us, mentally. His life became a torment. He didn't sleep for a year. He died in November 2008, in my mother's arms, with his children around him. They had been married for fifty-six years.

My mother was flattened, as I had never seen her, by my father's final year. Always thin, now she was gaunt. She resumed going out—to concerts, plays, movies—with friends, with me. She was still an enthusiast—I remember how intensely she liked *Winter's Bone*, how thoroughly she hated *Avatar*—but her lungs began to fail her. She had bronchiectasis, a respiratory disease. It causes, among other things, shortness of breath. It sapped her strength. A lifetime of Los Angeles smog was implicated. We took her on vacation to Honolulu, renting a house in the old neighborhood near Diamond Head. Her room looked out on the water. Her three granddaughters curled up on her big bed with her. She could not have been happier, she said.

She and I had a funny moment the following summer. It was the last time she went to the beach—a cool, sunny afternoon on Long Island. She was so frail that we bundled her in blankets and tucked her in a sun trap, out of the breeze, overlooking the waves. Her granddaughters were tucked around her for extra warmth. I mentioned that the waves, though terrible, looked ridable. The west wind was kicking up a running, waist-high right just off the sand. "Go surfing," my mother said. I didn't have a board with me. But Colleen had a longboard in her truck. It was an enormous, ancient log, bought at a yard sale for purposes undetermined. Caroline, though rolling her eyes, gave me the nod. I ran out and caught a few waves. The log was ideal for racing the shorebreak, and I flew down the beach, throwing old-school moves on the ratty little waves till I crashed on the sand. I ran back to our little encampment in the dunes. My mother's blue eyes were bright. I felt about ten years old—showing off for Mom—and she said, grinning, "You looked just like you did when you were little." It was the antique longboard. Everyone else was chatting and laughing. Had they seen my waves? "No," my daughter said. "Go get another one."

As my mother became less steady on her feet, she walked faster. She had always walked fast, but this was different: a headlong tottering rush that made you want to run after her to prevent a crash. When she finally did fall, I blamed myself. We were coming home from the pulmonologist, and I left her alone, unsupported, for a few seconds on East 90th Street. I turned and saw her trying to negotiate a step that was too much for her. She toppled backward before I could reach her, cracking her pelvis. With that, she was bedridden. Mollie and I started spending nearly every evening with her. Old friends from California visited. Michael, who was now at the *Los Angeles Times*, came as often as possible. So did Colleen and her family. Kevin and his partner.

Most nights, though, it was just us—Caroline was stuck on a long federal trial. We were a cozy trio: Moll curled up with a book, my mother and I reminiscing, or watching TV, or solving the world's problems. My mother retained a keen interest in my projects, and she did not euphemize when I showed her drafts that she found sluggish. Her wryness was intact. She had always made wicked fun of clumsy savoir faire, and one of her bits was to stick her tongue in her cheek, bob her head, toss her hair, and say, "See ya tomorrow." That was what people who didn't have much going on, whose worlds were small, said to each other, airily, on parting. One night, as we gathered our things to go, she gave me the old head bob and, to my amazement, said it—"See ya tomorrow"—with an extra crinkle of sad amusement. So we were that family now. Our world had certainly shrunk. My mother was changing. She could look right through me now. Fearless love, unwavering. She and Mollie seemed to be, if possible, even more deeply in tune. My mother didn't believe in the afterlife. This was it.

Chronic nausea got her. It killed her appetite, and she wasted away. Her forward-lookingness faltered, finally. We scattered her ashes, and my father's, at sea, off a place near Sag Harbor called Cedar Point, which they had often sailed past in their boat.

YOU HAVE TO HATE how the world goes on.

I FOUND MYSELF getting more reckless, even before my parents died. In Dubai, chasing a story about human trafficking, I stepped on the toes of Uzbek slavers and their local protectors and had to leave the emirate in a hurry. Reporting on organized crime in Mexico, I edged further into the lion's den than I should have. This was the sort of work I had sworn off when Mollie was born. The same impulses were showing up in my surfing. I went to Oaxaca to ride Puerto Escondido, which is generally considered the heaviest beachbreak in the world. I snapped two boards and came home with a perforated eardrum. I wasn't turning into a big-wave surfer—I would never have the nerves for that—but I was pushing into places where I did not belong. On the bigger days at Puerto, I was the oldest guy in the water by decades.

What did I think I was doing? I liked the idea of growing old gracefully. The alternative was, after all, mortifying. But I rarely gave my age a conscious thought. I just couldn't seem to pass up even a slim chance of getting a great wave. Was this some backward, death-scorning way to grieve? I didn't think so. A few weeks after my sixtieth birthday, I pulled into two barrels, back-to-back, at Pua'ena Point, on the North Shore of Oahu. They were as deep and long as any tube I had ridden since Kirra, more than thirty years before. Both waves let me out untouched. Being adjacent to that much beauty—more than adjacent; immersed in, pierced by it—was the point. The physical risks were footnotes.

For obsessive before-it's-too-late wave-chasing, Selya made an excellent companion. He turned forty and the leading-man parts started to dry up. He could still leap, and lift and catch his partners, and perform as well as he ever had, he said. But younger faces, younger bodies, were preferred. He had a big role in a 2010 Twyla Tharp show built on Frank Sinatra songs. The best number in the production, I thought, was his solo dance set to "September of My Years." It was restrained, almost meditative, elegant, and nobody could miss the symbolism. "I wanted to make the solo very John," Tharp told the *Times*. After 188 performances on Broadway, Selya took the show on the road as resident director, while still dancing in it. He was choreographing, teaching, writing a screenplay. And yet things were winding down for him as a dancer. I overheard someone at a party ask him about his upcoming projects. Selya mentioned an asteroid that was in the news; it was alarming people by coming too close to Earth. He was hoping for a direct hit, he said. That was his best-case career scenario.

He channeled his fury into surfing. He turned days of Long Beach dribble into skatepark-style clinics, milking waist-high waves for every ounce of juice. Was it possible that he was still improving? His attention to the finer points of technique was unblinking. He was driven and endlessly patient, both. Smoothing out his style, making it look easy, while also pushing harder. He saw performance subtleties that I had been missing all my life. West Coast guys, after a successful wave, ran a hand through their hair on the pullout, according to Selya. Australians, in the same situation, made the same claim by wiping their noses. This seemed too silly to be true, but, watching a surf video, he would say, "Nice! Now wipe your nose," and, right on cue, the rider would do it. "*Stylin'.*"

Every nor'easter, if he wasn't stuck in Denmark or Dallas, Selya was ready to run east or south, depending on the winds. He got subtle tips about which bars and jetties might be working from the Instagram posts of certain local pros, and they rarely steered us wrong. When Jackie was working out of town, Selya would go keep her company, but if she was anywhere near the coast he would take boards. He was in Boston for a series of swells that seemed to light up every cape in New England. His text messages were ecstatic.

One of those swells was Hurricane Irene. I caught the front edge of Irene at Montauk. It was excellent. Then I ran home to spend the night of high winds with Caroline and Mollie. In the morning, with the storm passed inland and tearing up Vermont, the winds swung west and I, with my family's permission, drove alone to New Jersey. East Coast surfers have a ghoulish relationship with Atlantic hurricanes, panting eagerly as they rain destruction on Caribbean islands and, occasionally, the U.S. East Coast itself. Irene was bad that way. (Sandy was far worse.) New Jersey hadn't been hit hard, but when I arrived the beaches were still closed, pointlessly, on the governor's orders. (Chris Christie to the public, pre-Irene: "Get the hell off the beach . . . You've maximized your tan.") The surf was big and clean, the wind dropping. I parked a few blocks inland, tiptoed to the coast, and surfed for hours. My favorite wave in the East, a wailing right off a jetty, started to work in the late afternoon. It was almost too big, but I was alone in the water, which meant I could pick my waves carefully from the groomed, multitudinous sets. I picked the ones that tapered to the north. They were dark and throaty and ridiculously good. There were police lights flashing, red and blue, in the gloom on shore. The whole scene had the flavor of a dream—except my surfing dreams are always marked by frustration or fear or a special brand of anguished almost-remembering, never by great waves actually ridden. I didn't know if the cops were waiting for me, but, to be safe, I stayed out till dark, and then paddled two jetties north and slipped ashore there.

I USED TO THINK of my work as the antithesis of show business. Now I'm not so sure. Seeing my dad on the set, or out on location, when I was young, was like seeing his other family. A movie crew is a world, full of emotion, purpose, big personalities. People thrown together, getting intricately, tempestuously involved, temporarily. *Let's get this thing made.* Most of my projects—long narrative pieces, certainly—have a similar arc. I lash myself to people I want to write about. We knock around together, talk our way through their world. Then, at some point, it's published, the story's out, we're done. Strike the sets. Sometimes we stay in touch, even become friends, but that's the exception. Selya lives his version of this with every show. I'm lucky: I have a home team, the magazine where I've worked for decades. Most of my friends, now that I think of it, are writers or surfers or both. I've always disliked mirrors, but when I catch my own eye in a reflection nowadays I often think I see my father there. He looks worried, even ashamed, and it pains me. He had so much drive. He once told me that it was all just fear of failure. When he was older, waking up in the hospital after a knee operation, he looked at me indignantly and said, "When did your hair go gray?"

Mollie has our attention in a way that's different from what my parents paid me. She is adored, included, closely attended, carefully listened to. I used to worry that we were overprotective. When she was five or six, she and I were diving under waves on Long Island. I misjudged a bigger wave and lost her little hand. The moments after I came up and she was not in sight were for me a solid wall of panic. She surfaced a few yards away, looking scared and betrayed and crying, but no, she didn't want to go in, thanks. She just wanted me to be more careful. I was more careful. I remembered my fetal meditations under the booming brown waves at Will Rogers, before I could even bodysurf. Was anybody watching for me to come up? I never thought so. Certainly you only learned your way around waves by getting your ass kicked for every mistake. But I couldn't imagine letting my darling take her lumps that way. Luckily, although she likes to porpoise around, she has no interest in surfing. She does have, allaying my worries, a wide streak of independence that needs no encouragement. When her parents drop her at summer camp, they are the forlorn ones.

She started riding the crosstown bus to school, alone, at twelve, with quiet joy. We've drawn the line, for now, at the subway.

Do I not think of my daughter when I take stupid chances? I do. In March 2014, I ran out of air, unexpectedly, under two waves at a once famous break called Makaha, on the west side of Oahu. It was a rainy, windless day. I had just finished a teaching gig in Honolulu and had a few hours before my flight home. Makaha was big, the reports said—ten to fifteen feet—but it sounded more manageable than the North Shore, and so I headed there. From the beach, all you could see was whitewater and mist. The ridable waves were outside somewhere, beyond the foam curtain. I hadn't brought my gun to Hawaii, which was a mistake, I now saw. There were a few guys paddling out, angling through a wide, easy channel to the south, but they were all on massive big-wave boards. I had a thin, four-finned 7'2" that I loved—it was the board that had carried me through those two barrels at Pua'ena Point the winter before, with the inside fins holding the scooped-out lower face like lancets—but it was obviously not the right board for today. I paddled out anyway. I figured I would regret not going out more than I would regret going out—and regret it in the corrosive, self-hating way that I still recalled from not paddling out at Rice Bowl when I was fourteen. It would be different, of course, if I could see the waves. At Puerto Escondido, on the biggest day I saw there, I never considered paddling out. People were surfing, but I would have drowned. I could see that plainly. At Makaha, a less fearsome break, I at least had to see what was out there.

It turned out to be weirdly beautiful. The channel, which was just big, smooth, well-spaced swells, felt momentous, orchestra-warming-up. The lineup, when it came into view, was an unexpectedly spacious field, quite uncluttered, at least during a lull, with a small clump of guys out at sea and another, smaller clump of guys maybe two hundred yards farther up the point. The near clump was gathered to ride the Makaha Bowl—an enormous end-section that was constantly featured in the mags and surf movies of my youth. The far clump was for Makaha Point, a rarely photographed wave. The two spots are connected, on big days, by an extremely long, hard-breaking wall that is rarely, if ever, makable all the way across. The Bowl lost its cachet long ago to hollower big waves that break closer to shore. The Point retains a strong underground rep. I took a cautious route to the Bowl, staying out in deep water to the south. Smaller waves, which were not small at all, were steadily breaking across the inside, obscuring the shore. I kept a wary eye on the horizon. The rain was light, the sea surface glassy and pale, almost white—the same pale gray as the sky. Approaching swells were darker. The darker they were, the steeper they were. It was all on an unusually precise black-and-white scale.

The group at the Bowl was, on average, old. A couple of guys were at least my age. Nearly everybody was on a gun. The mood was both giddy and serious, not unwelcoming. I got the impression that these guys, most of them West Oahu locals, lived for these waves. I followed the pack, moving out as big sets approached. When the swells turned dark far out at sea, I sprinted for the channel. As waves got ready to break, the faces turned practically black. My board was completely inadequate. There were only two or three guys who really wanted the biggest waves. An older Hawaiian on a huge yellow gun stroked calmly into several monsters. I caught three waves in three hours. I made all three, but each drop was late, and exceedingly sketchy, my board fluttering under my feet. On all three drops, despite myself, I screamed. My waves weren't especially big, and I didn't surf them especially well.

There were a couple of cleanup sets: twenty-foot walls breaking way outside, in deeper water. We were all caught inside. I stayed calm, diving early and deep. One of those tore off my leash. A lifeguard on a Jet Ski, idling in the channel, dashed into the impact zone when boards or leashes broke. He retrieved my board from inside. As he handed it over, he gave me a long look, but all he said was, "You okay?" I was half-ecstatic, thanks. I was scared, and on the wrong board, but I was seeing things out there that I would never forget. On the black wave faces, the colors of boards became important. The guy on the red board is not going. The guy on the orange board is going. See his orange board stuck on the black face, trying to get traction to make the drop. The old Hawaiian on the yellow board was painting the most brilliant, passionate strokes across the tallest, blackest walls. Some waves, just as they broke, went cobalt at the top, under the lip. Others, the big set waves that barreled in the peak, went a different, warmer shade of navy blue in the shadowed part of the maw. It was as though, at that point, the gray sky was no longer part of the color scheme, as if the ocean was providing its own submarine hues.

Then there were the guys at the Point. They were shortboarders. The waves up there were not quite as big as the Bowl behemoths, but they were long, long, roping gray walls, with these tiny figures falling out of the sky, pumping down the line, deep in the shadows under the lip, ripping huge, heaving waves with a kind of respectful abandon, surfing at the very highest level. Who *were* these guys? I was too scared to paddle up there, and I would never in this life surf like that, but seeing these things filled me with joy.

My little fiasco at Makaha came partly from impatience, partly from watching those shortboarders, and partly from a deeply foolish leap of faith. I was like a somnambulist, regressing. I left the channel edge of the Bowl, where I had been hunting last-second on-ramps, and paddled deep into the impact zone. Big gorgeous waves, coming down from the Point, were regularly roaring unridden through there. They looked catchable, possibly, on my board. They were empty because their takeoff point was in a no-go area, inside the Bowl and upcoast—the absolute wrong place to be when a big set came. I snuck over there on a little bet with fate: that I would snag a great wave before the next big set came. It was a bad bet, a lazy bet, and I lost. The waves that caught me inside were mountainous. I thought I might be okay because the water still felt deep. I swam down hard, but couldn't escape the turbulence. Great columns of violence fired downward and pummeled me. I didn't panic, but I did run out of oxygen.

I had to climb my leash long before I thought it was safe to do so. It was difficult to catch a breath when I surfaced—there was too much foam and whiplashing current. But I only had time for a couple of breaths because the next wave was bigger and already breaking, preparing to obliterate me. That was when I had a very clear thought about Mollie. Please. Let this not be my time. I am needed.

It was age, I later decided. My quick calculations, my solid intuitions about my own lung capacity were off. I survived that second wave, obviously, but again ran out of oxygen many seconds before I expected to. The interval that day was long, which helped me avoid a two-wave hold-down, which I would probably not have come up from. As it happened, the third wave was smaller. I scrambled back to the channel. I felt peaceful afterward. Ashamed of myself, deeply exhausted, but newly decided not to do this again—not to bend my neck, not to commend my soul to the ocean at its most violent in the hope of some absolution. My nose was still dripping seawater in the taxi home from Newark.

IF I'M NOT on the road or surfing locally, I try to swim a mile a day now in a basement pool on West End Avenue. This humble routine, and the dry-land workout that goes with it, are my surf salvation. Back when I could get away with it, I subscribed to Norman Mailer's view that exercise without excitement, without competition or danger or purpose, didn't strengthen the body but simply wore it out. Swimming laps always seemed to me especially pointless. But I can't get away with that attitude now. If I don't swim, I will be a pear-shaped pillar of suet. My regular slog through the chlorinated cross-chop of the water aerobics class is all that stands between me and a longboard-only existence. Forget big-wave-level lung capacity. I just want to be able to paddle, and pop to my feet. When I first felt too old to surf, whipped and discouraged in Madeira in the '90s, I had never swum a lap or touched a barbell. I'm more physically fit now than I was then. But the pop-up still gets trickier, more effortful, every year. This isn't even maintenance, as Selya would say. It's just trying to slow the rate of decline.

Selya, a true son of the Upper West Side, thinks Jerry Seinfeld is a genius. Seinfeld, who doesn't need to work, still does stand-up comedy, fine-tuning his bits obsessively, averaging close to a hundred shows a year. He says he's going to keep doing it "into my 80s, and beyond." In a recent interview, he compared himself to surfers: "What are they doing this for? It's just pure. You're alone. That wave is so much bigger and stronger than you. You're always outnumbered. They always can crush you. And yet you're going to accept that and turn it into a little, brief, meaningless art form."

Selya recently developed arthritis in one hip. He could still dance, he said, and teach, but he couldn't surf. It hurt too much. He got resurfacing surgery. During the period when his hip wouldn't let him surf, he still came along on wave runs. While the rest of us surfed, he bodysurfed. It beat being stuck on land, he said.

TOWARD THE END of my ignominious run as a paying customer on Tavarua, I destroyed the last of my Owl boards. Cloudbreak first bent it, opening hairline cracks across the bottom. Then, while I was riding a wave, it abruptly stripped four feet of fiberglass off the planing surface, all the way back to the fins, one of which tore out. This was in 2008, late in the week, and the swell was building. Selya, as luck would have it, had also brought an Owl to Tavarua that week as his big-wave board. His was blood-red but otherwise identical to mine. After the morning session that trashed my board, a nasty little north wind came up. It would be side-onshore, a terrible direction, at Cloudbreak. The boats stopped running. I wanted to go take a look, at least, but no one else was interested. I was suffering from the mania that Cloudbreak often infected me with. I needed to go. I talked a couple of boatmen into running me out there. Selya loaned me his Owl, in case we found something. During the run across the channel, the north wind quit and the sea went glassy. I was thrilled, though the boatmen remained noncommittal. Selya, I later learned, planted himself in a watchtower, a little shaded platform above the trees on the southwest side of the island. He kept binoculars on us the entire time we were gone.

As we pulled up to Cloudbreak, the waves looked phenomenal, I thought. Some residual bump from the north wind, maybe, but cleaning up fast and pumping. It was a couple of feet bigger than the morning, and the lines of the swell were as long and unbroken as I had ever seen out there. One boatman, a square-shouldered goofyfoot named Inia Naka-levu, jumped in the water with me. His partner, a Californian named Jimmy, stayed in the boat, which he moored in the channel. He might join us later, he said.

My first two rides were warm-ups, testing the board, testing the wave. The board was perfect—stable but loose, familiar, fast. The waves were meaty, double-overhead, bending far down the reef, extremely fast. I rode them carefully, made them easily. Inia was paddling, I noticed, extra-hard after his waves, shaking his head. I knew the feeling: this was too much, too good. There was still a little chatter on the face, but it only increased the sensation of speed. My third wave was bigger, more critical. I rode deeper, under the shadow of the lip, doing long-radius speed pumps, going as fast as I knew how to go. It was not a complicated, technical barrel. I just had to keep the board going flat-out and stay away from the bottom, where the lip was landing with a continuous loud crack. I finally raced out into sunlight far inside, and did one last S-turn to exit before the wave shut down on shallow reef. Coasting to a stop in the flats, I tried to remember the last time I had ridden a wave that good, that intense. I couldn't. It had been years.

Pride goeth, and I took my next wave far too lightly. I drove extra-hard into my first bottom turn, not bothering to look over my shoulder to see what the wave was preparing to do but concentrating on my unusually all-out turn. The nose of my board must have caught a stray bit of north chop that I never saw. I went down hard, and so quickly that I didn't even get an arm up to protect my face. The side of my head struck the surface with such force that it felt like I had hit, or been hit with, a solid object. The wave shrugged me off; it did not suck me over. I had managed this high-speed splat before the wave was even ready to break. I reeled in the board, started paddling, head ringing, stunned. I coughed and saw blood. It was pooling low in my throat. It didn't hurt, but I had to cough it out to breathe. I reached clear water and sat up. I kept coughing blood into my hand. The ringing in my head diminished. Now it just felt like I had been slapped.

"Bill!" Inia had seen the blood. He wanted to head for the boat. "Can you paddle?"

Yes, I could paddle. I felt fine except for a headache and the urge to cough. I was okay, I said. I wanted to keep surfing.

"No, you cannot."

Inia looked frightened. It was his job to look after guests. I felt bad for him.

"I'm okay."

Inia looked into my eyes. He was in his late twenties—a man, not a boy. His gaze had surprising weight. "Do you know God, Bill?" he asked. "Do you know God loves you?"

He wanted an answer.

Not really, I murmured.

Inia's frown changed. Now it was my soul, not my cough, that concerned him.

We made a deal. We would keep surfing, but he would stay close to me—whatever that meant—and I would be careful, whatever that meant.

The swell was getting bigger, the lines even longer. We paddled over a very big set that looked, from the back, like it closed out. Inia studied it. Another worry.

My head felt fine now. I wanted a wave. There was a great-looking wave coming, already cracking far up the reef. "No, Bill, not this one," Inia said. "It closes out."

I took his advice and paddled over it. The next wave looked identical. "This one," Inia said. "It's good."

So this was what our deal meant. I would rely on Inia's judgment. I turned and dug for the wave. His judgment was extraordinary. The wave I caught peeled down the reef. The wave before it, identical to my eye, had in fact, I could now see, broken all at once. I surfed conservatively, just heading for the greenery. When I pulled out, I saw that Inia was on the wave right behind mine. So this was how he was going to stay close to me. He was surfing hard, right at the edge of his ability—the opposite of con-servatively. His expression was ferocious, his eyes like searchlights. Inia, I saw, had it bad.

As we paddled back out together, I asked, did God love everyone?

Inia looked delighted. The answer was an emphatic yes.

Then why did He allow war and disease?

"Shall not the Judge of all the earth do right?"

Inia was a lay preacher, with a mind full to the brim with scripture. He was grinning. Bring on the theological debate. He would convert me yet. This was a double reverse Hiram Bingham, I thought, with the dark-skinned evangelist surfing his brains out.

And so it went. Inia called me off some waves, called me into others, and he never got it wrong. I couldn't understand what he was seeing, couldn't see the distinctions he was making. It was a supreme demonstra-tion of local wave knowledge. It was also keeping me safe. I tried to surf prudently, and I didn't fall off once. I saw Inia, going for broke, get a huge barrel. After he pulled out, he said it was the best wave of his life. Praise the Lord, I said. Hallelujah, he said.

Selya later told me that all he could see, from a mile away, were the takeoffs, his tiny red board bright against light green waves. After that, as the waves bent onto the reef, there were only our wakes: thin white threads unspooling down the line.

The waves kept pouring through, shining and mysterious, filling the air with an austere exaltation. Inia was on fire, as a surfer, as a preacher. Did I still doubt? "We will not fear, though the earth give way and the mountains fall into the heart of the sea, though its waters roar and foam."

I continued to doubt. But I was not afraid. I just didn't want this to end.